born under *an* assumed name

RELATED POTOMAC TITLES

Generation's End: A Personal Memoir of American Power After 9/11
—Scott L. Malcomson

Spymaster: My Life in the CIA
—Ted Shackley, with Richard A. Finney

born under *an* assumed name

THE MEMOIR OF A COLD WAR SPY'S DAUGHTER

SARA MANSFIELD TABER

POTOMAC BOOKS
WASHINGTON, D.C.

Library of Congress Cataloging-in-Publication Data
Taber, Sara Mansfield.
  Born under an assumed name : the memoir of a Cold War spy's daughter / Sara Mansfield Taber. — 1st ed.
    p. cm.
  ISBN 978-1-59797-698-5 (hardcover)
  ISBN 978-1-59797-827-9 (electronic edition)
  1. Taber, Sara Mansfield—Childhood and youth. 2. Taber, Sara Mansfield—Travel. 3. Taber, Sara Mansfield—Family. 4. Cold War—Biography. 5. Daughters—United States—Biography. 6. Fathers and daughters—United States. 7. Intelligence officers—United States—Family relationships. 8. United States. Central Intelligence Agency—Officials and employees—Family relationships. 9. United States. Central Intelligence Agency—History—20th century. 10. Espionage, American—History—20th century. I. Title.
  CT275.T137A3 2011
  973.92092—dc23
  [B]

                                                                        2011028462

Printed in the United States of America on acid-free paper that meets the American National Standards Institute Z39-48 Standard.

Potomac Books
22841 Quicksilver Drive
Dulles, Virginia 20166

First Edition

10 9 8 7 6 5 4 3 2 1

for Maud and Forrest

in memory of
Charles Eugene Taber

The air rushes down my nose and throat—the cold air, the salt air with the smell of turnip fields in it. And there is my father, with his back turned, talking to a farmer. I tremble. I cry. There is my father in gaiters. There is my father.

VIRGINIA WOOLF
The Waves

CONTENTS

ACKNOWLEDGMENTS

While I am not given to spy craft, in CIA tradition, I have changed the names of most of the people who appear in this book. They did not ask to be written about. I wish to preserve their privacy and acknowledge their own undoubtedly different versions of events. I thank them for their parts in my rich childhood and for their gifts of friendship and life lessons, however joyfully or painfully gained.

I also wish to acknowledge those people vitally important to my childhood who do not appear in these pages, disguised or otherwise. A writer must preserve some experiences just for memory. Those unmentioned, too, have contributed crucially to my life and this story.

I would like to say a word or two about the writing of a memoir. Because of the untidy and kaleidoscopic nature of life, memoirs are, in a sense, never really complete; this one is no different. Every time I thought I'd opened the last door in the story, another colorful door would appear. The story could also have been slanted any number of ways. Several quite different stories of my childhood might have been fashioned. Eventually one has to stop. Another critical point: I chose to write this book from a child's point of view. I only report on my experience—what I made of what I saw as a child and what I've made of it since. I did not try to obtain CIA files or my father's records. I don't know much about what my father did or what went on, so, even when one takes into account the subjective nature of truth, there are inevitably vast limitations and flaws in my description of his work. Another book could be written about my father's work and experience. Finally, there is one other very important fact about the writing of a memoir: in a sense, we are all fictions for one another. No matter how very hard we try to see the truth, owing to the shadings of our psyches, others are, in part, figments of our own conjuring imaginations; in a way, we—innocently and inevitably—assign all others assumed names.

I won't name them, but I wish to thank my parents' friends and the people I grew up with for their friendship across continents. Friendships forged in far places and challenging circumstances are among the most enduring and precious. You know who you are.

I must extend a huge thank-you to all my writer friends and advisors. A close reading of one's work is the greatest gift anyone can give to a writer. Therefore, I thank: Beth Baker, who zoomed to my rescue right when I needed her; Ann Harvey for immeasurable gifts of the very best kinds; Elaine Klaassen, always there with musical notes; C. M. Mayo, *compañera*, for wise advice from near and far; Kate Phillips for generous, smart, and specific comments (the writer's dream) while raising two very young sons; Alison Townsend for her in-the-bone understanding; Amy Troyansky for steady, lovely commiseration; Oliver Tessier for his belief in me and for always excellent counsel. I also thank, for writerly aid along the way: Sandra Dibble, Nadine Epstein, Bill O'Sullivan, and Mary Stucky.

The Aislings, dear friends and co-conspirators, offered sustaining, sage, good-humored counsel.

My erstwhile writing group—Jenny Brody, Mary Carpenter, Ellen Cassedy, Sally Steenland, and Natalie Wexler—offered unfailingly sound editorial advice as well as reviving chocolate cookies over the course of ten years.

Consummate editor Bill Strachan, who edited my first book in 1989, continues to provide never-failing kindness, knowledge, and wisdom.

I must also give my friends heartfelt thanks. They have helped me and this book, in countless ways, during its long gestation: Claudia Ahrens, Kristine Aono, Anne Marie Atkinson, Jana Belsky, Nancy Blum, Renee Burgard, Janna Butler, Madeleine Cardona, Susan Chase, Dena Crossen, Gretchen Cudak, Mary Diamond, Betsi Dwyer, Cindy Eyster, Juliette Fournot, Nan Fuhrman, Eiko Fukuda, Miki Garland, Val Giddings, Harriet Gordon Goetzels, Mary Gorjance, Anne Gray, Sheila Harrington, Mary Horton, Bruce Johanson, Marcie Jefferys, Linda La Pierre, Marielle Marsac, Selby McPhee, Breck Milroy, Kay Neer, Susan Perkins, Wendy Pollock, Snigdha Prakash, Fiona Reid, Greg Robb, Stasha Seaton, Cindy Snyder, Jim Symons, Jim Taggart, Wendy Weil, Bob Winship, Lauren Rader and all the women in her wonderful and nourishing classes, and those I have unwittingly forgotten to include in this list. Dear comrades all: *domo arigato, xie xie, dank je wel.*

Special thanks go to my old friend Sara Middleton, who generously agreed to appear without an alias.

Dr. Ralph Cohen, the man who transformed my life and has continued as a treasured friend and mentor, also agreed to appear sans cover.

Bob and Nancy Traer rescued me at the crucial moment. They remain wise and inspiring friends.

In my father's absence, John Horton, his dear friend, gave me the go-ahead to publish my story of the CIA.

My professors, Henry Maier and Sharon Berlin of the University of Washington School of Social Work, and Robert LeVine, Sara Lawrence Lightfoot, and Max Katz at Harvard helped me to understand human development and behavior, and the fascinating intersection of personality and culture.

My students—their honesty, and their brave and stunning work—endlessly renew my faith in the goodness of human beings.

I also wish to thank members of the Foreign Service Youth Foundation, who very early on expressed enthusiasm for my perspectives.

The Writer's Center in Bethesda has sustained me in multiple and basic ways for over fifteen years. Sunil Freeman has been a wonderful, never-failing friend and employer.

The Virginia Center for the Creative Arts provided residencies that allowed me to gather my thoughts in the fertile garden of other writers.

Susan Schulman was an early, helpful supporter of this project.

Elizabeth Demers at Potomac Books is a wonderful editor. She immediately "got" the book and helped me, through her wisdom and expertise, to make it do its job in the best possible way. Kathryn Owens efficiently and cheerfully ushered the book through its production phase, and Aryana Hendrawan was an expert copyeditor. I am very thankful to all three.

I also wish to acknowledge my debt to these books: *Ike's Spies* by Stephen Ambrose, *The Agency: The Rise and Decline of the CIA* by John Ranelagh, *Vietnam: A History* by Stanley Karnow, *The United States and China* by John King Fairbank, and *The Espionage Establishment* by David Wise and Thomas B. Ross.

As for the Chinese romanizations used in this book, Taiwan has now adopted pinyin for most words, with some exceptions, such as for place names. To conform with this, I have used pinyin romanizations for simple nouns but the romanizations used during my time in Taiwan for the places and streets.

Special thanks, of course, must go to my late father and mother, and to my brother, whose versions of this story, as in any family, would be very different. In what manner does one thank one's family? This book is a testament to what my father gave to me. Oddly, my father, the spy, holder of secrets, was all in favor of my writing. He believed everyone has a right to his or her story. His endorsement in this and all things has made all the difference. He wrote his own book about his exodus from Vietnam: *Get Out Any Way You Can: The Story of the Evacuation of House Seven, the CIA Propaganda Force in Vietnam, April 1975*, by Charles Eugene Taber. My mother was a plucky Indiana farm girl who could make a community anywhere in the world. Among multitudinous gifts, she gave me a basketful of love, invaluable advice for life, and a wonderful helping of gumption. She deserves her own story. My brother, Andrew Taber, was my youthful partner in crime; and besides, he wore that floppy hat in high school.

Last and most, giant hugs to Peter, both mate and sea anchor—and Maud and Forrest, my miracles. All three met my obsession with never-ending support and grace, and kept me ever-aware of the world's best and ongoing delights.

PREFACE

The Secret and the Sea

I was born under an assumed name.

It was in Kamakura that my parents first went under. "Mr. Brown," a colleague, met them at the Tokyo airport after the endless flights from Washington. As he was driving them the forty miles to Kamakura near the coast, he asked them to select a surname. Once they arrived at their new home, nestled into a mountain slope beneath an ancient, three-story-high Buddha, they settled into their new identity.

~~

Two years later, on that piney slope, I emerged into the world. It was 1954, and the world was seething. McCarthyism, Soviets, massive retaliation, Red China, Mao Tse-tung, Ho Chi Minh: these were the maelstroms of my first world. All through my childhood, my father's shifting identities and covert missions ruled us, as we moved from continent to continent. During the first five years of my life, we changed locales five times—from Kamakura, Japan, to Okinawa, to the Philippines, Taiwan, Connecticut, and back to Taiwan.

Always, the secret was there, like an invisible molecule suspended in the deeps of the sea.

~~

A person who loses worlds, whose truths are murky, whose identity wavers, is hungry and given to remembering—to tracking down and naming sensed truths, and to fashioning scenes and whole landscapes around an image of a pea soup–green Dutch canal or a dimly recalled whisper in the Taiwan night. To retrieve the girls I used to be, to stitch my life together and claim my own name, I collected half-recalled fragments of long-ago moments, cities, and people, and awakened from deep memory, with imagination's assistance, the sights and sounds and smells that surrounded them. In order to understand my father, and thus myself, I had to fathom not only the kaleidoscope of my own life, but American soldiers, American spies, my country, and its role in the world. This was the only way I could sort out what it was to be an American, and even more, what it was to be human.

PART I. THE SEA

Book 1

DRAGONS
Taipei, Taiwan,
1961–1962

1

the wall

China—age seven, age of clear memory—was the place I became
aware of my strange perch in the world.

The sun was warm on my cheek. My legs shifted under the sheet. I squinted
my eyes open, sensed a ray of watery shine, shut them again. There was the smell
of cooking rice and the green-mud smell of padi—the smells of Taiwan, of "Free
China," as my father called it. Snuggling under my covers, I listened. There was a
soft scratching sound. The scratching sound of earth being dug.

I kicked off the sheets, opened my eyes, settled them on the soft grey, plain
walls of the room. The air was cool and moist, playing on my flung-out arms and
legs. It wasn't hot yet. The atmosphere inside and around my body was soft and still.
No one else was awake.

Pulling my nightie down, I sat up. There was the scratching sound again. I
tugged the filmy curtain aside and peered out the window. The guard was squatting
in the dirt across the small patch of garden, wearing his sunny-side-up, straw coolie
hat and his loose cotton pants. I could see his thin ankles and the thick, corded
veins of his weathered, caramel-colored arms.

The yard was ragged—a thin rectangle of dusty grass edged with a bare, tan bed
of dirt. My mother had asked the guard, who was on round-the-clock duty but had
little to do except twiddle his thumbs at his post near the gate, to plant some flowers. At the back of the dirt bed rose a high cement wall, with little chunks of clear
broken glass on top like ice teeth. This was the wall that kept my family safe from
thieves and other unnamed dangers. I often imagined what it would be like to be

a thief trying to climb over the wall into my family's yard and finding his fingers and the fleshy parts of his legs and his feet sliced by the glass shards.

The guard was standing up now, his spade and pail lying on the ground beside him. He shifted slightly. The moves were quiet. Now he was staring at the earth; he was gripping his rake. All of a sudden, his skinny arms and upper body were twisting something, and, a second later, he was turned around, looking shyly into my face. He was holding, on his rake, a coiled, long, fat, dead brown-and-black snake.

I was transfixed by the sight, but my insides shrank down very small with fear.

During the time that the guard was standing, looking into my face, our bodies were only three paces apart, but it seemed like the old Chinese man and I, a seven-year-old American girl, were separated by a distance as large as three oceans. Even so, I wanted to open and climb out the window, to join the guard, to see the snake. *What would its eyes look like, up close?*

But I was frozen. I couldn't go out the window to the guard and I couldn't step back into the coolness of my room. I was at a juncture. I could stay in my room and remain an American girl with patent leather shoes and smocked dresses, or I could clamber out the window and become a Chinese girl who could kill snakes and spy dragons in the air. I stood at the opening, holding my breath.

Then I heard my father's voice calling. "Girl-child, time to get up. Time for breakfast."

A little while later, when our cook, Yuki, was clearing my sugared rice porridge, my father put down his Chinese newspaper and told me the guard had knocked on the door to say that a snake had slithered under the wall that morning.

"It was a krait," he said, beckoning me onto the lap of his khaki suit. "A twenty-stepper."

"You run inside, Sara, if you *ever* see anything moving in the yard," my mother said, leaning her dusky-blond bob toward me and pulling her Japanese *yukata* around her, her voice trembling, vehement. "Besides kraits, pythons and bamboo snakes are about. They're poisonous too." Andy, my brother, two years younger than I, was born right after my father drove over a thirty-foot python that was sleeping in the road.

"And," my mother went on, uttering the words I had heard many, many times, "don't *ever, ever* go outside the wall by yourself. It's not safe beyond the wall."

"But don't worry," my father said in turn, as he always did. "Snakes are rare. Almost all the time Free China is a very safe place."

My father had told me that, like the king of the beasts, America was the strongest country in the world and could save us anywhere, anytime, from anything—even, as I imagined now, from poisonous snakes.

My father had told me, too, that the Chinese thought of their country as ruled by a dragon—a wild and powerful dragon curled over a continent. I lived, thus, in a land of enchantment. Always, my father could change the look of something. He was my private magician.

~~

Later that morning I watched from the window again as the guard placed foot-high piles of dirt along the inside perimeter of the wall.

~~

As a child, I lived in a walled, American world within the island of Formosa, as Taiwan was then called. In one way, this world was bright and spotless and upright as a battleship, but often, when we stepped outside its walls, or bits of the outer world slipped in, that sterling picture became jumbled and tarnished. Living in a closed American world within another country has its inherent brittleness.

When you live in the country of your passport, you can take nationality for granted. You breathe it in with the air. When you grow up abroad, however, surrounded by people unlike yourself, the question of what country you belong to arises every day. You have to piece together nationality, painstakingly put it into words and build it block by block, like a foreign language. As a girl, I learned what it was to be American by watching Americans, by watching the world, and by watching my father. And my father was a certain kind of American, with a certain kind of job, a job that could make being an American into a hot potato.

~~

My father went to work every day at the NACC, the Naval Auxiliary Communications Center, a plain, rectangular building on a base surrounded by a high wall in the sprawl of Taipei. As long as I could remember, my father had described his job to me as "China Watcher." This meant his duty was to keep a close eye on Red China for the American government. China Watchers had a secret mission that was very important to Washington, he told me, but I hadn't a clue, at seven, what exactly my gentle father really did. His official title was "naval attaché," but, unbeknownst to me, my father's actual portfolio, as a clandestine human intelligence officer, was to "debrief" escapees from the Mainland and to recruit and run agents with close ties to Red China. China then was almost completely closed to the West. In addition, my father and his associates were training Nationalists from the Mainland to infiltrate back into their homeland and build a democratic opposition movement.

In Taiwan, my family lived not under an assumed name, as we had when I was born in Japan, but we would throughout the rest of my childhood live under the cloak of "official cover." All through his thirty-year career—I wouldn't know this until I was a teenager—my father described his job as something somewhat altered from the truth. And every day in his work as a covert operations officer in pursuit of Communist secrets, he used false names and assumed secret identities.

Until I left for college, in tandem with my father's shifts in identity, and by virtue of family membership in the strange league to which my father belonged, I too lived under identities not of my own choosing. This way of living had many benefits but also high and painful costs for both me and my father—sacrifices that would eventually, for each of us in different ways, call in their chits.

It was in the crumpled and beauteous hinterlands of postwar Japan, at the point my father entered the clandestine service, that my father's secret work commenced its own clandestine job of slow and subtle tainting. The secret work my father did was like a branding on his chest, predestining his rocky and ambivalent, fascinating and tortured career. For me, his daughter, his secret work was like a stamp on my passport. Indelibly, it shaped my girlhood, turning it into a glamorous life rich in foreign cultures, delicate beauties, and startling joys—and burdened by strange silences, heartsickness, constant change, and loss.

Now and then, I sipped tiny tastes of my father's clandestine activities—they were like the little sips of scorching Chinese tea my father shared with me from his glass—but I didn't know that I was sipping. Most of the time, my father's secret was as imperceptible as a droplet in a rising tide.

~~

In my father's soft-worn British atlas, Taiwan was a tiny rice grain in the Pacific Ocean just off Red China. The island was a dictatorship propped up by the U.S. government, patrolled by military police and on constant alert for Red Chinese attack, but for me it was a place of limpid airs; of lime-sparkling padi and scarlet lanterns; of fast-talking people in tattered clothes; of the delicious smells of pineapple and soy sauce shrimp; and the stink of fish and water buffalo dung. I had spent most of my seven years in Asia. This, to me, was how a place should look and sound and taste and smell. This poverty-burdened and shimmering padi-land—yanked around by the big powers in the Cold War—would stay in my bones, and draw and disturb me for years to come.

~~

The Taipei in which my family lived was a cluttered city—half poverty-crumbled, half rebuilt with American money—sprawled at the foot of Yangming-shan, a beautiful, steep-sloped mountain named for a Chinese philosopher, and inhabited by deer, mountain pigs, and wealthy Taiwanese. According to my father's orders, our tour of duty in Taipei was two years, but, as my father said, whenever Washington cabled—and it could happen at any time—our job was to serve the U.S. government and board the next boat. (One day when I was settling into a new dormitory in a Midwestern college, feeling homesick for our recent home in Tokyo, I would ask my mother how she felt about having left so many places. "Oh I miss every home we've ever lived in," she'd sigh. Then she would count up the temporary billets and embassy houses we had lived in over the course of my father's career. We'd have moved, by then, thirty-one times.)

Our house was in a neighborhood called Renai Lu, Section Four. This was a new housing district on land that used to be rice padi: a crisscross of narrow streets lined by compact houses, each boxed within its own high wall. Many Americans lived in a U.S. compound, but our neighborhood was mostly Chinese save for the Tanners, another U.S. government family.

Our house, enclosed within its wall higher than my father's head, was made of concrete. It was small, square, and tight. The bare rooms were provided with embassy-issue furniture made of bamboo with grey duck cushions: a two-person couch and two chairs of the same grey duck, and a low coffee table. We also had one armchair, with a flowered slipcover, a sprig of prettiness to cut the institutional grey. Andy and I each had a plank bed with our own covers on them—olive green army blankets and white sheets. My father loved army blankets because he had served in World War II—when he'd first visited Asia—and his army service was one of the things of which he was proudest. There was a scroll on the wall in the living room. It was of Chinese characters in calligraphy presented as a compliment to my parents by one of my father's Chinese colleagues. The characters meant either "America," or "beautiful place," my father told me, depending on how they were translated. He delighted in the double entendre.

America was my country, but I really couldn't say if it was beautiful. I had last been there when I was four. Taiwan was the only home I remembered with any clarity. I knew America made good hamburgers and vanilla ice cream, because we ate them at the snack bar at the base, and I knew America had friendly soldiers with crew cuts, because we saw them all the time, both at the base and on the regular Chinese streets. What I didn't know was that my country had another, darker side.

My days in Taipei clicked along to a rhythm like my piano metronome, put into motion by my mother's orderly hand. My mother was often busy with her work as a physical therapist with Chinese polio victims and orphans, and as a teacher at TAS, Taipei American School, so our family had three servants: Yuki, a cook; Aduan, a maid; and Mary, our amah who took care of Andy and me. My mother and Mary knitted our household together. It seemed as if Mary had always lived with us. I loved her. She had fluffy black hair that she let me pin up with barrettes. She cooked special sweet rice snacks for us and played Old Maid as many times as I asked.

When we lived in America, my mother explained, we couldn't afford household help, but when we were in foreign countries, it was different. Because of my father's "representational duties," our family received an extra allowance for servants.

We lived in China but I hardly ever went to Chinese people's homes. On weekends we visited other Americans who lived in Taipei—missionaries and other government families. Some of them had sandboxes and swing sets like back in America. When I went to my best friend Laura's, we sat on the couch side by side, and drew pictures.

My parents did have Chinese friends. My mother had her Thursday ladies' group and my father had lots of Chinese friends. One of them was Mr. Chu, a man I had never seen—his special Chinese friend. At odd times—a drowsy Sunday midafternoon or a Thursday morning at five o'clock before the roosters had crowed—my father sometimes went for a walk with him. I imagined the two of them walking along hidden back alleys that smelt of blossoms and garbage, or along misty forest paths, their heads leaning toward each other, speaking of private things known only to the two of them.

~~

We hired two pedicabs on Renai Lu, the big street near our house, and the skinny drivers cycled us into the center of the city. We were going downtown because my father loved to walk the streets of Taipei.

I watched the old man who was pedaling my mother and me. The muscles of his bare back strained and stuck out in rubber bands, and his leg muscles were carved into curves as they pushed up and down on the pedals. I hoped the ride would finish soon because it looked like it was difficult for him to carry us. When we got to the downtown, we paid the drivers and proceeded on foot through the close streets. One of the roads was called "Losefalu," the Chinese way of saying Roosevelt.

The streets as we walked were a whirl of stink, color, and cry. I liked all the swirling colors and rotten and fruity odors, and walking along holding my father's strong hand.

Long vertical banners of cloth with big Chinese characters fluttered in front of all the small, jumbled shops set side by side on the crowded, narrow street. They were messy places piled with plastic toys and buckets; cascades of rubber shoes; stacks of hard Chinese pillows; bolts of cloth; and tubs of smelly fish heads, noodles, and chicken feet. They also sold items like black furniture carved in geometric designs and shiny pots in a thousand sizes. But most of all, for me, looking around holding my father's hand, the street was teeming with people. Hundreds of heads poured into the distance ahead of us, and when I looked back, a long, oncoming wave of faces pushed toward me. They were a smudge of bright brown eyes, butter-brickle skin, and ink-black hair. I could hardly distinguish one person from the blur until my eyes got used to it. Then I could pick out people one by one: a hunched woman in a black dress shaking her finger at a man standing by a shelf of pigs' heads; a man selling fortune-telling sticks; a boy chasing a scroungy brown dog; an old man squatting, fanning himself with a broad fan; a sea horse seller; a man falling off his bicycle because no one would let him through; a pedicab driver leaning against his cab in the middle of the street; a water buffalo wandering in and out of the people, its tail flicking.

Mixed in with all the other people on the street were American and Chinese soldiers. They were bunched in groups of two or three. My father had told me that the guns both the Chinese and the American soldiers carried were American M-1 rifles and American 45-caliber pistols. The Chinese soldiers wore khaki the color of old bamboo. The faces of both the American and the Chinese soldiers were serious until one of their group pointed and told a joke, and then their shoulders swayed and they laughed.

The air around me squabbled and banged. Chinese people were talking, in a racket of chattering and yelling and scolding. I could only understand words here and there. TSE CHAW SHUR HOW CHOW CHO, harsh, chopping consonants strung together in rapid, spat-out sentences. Cows lowed, roosters crowed, buffaloes snorted. Hawkers shrieked out the names of the wares they were selling.

As we walked deeper and deeper into the street the smells grew stronger. The street reeked of rotting fish, rotting eggs, vomit, and dung. The air also smelled of fresh-cooked chicken and spring onions, spring rolls, and sweet candy.

Through the chaos, my tall father in his long, baggy shorts and sneakers, my mother in her pale green shift, my brother with his short legs sticking out beneath his shorts, and I, in my smocked, flowered dress, made our way. My father, walking with his head high and his eyes directed outward, looked exhilarated, my mother looked both interested and concerned about the poor people, and Andy pointed at everything and talked nonstop. I was easy and curious, and bubbling with confidence. I knew all these Chinese who saw us would know, just by looking at us, that we were American: inherently different, richer, and superior to them.

As we walked along the street, we were frequently approached by ragged children: boys in nothing but frayed black shorts, girls with pus-filled eyes, and twig-thin toddlers. They pulled on my father's pant leg, or they hung on to my mother's arm, or tugged on my dress. And they looked at me with their dark, sick-sad eyes. I knew that if we gave one child a coin, we would instantly be mobbed, but at some points, if a child was alone and there was no crowd about to pounce, my father spoke to the child softly in Chinese and handed me a coin to give.

This time, a little girl in a tattered frock stood in front of us holding out her dirty hand. My father dug a couple of coins out of his pocket and put them in my hand and nodded toward her. Her eyes were black pools.

I had been around poor, diseased children all my life, but still it was difficult to look her in the eye—I felt ashamed of both my pity and my pride—and I tried to avoid looking at her scabby, poxed arms and stained, ripped dress.

My father had said to me many times, "We are lucky to be Americans. The Chinese are very poor, and so we should help them whenever we can." But the children of the oozing eyes and scabby arms climbed into my bed with me at night. With dull eyes, they begged in my dreams. Dreams that would return—issuing sharp pangs of sadness, and lacing me back to Asia—for years ahead.

~~

After our walk, since this was Saturday, we drove in our flag-blue Rambler for lunch at the NACC Club, a low white building inside the blocks-long, cement-walled American compound where my father worked. In the cool dining room with white cloths on the tables, we sat near the window. Andy ordered a hot dog and french fries. My father and I ordered Salisbury steaks, and my mother ordered liver and mashed potatoes: all good old American food. As we ate, I observed.

The club was filled with American military men, and outside the window a steady stream of soldiers, marines, and sailors passed by. I could tell that a little World War II thrill trickled through my father's body whenever he saw a uniform, and he had taught us to identify men by service and rank. I was good at navy men: Enlisted men had navy, white, or sometimes khaki uniforms with chevrons on their sleeves; ensigns had one stripe on their shoulder boards; lieutenants had two stripes; commanders had three stripes; and captains had four. Admirals had stars, from rear admiral with one star to full admiral with four. A hush, like a pause, stopped my body whenever we saw an admiral. The navy men, I knew from my father, were from the Seventh Fleet. President Truman had sent them to Taiwan after the Korean War to patrol the Formosa Strait, which flows between Taiwan and the Mainland, and to protect Taiwan from Communist attack.

Sometimes at the Club we were seated at a table next to a captain and his family. My father had an important job, but because he was a civilian, he didn't have a uniform. Sometimes I wished he did, so everyone would notice him like they noticed the captain, with creases sharp as knife blades and black-reflecting shoes. But my father didn't want to be noticed. He had a way of standing at an angle and gazing far off, deflecting attention from himself, like light bouncing off a mirror. Years later I would realize my father was a master of "hiding in plain sight."

~~

While we swizzled up the last of our ginger ales through our straws, my father shifted forward and I could tell he was about to talk to us about the world. At mealtimes, my father taught us about history and current events—particularly about the actions of our country. Even though we were children, he wanted us to know about the world and to think about what was occurring. The year before, when I was in first grade, John F. Kennedy had been elected president. He was young and handsome, and he had a beautiful wife who wore hats that matched her nautical dresses. He also had a fluffy-haired daughter, Caroline, who was three years younger than I was, and a little son named John-John, who wore wool shorts and had knobby knees and brown shoes, like Andy's.

When we received our tulip cups of American vanilla ice cream—I liked to swirl mine into a cool, smooth soup and then eat it very slowly so that it lasted a long time—I said, "Tell us again, Pop, why America needs to be here to help Taiwan." I loved this story of China and America. In it, the countries seemed like characters in a book: bad guy China and good guy America.

My father looked at me, his soft brown eyes intent behind his horn-rimmed glasses. He clasped his hands on the table and leaned toward us. "Well, before and through World War II, China was a feudal society. That means landlords owned the soil, and the peasants—and these were most of the Chinese people—worked like slaves for them. The peasants were extremely poor, and had to give most of what they grew to the landlords in exchange for using the land. It was a desperately unfair system, with the vast majority of the Chinese wearing rags, living from hand to mouth, and being maltreated by the few who lived fat and wealthy like kings.

"Then, during World War II, while the Japanese were occupying big hunks of China, a civil war kindled between the Nationalists—commanded by Chiang Kai-shek—and the Communists—inspired by Mao Tse-tung—and once the Japanese were defeated, it flared up.

"Now, the Communists, as I've told you, believe in the principle, 'from each according to his ability and to each according to his need.' This means that they believe everyone should work hard for the welfare of the country and, in return, everyone should have all their basic needs met by the government. Under communism, governments own all the land and factories, and are responsible for supplying their people with jobs, housing, food, medical care, and old-age security. This idea appealed to the followers of Mao, who wanted to make things more fair and more equal for the peasants of China." My father unclasped his hands, placed them flat on the table, and straightened up as he continued.

"Now, our government objects to the idea of governments controlling industry and people the way communism does. In China, the government dictates where people live, what work they do, what food they get to eat, and how much money they make. In America, we believe that people should be able to own their own living quarters and own their own businesses, and have the freedom to choose their own jobs, and make as much money as they wish to through their own hard work."

The Chinese waiter in an American waiter's uniform arrived at our table and asked if my father wanted coffee. He said, as always, "Yes, Black, please." As my father said this I experienced a little shot of pride; his bitter choice was, to me, a signal of his courage: in matters small—and large.

My father took a quick sip of the reflecting black liquid and then returned to China's story.

"So, when the civil war fired up in China, we Americans supported the Nationalist leader, Chiang Kai-shek, because, while he, like the Communists, wanted to change the feudal system in China, he wanted to install a democratic-capitalist system like ours."

My father explained then that at the outset, in 1946, when China's civil war had started burning hard, the Nationalists had 3 million men to the Communists' mere 1 million, and Chiang's forces seemed destined to win. The American government poured 6 billion dollars of money and weapons into the Nationalists' hands, but, to America's surprise, the Communists triumphed, and the People's Republic of China was proclaimed in October 1949. "This Communist victory was a shock for our government," my father said. Now the United States was terrified of communism's spread, and prepared to take extreme measures to contain it.

"But even though the Communists took over the entire Mainland and the Nationalists had to flee here to Taiwan, we refused to give up," my father said.

"This brings us to why we Americans are in Taiwan. . . . We are committed to helping the Nationalists retake China and make it a democratic country. But the truth is, this is a very difficult undertaking. As of now, the Mainland and we, with Chiang, are in a deadlock. Neither of us accepts the division of China. The simple answer to your question is: we are here to help the Gimo's forces retake China." Everyone called Chiang Kai-shek, the leader of Free China, "the gimo," which was short for "generalissimo." To me the word "gimo" had a powerful and harsh sound; it gave me goose bumps.

Hearing again this tale of the troubles between Mao and the Gimo made my heart thrill with a mix of excitement and fear, but tucked here at the NACC Club, I felt completely cradled and safe. At the commissary, where we bought stateside groceries like Carnation instant milk, Nabisco's Nilla Wafers (my favorite cookies), and Sara Lee cheesecake—Yuki bought our cucumbers, snow peas, tangerines, and shrimp at the local market—I felt at home. At the PX, the Post Exchange at the Military Aid Mission on Chung Shan Bei Lu, where we bought my father's shaving cream and my snow-bright American underwear in neat little packets, I knew I belonged, and among the army men in all these places, and on the Taipei streets where they strode tall with their weapons, I felt protected.

~~

After lunch, we went to the Grand Hotel for a swim. Since we lived in Taiwan's steamy tropics, we swam every day. The Grand Hotel looked like a magnificent, broad pagoda, at the foot of Yangmingshan. Families of American officials swam there, in the pool, alongside the families of rich Chinese people. We splashed around for a couple of hours in the cool, pearly water, and then we drove home, through streets of pedicabs, bullock carts, stinky smoke-spewing buses, and the many rag-clad Chinese on foot, to our house behind the wall.

~~

When we stepped in the door, I went to my room and put on my white cotton Chinese pajamas—beautifully ironed by Aduan and embroidered with little Chinese children watering plants in gardens. When I emerged for dinner, bowls of fried rice, prepared by Yuki, were steaming on the table.

My mother had taught Yuki to boil all our water for twenty minutes, following the rules sent out by the embassy medical unit. The boiling, followed by filtering, was performed to eliminate parasites, hepatitis, giardia, dysentery, and other dreadful diseases.

My mother had a habit of diagnosing by sight the ragged, ill-looking children on the streets. Rickets, malnutrition, polio, cholera: these were some of the serious diseases my mother, as a medically trained person, could spot, and of which all American mothers lived in fear. We were constantly inoculated against these dire illnesses but infections, lice, worms, and boils were part of our daily lives. At school, we pressed our cuts with our fingers and showed each other the white-with-a-touch-of-yellow pus oozing out. We scratched our scabs and our boils and our mosquito bites and made them bleed. The Chinese children on the street had lots of sties and boils and sores like we did, but also more serious sicknesses. My mother said it was because in China there was a lack of sanitation. She often pointed out people taking baths at the open sewers that lined the Taipei streets, and children dipping water to drink out of those same sewers. "That is why, Sara and Andy, you *must* wash your hands when you come in from outside."

To prevent all these problems of sties and filth and throwing up, in addition to hand washing, my mother had us drink milk: powdered skim milk from the commissary. Milk was like a holy drink. We drank it with everything. We loved milk. There was something American about milk, something protective, and we drank and drank it.

When we were sick, we went to the NACC dispensary on Yangmingshan, or to the American military hospital in town. I had my tonsils out at the five-bed dispensary on Yangmingshan, afterward eating lime sherbet on Dr. Dawson's lap, while he talked to me in his Texas accent. Americans never went to Chinese doctors.

~~

I was being raised in a world that made Americans seem inviolate. But one day, I'd overheard my mother talking to her friend Mrs. Munger in the living room. "I worry that one of those crazy groups will snatch them off the street," she said in a low voice, making sure Andy and I couldn't hear. But I was listening from my bedroom; children always know a mother's worries even when she tries to hide them. Cobbling fragments of sentences, I figured out that my mother's fear had to do with my father's work for President Kennedy: a fear that Communists or other shady groups would kidnap the children of Americans, and hold them for ransom. It was a fear, as I'd know later, that my mother, and even my father, would secretly harbor all through our growing up.

Another afternoon when we were out taking a walk, the market crowd was so thick that I lost sight of Andy and my parents, and an icy fear streaked through my body. *If I were to be swept up by the crowd and kidnapped, I wouldn't be able to speak enough Chinese, no one could help me and I would never get home.* I was paralyzed and sobbing by the time my father found me and took me in his arms.

Once home, my father scoffed about the possibility of our being kidnapped. He looked at Mom, as well as us kids as he said, "I don't want any of you to worry about that. It is about as likely as the Pacific Ocean drying up." And then our father taught us to say, in Chinese—as he later would in other languages, "Please take me to the American Embassy." Our country would always keep us safe.

~~

This was my life in Taiwan: My father and mother went to work; I went to school at TAS and Andy went to his Chinese nursery school, where they wore blue smocks with hankies pinned to them and red characters embroidered on the breast. We bought donuts and Kellogg's cornflakes at the commissary; and we took outings around Formosa to, as my father said, "sample the riches of China." And while we did all these things, every minute, the American government was like an invisible dome over us, protecting us from all dangers. The government provided this for us because of my father's important work. He knew important information, he passed on important messages, he met with important Chinese people, rich and poor—in the day and in the night. All of this, I knew, was to help the Free Chinese take Red China back from the Communists. To my seven-year-old mind, this seemed logical, and, tucked in our house behind its high, concrete wall—topped with broken glass to stop unnamed bad men—I felt utterly safe, as safe from vultures and eagles as a sparrow in an aviary.

~~

Fried rice and milk downed, seven o'clock, window locks checked by my mother to keep out the thieves who frequently stole into American households, and goodnight-hugged by my parents, I lay on my bed, watched the green and grey geckos skitter up the wall for a few minutes, and then snuggled down to read. I was reading a book about Raggedy Ann and Andy and their adventures in a land with lollipop bushes and root beer pools. The stories in the Raggedy Ann books were set somewhere in England, but the books were printed on Taiwanese paper. I loved the Taiwanese books, even though the words were sometimes spelled wrong. They had slick, greyish paper and a strong, good, leafy smell. My father said they were pirated, that "the Chinese are masters of piracy." The Encyclopaedia Britannica was sold, my father said, "for a pittance, just a few New Taiwan dollars," for instance, and an American bestseller, the day after its release, was on the Chinese market, ready for our American sailors, in a cheap pocket edition. *America has the best writers; that's why they copy us*, I thought as I sank into sleep.

2

the chicken village

For most of my childhood, I lived an American fairy tale. I was a princess in a crystal coach, floating through the airs of various cultures, gliding down foreign streets. As the child of an official American in poorer countries, I was automatically "more important" than the local people. Here in Taiwan, because I was wealthier, well fed, had nice clothing, went to the NACC Club, swam at the Grand Hotel, and rode in a sleek embassy car, I was like a girl in a movie. This sense of elevation and difference inscribed in me a consciousness both of shining privilege and of fragility, unreality, and apartness, a habitual sense of odd specialness that was hard to shake even after the crystal coach shattered, and I landed—*thud*—at age eighteen, on hard American turf.

As an American girl being raised in Taiwan, I took note that American servicemen protected Taiwan from invasion; American men towered over Chinese men; and crowds of Chinese people moved back from American cars in a wave, as though we were royalty passing through. My conclusion was that Americans were a superior people.

Because Americans had the obvious advantages as I saw it, we were inevitably happier than the Chinese, smarter and more talented. And most of all, Americans were more powerful than the Chinese—and so, omnipotent and safe from any peril. Like most seven-year-olds, I was a natural social Darwinist. And there is nothing to match the purity of a young child's ardent patriotism. But in the course of my daily life, from time to time, pebbles tossed by the outer world pinged the windows of my crystal coach, and one day, in a village of skittering chickens, rocks pelted.

~~

I climbed into the low-slung black embassy car. The driver, Mr. Wong, backed it down the dirt lane—our house was recently built, the road fresh-cut for the tic-tac-toe lanes of new houses—and then whisked me off for the half-hour ride to TAS, where I'd begun second grade a month before.

As always, as we drove, I felt like a protected witness. Whatever my father might be doing in the messy Taipei back streets, sitting in my clean dress with my book bag beside me, I was an orchid in a small, private, traveling greenhouse—protected, but also alone.

As Mr. Wong maneuvered the long, wide car through the narrow, tumbledown streets of Taipei, I watched the pedicabs and bullock carts nearly colliding as they hauled their loads of people and burlap sacks of goods, and I followed, with my eyes, the black-haired people in thread-bare, baggy clothes moving this way and that.

As we left the city proper, I gazed out at the scenery that changed from city outskirts to little farms to rice padis, set against the wooded, massive, black-green slope of Yangmingshan.

The school came into view: a low, sprawling white-block building, set among the vast fields of rice. It was newly sprung out of the padi, like our house. American buildings were always fresh and modern—and better than Chinese ones.

~~

I loved TAS but sometimes at school I felt not like an orchid, but like a little sparrow inside a cage. I felt my face grow hot and red if the teacher called on me, and I answered arithmetic problems in such a quiet voice that Mrs. Johnson asked me to repeat myself, which made everyone turn around and look at me.

I was a girl who liked to be at the edges. When in a twosome I was fine, but I didn't like big groups of people. I didn't like being looked at or watched; when my broken arm was in a cast, I didn't want anyone to notice it. But I hated being called shy, as adults were wont to do. It seemed like being called bad or weak. I wanted to tear up the word like a piece of paper.

Sometimes, if I couldn't find my friend Laura, I sat on the grass at the edge of the blacktop and looked off across the padi until the bell rang. But today I was excited to get to school. It was Friday, the day of the weekly spelling bee.

The car pulled up in front of the school. Children—most of whose fathers worked for the army, the embassy, or some other American office—were milling around. We all gathered around the flagpole, put our hands over our hearts, and watched as two sixth graders raised the American flag up the pole. We sang "The Star-Spangled Banner," and the Nationalist Chinese anthem, *"San Min Chu Yi . . . ,"* screechy high notes climbing into the air. My father told me the anthem was about the "three people's principles," advocated by Sun Yat sen, the famous Chinese leader. He believed adherence to the principles of nationalism, democracy, and social welfare would make China a free and powerful country.

I could feel the bow of my sash bouncing behind me as I hurried to my classroom of twenty or so American and three Chinese children. I slipped into my chair and got out my list of words, to practice them one last time before the bee, which would be held first thing.

I was one of the quietest of the students, but I was proud because I was one of the best readers and spellers. In my special shoe box at home, I had several prizes for winning spelling bees: a book of postcards of the monuments in Washington, D.C.; a Donald Duck pencil; and a box of Crayola crayons Mrs. Johnson had gotten from the PX. My only rival was Mei-Lin, a Chinese girl who, like me, wore two ponytails bouncing out above her ears—but, instead of being wheat-colored and fluffy, hers were black and as shiny as two slim, lacquered vases.

Mei-Lin and the two other Chinese girls in my class never played with the American children, even though they spoke English. I sometimes wanted to ask them to play with me and Laura— my parents said to always include people—but I never did. The Chinese girls seemed contained, complete, tight-stitched in their small, tidy bodies and shiny, flopping ponytails and top-knots. In the hall, they stuck together in a bundle of three and chortled with one another, sounding lively and carefree in a way they never did in class, where they were quiet as padi birds. On the playground, too, they kept apart, making dolls and animals out of bits of paper with their skillful hands. Clustered tightly near the building, it was like they were huddled in a little hut that you could see into but not enter. Sometimes in class Mei-Lin gave a shy smile or said a quiet "thank you." She seemed nice but I didn't go over to her or the other Chinese girls. I didn't have the need. I was in the sway of a security that came from being one of the blond children, one of the majority.

I scolded myself sometimes for not making friends with the Chinese girls. I thought it showed weak willpower. My mother's favorite saying was, "You can do anything with willpower." I didn't realize that I was in the hands of something larger: human nature—people usually stick with those they know; and geopolitics— Mei Lin and I were stuck behind the fortifications of our groups on either side of a deep ravine. It was not as deep a ravine as that between America and Red China, but we didn't know how to get across the gorge. These were forces a seven-year-old couldn't easily defy.

~~

My father had told Andy and me about the world's great ravine, the Cold War: a war without shooting, but full of threats, which the U.S. government was fighting to prevent the Russian and the Chinese Communists from gaining control over the world, or using the atom bomb. "This is the biggest danger in the world," my father said. He'd explained that the conflict between America and China was being played out in different locales, with each side trying to dominate Asia. In the early 1950s we had fought the Chinese during the Korean War, a war that had ended with a country split in half.

In addition to the thrust into Korea, Peking had taken over Tibet, which was until then an independent state, and we were giving massive military aid to Taiwan and South Korea, trying to contain Communism. Every time one country fell to Communism, we feared it opened the door to another falling into the enemy camp.

"And now we have turned our attention to another Asian country, the country of Vietnam," my father said. "Vietnam is a place where some Communists, similar to the Red Chinese, are trying to take over." The year I was born, he said, Vietnam— a little place shaped like a sea horse in the South China Sea—was divided in half. Its head was sliced, just at the belly, from its curvy tail—he sketched the belted sea horse on one of the flash cards of Chinese characters he kept in his pocket—and it became two countries: the Communist North and the Democratic South. The Americans and the Communist Chinese, had, ever since, been positioned at either end of the country—the Americans like a white whale at the tail, and the Chinese like a red whale at the head, each ready to gobble up the whole country the minute the other one tried to take a bite.

"President Kennedy has just sent a force of specially trained troops to Vietnam," my father said. "These fighters, the Green Berets, will help in our mission of fighting the spread of Communism in Asia. . . . But the basic fact is, Vietnam is a plaything for the big powers in the Cold War."

The conflict between China and America could be worrying, he said, but we had wise leaders and the finest government in the world, and so we Americans were secure despite the divide.

~~

I felt flutters in my belly as Mrs. Johnson held up the prize for the winner of the bee. All the girls let out an "Ooooh!" when they saw the plastic pencil case that Mrs. Johnson held in her hand. We lined up in two rows.

Before long, Mei-Lin and I were the only two students left standing at the front of the room. We spelled our way through *hippopotamus, gigantic, alphabet,* and *tyrannosaurus,* and then it was my turn again. Mrs. Johnson said the word: *peculiar.* For the first time, I did not immediately respond. Into my head came a picture of myself: skinny, shy, with two short messy ponytails: peculiar, that's what I am, I thought. For a moment, I was lost in a spinning whirlpool of thinking and worrying. Then I hurriedly spelled out the word—wrong.

At the end of the school day, the last bell rang. As we gathered again at the flagpole I tried to hide my shame. As the other blond, ginger-haired, brunette children and I bunched up, I was aware of Mei-Lin, Nancy, and Da in a little clutch off to the edge. A first-grade boy and girl solemnly lowered the American flag and then folded it into a tricorne. As they slowly folded the Stars and Stripes, my heart pattered with pride, but I also thought to myself, *I am American. How could Mei-Lin have beaten me?*

~~

At the NACC Club, we ordered hamburgers and the Chinese waiter had just brought Andy and me our ginger ale when I asserted what I assumed was a simple fact, "We're better than the Chinese, aren't we, Pop?"

Sitting and sipping my sparkling ginger ale with its Maraschino cherry, I was utterly sure of myself. I knew Mei-Lin was smart, but even so, my conviction was fast and I wanted to revel in it: our president bossed Chiang, and we had more modern things and were richer, so we must be better.

My father, however, was from a family whose fortunes had plunged into deep valleys and mounted to the summits of steep mountains—like the landscapes in Chinese scrolls—according to the successes and failures of his father's sales jobs and inventions. During the Depression his family of eleven had sometimes lived as squatters, and had ended up, on one of my grandfather's successful ascents, in a big, yellow house at the edge of the Washington University campus in St. Louis. My father had taken advantage of the GI Bill to go to college. My mother, the ninth child in an Indiana forester's family, had tutored wealthy sorority girls in math and science to get herself through both college and physical therapy school. My parents knew firsthand the roles of luck and class in socioeconomic standing. In Taipei, unbeknownst to me, we lived month-to-month on my father's government salary, and my mother did all her physical therapy work with Chinese orphans and polio patients in Taipei for free. But among the impoverished Taiwanese, to me, we seemed as rich as Rockefellers.

I assumed my father saw things as I did—I knew his heart hummed like mine did when he saw the Stars and Stripes fluttering on a pole—and I expected him to agree that Americans were superior to the Chinese. But he said, looking at me with his intent brown eyes, "No, Sara, we're not better. We and the Chinese are just human beings, and all human beings are the same."

As the waiter set down our hamburgers, my father launched another of his history lessons. "We're not better than the Chinese. We're just more fortunate. The Chinese people are good, smart people who have been through terrible times and are now struggling for freedom. On the Mainland, as you know, the citizens can't criticize the government or they will be jailed or killed."

I was confused. It still sounded like Americans were better.

"We Americans are here in Free China to help the Chinese develop a government and a way of life," my father went on, "where they will be freer and also better off so they can afford to live with more comfort—like we have. The Chinese are struggling and poor, but they are basically just like us. We Americans *are* very wealthy compared to the Chinese, and as wealthier, luckier people, it is our responsibility to give to poorer people, but this does not mean that we are better. I believe, as Teddy Roosevelt said, 'To whom much has been given, from him much is rightfully expected.'"

I began to absorb my father's meaning now.

"Above all," my father said, "we must respect the Chinese culture. The Chinese are very hard workers, and we have much to learn from the Chinese ways: their music, their religions, their bravery. You've seen how hard they work in the padis, Sara, how fast a Chinese storekeeper can spin the abacus beads. You've seen their magnificent pagodas. The Chinese have a strong, fine, ancient culture."

Even though my father told me this, I didn't quite believe it. I believed my eyes, which absorbed most readily shiny things.

~~

We crossed the dusty yard of Yi Kuang, the orphanage established by a Chinese legislator's wife, where my mother worked, in addition to the polio clinic she had set up in Taipei. Many of the children at Yi Kuang, my mother had told me, had crippled legs and inflamed brains, and the parents of the children, a large number of whom were from the Mainland, had died, or were too poor to feed them. Some of them had been abandoned, like kittens, on Yi Kuang's doorstep, wrapped in old rags, in the secrecy of the night.

Your order of January 16, 2012 (Order ID 103-5816247-4134628)

Qty.	Item	Item Price	To
1	Born Under an Assumed Name: The Memoir of a Cold War Spy's Daughter	$19.37	$19
	Hardcover		
	(** P-2-F32A452 **: 1597976989)		

Subtotal		$19
Order Total		$19
Paid via credit/debit		$19
Balance due		$0

V3

This shipment completes your order.

Have feedback on how we packaged your order? Tell us at www.amazon.com/packaging.

193/DQFqNFIKN/-1 of 1-/1SS/Second/8668090/0212-12:30/0211-08-27/snem

We visited a room full of babies lying in wicker cribs lined up, one smack against the next. In the next room, the children were bigger—maybe two or three years old—and paired in their cribs. Each of them had polio or cerebral palsy or spina bifida, or some other condition that made it hard for them to learn to walk. My mother put down her bag and began to examine the children closely. She leaned into each bed and moved each child's arms or legs. The children were strangely silent as she coaxed them, gently massaging their too-curvy or too-bony legs with her long-fingered hands. Here and there she commented to the nurse that a child needed more eye ointment, a pneumonia check, or some medicine that she took from a box in her purse.

In the Yi Kuang dining room, while my mother talked to the cooks about nutrition, I stood near the wall, watching the children eating their rice, fruit, and tea. At the low table nearest me, one of the little orphan girls—about four years old, her hair cut into a sharp upside-down bowl at her ears, her bright, quizzical eyes forming little teepees in her small face—looked over to me and held out her bowl of rice and bananas. She grinned and motioned with her chopsticks that she would be happy to share with me. I shook my head I knew I shouldn't take food from a hungry orphan and the food looked horrid—but the girl's happy smile and extended bowl traveled into me and established a station there. This is my first memory of the astonishing generosity of the poor—an experience I'd have regularly over my childhood. I was startled and ashamed. It was I who should have shared the candy I had tucked in my pocket.

After this visit, I developed an eye for stray kittens. I spotted them everywhere, and, when my parents relented, took them home and fed them milk with an eyedropper until they could survive on their own.

~~

We were riding in the embassy car. The car wound down a narrow street between rows of shabby shops. High screeching Chinese music, from the street sellers' radios, assaulted the car, even though the windows were rolled tight. As we glided along the trash-filled street, dirty animals—doves, dogs, chickens, cats, and pigs—and hordes of people roiled and blocked our way. The driver honked continuously.

As we crawled along, I watched a slender boy, naked to the waist, racing up and down the street. Suddenly he separated from the throng. He came up to our car, displayed his polio-damaged, limp left arm three inches in front of my eyes, and pounded on the pane with his useful hand. I forced myself to look into his face. The boy's eyes met mine and our eyes latched for an instant. I was amazed: His mud-brown eyes and his crooked mouth were laughing. His face and his whole body seemed to shout out with merriment.

Before leaving the side of the car the boy took a little wooden flute out of his pocket with his one hand and played a tune. He went off flipping the coin my mother gave him high into the air.

As the boy sauntered off, I watched, deeply intrigued at how a Chinese boy, all alone, with dirty legs and no shoes and a useless arm, could laugh to the sky.

~~

Such moments of admiration for the Chinese were tinkling sounds against my crystal coach that didn't chip its glass—until, carried by my father's eagerness to get out "to see the real people," we took a journey to a small village at the foot of some mountains where the villagers made vases and urns.

In the black, motor pool Chevy with the driver, we glided through the poor, jumbled streets of the villages along the way. Feeling like I was riding a float in a parade, I wanted to wave an American flag and shout "Here I am! Look at me. I'm an American."

Andy talked the whole journey long, narrating everything he saw. "Look, Pop, a jeep!" and "Look, Mom, a man on a donkey!"

As we rode along the twisty dirt roads, we got to talking about John Glenn and his first-time orbit of the earth. To me, this showed definitively that we were the smartest country. I didn't know about Sputnik or the arms race. Then my father started telling us about other world events. Communist Cuba had stopped our country from taking it over, he said: something called "The Bay of Pigs." Another thing that happened—a more concerning thing—was that Russia exploded a test nuclear bomb. Bombs like that scared me, but my father said, "Don't worry, our American president knows exactly how to handle these kinds of things."

As an adult I would wonder about reassurances like these from my father. Did he really believe what he was saying? Was he truly confident and optimistic about American wisdom and omnipotence, or was he protecting his small daughter from fear? Perhaps back then, still brimming with the afterglow of World War II, he believed America had the corner on nobility. I know that not too long afterward, his thinking shifted. And just as my father's perspective would alter—one's sense of one's country fluctuates over time—my own blindered patriotism would swing.

Soon, my mother was singing, leading us in croaky renditions of the servicemen's anthems: "Anchors Aweigh," "The Caissons Go Rolling Along," and "America the Beautiful." Singing them, I felt as indomitable as General MacArthur wading ashore in the Philippines.

Stacks of terra cotta pots—vases and plates and bowls and huge urns—stood in firewood-like piles along the walls of the buildings, up to the roof of every house in the village. Children in tattered clothes ran to and fro. Bicycles leaned against the fronts of the houses, chickens wandered, and old men with long white beards squatted along the street in twos and threes.

We drew into the center of the village, up the single dirt street, and innocently got out of the car to ask directions to the central pottery workshop. The moment the car pulled to a stop, the people of the village converged, coming from every direction like specks of iron shooting toward a magnet, into a whirlpool around the sedan. It was as if they had never seen pale-skinned people before. By the time my feet touched the ground the vehicle was surrounded, six people deep on all sides. Instantly, I was pressed against the car's rear fender, bodies pushing against me every which way.

I felt I was being smothered. Fingers grabbed at every part of me. Boys and girls of all sizes, in tattered shirts, with sores on their arms and bright, watery eyes, shouted to one another as they pinched my arms and shoulders and hands. Each time one hand was withdrawn, two more replaced it. A woman with needle-thin wrinkles all over her face and eyes like bright ebony slits grabbed a piece of my hair and pulled. She squabbled something to two other women, who then reached out their arms to do the same. I couldn't escape. I tried to shelter my face, but the strangers grabbed my hands down again. Babbling lots of Chinese words, one old lady pressed her face close. She had blank eyes that I couldn't see into. Suddenly she yanked my ponytail and put it in her mouth, as if to taste it.

The crystal coach had now vanished entirely, and with it dry land. I was in a new, terrifying element: an ocean of fear. Underwater, caught in the welter of a constantly surging sea. I was panting now, trying to get my head above the swells—gasping, gasping for air.

Just in time, the embassy chauffeur barked out a fierce-sounding phrase over and over. He waved his arms like fan blades, and the crowd pulsed back.

~~

The crowd shrank into the stoops and pockets of the village, but I could still sense the gleaming eyes watching us as my father and the embassy driver led us down a dirt alley to the pottery shed we had come all this way to see. After viewing the many pots, adorned with intriguing, hand-painted, looping-tailed dragons—

my mother bought a flower pot and an urn—we rested for a while, under an umbrella at the back of the village leader's house. While sipping a cool, fizzy drink, I listened to the other side of my home of Taiwan: the familiar, soothing, human and natural sounds of the countryside—chickens clucking, boys shouting, old people yammering at children, the rush of a nearby Chinese stream.

~~

My body could suck the right amount of air again, now that the people had shrunk back. But standing in the middle of the messy, fish-smelling street, I had changed from one kind of girl to another. In an instant, the disturbance inked itself into my brain, and into the chambers of my heart. Indelible now, in my ideas and on my skin, was the girl seen by the eyes of an old Chinese woman: an odd, funny-looking misfit. Now I was, not a royal American, but an ugly little sparrow, who, when spied, would become prey to a swarm of vultures wanting to skewer her with their insatiable eyes and pluck off her wings and legs.

Forever after—through my childhood and into my grown womanhood—I would not be able, ever, to lose the frightening image of the wild-eyed old woman pointing at me and nattering to her friends with an exhilarated laugh coming out of her mouth—nor the animal urge to flee to the safety of our American house behind the wall. From this moment, I would strive, by power of will, to make my face and my dirty blond hair and my skinny body and arms and legs invisible. I would try to shrink narrower and narrower, until, like a pencil line in the air, or a slit into another world, I was too narrow for other people to see.

~~

The safest thing, I decided as I sat by the trickling Chinese stream, would be to become a mole in a burrow, or a girl behind a Made-in-America, one-way glass wall, who could spy out and see the world, but could not herself be seen.

~~

Back at this juncture—1961—I couldn't even begin to imagine that this China of rag-clad peasants in coolie hats might one day be a veritable dragon—an economic and political one—with a strength superior to that of the United States. It was inconceivable—to me, my father, and my country—that American arrogance could circle back and get us, and that China might one day be on the brink of owning *us*.

For now, here, age seven, in this Taiwanese pottery village, I had learned a stark, permanent-ink lesson: to be American was to be a unique, strange being—superior but in danger.

3
whispers

One steamy night, I was asleep—deep in the velvet, tropical darkness—when the phone trilled. I heard rustling, the click of the phone receiver being picked up. Then: my father's low voice. Whispers drifted into my room and trickled down my body. And danger fluttered, like a fleet, invisible bird, winging through the damp, dark air.

~~

My childhood was full of whispers. Secrets tingled at the rim of our Taipei life, but most were so well concealed that they were mere ripples in the air, pulses on the skin like the caresses of a lost, wayward breeze. I hardly noticed them; I assumed shushes and asides, innuendos and hints were part and parcel of every family's life. But on this particular night, the whispers became loud and ominous. I witnessed distress in my father's face, and danger itself slipped briefly into the open.

~~

My life was a clear sky.

My father arrived home from the mountain. His shirt-back was wet through with sweat. His dark, wiry hair was still wind-stunned, despite his efforts to finger-comb it down. He slumped his equipment to the floor: his canteen in its army-drab sling, his canvas rucksack and bedroll, his belt with the knife and hatchet hanging down. He looked up at me and at Andy. We were eagerly watching. His face and his knees were bright red, from sun, but his face was lit by vigor, by joy.

Handing us sugary rice candies, he said, "You'll come next time. Yu Shan, Mount Morrison. A splendid climb."

At our rice and tofu dinner he fastened us with the stories. The buck seen deep in the woods, an eagle soaring over the highest rocks, the intense thirst he felt on the descent. The thrill of hurling himself, naked as a deer, into the stream at the foot of the mountain. After dinner, he showed us his blisters—his "merit badges," he called them. For us, they were as good as war medals.

When he was taking his shower, I went over to the pile my father dropped beside the door. I dug into the pocket of his pack. "I found 'em," I said to Andy— tossing him another of the pink candies my father kept for quick energy. Their scent was almost sickly sweet.

Putting a hunk of the hard candy in my mouth, I settled my back against my father's pack and took a swig from his canteen. As the cool water mixed with the sweet candy taste in my mouth, Andy and Mom and the whole house melted away. And for a few delicious moments, I was *him*: my invincible, brave father.

～～

In the morning, as I sat on my parents' hospital-cornered, army-blanketed bed, my father put on his baggy khaki pants (some days, if it was extra hot, he put on his baggy khaki shorts), his airy, white, Chinese-tailored cotton shirt, his tie, his khaki jacket, and the light tan Clark's desert boots he bought before I was born, when my parents were on TDY—Temporary Duty—in Hong Kong.

Even at seven, I knew his two pairs of British-made desert boots—one tan, the other chocolate-brown—represented something important, private, to my quiet, elegant, self-denying father: an intellectual seriousness, a sturdiness, a person's right to a few small preferences. Later I'd know my girlhood sense of reverence for my father's boots was on the mark: they were symbols of his deepest affiliations, of the inner self he too often had to keep under wraps. Those supple, hand-sewn shoes stood in for my father's Anglophilia, his admiration for the elegance of British rhetoric, his belief that a pair of stout walking shoes was a person's most essential item of apparel: they could carry you out of any swamp of difficulty.

～～

After a breakfast of donuts from the PX, my father paused at the door to wipe his horn-rimmed glasses and gave us all kisses before he set out the door to work. He left on foot into the steamy heat, to do his important work for President Kennedy and the Gimo.

～～

Much of the work of the American intelligence community in Taiwan at this time was on the up and up. About China, the outside world heard no more than rumors . . . about Mao's campaigns to militarize his people, about weapons programs, about plans for further conquest in Asia. The CIA's main mission was to run down hard facts about Mao's activities and intentions and to support Chiang in thwarting them.

But another aspect of the Agency's agenda was much more devious. While with one hand, the American government was stacking the repressive leader's deck, with the other, fingers crossed, it was seeking to undermine him, even to reshuffle the deck entirely. Even as it backed the repressive Chiang regime, it was giving clandestine support to secret "Third Force" anti-Chiang opposition groups, a dicey activity at best.

~~

At six o'clock, as soon as my father came in the door, and after hugging each of us—he whirled me in the air like a Sikorsky rotor—my father took off his socks and his desert boots and donned a pair of black cloth Chinese slippers. He breathed a sigh of relief, like he always did, and then I knew I could have his full attention.

While my mother went into the kitchen to see how Yuki was coming along with our dinner, my father read to Andy and me. He was reading us Chinese folk tales. In the past he'd read us books like *Winnie the Pooh*, the *Better Homes and Gardens Story Book*, *Timeless Tales of Gods and Heroes*, and *Tales from the Arabian Nights*. During this delicious after-work hour my father always played whatever game we begged him to play. Sometimes it was Chinese checkers, sometimes it was American checkers, sometimes it was Rogers' Rangers—which meant wrestling on the floor. We threw ourselves on my father's hiking-fit, hard body and tried to wrestle him to the ground, in the best game of all.

After dinner—today we had rice with tofu and beef and bamboo shoots—my mother herded us off for our baths and my father entered his study.

In my father's study there were lots of books, books like *Red Star Over China*, *The Chinese*, and *Socialism of Our Time*. On the bookshelf there were also piles of Chinese newspapers. The study was where my father did his tai chi, practiced his Chinese characters, and met with the men who visited him. His study was also where he just enjoyed being with himself. There was a stone head of Buddha and a framed, signed photo of the Gimo on my father's desk. The Buddha had whorls meant to be snails on his head, snails that kept him cool in the heat, my father told me, as he meditated on the world's suffering. Snails were always crawling around in Taiwan—on the walls in my rooms and on the padi stalks—so I could imagine them planting themselves on the Buddha's head. My father loved the rough-stone Buddha head with its deep, kind expression.

But my father's eyes didn't have the same, happy-hearted sun glints in them when I asked him about the portrait of the Gimo. To me it seemed a wonder that my father possessed a portrait signed by the Gimo himself, but it was like he had stuck it on his desk out of obligation—like the presidential portraits mounted in every embassy in the world. He explained that, yes, the Gimo was the leader of Taiwan, and we Americans supported him, but "he is not the noblest of men."

Most Americans in Taiwan agreed about Chiang's questionable morality—he had had his followers trained by the Nazis, and he was a dictator and a crook—but he'd led the anti-Communist fight on the Mainland, and though he'd lost, the American government had deemed it "in our interests" to put its eggs in Chiang's basket. In this era of Red Devils, fascist dictators were preferred to Communist ones.

When I studied it up close, the uniformed man in the photograph seemed to emit trickiness through his stern eyes. These slipped-out doubts about the Gimo from my careful father might have served as my first clue that something was not as it seemed—that work in support of ruthless dictators is not to every American official's taste—but a seven-year-old who adores her father is not on a search.

To me, my father's study was a place of solemnity and magnetic fascination. Once I was dressed in my white cotton pajamas, and with my wet hair combed slick along my head, I went to sit on a flat, square *zabuton* cushion on the floor beside my father at the low, shiny table my parents bought in Japan, near where I was born. Spread in front of him was a Chinese newspaper, of many sheets, covered in characters columning up and down the long pages, and to the side there were two open, large hard-backed books also covered in characters. Over these my father was poring. Beside him, in low stacks, and in high-toppling stacks, were small, square flash cards, each with a Chinese character on one side and an English word, penned in my father's light, sketchy bird-foot print, on the other. As he read, my father consulted the cards. His absorption in his work was so complete that he didn't seem to know I was there. I just sat quietly, enjoying his soft rustle and the scent of his woody, paper and ink smell. Soon, though, he patted me briefly on the hand. He gave me a small pile of his flash cards with Chinese characters to practice copying.

Sitting beside my father during that brief hushed period of night just before I went to sleep, a longing to study, to pore over books as he did, grew in me like a plant pushing inside its pot. In the afternoons, my mother and I made flash cards of my English spelling words, and as my mother said them to me, I spit the spelled-out words back to her in the fast, expert, gunshot way that my father spoke Chinese. Because our government had sent my father to Yale University to study Mandarin for a year when I was three, he could read the long pages of picture puzzle characters and speak Chinese with all the right tones.

Sometimes, in the evenings, my father held a gathering of his work colleagues: tall American men with butch-cut hair, the spectacled missionaries from the local hospital, or some earnest Chinese men. I heard them speaking, louder and louder, in Mandarin Chinese's sharp, piercing high and low tones, as I tried to sleep. Once in a while, the men broke into hard, strong laughter, and I could hear my father's laugh mingled with the others'. "The Chinese loved your father," my mother always said. Hearing the men laughing in their own special world, I longed to grow up to be one of them, laughing boisterously in another language.

A deeper, soft-tissue residue of my Taipei men-watching stints was a sense that men possessed a sacred, hidden knowledge—and also, a deep inner reserve, a granitic strength. I saw in these men of secrets and plots a kind of special force characterized by a supreme capacity for self-denial, an ability to live with duality and ambiguity for the sake of something beyond themselves. These were the groping, unreasonable idealizations of a young girl. Most girls worship their fathers—at least for a time—but my own adoration had, perhaps, a peculiar power, reinforced by the scent of secrecy.

～～

Those days, peering from the doorjamb, I was perhaps seeing my father at his height, at his most buoyant. His laugh was loud and carefree with confidence and optimism, unburdened by the doubts that would later weigh down his pockets like stones and turn his laugh into a startling, rare joy.

～～

The whispers were always there: momentary surfacings of my father's true affinities and convictions; hints of the secret nature of his work; intimations of his doubts about his engagements; and scents of their perilous nature—all of which had to be concealed. The stirrings were there if I could have read them, but I was yet seven, still reading the *Weekly Reader*. There were so many levels of secrecy that, now when I put my mind to it, they seem to mushroom until they fill the world.

~~

One of the whispers had to do with my father's views of Communism. One night at the NACC Club, my father mentioned again Mao's determination to make all his people equal. This story of Mao's actions puzzled me. It didn't make China seem as bad as an evil king in a fairy tale. "What's so bad about Communism, Pop? It sounds kind of good."

He explained that, in order to have all his citizens contribute to the production of food for their poor country, Mao had moved thousands away from their homes and careers to toil as peasants on remote farms. "This is a good ideal, but it is wrong-headed because it denies Mainlanders the freedom to follow their dreams and build their own lives." But the worst thing about Mao's policy, my father said, was that millions of people, including great thinkers and scholars, had been executed or sent to the countryside sentenced with cruel hard labor for disagreeing with Mao. "In the free world, we believe people have a right to disagree with their leaders, and it is wrong to murder people who do so."

Still, he said, it was difficult, really, to know which system was best for China. Life under the old-style tyrannical landlords was bad for the common man. Perhaps this time of terrible disruption was necessary for China to move toward something better, and in the end there would be a better life for the Chinese people.

"Relations between our country and China are complicated. However," my father said, like he was netting back some escaping fish, "the most important thing for you to know is that President Kennedy is an excellent leader—the best in the world—and that our government is the best, most powerful, and most trustworthy on earth."

If I had been older, I might have been able to detect, like a telltale black strand in a head of blond hair, the ambivalence within my father's reportage. I might have sniffed out, during these dinner table talks, the deeper truth that any good spy knows lies hidden within another man's cover story. I might have sensed my father's interest in Communism as a legitimate social experiment—especially in a country long plagued by crushing inequity and poverty. I might have known that, even though my father's Taipei job was based on fighting Communism, internally he was giving Communism the benefit of the doubt—and that this was risky. The young intelligence officers at work in Taiwan could not but be affected by recent ideological trends in Washington. During the McCarthy era, there had been a vilification of both official and academic China specialists, who were suspected of pro-Communist sympathies. In government in the 1950s, it was obligatory to be fiercely anti-Communist, and the Taipei operation was sunk neck-deep in this conviction. This ideological conformity, and the atmosphere of fear that spawned it, were to hamper official China policy, and bind and twist intelligence officers like my father, for a long time to come.

In a few years, my father's political views would become apparent to me—he would be like a man stepping out of a fog in a movie—but, for now, he was the man who held my hand on pedicab rides and pointed out glittering temples, who ate Chinese octopi like they were donuts, and who, with his soothing hug, could make any carsick ride better. I was a child, wide open, simply absorbing the most obvious meaning in my father's words: America stands for freedom. And those were the meanings he intended me to hear at this point in my life. They were the clearest and, most important, safest.

~~

Here is another of the signals I could have noticed: the soft nosing that told me of my father's love for China—and of the danger associated with that love.

My father deeply admired Chinese culture. He studied Mandarin with a passion and his eyes always squinted in a grin when Andy spoke the Chinese words he was learning in his Chinese nursery school, or when I ordered *pi jiu* or *jiao zi*, beer or dumplings, in Chinese for him when we sat in noisy, dirty, delicious restaurants. (My parents believed that the filthiest restaurants always had the best food.)

Our house was filled with Chinese art. We had scrolls of old men drinking tea, of frogs and pine trees and crabs, and of poems in beautiful twirling characters that my father loved to translate. One of the poems started, "Life is but a dream, why should we be toiling?"

We also had *shan shui*, "mountain-waters," which was what the Chinese called landscapes—beautiful scenes of ghostly mountains with scholars' huts tucked into forests, and wending rivers down below. Looking at these scrolls, I always imagined that I was the man in the hut, writing in a beautiful silence with only the sound of water flowing, and maybe a few cricket chirps. After Taiwan, in future places far, far away, such as the Sackler Gallery in Washington, D.C., when I came to gaze at a Chinese shan shui, a cool, calming river of deepest contentment would ripple through me.

My father's favorite piece of art was a painting of a caravan of camels trudging across the snows of a wild, empty land. He had admired a similar painting at a Chinese man's house. A week later, the man appeared with the painting's twin under his arm. He had gone to the artist and asked him to paint a replica for our family.

My father loved many things the Chinese thought and did—their splendid architecture, their ancient and beautiful script, and their respect for the scholar. He admired the wise Confucian virtues of patience and contentment with little, and the Confucian belief that man was fundamentally good.

And my father loved the Chinese landscape itself. Sometimes he took me down to the padi at the end of our lane when he got home from work. We gazed across the purple-bright mud, the yellow triangles of the rough straw hats of the people working, the infinite, soothing green. The padi was like the French painting of poppies my father showed me in a book, only instead of flowers there were yellow straw hats bobbing about in the padi's green. As we stood in the blue and yellow twilight air, I knew, via an inner tingling, my father's deep sense of peace.

~~

Was my father's feeling properly called love? Or was this quickening that put a bounce in my father's stride and shine in his eyes better called invigoration: the tumbling, the relief and pleasure that are roused when a person finds a hidden part of himself awakened and nourished by another culture? Was it the ardor that a Foreign Service officer often feels for early posts? Or was it the intellectual fascination that bubbles up when a person finds another culture simply paints each aspect of life with a different brush, in an unexpected tint he has never before known? Or was it simply the emotional sympathy of a judicious, sensitive man for those with less? Perhaps it was all these things. My father was always quiet about his pleasures. But to me, even as a girl, my father's passion seemed ardent, like love—a dangerous love, it turned out.

~~

Even at age seven, I could smell the salt of danger in some of my father's proclivities. First: Chinese shoes. My father loved his desert boots, but he also loved his black peasant shoes, the plain cloth slippers, so cheap any Chinese urchin could obtain them. Other fathers, I sensed, would not wear those shoes. Not Mr. Mason, for instance, or Mr. Summers. They wore suits like my father, and on the weekends they wore shorts and sneakers like he did, but they would never put on those Chinese shoes. I sensed that they were holding a line that my father didn't see a need to hold. But my father was different from many of the other American fathers. Like the way he carried flash cards in his pockets and went for walks through the market streets in the early weekend mornings, and the way he didn't worry about washing his hands like Mr. Mason did—first thing when he got in from a trip through the Taipei streets. There was a uniqueness to my father's choice of slippers, something earth and salt.

And then there was the doll-seller at the door.

One Sunday afternoon, we were sitting in our tiny garden as the bell rang at the gate. When my father opened the door, a peddler was standing there. Shoeless and shirtless, in a pair of shorts held up by string, he was holding a bouquet of home-made, colorfully painted paste dolls on sticks.

I said, "Oh Pop, can I have the one that looks like a clown?"

My mother said, "Charlie, don't you dare buy one of those dolls for her. That paste is poisonous. If Andy were to eat it . . ." Mom was keenly, and hourly, aware of all of the possible diseases that could strike and make us fall dead before bed-time. I felt the fear in her voice, like a small tremble inside my own body.

My father said, handing the man a few coins in exchange for the clown doll, "It'll be okay. Andy doesn't eat dolls anymore. And, he's poor," he said, turning to-ward my mother. "This will help him feed his family tonight."

The same thing happened when the typewriter was stolen from my father's study. My mother was worried and mad, but my father said, "It was probably some poor man trying to find a way to feed his children."

~~

A pair of shoes, a doll-maker at the door, a typewriter: Why would these mo-ments carry a whiff of riskiness so strong that they would tickle a child's heart? Why was there a slip of furtiveness to my father's simple enjoyment of the place he lived, the land to which he'd been assigned by his own government?

Back then, I didn't know that employees who differed from the accepted doc-trine, who had socialist sympathies, or who just took a keen interest in the Chinese viewpoint, had been marginalized, had their careers ruined, or been pressed out, at the outfit where my father worked.

My father was a sensitive man and his sensitivity extended to the Chinese. Was his too deep a sympathy? Later I understood that American officials were expected to study and take an interest in the countries to which they were posted. But their sympathies and outlook were always to remain strictly pro-American, their perspectives limited to promotion of American interests. Was my father in danger of "going native"? Is this why he would later have trouble getting promotions from the China Desk? It strikes me, looking back, that my father had to conceal so many things. He had to veil even his most elemental pleasures, like gazing at a Chinese vista. And it got dicier from there. His socialist leanings, his empathy for the poor: these could be misconstrued, or used against him.

Of course, at age seven, I couldn't have begun to plumb the subtle anxiety associated with my father's feeling for China. It wouldn't have made sense that loving another people should be a risky matter. So I overlooked the whispers. They were the background hum of my childhood, unattended to as the singing frogs in a swamp. I could only assume, like most children, my father was always safe.

~~

But then came the steamy night—a night like one hundred others—when the whispers that had been encircling me became loud enough to hear, when they staked out a claim in the material world.

Soon after the deep-night phone call and my father's urgent whisper, from my dark bed, I heard an odd and disturbing sound. I heard my father quietly open the front door. I heard low voices in the study: my father's Chinese and a Chinese man's Chinese. I tiptoed into the hall and saw a man with a worried face being given a cup of tea by my mother. She and my father wore their Japanese yukatas. I could tell by the way my mother was standing with her arms wrapped tightly around each other that she was afraid.

Then, suddenly, my mother turned and saw me. She rushed toward me and hissed, "Come here, Sara. I'm putting you in Andy's room tonight."

"But Mom!" I said.

"You do as I say," she said, her hands shaking, pushing me out of the hall. She hurriedly made me a pallet of rush mats, blankets, and sheets on Andy's floor and made me lie down.

"Now go to sleep. Don't say a word." And she rushed out of the room. Then she did something she had never done before: I heard her lock the door.

Feeling my mother's haste and terror in my own body, I couldn't close my eyes. On my pallet, I listened to my parents and the Chinese man speaking in the hush. There were long yammers and then whispers, and then slower yammers in a string. I heard my mother hurriedly tiptoeing around and closing doors. Then the Chinese became lower and lower, like an eel lashing in the sea.

In the early morning I heard rustling again, but by the time I got up—though I could see my bed had been slept in and roiled by someone other than me—the Chinese man was gone.

At breakfast, my father's face was drawn. He looked like he might cry. My mother was only drinking coffee for breakfast; she usually had toast and a boiled egg. Her face looked tired, but she was pulsing like a pot of milk about to boil over. Her eyes were shooting streaks of fury.

Finally, she had to overflow, even though Andy and I were there.

She hissed to my father through clenched teeth, as though she was continuing a conversation already begun, "'That poor man,' I agree, but why didn't they send him to the Townsends? They have grown children. I can't believe they'd send him to us—putting our young children at risk . . . " Her voice was like shrieks of lightning, and also like stones scraping down a hill.

My father's eyes went narrow, but then he reached out his hand. "Okay," he said. Then he pulled my mother's pushing-away body into a hug and said, "It's all right, Lois. We had to help. He could end up like Lee or the others, Lois."

My father looked sick. "What else could I do? . . . What good do we do these well-meaning people, our friends?"

"But isn't it his choice?"

My father's lip trembled, as if he might burst into tears. "Yes, but Chu doesn't know what choice he is making. As Lee didn't. We're giving them a false choice because we're giving them false hope. These people think they can rely on us."

Lee was someone something had happened to back when we lived in Japan, when I was born. I saw now, for the first time, the look of utter sadness that I would see shadow my father's face, out of the blue, at Lee's name, for the rest of my life.

So the man had been Mr. Chu, my father's friend?

My mother nodded now and sank into his hug at last, but her eyes had turned into black pools.

My father patted her again on his way out, and said, "I'll call you later, when I hear any news."

After my father left, my mother quickly turned around. Her face was all angled up with tension. She looked us so fiercely in the eyes that I felt fear like a ghost steal into my body. "Sara and Andy," she said, "I want you to listen to me. If *anyone* with a Chinese voice calls and asks for a Mr. Someone with a Chinese name, you say to him, 'There is no one here by that name,' okay? Do you understand?"

We stared at her and nodded.

My mother then sat down at the table, heaved a big sigh, and sipped her coffee, like everything might be all right. But now, eating my rice cereal, I had in my mind a fixed picture: a Chinese man, quaking inside our house, his face, in the low lamp light, damp with sweat. Into my belly dropped little nameless jumping beans of fear.

~~

My father told me thirty years later of the unease still in his gut from the events of that night in Taipei. The man who'd come to our house that night was an important anti-Chiang newspaper editor, a member of the "Third Force," a political group situated between the Communists and the Nationalists, being pursued by the jealous Gimo's ruthless police. The police could have broken down our door, dragged him out of the house, and tortured him to death. The editor escaped being captured that time around. "But by supporting him," my father said, his eyes soft, his brows bent with concern, "did we do that man any favors? It may be that all we did was put him in great jeopardy."

In my father's effects, after his death, I came upon a packet containing a ream of documents about the trial of a Chinese editor who had doubted Chiang's ability to overcome the Communists and suggested that Taiwan work out some sort of compromise with the Mainland. He'd been sentenced to seven years in jail for his outspokenness. I wondered whether my father or others in the CIA had suggested or even written his copy. I also wondered why my father had reserved these documents from the many he could have kept. It implied a significant attachment.

For the anti-Chiang people in the underground press and the other Nationalist Chinese operatives, my father himself brought me to understand, we Americans were lifelines, life buoys. We were also like matches to their grenades. And, at worst, we were children tossing them time-release suicide bombs. To Washington, what was the loss of one man in a fight for the good? As Graham Greene put it in *The Quiet American*, "How many dead colonels justify a child's or a trishaw driver's death when you are building a national democratic front?"

The night of the Chinese man's visit was the first whisk of the tail of the secret tiger of my father's work, the first hint to me of the secret plots in which he engaged—and of his doubts about some of these actions. The tail grazed my cheek, and the animal passed into the night—but the sensation of flicking fur remained.

~~

In addition to secret and dangerous acts, there were other murmurs in the ear: dark hints about my father's relationships with his boss and his department.

An evening soon after the secret visitor, when my father got home from work, there was a fretful feeling in the house. My father had come into the house in a hurry and immediately gone into the bedroom with my mother.

I overheard my mother saying, "Charlie, why on earth did you have to tell him your doubts? You shouldn't be so trusting. He's a climber and a brown-noser. He'll do anything to get ahead. He's an ideologue; you know that. He'll always think he's right, and he'll always come out on top. If you're right, he'll sacrifice you."

At dinner, my mother's face was closed, her eyes looked watery, and she kept rushing to her room. While my father acted as though nothing had happened, my mother seemed scared; her eyes either looked out into the distance, or down toward the ground.

A day or two later, my mother got suitcases out and began packing them. My father went into the room and closed the door. I could hear his soothing voice through the wood of the door. Only then did my mother unpack her slips and blouses.

I would learn, years later, that my father's Taipei boss punished those who differed with his aggressive anti-Communist schemes. My father didn't know it, but at a particular instant, on one of these days, in this stretch of time, a black dot was stamped on his file, an ink mark that would blot the white cloth of his career and spread into an indelible stain of frustration. Another way to see it: an invisible thorn was planted in his body—a thorn that burrows deeper and deeper until it stabs the heart.

My father was thirty-four. He did not know that, in an instant, the course of his life was laid out. The knots were cinched. And he was from America, the place where a man makes his own destiny.

~~

Decades later, I asked my father why he picked the career he did.

I had read *National Security Council Directive 10/2*, issued in June 1948, which defined covert operations as actions conducted by the United States against foreign states "which are so planned and executed that any U.S. Government responsibility for them is not evident to unauthorized persons and that if uncovered the U.S. Government can plausibly disclaim any responsibility for them. . . ."

The document further explained that the CIA was authorized to carry out clandestine activities, including "propaganda, economic warfare; preventive direct action, including sabotage, anti-sabotage, demolition and evacuation measures; subversion against hostile states, including assistance to underground resistance movements, guerrillas and refugee liberations [*sic*] groups, and support of indigenous anti-Communist elements in threatened countries of the free world."

"It was the patriotic thing to do," my father said, in answer to my puzzlement about how a caring man of conscience would choose a job in covert operations. "We'd just come out of World War II. The most important contribution a person could make at that time, it seemed to us, was to stop mad men like Hitler. Government was *the* place to be back in the fifties." In fact, the CIA, and its predecessor, the OSS, was, at that point, an elite club engaged in a fight against fascism and communism. A stronghold of those with social power and wealth, it drew disproportionately from the Ivy Leagues. In 1943, for example, at least forty-two members of the Yale graduating class went into intelligence work.

"In addition," my father went on, "it was a good job, even a fascinating job, with security and excellent benefits. Your mother and I had been through the Great Depression, you must remember."

Both of my parents had grown to adulthood on the watery oatmeal of the Depression. During the thirties, my father's ten-plus extended family had had to live in a boiler room because they had nowhere else to sleep. While my mother's family of eleven grew their own food and always had shelter and enough to eat, they lived hand-to-mouth. My grandmother served meals to desperate homeless men who wandered onto their Indiana farm at dusk.

My father, an artistic Washington University political science graduate with a thick brush of dark hair and warm, hazelnut eyes behind horn-rimmed glasses, grew up in St. Louis, the son of two Missourians. As I remember them from infrequent visits, his father was a now doting–now irascible man, and his mother as sweet as her German chocolate cake. I have since heard, though, that they could be tough on his younger siblings, and the household was not a serene one.

When my parents met, my mother, sharp as an egret, with eyes of greyed moss, was a newly minted physical therapist sporting a perky, blond ponytail. She was the ninth child of a gentle Indiana forester father and a mother who, overwhelmed by her enormous brood, sewed her children's underwear from flour sacks. I can imagine that government service (wives were considered part and parcel of a man's available resources when he took an assignment) seemed a perfect arena for my mother to employ her rigorous, patriotic, eager-to-sacrifice, Midwestern bravery, her compassion for the poor and the disabled, and her can-do optimism, and for my father to apply his talent for languages and his innocent intellect, shiny as a fresh quarter. Leaving behind their stressed families, my parents were game for adventure, and had much to gain, and nothing—they thought—to lose. The new job looked like hope, a secure future, and glamour to boot.

"We didn't really think about it," my father said when I asked about whether he and my mother had thought about what covert work would mean. "We were young and just glad to have a good job." They had been recently married, at twenty-four and twenty-six—by a justice of the peace in St. Louis—and had traveled to Washington, D.C., on their honeymoon. My father had been accepted to a political science graduate program in Syracuse, and my mother was set to put her physical therapy degree to use. For a lark, during their honeymoon, my father put in an application at the government, and lo and behold, he was offered a job with the U.S. Information Agency. When soon thereafter he was offered another job with the new intelligence service it seemed like icing on the cake.

Nevertheless, it strikes me as strange that my parents didn't consider, as they signed on the dotted line, what they would be doing, what secrets could mean, how secrets could multiply and corrode—or about how work that requires shading and two-sidedness, and unquestioning adherence to a policy dictated from on high, could gnaw at a man's heart.

Furthermore, my father joined an agency where abandonment was in the contract: *We owe you nothing. We will not be there for you, and furthermore, you are muzzled.* Is any idea pure enough for this?

From their stories, I know my parents arrived at their first post in Asia eager and optimistic. It was as if they were walking under a magnificent, towering *torii* gate into a glorious Japanese garden.

~~

All through my days, I watched my parents, like a monkey in a tree overlooking a hut. In Taipei, it was like our whole family was on a stage in front of the Chinese. My mother's roles were American embassy hostess—gracious server of tea and cookies to Chinese ladies and other embassy wives, and health worker—saver of Chinese orphans and polio victims. My father's role was to save the world from Communism. To me, as a child, both of these roles seemed straightforward.

But as a twenty-year-old visiting my father in Vietnam when the sham of American pretense was in clear sight, I would look back and see that my father's role was not as simple as my mother's. Each day, he received his orders from Washington ready to do his duty. But then he also sat alone at his desk and thought through the implications of what he was being asked to do. When he had joined the Agency he'd been eager to fight fascism. But, as it turned out, fighting fascism wasn't clear-cut: when did covert operations against fascists become fascist themselves? He couldn't quite be the "good soldier." He was tender and sweet—my mother always said "too sweet for this world." My mother could squat down in the orphanage pigsty and feed the pigs, and know she was doing good. My father, on the other hand, was tangled in the meddlesome strings of the American puppet master. It was a sticky web that placed everyone in jeopardy—the Chinese the Americans supported and those Americans themselves.

~~

There were those bedroom-door murmurs of the troubling nature of my father's employment. Also swirling around were other hushed truths: wisps of my father's vulnerability, of the fervid emotions that dwelt deep in the calm brown pools behind his eyeglasses. Unlike some of the other hints, these stole down to my bones even as a young girl, because they sprang from ardor, running clear and crisp as a mountain stream: my own and my father's. They forecast the way the story would play out.

~~

We were at the Grand Hotel on a Taipei afternoon when the sky was bright as sapphires. Swimming in the shining turquoise pool at the mountain's knee, I was happily climbing all over my father, as I always did, when I heard my mother shrieking from the poolside. Suddenly, the Chinese lifeguard came roaring across the pool, reached for me, and, to my shock and hurt, tossed me out of the way. He then put his arm around my father, who was gasping for air and gulping in water.

When we were back at the poolside table, dripping, wrapped in our monogrammed Grand Hotel towels, I asked my father, "What was wrong, Pop?"

"You were pushing my head under for long periods and I couldn't touch the bottom there, Sara."

A shudder passed through my body. I hadn't known. I hadn't known I needed to know. I'd thought my father could touch the bottom of any sea.

I held my arms stiff at my sides while we rode home in the car. I couldn't forget the look of my father gasping for air.

I would always think of my father as strong, but forever now, I would know a delicacy, a fragility, in my father that caused me to tremble inside. This was a sense that would ripple into a deep-lodged fear for my father's safety, for the safety of men. A strange sense that—sensitive beings that we both were—it would be up to me to save my father. I dashed it away, but it sank and stayed—lurking like a terrifying giant squid, like a warning—in my deepest waters.

~~

My father pulled our navy blue, round-fendered Rambler up beside a high, dirty concrete wall topped with barbed wire and broken glass that extended as far as I could see on the left side of the car. The wire and glass looked almost like a tangle of Christmas tree ornaments. My father told us to wait in the car. He was going into the building to see if he could identify the man who stole our radio and binoculars a few nights ago. My mother gave him an encouraging pat on the shoulder as he climbed out. He entered a door in the long concrete wall. My mother told us the grey-block building was a prison. While we waited, Andy and I tickled each other. We were having fun, but Andy started crying and told my mother, "Sara hurt me."

My mother waved her hand back over the seat. "Hush. Behave yourselves."

My father's face, when he emerged, was as grey as the wall and his eyes were narrowed and sad, like he'd seen a snake or a ghost. He said to my mother, "I wish I hadn't done it." He then whispered to her several more sentences. I heard the words "shackles" and "beaten."

My mother shook her head and touched his neck. "You had to do it. There has to be a line. There's no excuse for stealing."

At the wheel of the car, though, my father rubbed his eyes. I had just seen how the strains of his work were starting to play in him. Month by month, year by year, his lights would become a little dimmer.

In the darkness of night, and now in the bright of day, I sensed the pain playing through my father's lean body. Over the next twenty years, his life would become one of inner torment and outer slippery slopes—until he seemed to be suffocating with the effort of keeping quiet.

~~

These painful moments in Taipei were a whiff of the troubling nature of my father's special work: of the inordinate exposure and extraordinary hiddenness that were by-products of signing the loyalty oath, the mix of internal conflict and external threat that were part and parcel of my father's chosen profession. They were also the first intimations of my father's sensitivity and vulnerability: a sense that would grow in me through time into a strong, fumbling, inarticulate urge to protect him.

~~

This is the scene I hold tight.

One day, a Friday afternoon, my father insisted we drive hours through rugged mountains to Sun Moon Lake. "The moon will be full," he said to my mother. We stayed in a small, clean, white lodge that seemed like a castle compared to our little government-issue house. Flowered beauty was everywhere. There was an outbuilding with two huge Chow dogs barking threateningly on chains—the chill of menace that was always lurking in the Gimo's Taiwan—but they were secured behind a high metal fence.

For a wondrous weekend we romped in light-lanced woods. I rode my father piggyback as he galloped through paths of ferns. Nothing in the world was more fun than this. My father was my comfort and I was his. It was as if we were the only people in each other's lives.

Jouncing along, I was sure it would be this way always: My father would always be happy and so would I. Life would always be clear like the sky of this day, and love would always be a gold, unknotted thread. All my life, I would live in Free China, playing with my father.

At evening, we dined near the lake, and the moon was reflected like a gold medallion in the shimmering black-purple water. When noon came on Sunday, we loaded into the car and set off, spirits high, down through the green humps of mountains.

Along the way, old cars were stopped along the road, steaming or with flames leaping out of them, and people hurrying down the road or scurrying around with buckets. About halfway down, on a steep incline, my mother smelled smoke. My father stopped the car and opened the hood, which released a large, black, billowing cloud just like those coming out of the Chinese vehicles. My mother pulled us out of the car, yelling and beating at us to come faster, and we ran down the road. My mother yelled back to my father, "Charlie! Get away from that car!" but my father had already grabbed a tin bucket from the trunk, jumped down the ravine, dipped some water from the stream passing below, and thrown it into the radiator, dousing the flames.

It was at this moment that I knew one thing for certain: we were all safe, and my father was not only the handsomest and smartest but the bravest man in the world.

4

night soil

When I was a child we had few photographs, but there was one of my father on a hike through Formosa's mountains. In the black-and-white picture, my father, in a coolie hat, was walking across a rickety bridge of two bamboo poles suspended high over a gorge at the bottom of which was a boulder-strewn, churning river. He held a walking staff, as a balance.

For any person living in a foreign land, even a young child, something pure and strong and astringent rises up: A wish to cross the invisible chasm between herself and the native inhabitants of the land in which she lives. A wish for proof that unities, commonalities, and love are greater than all the differences that can be seen and smelled and touched.

~~

There are two kinds of loneliness: personal and national. At age seven, I was struggling against both—and striving for a place to rest in both the emotional and geopolitical realms. I needed a sense of belonging in China to set against the people in the chicken village. I longed to find one person who could merge my need for belonging.

In Taipei, I could claim to know only one Chinese person well: my amah, Mary. To me, with Chinese people here in Taipei it was too close–too far, too close–too far. Except with Mary. She was the only person holding a stick that might be laid across the chasm, for me, between America and China.

Mary was one of a string of amahs, nannies, and housekeepers who were important in my life: women whose patient eyes and gentle, helpful hands I would still be able to sense on my skin—like small, whispering, wafting gifts—forty years later.

Under her curly black hair, Mary had a sincere face, with solemn eyes that squeezed together and glinted with pleasure when I asked her to play with me. Her eyes were nothing like the fierce eyes on the Taipei streets. They were M&M eyes: quiet and melting with love.

My amah's devotion had no dark line holding in its colors. One late afternoon I was drawing on the couch and Andy was playing cars with Mary. When my mother came home from her day at the orphanage, she opened the door and stood inside the doorway for a moment. At that instant, Mary was crouched under the rug in the living room, forming a mountain for Andy to drive his cars over.

"Andy!" my mother said with a shocked tone in her voice. "Stop that right now. Think about poor Mary!"

When Mary emerged from under the rug, my mother said, "You mustn't do that ever again, Mary. You'll spoil him. You'll turn him into a little prince."

I knew, though, that Andy *was* Mary's prince, and that I was her princess. My mother didn't know about the candies of every color that Mary kept in her housecoat pocket, or about the trips to the market when Mary carried Andy on her back, gripping my hand to shield me from the Chinese women who wanted to stroke my hair. She taught us how to ask for sticky sweet noodles or the delicious grilled corn that the sellers were delighted to push into the hands of foreign children. Mary loved to show us off to the market ladies, but she held us tight.

~~

Each day Mary appeared at our house with the same grey skirt and pressed white blouse, and wearing a gold cross around her neck. Once, my father had told me Mary's story: about how she was the eldest in a family of girls, that the grandparents she lived with were old and frail, that she'd had to go to work at age ten to support her family. "The job we offer to Mary is a very good one for her, for her place in life," my father said.

With the light off, watching shadows drift across the ceiling of my bedroom, I wondered about my amah. What does "place in life" mean? The next day, I could not put out of my mind the picture of Mary, as a girl only two and a half years older than I was, mopping some American lady's floor. It gave me a strong wish to totter across the rickety bridge into Mary's life. I studied Mary's face while she was neatening up the living room. Her cheeks were soft and her movements gentle, but it was as if she had seen many things that I had not and could see a future I could not imagine. The look she returned was awash with longing and sadness.

~~

Mary was the only Chinese person with whom I had a sense of closeness, but it was not equal. Even to my child self, the inequality of my and Mary's relationship was worrying. And as an adult—when I'd come to know that the amah-employer relationship was age-old and existed all over Asia—I'd find it still more disturbing. Though the relationship between the amahs and us American children was mutually agreed-upon, it was a stretched-thin version of human relations, an odd seesaw economy. On the one hand, we children were more vital to our amahs than they were to us: they required our parents' money for their livelihood—and were all the more vulnerable because we might be spirited away at any time. On the other hand, we American children were utterly dependent on our amahs for our daily needs and our very safety. It was a crude exchange—money for love—and yet, love miraculously survived the contortion. I know this for certain—I see it in photographs of Mary holding a small American girl. Perhaps this amah-child love is prime evidence that human commonality trumps human difference.

~~

I had Mary, but I still desired a Chinese twin, someone my age who loved to draw like I did, who felt uncomfortable speaking up in groups of people, who knew what I felt at the exact moment I did. This was a hunger so deep—deep and bottomless as the ramshackle well my father and I once discovered in a deer woods—that sometimes I thought it might never go away. If I had such a Chinese friend, no matter where I was, everything would always be okay.

I made a resolve to keep a lookout. "I may be what other people call shy, but I am also a close watcher," my thoughts went. "My eyes are my brave part. They are not afraid to look down the steep drop-off of a mountain, or to observe poor Chinese people soaping their bare bodies in tubs in the street. Listening and waiting and viewing: I am good at them.

"My eyes—I will never close them," I thought. And, despite the habit they had of drinking in unsettling and contradictory sights, I was rewarded with strange magnificences. At the Grand Hotel I loved to watch a beautiful Chinese lady who wore a scarlet-and-gold robe over her bathing suit. On the way up Yangmingshan to the embassy dispensary, I always looked for a hut of branches at a certain place in the forest, where I often saw a girl my age weaving baskets.

I did not ever want to close my eyes. Something beautiful and small, like the pearl I'd once found hidden in an ugly, horny shell on the beach at Tan-Sui, might be lost. And the lost thing might be a dragon pearl, a miniature lustrous orb that would hatch into a glorious winged beast. And it seemed to me that though they isolated me and sometimes made me feel like an outsider, what my eyes gave me might be all the wealth I had.

I thought again of the gazes of other people. They were a grand part of the wealth my own eyes hauled in. On the streets I saw fearful eyes or sharp ones or the terrifyingly eager ones in the chicken village, and then there were Mei-Lin's eyes, leaping with playfulness, and Mary's, chock-full of love.

Placing my hand in Mary's allowed her to lead me into the lacquered world of China, and into the midst of my own part-Chineseness—and made it possible for me to find, by keeping an eye out, on the curb of a downtown street, the Chinese person that I had been most wanting.

~~

I was walking down the street called Chung Shan Pei Lu with Mary. She was searching for the right fish. The strong, pungent smells were familiar and comforting to me, but so strong that I would forever be taken back to those streets whenever I smelled fish.

My teeth were all sugary from the watermelon-colored candies I was popping into my mouth—the candies my mother hated me to eat, because they might be dirty or poisonous or rot my teeth. I'd seen the Chinese market children unwrapping and eating them, and when I was with Mary I forgot everything and was sort of Chinese myself. At one stall, I spoke my best Mandarin and asked for a ball of chewing gum. The stall woman was so pleased that I'd asked in Chinese—she chortled, smiling and pointing at me to Mary—she gave me a whole sack-full.

I waited for Mary outside a shrimp shop on the crowded, narrow street. As I chewed my candy, I watched. I was an island in the swirling waters of scores of people with black-gleaming hair. I felt conspicuous and alone. A part of me wanted to be invisible and ordinary, ordinary as that little girl jumping up and down in the band of children playing with plastic fish on strings. She was not thinking about anyone else—just shouting and laughing.

Then it happened. The thing I had been yearning for—the thing I would possess forever. Across the narrow alley of men pushing bicycles, and hawkers, and people shoving by with market baskets, I saw a girl about my age sitting at the curb. Her skinny, scabby legs were tucked under her, making a vee, with her knees forming the point. Her hair was messy, but shiny black like the sea sparkling at night, and she was wearing a faded, ragged shift.

Clutching a book along her thin forearm, she was drawing quickly with a pencil, her face bent close over the page. Then, at one random instant—caught from the flash of time—she looked up. Our eyes locked. Her face was clear and clean. Her eyes were gentle and dark brown, and seemed very, very true.

As our eyes melded, we searched for something. And suddenly we found it. It was, simply, there: a friendliness. Chemicals tingling across the boundary between two human bodies. We understood each other without speaking. We looked different—brown eye to green—but inside her body she was exactly like me. It was like she was American and I was Chinese; we were both, both.

An old Ford suddenly roared between us, scattering the passersby, and afterward the raggedy girl was gone. I would never see her again. But something had shifted. It was like the drawer in a Chinese puzzle box had suddenly clicked open. I felt something invisible but strong and sinewy connecting the Chinese girl and me. A small, refreshing wind blew through me.

~~

Bedtimes, all through my Taipei years, I heard the screech of the night soil man. His singsong cries and the squeaks of the wheels of his cart were my lullaby. My father had pointed him out, an old man with knobby knees making his rounds with his wooden buckets in another part of the city during the day, but I thought of him as a nightwalker, a mountain cat that snuck through the city after dark.

My father had told me what night soil was, and I imagined his secretive, deep-night activities. With a bullock at his side, with his sloshing buckets swinging on a pole and jumbled in his creaking cart, he finished his rounds—he spent all day dipping his product out of people's sumps and mixing it with water—and stopped at the outskirts of town.

Then the night soil man worked his magic at the edge of the padi.

He poured out his brimming buckets into the mud and the green spikes sparkling under the moon, and the dung—my own dung mixed with that of the Chinese girls and boys and mothers and fathers—began to glitter. In the blackness, the sparkle grew, the sparks rose higher and higher, until there was a low fireworks display of gold, purple, emerald, and magenta across the stretch of the padi.

That is how the rice grows, I thought, deep in my bed at night. *I, and the Chinese people, make the night soil that makes the rice that pads out my body.* I felt a calmness like cool dawn inside me. As my mother said, "Chinese and American, we nourish the earth together."

Over the years, China had crept into my body without my awareness, pouring in through my eyes in the day, and through my pores as I slept at night. The lively, jabbering, black-haired people; the cluttered, stinking streets of the city; the expanses of padi; the velvet blackness of the mountains had nestled into my mind. The small, tidy house inside the wall, my plain-walled room with its window to the garden, the very concreteness of the wall itself were a familiarity, a deep but unconscious comfort to me. They were the soil, the home among all possible others, of my early childhood.

~~

At this point in my life, I could love both China and America. The expatriate life was really the only one I'd known. To be American and to be Chinese were one to me. Doubleness was not the problem it would be for me later, when logic and competing viewpoints and a need to choose kicked in. It was a naïf's view of the world, but an emotionally true one. At seven my staples were Chinese rice and American milk. I could both wear my patent leather shoes and look into the eyes of snakes.

Or perhaps because it was a given that America was above Taiwan, this ordered my life: all was right with the world.

My father once took me to the central plaza of Taipei where a road circles a gigantic, heroic statue of Chiang Kai-shek. My father was almost running as we set out from the house. As he piggybacked me to the pedicab stand, I could feel his excitement—the shiver inside his body and a bounce in the middle of his paces. As he trotted, he told me we were going to see the great American president, the leader of the Free World: President Eisenhower. After the pedicab man let us out at the roundabout, we were standing in a crush of what must have been thousands and thousands of Chinese people. My father, who couldn't see beyond the throng, put me on his shoulders and told me to look for a man standing up in a convertible in a motorcade.

Little did I know that I was waiting for the man who would warn my country, in the final days of his presidency, of the dire danger associated with the ever-increasing power of the "military-industrial complex." Eisenhower foresaw—looming like a dark and all-too-probable specter—the troubling consequences of a focus on commercial and military might over human considerations.

After a long line of low, dark cars passed and people pushed forward in a scary, suffocating pulse, my father asked me, "Did you see him, Sweetie?" All I'd seen, floating above the open-air car, was a bald head. The most powerful man in the world had a large, shiny head. It looked like a perfect, gleaming, white-marble globe set on a pedestal.

~~

All around the edges of our years in Taipei, as American friends and colleagues came to and departed from the city, there was a vague, unspoken possibility in the air curling in and out like an invisible dragon's tail. *Will Pop get new orders? Will we receive an assignment to leave Taiwan? Will we return to the States someday?*

~~

Then, one night, as my mother was dishing out the fresh, steaming rice, my father told us we would soon be leaving Taipei. We would be returning "home": to America. "We'll take a ship! It'll be fun, a great adventure!" my father said, his eyes ablaze with excitement. "You'll love it!"

~~

My father acted about the move like he did when he was about to embark on a hiking trip: his step was springy and his eyes darted with excitement. My mother's eyes, though, were downcast. Years later she would tell me she hadn't wanted to leave Taiwan. She loved her work at the orphanage and at the polio clinic. She felt needed—she was making a real contribution. "But your father wanted to move on." My brother told me that my father had told him the Taiwanese government had uncovered the fact that the United States was supporting dissident groups, arrested many of those the United States had supported, and had declared that the associated American officials were no longer welcome.

Had my father been forced to leave or was it his choice? Could he say, like my mother, that he had been making a contribution? Was he, instead, disillusioned by his work? At that point had he faced down his fears about harming his Chinese colleagues and informants, or had the fears, perhaps, grown? Had he managed to fashion any bridges across the Chinese-American strait? Did he feel he had helped build freedom or democracy? Or, by moving, was he trying to escape his doubts about his own and his country's efforts? Or—was the motivation behind the move primarily to escape his boss? Or did he just want to move on? Did he simply want to taste the whole world?

~~

After the news, the air I breathed was faster, full of rush and jitter. People talked to us of nothing else. At TAS, all the other children exclaimed how lucky I was: In "the States" I would get to eat all the Hershey's bars I wanted. I would look and be exactly like everyone else. The excitement, the pulse of movement, the regular migrations I had absorbed into the fibers of my body over the six moves we had made since I was born, took over my being, billowing the sense of adventure and hushing the sense of loss. The soy-sauce-and-tofu familiarity of my Taiwanese home was flattened under the practical adventurer's boot. The air was Magellan air.

I thought about the objects I would put in the suitcase Santa Claus had given me for Christmas: one of my spelling tests marked with a big "A," my collection of wooden Chinese dolls, my pad full of ballerina drawings, and my bell from the Temple of a Thousand Steps.

But I would be packing much more: indelible pictures of my father speaking rapid-fire Mandarin, striding off in the hushed morning cool to meet a Chinese man on a back street of Taipei, spark-eyed and invigorated after mountain hikes—a young man in his prime, confident of his abilities, optimistic about the fairness of the world as he might never be again.

Into my suitcase, weighty but invisible, I would also be packing a reflex love for Asia. For after Taiwan, every time I saw an Asian face on a street anywhere in the world, I would feel an instant crazy bond. I would smile familiarly as I approached, feeling a cousinship with the passing person based purely on gleaming black hair and features set in a particular plane.

I would also carry with me a peculiar collection of smells, sounds, and a certain look to things: the red-and-black lacquered roof curve of a layered pagoda; the light-brushed, up-to-down beauty of a shan shui; the rough-textured straw of coolie hats; the strangely reassuring Chinese scent of fish and soy sauce mixed with chickens, bodies, and lotus blossoms; the squabble of toothless women; the shouts of joyful, patchy-clothed children; and keening music. Never again would I have this riot for the senses. All down the years, I'd hunt for it in Chinatowns, Chinese restaurants, Asian emporia, and films. I'd haunt Asian art museums, a stalker after a disappearing slip of harlequin cloth. Whenever browsing through a magazine I came across a photo of a padi, my heart would pause and drink in a great draft, as if it had been thirsty for a long, long time.

After Yi Kuang, the raggedy girl, and the street children of Asia, I knew dirt, poverty, and sadness were real; life wasn't always clean like an American mall or beauty parlor or Episcopal church. This early acquaintance with poverty led me, in my twenties and thirties, to work in the projects of Somerville, Massachusetts; a psychiatric emergency service in San Jose, California; and the Hispanic slums of St. Paul, Minnesota.

My sojourn in Taipei—and my family's later stints among the poor of Malaysia and Vietnam—also instilled the conviction that I should live without. I should be able to live as simply as the poorest person in the world. I would be thoroughly content when, in my late twenties, I lived in Patagonia—in a corrugated metal Quonset hut where a natural gas canister for heat, light, and cooking; an outhouse; and a handful of poor sheep farmers for friends met all my basic needs.

From Taiwan, I left with a child's naïve assessment that, at the very least, I had an obligation to devote a part of myself, at all times, to the hurts of the world, like a kind of prayer, a bow of loyalty, respect, kinship, and acknowledgment to all those who would never have American abundance or freedom or optimism. For a long time, I would keep sadness with me, like a signet ring—or a sailor's stripes—so as to know what I knew, to know who I was.

~~

One night, I came upon my father hugging my mother in the living room. Boxes of the clothes she collected for the orphans were piled around the living room floor, and she was dabbing her eyes with a crumpled up hanky. When she saw me, she immediately straightened up and said, "Oh, Sara's here."

She wiped her eyes and said, "Go back to bed, Sweetie. Everything's okay." But I knew it wasn't: my mother was sad that we were leaving Taipei. I knew this like I knew padi was rice.

I lay with my eyes open in the hot, chirping dark for a long time.

The next day when we left the house to go see friends, my mother wore her dark glasses.

~~

A few weeks later, on a bright day after school, my father and I looked out over the broad, lettuce-green padi that seemed to stretch forever into the distance. As my father squeezed my hand here on the muddy dike that stretched for miles along the town side of the padi, looking out over what seemed the entire expanse of China, I felt a sublime contentment. My whole self rushed out over the land, like a fast swooping hawk, to join it. I stood for a few moments, just watching the straw hats of the people squatting far off in the mud, and inhaling the warm, stinky-soft air from over the expanse before me.

I did not know it yet, but this was how it would be forever. Just before leaving each place I lived, I would be out walking and a surge of contentment would rise within me. Somehow, the country, its people, my life in that country and among its people, would spread out before me whole and verdant. The land would shine, all its beauties apparent for the first, and final, time.

~~

The morning we left Taiwan, the air was sweet as ginger ale, bubbly and clear.

I awakened well before dawn, before anyone else was awake. Mary helped me put on my traveling clothes. People in those days dressed up for plane journeys. She brushed my hair free and put on my headband. She handed me a rattan purse filled with candies—her gift to me. I felt like a princess in my puffy, light green dress with its crinoline underneath and my necklace of pretend pearls, holding my purse—but my stomach was a sour, uncomfortable, cold pool.

At breakfast, I couldn't eat, I was so excited about going on the airplane. Andy ran around the empty house in circles. My mother asked my father ten times if he had the orders. He kept patting the passports in his hidden chest pocket.

Finally the embassy car came, along with friends in another car. We had to get to the airport four hours early, for processing and all the good-bye formalities.

In the grey-furnished living room, now stripped of any sign of our life there, Mary stood in the center of the hemp carpet. My father, dressed in his smartest suit, hugged her, patted her shoulder, and handed her an envelope. He made a last-minute check of his pockets—passports, tickets, orders, money—a gesture that would become familiar as breakfast through the years of my childhood. Then he stood by the door: the spruce American official readying himself for his next assignment.

My mother in her pretty belted flowered dress, her handbag over an arm, embraced Mary's small, thin form. All she said was, "Oh Mary, thank you." Tears trickled down Mary's cheeks and wetted her neck. My mother's torso shook and she put on her dark glasses. "The Browns will love you," she said. "You'll be okay." Mary nodded her head, her body shuddering.

Then Mary grabbed Andy, who was still running around the room. She hugged him as if she would never stop. Then it was my turn. Mary bent down and took my hands. Her voice was thick. "Eat lots of candy, Sara," she said, and then she hugged me.

Though I was too excited to pause for long, the look in Mary's eyes that morning would stay with me forever. Her young face all crumpled up, her eyes creased as the tears poured down her cheeks. In her deep brown eyes: all the losses of the world, and all the worlds yet to be lost. This was the precise moment when the tincture of loss that would tinge the rest of my Foreign Service childhood trickled through my open eyes and into my blood.

~~

Leaps later in time, seeing Mary's eyes, shining still, in my mind, I would be seared by her vulnerability to our departure: *What became of her? . . .* And by my vulnerability to the loss of her: *Where did the hugeness of my love for her go?*

So strange, the way we Americans—always moving on—minimized the loss of these amahs who'd been, for years, quiet but essential dispensers of love and service in our households. Perhaps we just weren't trained to know what to do with sadness of the size and shape of these women—and so, we could only flee.

~~

This departure from Taiwan, and from Mary, would leave me, not only pierced by loss, but thirsty for it. All my life, I would feel as though I must travel, or die— and simultaneously as though, once I departed, either I would perish, or I'd never see my loved ones again.

~~

At the airport, it seemed like one hundred people were gathered to see us off. I found a wall to lean against, dug my hand down into Mary's purse, and got out a hard, red chunk of candy. My father, who seemed busy and removed, shook hands with, and slapped the backs of, lots of close-cropped Chinese men in uniforms and clean, starched suits.

One day, in my twenties, watching some cheap film about a Banana Republic in a California movie theatre, these Chinese men in their uniforms and sharp-crisp suits would suddenly spring into my mind, and it would seem as though they, and we, were in a movie of crooks and gangsters parading as legitimate officials—the American government, justifying itself as choosing the lesser of two evils, too often in pacts with highly questionable characters. The same image, and shudder of recognition, would pass through me over and over again through the years: Pinochet, de Klerk, Somoza, the Shah, the Saudi princes, the Taliban, Saddam Hussein . . . Even at this juncture: here, back in Taiwan, 1961, the Algerians had just declared independence from their colonizer, France. Couldn't the American government have taken note?

~~

Finally, we boarded the Northwest Orient Stratocruiser that would transport us to Japan for the three-week ship voyage "home." Foreign Service officers had a choice of returning either by ship or by plane. As my parents loved ship voyages, we were going to sail home from Yokohama on SS *President Cleveland*.

I spread out my petticoat and smoothed my green gingham skirt. A little nervous now, I leaned against my father, who patted my hand. He appeared calm as a mountain, confident about this return to Headquarters. My mother, across the aisle, gave me a quivering smile from behind her dark glasses. Andy squirmed and pointed out the window to my mother, and we all waited for the plane to start taxiing.

The airplane was long and fancy. We were traveling first class, and as we taxied down the runway, the stewardesses treated us with honor. They passed down the aisles with big rattan platters of candies and gum, and they handed out slippers. The bathroom was furnished with little piles of soap and perfume that we were allowed to keep.

~~

As we rose into the sky, for a fleeting instant I thought I heard the screech and clang of Chinese funeral music. Almost immediately, though, it became the drone of the plane. And a few minutes later, when I looked out the window, I saw only clouds. Taiwan was gone.

Book 2

GUM
Bethesda, Maryland,
1962–1964

5

cross my heart

Sometimes, in life, there is an opening in the sky: an aperture like a porthole through which your crystal coach could pass. Through the spiracle in the air, you can see your other life: a toy-sized village with a main street and smaller lanes with porch-fronted cottages, a place where you know everyone and where everyone carries a little portion of your history in his pocket. A place where, at ten, you and your friend Charlotte ate worms, where at thirteen you and Charlotte gagged on Camels behind the dilapidated Atkinson barn, where at sixteen the two of you sewed Juliet dresses like the ones in Zeffirelli's film for the junior-senior prom, and to which you returned from college to see your old friend and picked up talking in your mother's old linoleum kitchen like you'd never left.

There is this yellow-bright opening—this chance—and then the moment passes and you're swept by.

~~

Embarking up the long, awning-covered gangplank and stepping onto the C Deck of SS *President Cleveland*, I found myself in a sparkling, floating luxury planet. The walls were clean-spanking white, the railings that lined every hallway and deck turned of gleaming brass. While waiting to set sail, we explored the top stories of the ship: the gilt and white ballrooms; the brocade and velvet lounges; the dining room of tables set with starched, white tablecloths, hundreds of crystal glasses, and thousands of pieces of sparkling silverware; the bursar's shop with little Japanese boxes, folders, and fans, and Hawaiian muumuus and leis, and Hershey's bars. As we passed up and down the shining, waxed stairways, and in and out of the magnificent rooms, I was now, for real and at last, a princess.

~~

The moment we set sail—I recall the voyage in my fibers like a tonic of memory—Taiwan seemed to wisp even further away on the Pacific breeze, and Washington, waiting on the other end of the blue and secretive ocean, seemed far off, invisible somewhere beyond the dazzling blue horizon. The three weeks of the journey lulled the whole family. Andy played with military toys and I with dress-ups in the well-equipped nursery, and my mother lolled and chatted in a chaise lounge on the Promenade Deck, while my father took bracing constitutionals around and around and around the D Deck, his head held high, as if he were Columbus sure of the Indies. Only one thing on the journey unsettled me: a glimpse of a girl down the gangway leading to the second- and cabin-class staterooms. The passengers in those lower decks of the ship, I learned, were prohibited from entering our first-class realms. This was my first acquaintance, other than knowing the military ranks, with a caste system within my own kind.

That jarring moment aside, the blue-rippling sea, the balmy air, the gentle undulation of the ship, and the shrimp cocktails on deck as we watched the sun set rocked me and the rest of my family into drinking in each day as if it were fresh fruit nectar. The twenty-one days were twenty-one gifts of blessed, luxurious leisure, of time stolen from time. These were the days before long-distance calls, when the world still offered pause.

Every blue-bright, Pacific day of the voyage, my father took Andy and me up on the fore deck of the ship to look toward America—a morning ritual. With the spray hitting our faces, the green ocean glinting, the sky a clear, endless Neverland, we saw nothing but more sea. After a long gaze, we returned—holding our father's hands—to, respectively, our flouncing, metal tanks, and deck-walking.

Then, after many days of this routine, one day up on deck, there it was: in a growing, tawny strip at the far edge of the sea. "That's your home, Girl and Boy— the United States of America!" my father said. As I looked, my chest swelled with air so crisp and delicious it seemed like it came from a newborn planet.

~~

From San Francisco, we flew over the continent toward my father's new job at the China Desk in Washington, D.C. Over the droning hours of the flight (these were not jets we flew on), I looked down upon the vast, spreading lands of America as they changed hues from tawny at the coast, to evergreen, to tawny again, to sandy-brown, to evergreen once more, and then to a rambling stretch of yellow and green. As we banked to land, the earth all bright green now, ribboned here and there with glinting blue rivers and streams, my heart thumped with excitement. My mother patted my arm. "We're almost home!"

~~

But as it turned out, Bethesda, Maryland, was another foreign country. I supposedly belonged here but I almost felt as much like a lone scarecrow among regular Americans as I had in Taiwan surrounded by poor Chinese. The SS *President Cleveland* had thick, silky cords to grab onto. Here in Bethesda, there was nothing to keep me steady. I hung on to my father's arm and stood close against my mother wherever we went.

It was strange to have everyone around me speak English. The world was loud and frenetic and distracting when I understood all the words swirling around me. And America looked different from Taiwan. The houses were mostly brick and had squares of green grass and big trees in front of them. There were no walls around them, so the houses didn't protect you from robbers or give you turrety privacy like in Taipei. Here, everyone could see everyone else. Also, there were more cars than people in the streets, and the parked Buick, Chevy, and Ford station wagons took up half a block. There were no pedicabs and only children rode bicycles. The buses were new and didn't spew smoke, and people didn't throw up out the windows. There were no coolies in stiff, straw hats; no poor, butterscotch-skinned people in rags; no chickens skittering near your feet; and no water buffaloes. There were just ladies in curlers with four or five clean-noisy children in shorts trailing them at the grocery store, or shouting on the green-patch lawns with squirrels in the trees.

In America no one ate rice. They ate steaks and potato chips, which were very good, but I missed Yuki's fresh-cooked fried rice, served in a white bowl decorated with brushy blue fish. In Bethesda, it never smelled of fish, pee, or lotus blossoms. It smelled of gasoline and barbeques. There was no flashing crimson or scarlet or gold, and I never saw a lantern swinging in the dark night air.

~~

Two weeks before school started, and after we'd unpacked our HE—government talk for Household Effects—into our standard, red-brick colonial house, with a front and back yard, on Wilson Lane, we drove in the sweaty car to sweaty

Indiana—it was August and there was no air conditioning in our Rambler (few had it back then)—to see some of my mother's relatives. Overseas, we were a self-contained mobile unit and my parents hardly ever mentioned relations. I had a lot of aunts, uncles, and cousins, but my parents didn't nourish the ties. I didn't understand their lack of interest in family; I was hungry for it.

We met up with Uncle Carl (my mother's brother), Aunt Fran, and their son Scotty at a camp site in a state park. At the picnic table, we ate hamburgers my mother and Aunt Fran patted into wet, pink rounds and cooked on the fireplace grill. The meat dripped fat and made the fire spurt, and they smelled delicious. Scotty talked about rocket engines and propulsion all through the hamburgers, the potato chips, and the marshmallows. I liked Scotty by definition; he was my cousin.

"It's hot as sin," my mother kept saying as the sun dipped into the trees, and the mosquitoes were "eating us alive." In desperation, we climbed into our tents well before dark. Then, in the middle of the night, the mosquitoes were stinging us so badly that my father lifted me and Andy up one by one, groggy and sticky-hot and whimpery from the itching, and put us into the car to sleep. In the morning, he commented to my mother, "Welcome to Indiana." Her face had three huge, angry-looking bites on it, her hair was scraggly, and she looked like she hadn't slept in a month. She scowled and whipped the dishcloth at him and said, "Humph."

This interaction, had I been older, might have revealed the reason I hardly knew my relatives. The Midwestern mosquitoes had just reconfirmed my father's conviction that exodus had been the best course. My father was relieved, on joining the government, to have shed the Midwest and left family obligations behind. He was the firstborn and golden boy, but one of his brothers who had run away to the marines at age fifteen was constantly in hot water; his grandmother, who lived with them, domineering; and his father unpredictable. When my father traveled to Japan on the troop carrier at the end of the Second World War, he had discovered his elixir: the boundless, strange, fascinating world beyond America.

My mother also had her grounds for escape. Family dynamics in her case, too, may have contributed. As the ninth child, she received little attention—or was viewed as a pest. Or it may be that my father's work made it too complicated to keep in close touch: relatives had to be lied to. I have heard that, because of this, Agency families are most comfortable with each other. Whichever it was, my mother was grumpy and my father was trying to endure, but Andy and I were happy to be camping and swimming in brown ponds with our cousin and eating sticky candy.

One night, we went to a drive-in with Scott, Aunt Fran, and Uncle Carl. Snuggled in the car in the dark, with my back against the sticky hot vinyl seat, with the wide black sky overhead and the Hollywood feature flickering on the screen, and with my brother and my parents near me munching cheeseburgers and french fries like me, I thought, "This is what's so great about America."

~~

From the state park, we traveled west to visit my mother's mother, her sister and brother-in-law (my Aunt Norma and Uncle Irvin), and their three children, Linda, Randy, and Brian. They lived in New Albany, Indiana, a tiny town set down in the flats near Louisville, Kentucky, in a white bungalow on a quiet street down which brown mongrel dogs moseyed bovine-slow in the heat. When I stepped out of the clammy car at my aunt and uncle's, my immediate thought was that I'd stepped into a book. The house and the street fit perfectly into the America I'd imagined when I'd sat at the NACC Club in Taipei.

The days in New Albany were glorious: hot, sweaty, and perfect. Every day, our cousins, Andy, and I grabbed our suits, ambled down wide streets lined with small cottages, cut through backyards and alleys, and wound up at the neighborhood pool. There, luxuriously parentless, we cannonballed and "dolphined" all day, watched over by a lifeguard who was the cousins' neighbor, and ordered hot dogs and Cokes whenever we felt hungry. Every now and then a neighbor kid dashed in, breathless, to deliver a message from my mother and Aunt Norma, instructing us when to come home, or when to meet them for a five cent cone at Ben Franklin's. But usually, during these dreamy days, we played in the cool, light-lanced turquoise of the pool until after five, returning home just as the platters of fried chicken and potato salad were being placed on the long picnic table in the backyard. At the pool, I was immediately accepted as one of the clan. The sense of being known, of not having to explain who I was, unlike in all the places I'd ever lived—Randy simply said, "This is my cousin," and that took care of it, no questions asked—was an ice cream sundae with a cherry on top for me.

At bedtime back at Aunt Norma's, we all took turns using the bungalow's single bathroom on the ground floor. Even the bathroom enchanted me. A sign above its door read, in down-home wisdom that still seems like Indiana to me: "When I works, I works hard. When I sits, I sits loose. When I thinks, I falls asleep."

~~

An evening, as we slurped ice cream in the darkening firefly air, I came upon a comforting thought. *I am a link on a chain of connected people. I am a link in the necklace of an American family, and I am also a link in the necklace of America.*

This thought seemed valuable and essential; it made my body feel like all my bones were sparkling-white, straight and strong, and the muscles that hugged them trim, taut, and limber. This golden chain would keep me from all harm.

But this magic chain, this precious sense of affiliation, was fleeting and flittery. Repeatedly in the years to come, the golden circlet would slip off my neck, leaving me adrift. I would recover it in unexpected places—at twenty-two as an intern in a warm-hearted, shoestring clinic for emotionally disturbed preschoolers in Cambridge, Massachusetts; in the unadorned seminar rooms and musty library stacks of graduate school in my mid-thirties; with a college friend on a white-rock, sweet-humming Wyoming mountaintop at forty-nine. But I could never simply will the circlet to be found. It only appeared when *it* wished to—its filigree clasp never secure enough to hold for long.

But here in New Albany, I, the girl raised among the scarlet and clanging funeral processions of Taiwan and the pine-scented hushes of Japan, wakened to a dream that would possess me forever afterward—that bountiful, rooted, family-stuffed, and, to the Foreign Service child, unattainable utopia. As we traveled from country to country, I would tow with me in my Pan Am flight bag a mental home movie of this New Albany summer, saturated with yearning.

All the way into my forties, even after discarding a quintessential American small city life in St. Paul, Minnesota, in favor of the worldliness of Washington, D.C., I would—perversely—long for small-town America. I would ache for a place I probably wouldn't fit in once there.

~~

On the drive back to Washington, we stopped at an amazing American place: a rest stop with a hamburger restaurant, a snack bar with milkshakes, and a little shop with dazzling souvenirs like baseball hats labeled "Ohio," American flags, and miniature license plates with children's names on them. Muttering about cheap trinkets and junk, my father said, "Oh, all right"—and bought us each a license plate. Mine spelled Sara with an "h," but I sat with it in my lap the remainder of the drive.

~~

When we pulled up in Bethesda, life, unlike in Taiwan, did not yield up oddities and curiosities, like sea-echoing conches and Chinese prayer charms on a shore. Every week was predictable. We did our shopping at Bradley Shopping Center, where we bought things at Bradley Food and Beverage, Bruce Variety—a wonderful shop jammed with buttons and envelopes and kick balls and gingham and frying pans and three-packs of socks and underwear and bobby pins and curlers and Halloween masks and every other useful item you could dream of—and at Strosnider's Hardware.

Here in America my father no longer wore his baggy khaki shorts to work; he wore suits. My mother wore practical shirt-waist dresses with belts, and I wore shifts and skirts, but not my smocked dresses. They needed too much ironing; we didn't have a laundry maid anymore. Being fancy was not a part of life in Bethesda, but I didn't mind. I was with my family and I was busy reading fairy stories, and playing "going on a ship" with Andy. Being American in Taiwan and being American in America were very different. The best thing of all about being American in America was that no one noticed me, and no one wanted to touch me. I adored being invisible.

In Bethesda, we didn't have any servants or an amah. My missing of Mary was like the gnawing feeling you have in your belly when you have skipped lunch. Mostly I tried not to remember her. If I said I missed her, my mother said, "I miss Mary too." Then she added her hallmark phrase, "But I try to think, *Wherever I am is best*," and so I tried to think that too. Cleaving to my mother's practice of stalwart optimism would stand me in good stead, particularly during this period of childhood when I had no say as to where I lived—until one evening back in Washington in my teens, when I would shriek at my mother and rush upstairs crying, yelling, "No, this place is *not* best!"

Every day was the same here: my mother and my father went to work and Andy and I attended Radnor Elementary School, five blocks away. My mother taught English to African and Middle Eastern students at Georgetown University. My father was gone for long days at work at "the State Department," a huge white building downtown with a thousand white corridors. I pictured my father at work in a cube-shaped office, locked deep in that mazelike stockade near the Washington monument. Years later, I would come to know that he was really working in an entirely different building in an entirely different location in an entirely different state, but, for now, there was no reason for me to doubt my father's words. My parents had always had secrets associated with my father's work—"things children don't need to know." I took it for granted that everyone's father's job entailed secrets.

Here in Washington, though, my father's work suffused little of the whispering or vague sense of menace that wavered around his Taipei job. There was no midnight rustling, no sweaty smell of fear. Any secrets that existed were offshore, floating around, invisible particles in the far-off sea.

My father worked at the China Desk, he said, and his work, even though we were now in America, was still China-watching, but from afar. Here my father seemed more tired than he had in Taipei. The China Desk at Headquarters didn't seem like my father's cup of tea, as my mother would say. He left for the State Department at about 7:30 in the morning and returned at about 6 p.m., and when he got home he just wanted a beer, and he didn't want to talk about his day at the office, even when my mother asked. He just said, "Same old, same old," and waved his hand as if to erase the tedium and the office politics—even though I heard my mother muttering about "that mafia." In Taipei he used to come home all fizzed up, like he had ginger ale bubbling in him instead of blood, and now it was as if the ginger ale had gone flat.

Foreign Service and intelligence officers—I would come to know—usually disliked their returns to Headquarters. When I was in my forties, working and raising children in Washington myself, I would often grouse to my father about the competitive, aggressive ethos in the city, and about the utilitarian view of people some Washingtonians seemed to have. With his penchant for using as few words as possible, he would offer his confirmation, "Washington is tough."

One day my father came home and it seemed like his ginger ale had not just gone flat; it was sour. I heard my mother saying in the kitchen, "Charlie Taber, you've got to keep your mouth shut."

"I can't say nothing if I know an action is wrong."

"You did that in Taipei and you saw what it did. All it did was hurt you. You can't expect anything different. That man only loves his 'Yalies.' Anyone who didn't go there has to kowtow even more."

My father's Taipei boss had returned to Headquarters too. The chipping-away of my father was continuing.

~~

By this time, the middle of 1962, China was finally beginning to emerge from the disastrous Great Leap Forward, which had taken place while we were in Taiwan. During the Great Leap Forward, Mao organized his people into work brigades on vast communes to maximize industrial production in rural areas. He had conceived of this three-year plan as a way to catch up with America and Britain, but the brutal collectivization he had imposed on the peasantry had led to agricultural stagnation, famine, widespread starvation, and desperate demoralization of the Chinese population. The Chinese people had been forced to eat husks and leaves from trees as the food they produced was taken away by force. Thirty million had starved to death while Mao had posed as the leader of world Communism, and made speeches about achieving a land of plenty through the force of will. A fair claim may be made that the Great Leap Forward was the largest man-made disaster in history.

Enthusiasm for the Communist revolution had flagged badly during this punishing social upheaval, and Mao had now begun a "revisionist bourgeois restoration," including the introduction of private agricultural plots to buoy his people's spirits and create incentives to productivity. While this mini and temporary recuperative capitalist thrust was underway, the cult of Mao was mushrooming, and the underpinnings of the upcoming, even more punitive Cultural Revolution being laid down. The China Desk, my father included, had the task of tracking these events.

As for events on other continents, many African states were gaining independence from their European colonizers. The Congo had already freed itself of the Belgians, and Uganda and Tanganyika would be independent by the end of the year. The Europeans had learned that imperialism had too high a price, while the United States, conversely, was just warming up to the enterprise. The Cold War was in full swing; the arms race was underway and U.S. spy planes were patrolling the air spaces over both the USSR and China. Khrushchev and Kennedy, the new imperialists, were engaging in the war of nerves that would lead to the Cuban Missile Crisis.

~~

Usual weekend afternoons, my father would relax in his black peasant slippers, reading a tan paper–covered Chinese book back to front and up to down. My mother would fix dinner: frozen vegetables and minute steaks or fish sticks. Andy would play out in the backyard in the huge, wooden packing crate stamped with big, black Chinese characters that came on the boat with our HE—which our father had hammered into a playhouse with, to our admiration, a ladder and a loft. I would draw a ballerina while I sat cozily on the couch in the living room, and the dog next door would bark.

Weekends were the only time I sometimes felt like the same person I had been back in Taipei, especially on the days when we went to the homes of other Foreign Service families to eat Chinese food. These evenings in Northwest Washington;

Chevy Chase, Maryland; or Vienna, Virginia—wherever our Taipei friends had set down—my father and the other men spoke Chinese and we all dove for beef and green peppers, cashew chicken, Peking duck, and spring rolls from the lazy Susan in the middle of the table. Hurling American manners to the winds, everyone reverted to the customs we picked up across the sea: the noisier the people, the messier the table, the better the meal. And my father's laugh when the men joshed around was confident and loud and hearty like it had been back in Taipei. My father told jokes, too, more than at home, when he was usually sapped from the office, in a conversational, confiding, folksy-but-man-in-the-know, slightly wry tone, and the men broke into hee-hawing, honking laughs. Even though they were sitting among their lipsticked wives and wriggling children, there was something private about the men and their half-English, half-Chinese jokes; in the way they leaned across the bosoms of the ladies to hear each other; in the way their eyes twinkled when they said certain words, when they mentioned certain people's names. "Joe sure lost his pants that time," one of them said. Or: "I never could tell if Chang was on the level."

Sometimes the wives chimed in. My mother always looked at Mrs. Thompson when she told a certain story. "Remember the time our two dumb husbands forgot the password and they were standing there, doubled over laughing like hyenas, in the middle of the street?" By the time the two mothers were halfway through the story, all the grown-ups at the table were clutching their stomachs and rocking back and forth like wild hyenas themselves—while we children just sat there and stared.

Back here in the States, we had to eat at other Foreign Service families' homes in order to eat Chinese food, because there were no smelly restaurants with tasty, soy-saucy dishes in Bethesda. But there *were* Twinkies, and there were raisin boxes, and circus car boxes of Animal Crackers, and accordion straws. McDonald's had just erected its golden arches out on Rockville Pike, and Howard Johnson's advertised twenty-eight flavors of ice cream. And, there were candy and chewing gum. Food was the one thing that was familiar here—since we always had American groceries from the commissary in Taipei. To eat food here that we ate back in China was comforting: it felt like Mary's hand smoothing my hair.

For the child uncertain of her reception on return to a country left behind, food can be the key that opens the door. Give a Frenchman his goat cheese, a Chinaman his rice bowl, an American his burger—or his Hershey's Kiss—and he's home free. American candy and gum: I knew just what to do with them.

America was candy heaven. Tootsie Rolls, both the tiny ones and the big ones with sections like fat worms: they stuck to your teeth and then turned into a soft, sugary, chocolaty squash in your mouth. Candy cigarettes: how cool we looked hanging them blasély from our first and index fingers. Cracker Jacks: the caramel made the popcorn stick to your teeth, and then there was the little present inside, a plastic gun or a little bell. And, of course, Mounds, Almond Joy, and Milky Way bars, the creamy, caramelly, coconutty, chocolaty staples of our lives: either nibble them so they last, suck them like lollipops, or peel the chocolate off the outside with your front teeth and then gobble the sticky insides fast.

Back at TAS, new students fresh from America would hand out candy bars like they were gold booty. Candy *is* America, I concluded back in Taipei when I was five—and now I finally had it all at my fingertips.

But gum was even better, the best of all—as American as all get-out, like Lucille Ball. In Taiwan, when I took my first piece of gum between my lips it was as though I was Columbus discovering America—and now I was in Gum Heaven. Perhaps because my parents didn't let me have it much—my mother said it was vulgar—I had a thing about gum. A gumaholic, I hid and hoarded it. I loved to chew gum while turning the pages of a book or twirling a ring on my finger. I loved the ritual of opening a pack with the zip string, fishing out a single slice, and then lingering over the luxurious decision about whether to roll it up first or simply wad it—with a slurp of sweet—between my lips.

And then there was the joy of choice—America is nothing if not the land of variety: Wrigley's Spearmint, or Doublemint, "Doublemint, Doublemint, Double-mint/Two Mints in One/Doublemint, Doublemint, Doublemint Gum," or Dentyne, with its thin, spicy slivers. And then there was Bazooka Bubble Gum: nothing could match the satisfaction of a big pink wad in your mouth and the dependable treat of unfolding the predictably bad comic you could barely understand. But Juicy Fruit was my favorite of all, that is, until I discovered Beechnut Fruit Stripe gum. What other country besides America would be clever enough to invent striped gum? *No country has gum as good as America*, I gloated, and so I chomped into gum like it was the main road home.

Here in Bethesda, at summer's end 1962, I was chewing my way to being American. My mission—it was as though the president of the United States himself had given me orders—was to prove that I was an American kid. *A wad of gum in my mouth, I solemnly swear. Cross my heart and hope to die.*

6
jap

I was standing on the playground the first day at Radnor Elementary School in my new white sneakers, holding my new pencil box from People's Drug Store. Hovering at the edge of these shouting American children playing hopscotch, throwing balls, and dashing madly, America suddenly didn't feel at all like home. I was the sparrow in the cage again.

First thing in the classroom, we stood and recited the Pledge of Allegiance, which I knew, but all through the first day I said nothing at all, unless Mrs. Hart, my teacher, asked me a question—and then I squeaked out an answer she couldn't hear. Mrs. Hart had kind, brown eyes that searched into yours, and a French chignon, like a soft bird's nest at the back of her hair, and she had a gentle voice, but I felt like I had a beak instead of a mouth and twiggy bird legs that didn't hold me up. My new sneakers were giving me a blister on my heel, and I didn't understand these American kids with their funny Southern accents. I wished someone could give me a recipe or a list of rules for how to be: what to do, what to say to people so that they would like me, so that I could just blend in.

My father joked to me when I was older that when I did ballet as a girl in Bethesda, I looked like a donkey on its hind legs. That's how I felt all through those first days at Radnor: goofy and awkward—until I finally realized it was safe to put my four hooves on the ground.

~~

After a week, I knew where to stow my book bag and where to find an extra pencil. I could locate, in the long corridor of doors, the library and the girls' room.

I was tentatively, gingerly, beginning to step down harder as I walked in my sneakers. But then, suddenly, the second week of school, something happened on the playground that whirled me into uncertainty about who I was.

The word had gotten around among the children that the new girl in third grade had come from Asia, and this day, a boy spotted me, ran across the blacktop, bustled up in front of me and said, swaggering, hands folded in front of his chest, "Are you a Jap?" His voice was sauced up with taunt and dare.

I knew it was very bad to be a "Jap," and I was struck dumb, riveted to this boy's puffy, fiery face—it looked like a terrible Halloween pumpkin.

Three other boys gathered around the first. "Are you a Jap?" "Are you a Jap?" "You're a Jap, aren't you?"

I was standing there with my two honey-colored ponytails sticking out from the two sides of my head. As the boys pushed me with their words, I could feel my eye pockets filling up like little sinks, with tears. I had to gulp and look high into the sky in order to stop them from overflowing. In Taiwan I had often felt different, but there I had been buffered by being a member of a select and superior elite. Here, in this place that was supposed to be my home, I was not supposed to feel this sinking aloneness.

The bell rang and saved me. I was so shaken by the boys' petulance, though, that only halfway through arithmetic did I realize I should have said, "No. I'm American." The whole experience fretted me. My nationality had never been called into question before. On the Taipei streets, jammed with black-haired people, my Americanness was very clear. Now I was confused: the boy who'd jeered at me was sandy-haired like me. *But, I thought, he's right. I'm not like him. Maybe somehow, in a way I'm not aware of, I am a Jap. I was born in Yokosuka. Maybe that means I have a hidden stamp on me that only other people can see.*

I felt shame, a gush of hot red blood, flushing my face. I'd been uncloaked, shown to be an imposter, an illegal spy trying to pretend she was American. I wanted to run away and never return. Only as an adult, looking back, would I become conscious of my own collusion with my American aggressors and ashamed of my betrayal of Japanese friends.

Suddenly, here as a seven-year-old, I had a longing so strong that my stomach hurt—for people with black hair, for the smell of fish and soy sauce and water buffalo dung. I wished I had a guard, like President Eisenhower had when he toured

Taipei, or at least a driver to chase people away, like Mr. Chang did for us in the chicken village. All through the rest of the day, I could think of nothing except going home to Taipei.

Simultaneously, I was run amok with questions: *Is Taiwan still real? Where is it?* I wanted to net my old country, pin it to a sheet of cardboard, like a butterfly.

Taiwan was now but a glimmer across the sea and sky. At home we rarely referred to Taipei. My family's creed, like that of most Foreign Service families on arrival at a new post, was to soldier on, adapt quickly, grab the possibilities before us and look to the future. Our motto was: *if you can't have tofu and mu shu pork, eat fries and hamburgers.*

When I came in the door from school, my mother saw my face and made me fried rice for dinner. Peas, eggs, soy sauce, rice, and a spoonful of sugar, cooked together into a colorful pile: she knew what comforted me.

When I told my father about the incident at dinner, he stroked my hair and roared with laughter at the boy's thinking I was Japanese. But then his face got serious when he saw I was about to cry. "Of course you're American!" he said, taking me on his lap and explaining that we had a law in America that decreed that anyone born to American parents, anywhere in the world, was American. "You're American as apple pie."

After dinner, less weepy but stilled inside, I trudged up to my room, and, trying not to make a sound—quiet as an orphaned Chinese kitten taking its first steps—I found a taped-shut carton under my bed and pulled it out onto the rug. As though I was on a secret mission, I noiselessly opened the box and peeked inside.

I removed objects from the box, grasping them gingerly, and then tiptoed to my dresser and placed them on its top surface. One by one, I arranged my bell from the Temple of a Thousand Steps; the oyster shell given to me by my mother from which I'd extracted a pearl; my collection of seven tiny wooden Chinese dolls; and a handkerchief Mary had ironed. Such arrangement of objects would comfort me throughout my life. With my head on my pillow, I looked across at them all, and as I did, I felt like a sea that was calming after a storm. The tears receded into their keeping pouches.

~~

Perhaps the most basic instinct of a child—and perhaps one of the most basic afflictions—is the wish to be the same as others. From the time of my birth in Japan, and all through my early years in Taipei, this yearning had been thwarted. Now at eight, I was a scrawny kid with knobby knees and side-parted, sandy hair coming loose from its ponytail. I looked a little like a scarecrow, in fact.

One day, as a college freshman in a leafy Ohio town, the knowledge would seep into me that my shy classmate from a small town in Minnesota felt utterly confident about her place in the world. Being the same was not an issue for her; she could take belonging to a country for granted. To me, my friend's possession would seem like a luxury more unattainable and remote than a palace in Tibet—which actually seemed attainable to me, the world-hopper. I didn't know that some small-town Americans felt as acutely out of place as I did. I would meet them as time went on— all those small-town kids who were too creative or unique for their surroundings. But here in this classroom of kids America-born and -raised, I was stuck on a pole flapping in the wind. My answer to the question, "Is it okay to be different?" was clear as my name: "no."

~~

The morning after the Jap incident, I had to count all my possessions three times before I could close up my book bag, I started brushing my hair three times, going to the bathroom three times, and checking that I had my homework three times before I went to school—I was making sure, making sure, making sure.

Now, routinely, I had stomachaches when I woke up. My mother, worried, took me to the doctor. He gave me x-rays and medicine, and one time I had to drink some horrid cement-like white paste—so that the doctor could look at my insides. But he found nothing physically wrong.

~~

Lonely afternoons these early weeks of school, my mother comforted me with the words that would be her refrain the rest of my childhood. "You can do anything for a year. Just do your schoolwork. The friends will come."

The raggedy Chinese girl with the drawing pad sitting on the Taipei market street floated into my mind as a promise, so I tried not to be shy, to keep a lookout. At recess, though, as I watched the swirling clamor and chaos and commotion, the loneliness ached. "Beggars can't be choosers," the saying went, but my mother said, like it was an asset, "A friend in need is a friend indeed."

As I would do in all the new places to come, here in Bethesda—without know-ing these were my criteria—I was watching for a girl who seemed strong, who had no doubts, who had no questions, a girl guide who knew how to be, think, and behave in the place I had landed—so that I could try to be her friend and step into her shoes.

One day I spotted her: Charlotte Hill was there playing hopscotch across the way, strong and sturdy, and waiting like the granite elephant statue at the zoo. She had been at Radnor since kindergarten. Generously, she took me on as her protégé. Almost instantly, we became "best friends."

Why some children reach out is a mystery—Charlotte was a gift to me, perhaps from the chubby, smiling Chinese folk god of good fortune. Or maybe she too was "a friend in need."

We began to do everything together. We sat on top of my Chinese embroidered bedspread and drew; we pressed Silly Putty onto our favorite Sunday funnies to make wobbly prints; we jump-roped and hopscotched on the path leading up to her tidy, white colonial house on Birch Street.

I fantasized that people might think Charlotte and I were twins. Charlotte was medium and I was skinny. We both had braids. Charlotte had brown hair and bangs, and mine was nearer to blond, but, even so, maybe we could be non-identical twins. My mother bought me a camel hair coat like Charlotte's at the Next-to-New. Looking like Charlotte fortified me eight ways like Wonder Bread on the commercial. Harry Stack Sullivan, the great psychologist of childhood loneliness whom I would read in graduate school, put his finger on it: the critical importance to every child of "the chum."

Another psychologist whose work I came to know, Heinz Kohut, wrote of the child's psychological need for a twin—of the basic and simple human requirement for reflection or "mirroring." In America, this basic instinct for twinning, however, is denigrated. The ideal, "strongest" American, as I'd learn in so many lessons, stands alone.

Charlotte and I went regularly to the impressionist galleries at the National Gallery of Art. Past the white marble busts of Greek gods, we entered the third gallery on the left and walked into a world of fluffy clouds, girls in full-skirted dresses, and rose and melon and lime gardens—all sun-shot and happy and light. We admired Monet's lacy pink, yellow, and lightest-blue Rouen Cathedral and Corot's deep black forests, but our official favorite was Renoir's *A Girl with the Watering Can*. I Scotch-taped a 25-cent print of her beside my favorite shan shui on my wall at home.

At school now, I felt confident and happy like the girl in the portrait, so long as Charlotte was near. I laughed when Charlotte did and scuffed my shoe along the ground at the same moment as she. I tossed my head as if I had bangs like hers. This copying assured me that I belonged in spite of my heretical background. But still, I was a new girl. Any hint of exclusion and the match flared: the feeling of being an outsider would flame up.

One day, Betsy told me she only wanted Charlotte to play Chinese jump rope with her and two other girls, and I felt, for the rest of the day, like I was a rock to be kicked out of the way.

Later, at home, my mother gave me a Twinkie and the sad look in her eyes made me think she understood. She said, "Sticks and stones may break my bones but words will never hurt me. Those girls don't matter, Sara." But then she added, "You're just being too sensitive."

My mother's comment made me feel as if I should wave my feelings away like a fairy godmother. I was supposed to play merrily all the time, no matter how other kids acted. But unable to conjure that kind of magic, all the little slights were like little slices on skin. Decades later, I would understand that my mother simply couldn't bear for me to suffer. But at the time, her wish to whisk away my feelings made me feel incompetent; I hated her for it.

One day after Charlotte went off to play jacks with Jennifer at recess, my mother found a note that I had written to my best friend tucked into the pocket of my camel hair coat.

The note read:

> *Dear Charlotte,*
> *If you don't like me, tell me how to be, and I'll change.*
> *Your friend, Sara*

~~

The note to Charlotte expressed a new girl's desperation, but since I would be new over and over throughout my life, the self-subjugation developed into a habit. I would hand myself to my friends for molding like a gift of clay. Luckily this girl was not the only one I was—but she was the one who would wrest the leading role in the next stage of my life. I would always have the sense that I had to earn friendship, and keep earning it, rather than it simply being there—or it would vanish across a sea.

This one-down position in friendship was a disadvantage, but, on the other hand, maybe the world would be a different and better place if everyone possessed the innocent need and devotion in friendship of that girl I was back then, that readiness for love.

Upon reading the note, my mother sputtered. "Sara! You're fine as you are!" But I knew that was not true.

~~

Tonight—it was mid-October now—my father shook his head, looked at my mother, tossed the newspaper on the floor, and leaned across the table, looking straight into our eyes, as if he had something important to tell us. "I want to explain something that you're going to hear more and more about," he said. "Right now, we are in the middle of an altercation with the Russians. What happened is that some of our recon pilots discovered Russian missiles, aimed at us, mounted on the island of Cuba. Since Cuba is right off our shores, that is of concern. But," he said, shuffling in his chair and glancing toward my mother again, "it is nothing for you to worry about. The president and his men are working like fury right now to get the Russians to dismantle them, and they will succeed."

My father knew about these things because he worked at the State Department, so I knew everything would be fine. But still, after this evening, my father whispered to my mother when he got home from work each day. It seemed like there was something about the missile crisis that pertained especially to our family.

During my father's kitchen reports to my mother, I caught the starts of her quivery sentences. "When . . . ," she said. "What if . . . " "Oh Charlie, what do they say about . . . ?" There were extra phone calls from my father's friends, my mother did extra shopping. She hauled in grocery bags of tuna fish, oatmeal, and dry cereal, and she filled old juice jugs and plastic cartons with water and put them on a shelf in the basement. My father watched the news like it was his church.

The standoff with Cuba was my first conscious sip of American-style power: of the U.S. government's use of posturing, threats, and swaggering; of the government's willingness to put the world at risk in the name of moral superiority. The Cuban Missile Crisis was perhaps one of the times when the use of threats was defensive and appropriate. The Soviet missiles were truly "a clear and imminent danger." But I wasn't afraid of the missiles because I knew from my father that President Kennedy was the wisest of leaders and America always did the right thing.

~~

Every week at school we had air-raid drills. We practiced going into the hall and lined up like sailors readying to board a ship, or we squatted under our desks like soldiers waiting in ambush. Being hunkered down felt familiarly American to me—like I was back in my Taiwanese house enclosed by the high, impenetrable, glass-topped wall, bunkered against the world.

One time, after we had all brought in cans of tuna fish, chicken noodle soup, jars of Tang (the drink of the astronauts), and Vienna sausages for the emergency stockpile, we hastened behind our teacher to the home of Mary, one of the girls in my class. We sat there in Mary's paneled basement rec room for a while beside the wet bar, the TV, and all the cans—imagining, between giggles, what it actually might be like to be bombed.

Mostly I just liked the excitement of the crisis—the hoarding of tins, the unusual, broken-up days at school. Life felt heady, important, like a flag was waving.

~~

One evening, at bedtime—the Cuban Missile Crisis finally over, but the exhilaration of conflict still in the air—my father told us the inspiring story about George Washington and his soldiers who suffered through the Valley Forge winter without food or clean water. He also told us about U.S. Army boot camp, where new soldiers had to slither on their bellies like snakes, while other soldiers shot over their heads with real bullets. As he told us of these men, his voice was hushed with admiration. He esteemed people who could do without, who could survive in "dire straits."

A Saturday with a sky shocked blue as the China Sea, my father took us on a six-mile hike in the Shenandoah "to build character." The woods were a festival of red, orange, and yellow mixed with pine green—and a carnival of crisp air; the smell of soft, crumbling mulch; and the rustle and crunch of dry leaves underfoot. We each carried our lunches in our Japanese rucksacks, our GI canteens slung over our shoulders. Andy and I gloried in the woods, dashing up and down the trail, hearts thumping, pretending to be fighters in the French and Indian War. We tromped up and down a slushy stream, looking for frogs. We ate bologna sandwiches and Fritos and swigged from our canteens while sitting on a log beside the path.

After lunch, we forged onward, trying to complete the circuit my father had mapped out for us. Soon, though, first Andy and then I started to flag. "Can't we sit down, Pop?" "I want to go back." "Can't we rest? I need a drink from my canteen," we said every five minutes. My father wouldn't let us do these things, though. "You may have a small drink," he said, stopping for us to take a swig of water. "But remember Valley Forge. Conserve your water. Just take tiny sips. On a hike, you only drink a little at a time because you never know how much farther you'll have to go.

"Water discipline," he said as though we were army men on patrol. "Water discipline is the key to survival." My father only rarely gave us absolutes to follow, so after that, we took only the tiniest of sips, even though we wanted to glug our tepid water all the way to the bottom of our metal canteens.

And then my father taught us another method for slaking our thirst. When the path led us to a brook, which we forded by jumping from rock to rock, he dipped from the trickling stream two smooth, glistening stones. (You could still drink from American streams back then.) "If you're ever in the wilderness and you don't know how far you'll have to go before you can next refill your canteen, pluck a stone out of a creek and suck on the stone."

I never questioned the logic of this instruction; its message simply registered in my bones. I would spend a lot of my life sucking on stones, in a sort of reverence for self-denial, even when there was water nearby.

7

the tomb

Who knows what causes an inner shift to occur. One day I was walking down the hall at school and the corset of tentativeness I had felt for months slid off me like a silky slip. I felt light-headed. I could walk down the hall and not worry about where to put my arms and didn't think about whether to look at the person I passed or to look down. I just walked down the hall.

By the last day of third grade, I had grown to love my school. I loved the hook on which I put my jacket. I loved the flap-top desks lined up in rows; I'd organized mine neat as a box of K-rations. I loved the walls of my classroom with our pictures of Paul Revere hung precisely, just so, in lines. I loved penciling my name onto the checkout card at the librarian's desk. I even loved school food, the astronaut-like trays with everything arranged in order: a neat peanut butter sandwich, a carton of milk, a small stack of carrot sticks. I loved best of all the half an ice cream sandwich I could buy when I brought in five extra cents. The Chinese word *binqiling* always popped into my head when I saw one.

In the school library, there was a deliciousness of books. The card catalog was like a menu of all desserts: Nurse Barton, the Bobbsey Twins, Nancy Drew, the Hardy Boys, and on and on. I opened one and sailed out over the world on a magic carpet. I cradled them in my arms like orphan kittens when I took them home. My father read aloud to me Frances Hodgson Burnett's *The Secret Garden*. This story of a little girl leaving her beloved India and drawing up to a mansion in the desolate English moors—and her accompanying sense of bewilderment and fear and curiosity—caught in my throat.

On the playground at school by now, I was mistress. I could lose myself sometimes—luxuriously, languorously—to eight-year-old pleasures. I dashed in relay races, jumped rope, and kicked a ball with my full might. In the game of Red Rover, I clasped my neighbors' hands with absolute determination not to let the runner through. Playing this game I became all grip and ferocity—as though I was a soldier in the Revolutionary army and if I let someone break the line the Redcoats would win.

~~

Even though Mrs. Hart was American, she seemed from a faraway place and an earlier time. A Mary Poppins without the stiffening. She wore soft, sweatery suits in shades like fawn and buff. She was very tidy, and she always had a fresh handkerchief tucked up her sleeve. Everything about her was reassuringly just-so. I would never be a just-so sort of person—I'd be a messy grown-up with one shoelace always broken—but I found organized people soothing.

One Saturday Mrs. Hart took Charlotte and me on a special outing to the zoo in our matching camel's hair coats and then to her home for tea in pretty China cups. I could tell by the sparkle in her eyes that she loved me.

I knew I loved her. She was like a good fairy and she was wise. I seized all of Mrs. Hart's stories and maxims and locked them in my heart.

"Always finish any book you start," she said, tapping *The Wizard of Oz* one day in class. "This is the only way to be true to the book and its author." How long would it take me to get over that one, to put a book down before reading the last page? Thirty years or so.

"Be a loyal friend," Mrs. Hart said another day. This aphorism was made for me, the girl who wrote to her Taiwan friend, Laura, every week, and considered friendship, once achieved, as something to be kept in a Chinese box decorated with alabaster inlay and guarded by jeweled dragon locks.

"And honesty is the most important thing of all," Mrs. Hart said. "Never tell a lie." Pulling our chairs into a circle around her, we listened to her read the story of Honest Abe. On another day we heard about George Washington and the cherry tree.

In class we studied American colonial history. We learned about the Indians, and how they could sneak through the woods in their moccasins without making a sound. We learned about Lewis and Clark and the pioneers. I loved to imagine the pioneers jouncing across the plains, with their whole lives in their wagons: wooden trunks of wedding china and embroidered linens, polished guns, and beautiful taffeta dresses sewn with perfect, tiny stitches. The stories of the wagons drawing into a circle around a fire at nightfall filled me with dreaminess and calm. I loved, too, the stories of the log cabins the homesteaders built. My mother had grown up in a log house in Henryville, Indiana, and had the do-it-yourself independence of a pioneer. She patched Andy's trousers with clippings of fabric from the trousers' inner hem. She taped her own broken nose together with Scotch tape.

These visions—of hardy people, well-provisioned wagons, and hand-hewn homes—would reverberate and feed my mind for years. When I was twenty-three and heading west for grad school, I'd get a more than ordinary satisfaction from neatly packing my blue Karmann Ghia with the full complement of my boyfriend's and my possessions and keep heading out on the highway, and I'd treasure a dream for years of building a cabin out of birch logs with my own hands.

In a study of frontiersmen, we read the Landmark biography of Daniel Boone. "Elbow room," said Daniel Boone. I tucked away, too, the heart-thumping tale of this roving man, who always had to see over the next mountain. In the future lying in store for me, the flags of curiosity and adventure would keep me loping, my head held high as I did what my wandering life required. What I gleaned from all the stories was that Americans were, above all, courageous. In pursuit of higher goals, they could improvise or live without.

My mother and father took us downtown on the weekends to see the museums and monuments to brave Americans. As we drove down Constitution Avenue and passed the Washington Monument with its circle of flying flags, my mother put her hand on her heart, and tears shone in her eyes. And then, on cue, infected by our mother's patriotic trembling, Andy and I cheered her up with a rendition of "The Pledge of Allegiance."

~~

. . . *Purple mountains' majesty and amber waves of grain* . . . Wrapped in scraps of songs and stories, America seemed to me like a green and fertile land where anyone could track down happiness, where any immigrant could breathe his lungs freshly full, open his hands to dropping apples, and fashion his dreams into mansions. We Americans, I reckoned—to use a Davy Crockett word—could conquer anything.

~~

Like he had done in Taiwan, my father talked to us about the news as we ate my mother's juicy hamburgers, our Kentucky fried chicken, or our Dinty Moore beef stew. From time to time, he read to us from the newspaper, the print smudging his fingers as he pointed to the articles and photographs—bringing the Cold War into the living room. "We discovered two Soviet spy planes flying over Alaska," he told us one night, "so President Kennedy has lodged a protest with the Russian president. . . ."

"Today," he said during dinner, "President Kennedy announced that he and the president of Russia have set up a 'hotline' between the Kremlin and the White House. This is a direct telephone cable between the two countries to prevent accidental nuclear war. If someone in one country mistakenly pushes the button to release the atom bomb, the president of that country can instantly notify the other so he can shoot down the bomb, and also prevent the other from shooting back. This is an excellent way to keep the world safe," my father said, his voice so confident I didn't even flicker. I envisioned handsome President Kennedy with his finger poised over a red button—through day and night—at any instant, able to save us all.

~~

"Some American army officers were killed a while ago in Vietnam," my father was saying now—pointing to another of the world's bubbling stewpots. "President Kennedy gave orders that our troops stationed there were to shoot back if fired upon. Now, the newspaper says, we are sending more aid to the South Vietnamese so they aren't taken over by the North Vietnamese Communists, who are being aided by the Red Chinese. . . . The Chinese are still a big concern to our government."

~~

In spite of the glowing hot spots in the world, and despite Mr. Smith, whom he talked to my mother about in the kitchen, my father's laugh has been mostly easy and free these days. One night, the Stanfords and the Constables came over—friends from our Japan days. The fathers reminisced about the hikes they had taken on weekends while their wives got together with all the new babies and toddlers, keeping each other company in a foreign land.

"Remember that crew of Japanese hikers on the top of Fuji?" Mr. Constable said.

"They looked like they'd waltzed up while we looked like wet mops," my father said.

"Those Japanese." Mr. Constable shook his head.

My mother said to Mrs. Constable, "Remember, Barbara, when I had a breast infection while the men were off hiking and you had to nurse Sara?"

"You did me a favor! I had enough milk for ten babies!"

My father's eyes grew misty as the men recalled the hikes through fir trees— and the hot spring baths at the end of the trail.

Then Mr. Stanford took a swig of beer, and the air in the room shifted. "Yeah. . . . Those were intense times. Hard play and hard work. . . . We were so young. . . . Did any of us know what we were doing?"

Mr. Stanford laughed, but it wasn't a hearty laugh, and my father's eyes, which had had dreams in them, clouded like they did when he thought of Lee, the Chinese man from back in those days in Japan.

~~~

In the spring of 1963, the end of my third-grade year, my father was given a three-month TDY assignment to Mexico City. There was something worrisome about it, a fact I picked up from my mother's fretful neatening up. The length of the trip accounted for a portion of her worry, but there was something more. I was used to my parents having secrets, but this was something different. I understood from fragments of their conversations that my father was trying out some new kind of work.

Before his trip, when I was passing the kitchen, I heard my mother say to him, "Of course you should go to Mexico City. Try it. You've got to get out from under that son of a gun. . . . It'll be good to be around some fresh blood." The son of a gun was my father's boss, Mr. Smith.

Forty years later, I would find out my father went to Mexico City on a special assignment, arranged by a friend at the Latin American desk, to explore whether it would be worth the United States setting up an operation there to monitor the local Chinese community. The idea was that he might shift to Latin American affairs if he found the job to his taste. It was an opportunity to escape the China Desk. But it was strange to me. *Why was my father going to Mexico? Pop speaks Chinese!*

The day my father left, he squatted down and looked into my eyes from his soft, brown ones. He said, "While I am gone, be brave, and do what Mom tells you, okay?" and then he gave me a hug that felt like the whole world was wrapping itself around me, keeping me safe.

The house seemed like it had too much space and too much lonely air when my father went away on his mission. My mother was like a soldier with a flagpole. She was organized and efficient, always looking after us, always doing her work, always doing her duty. One day I started to cry when I looked at my father's empty reading chair. My mother came over and said she knew I missed Pop, and hugged me against her bosom, making little circles with her fingers against my back. When the hug was over, though, she pulled her body up straight, and said with a hardened-up voice, "But we must keep our feelings private, Sara. People take advantage of any kind of weakness. In the government, if a man's wife and his children aren't perfect, the man can lose his job." I didn't know that, for most of my father's career, wives were graded on their husbands' efficiency reports, and the behavior of a woman's children reflected on her, and him, in black print.

"Do you remember Mr. Palmer from Taipei?" my mother said. "His son started acting obstreperous at school when he was on TDY, and the office sent him home for good." It was like something had clicked inside my mother, switching her from soft to fierce. "We all have to be brave," she said. "We miss Pop, but we have to just be brave and not show it, and put our best foot forward."

My mother's ideal was Jackie Kennedy, and mine was Caroline. We liked how tailored and beautiful they looked—like spruced naval officers in their white cord–trimmed navy dresses—and we liked what my mother referred to as their "carriage." As my mother said, they really knew how to put their best black pumps forward.

~~

"Hurry up, hurry up. You heard Pop, you have to do exactly as I say." I scurried as fast as I could. My mother had put on her best Hong Kong suit. It was as neat and trim as Mrs. Kennedy's.

We were going to Mrs. Smith's for tea. My mother said we had to show my father's boss's wife that we were a strong family. That we could carry on.

My mother was snippy when we headed for the car. "Come on, Sara and Andy, we're going to be late."

We sat stiffly, three in a row, on Mrs. Smith's couch. Mrs. Smith was cheery as she served us tea, Cokes, and Oreos, and my mother was polite. Mrs. Smith asked how we were doing while my father was away, and my mother said, "Oh, we're all doing just fine," with a big smile on her face. Then she asked about all of Mrs. Smith's children, and exclaimed about how proud Mrs. Smith must be of them, but I could feel her hips like hard rocks beside me, and I saw her jaw twitch against her clenched teeth.

I thought Mrs. Smith seemed nice, but when we got in the car, at last, my mother threw her purse on the backseat, heaved a big sigh, and said, "Well, I've done my duty for you, Charlie."

Then she said, half to herself, "Thank God that's over with."

Even though we were in America now, it seemed like my mother had in her mind the government rule, "It takes two, a man and a wife, to make a Foreign Service officer." It made for terrible pressure on her. If my father wasn't going to play the game perfectly, she would make up for it by being perfect herself.

My mother's tough childhood taught her you have to do everything yourself. She got scholarships and worked her way through college. Grit your teeth and do what it takes to get ahead: this was her practical view of life. While my father taught me receptivity, my mother taught me toughness. This would stand me in good stead many times later in life, when fortitude was a requirement. Fighting for my children. . . . brutal illnesses, rejection, resisting currents that weren't going my direction. She readied her children for the hard pull.

~~

One day while my father was gone, my mother, Andy, and I visited the Tomb of the Unknown Soldier in Arlington Cemetery. I watched the guard—in his spiffy navy high-collared dress tunic, his pants with the gold stripes down the legs, and his shoes shiny like black mirrors—march up and down the cement path beside the tomb. He walked up and back, up and back. First he stood still as a statue by the little guardhouse for a count of ten seconds. Then he marched ten paces to the end of the walkway. He clicked his heels, then spun on one heel, clicked again, then marched back down the path. March, march, march-click-spin-click, march, march, march-click-spin-click. As he marched, his back was so straight it seemed like he had an iron brace strapped to his spine, holding his back rigid as his rifle.

What riveted me to the marine were his eyes. As he marched, his eyes looked only straight ahead, as though no other people existed. His eyes didn't even flicker. It was sort of like what my Chinese ballet teacher taught me to do when I tried to pirouette: "Fix your eyes on a point on the wall," he'd said. To me, this was almost impossible to accomplish. But the marine was different. He walked with his eyes nailed, not on anything human, but on an invisible station in the air.

I wondered, standing there watching in my old cotton shorts and shirt and Keds: *would the marine stop, bend down, and help if a lady got sick or a child fell down?* I tried to spy into him, to see inside his brain, or inside his heart, but like a robot, he looked as if nothing could ever touch him or harm him. As if nothing ever, ever, would make him feel choked and lumpy with sadness.

This is what courage must be, I thought, standing with my knobby knees in my scuffed Keds. *This must be what you are like if you are a truly brave American.*

My heart tripped when I thought of being brave. It was bracing, like working for something high, for American glory.

William James wrote in his essay "The Moral Equivalent of War" that human beings thrive on hardiness, devotion, self-sacrifice, and "the strong life": heady emotions and a sense of high purpose most readily aroused in the face of war. He proposed that if human beings were ever to have peace—something he doubted would ever take place for any stretch of time—a sense of army discipline had to be preserved, since people were not rallied by the thought of a life of ease. "Martial virtues must be the enduring cement: intrepidity, contempt for softness, surrender of private interest, obedience to command, must still remain the rock upon which states are built. . . ." Even for me, a shy nine-year-old, thoughts of war and bravery made my heart sing.

~~

As a child I was simply absorbent, but the incongruity of the guard's behavior would strike me one day in my forties: the irony of stoicism at a tomb. The guard was almost like a tomb himself. I would imagine another culture where, at a similar tomb for unidentified dead soldiers, they might have a more appropriate, round-the-clock posting of keening and wailing men and women.

But here and now, watching the marine cemented in for me a core notion: that in America, you were not supposed to be tender. I had no way of knowing that this emphasis on stoicism was an artifact of government service: that it was perhaps government-issue instead of American-issue. All I could figure out was that, in America, any dark rustlings of sadness, chagrin, or anger were a sign of weakness. You were supposed be brave and act happy.

In school, I'd noticed, it was a dreadful thing to cry, or to blush, or to be bothered by someone else in public. If the other kids noticed you were about to cry, they'd say, "Look, Sara's crying," and point their fingers at you. If a boy got mad at another boy, the other boys would tell everyone to come and watch them fight.

Mothers kept their feelings secret too. Mothers in America were always happy. Everywhere in 1963 American mothers had big, red-lipstick smiles. No matter what they were wearing—flouncy dresses with nipped-in waists, pointy glasses and hairpieces, or mink stoles—their most indispensable adornment was a red-lipstick smile, like a smile of armor. Mrs. Johnson, the lady down the street who had six

children tumbling around in her big station wagon, was always cheery. Her bouf-
fant hair was perfectly sprayed, and when we met her at the A & P, she always
smiled and told my mother things at her house were "grand." And other mothers
were much the same. Even when you met them in front of their houses as they were
trudging in and out of their kitchens with their twenty bags of groceries, they didn't
show a drop of fatigue. They said brightly, "Isn't it a beautiful day?" even when it
was cloudy.

My mother's friend, Mrs. Lawn, came over one day and her eyes were all
smudged up from crying, but when she saw my mother and me, she said, "Oh Sara,
how are you, Sweetie?" like nothing was wrong, or ever would be. This, and the
other happy mothers, would leave me craving the true feelings hidden under the
lipstick smiles. I'd spend a long time during my early adulthood feeling allergic
to two-sidedness, and driven to shine lanterns into all shadowy corners; smiles
wouldn't count at all with me. They would seem like mere fakery, and only sadness,
to me, would seem like truth. My main goal in life during those days was to lift the
flap of a smile—to see into people. For a time in my life, as I imagine it, people probably ducked out of sight when they saw me coming.

Even when that brand of fanaticism died down and I realized perkiness had
its place, feigned heartiness would drive me crazy. I would eventually find refuge
in France where, it seemed to me, people were more honest about the mix of good
and bad in the world, about the existence of suffering in life. You could still have
joie de vivre (and perhaps even more of it) if you acknowledged the tough stuff. As
Khalil Gibran, the sage of my adolescence, wrote, "The deeper that sorrow carves
into your being, the more joy you can contain."

But stoicism would confuse and plague me through to the present. What to
show and what to conceal? There seems a basic doubleness to life: the secret you
and the you whom you can safely show to the world. What and in which circumstances is it safe to reveal? What if you disclose and other people don't? This often
seems to put you in a weaker position—particularly if you're with a woman with
that extra-large red lipstick smile. But then, on the other hand, the truth is, disguising can open things up to a level of intimacy and humanity unachievable by
any other means. Francis Bacon wrote in the 1600s of the vital importance in life of
"sharers of troubles." "A principal fruit of friendship is the ease and discharge of the
fullness and swellings of the heart."

But at eight, I was prepared to tuck away disquieting feelings and act brave. Emotions were enemies to conquer, their vanquishing a duty to carry out. The trouble was, I was born hypertuned to those around me, and this had been heightened by the necessities of a life of constant country swapping. No matter what I did to make them behave, a whole barnyard of feelings brayed, clucked, and yowled inside me, trying to get out, and having them raise a ruckus, even if they were deep inside and I could hush them up, made me feel inadequate, like a faulty American.

~~

When my father returned—it turned out the State Department had trained him in Spanish—he squatted down and said, "Thank you for being brave and helping Mom," and then he pulled from his pocket a beautiful bracelet made of silver Mexican coins that jingled when I moved my hand.

My mother said, "Thank God you're home," when my father embraced her, and she snuggled against his suit. He gave her a handmade bronze necklace she would wear frequently and refer to as her "lavaliere," which sounded like such a loving word—a word rolling with her love for my father. My father gave Andy a leather lasso that the Mexican cowboys used.

Later, I heard my father talking to my mother about his trip.

"Yes, Ed would be a much better boss. He is smart, honorable, fair—the best of men. But Latin America just doesn't interest me like China does."

"I think you should move to Ed's shop. I don't trust Smith like you do."

"He can do nothing to hurt me. Anyway, there's nothing to be done."

"You can transfer to Latin America," she said. "You could even leave. I can support us as a physical therapist. Go back to school and get your PhD in philosophy. Or get a law degree. You'd love to be a lawyer for the poor. . . . Maybe you don't really belong in that damned place."

My parents had an unusual marriage. Still, my father would have found it difficult to have let my mother be the breadwinner, even for a limited time. He had a keen sense of family responsibility and would have seen this as self-indulgent. And in the male-dominated world of the 1960s, even this culturally independent man would have felt diminished by such a setup. In another era, a different decision might have been made, and his life taken another course.

"It's a good life, Lois. Good work, with excellent retirement. And the new cultures, the language-learning, the travel . . . You loved Taipei and Kamakura. . . . And China fascinates me. . . ."

Then she said—like it was a ceaseless incantation in her head—"Well then, by God, Charlie, if you're going to stay in FE, you've got to play the game.

"If I can do my part, you can do yours," she added.

"Don't worry, Lois. It'll be fine."

But time would tell: it wouldn't. Troubles, once they've taken hold, don't tend to disappear.

My father's decision to stay in the Far East Branch was another flick of fate's fingers—the wrong fork taken. But, of course, my father didn't know this. He thought the world was good, that there was justice, that it was incumbent upon a man to offer his best judgments, that the CIA was a meritocracy. My father was such an idealist—a trait I would inherit, for better or worse.

~~

By the end of third grade, I had mastered the American trick. Now when a boy called me stupid or a girl pushed me out of the jump-rope line—instances that would set off Chinese firecrackers inside of me—I became the guard at the Tomb of the Unknown Soldier. I swallowed the tears and tried to imagine there was a pole holding up my back. "Shoulders back, eyes straight," barked out the marine. Through sheer, pioneer determination, Radnor Elementary had become my home. I had kneaded and pressed myself into the mold and achieved my goal: I had become ordinary.

8

america

In fourth grade, I wound all the strands of Americanness into a ball. One of the strands was resourcefulness, a trait I honed at Brownies. At our very first meeting, we made sit-upons—decorated squares of canvas sewn on three sides with a *Life* magazine inserted inside—for our weekly meetings and cookouts in the woods. For Christmas, cleaving to the Girl Scout motto, "Always be prepared," we filled milk cartons with sand, sealed them with tape, and then spray-painted them silver. These were for our mothers to put in the backs of their cars, for extra traction in the event of snow. At Girl Scout camp we learned to lash fortresses and walls out of sticks.

A few weeks after camp, my father loaded us up for a camping trip to Vermont. He'd wanted to take us camping in New England for as long as I could remember.

At Dogwood campsite in Calvin Coolidge State Park, a place of green, dromedary-hump mountains, with my new Girl Scout skills, I taught the whole family, with my mother's expert help, how to lash. All day long, we lashed long sticks from the woods, and by the end of the day we had created a gate that divided our campsite from the leafy driveway leading into it; we were safe from the rest of the world. I felt as triumphant as Daniel Boone.

In the future, this skill would serve me better than almost any: this lashing together of sticks. I would be able to lash any sort—Maryland pin oak limbs, Bornean palm branches, Japanese bamboo fronds—and make them into a home. As an adult too, I would fashion homes from a corrugated Quonset hut in Patagonia, a decrepit duplex in Seattle, and an old mill in Spain. Over the years ahead, over and over again, I would lash my way home.

When we left Vermont, following the instructions in the Brownie manual, we left our campsite cleaner than how we found it. I told Andy to pick a leaf off the grill and toss it into the woods. I was proud of how the campsite looked as we got into the car, and I looked back a couple of times as we drove off. Like spies in a movie, we hadn't left a trace.

~~

My fourth-grade teacher, Mrs. Levy, was teapot shaped and feisty, with a loud voice. She dared me to beat my book report record from the previous year. Racing myself, I gobbled books at a rate of three a week—my favorites were the Landmark biographies of famous Americans.

Most evenings, after I'd done my homework, in the dim coolness of the basement, I watched TV. I loved the cowboy shows: *Gunsmoke, Bonanza, Rawhide.* I adored the moment when Clint Eastwood, the cowboy hero, rode off on his horse into the sunset, that moment when it seemed a man, alone, could conquer anything, and all the world was set to rights.

I had a perfect 1963 American life. This was my fourth-grade routine: I went to Brownies, I went to school. I took art lessons at a low building in Rock Creek Park where I made clay ashtrays and painted pictures of the trees out the window. My mother and I shopped at Woodward & Lothrop ("Woodies," as it was called), at Best & Company, and sometimes we even went to Garfinckel's, the best department store in town. This was a hushed, somber-grey shop filled with tailored camel's hair and navy blue clothes with gold buttons, where my mother liked to go "just to look." I spent Friday nights with Charlotte. Snuggled in sleeping bags on the floor, we giggled until, suddenly, the Sandman sprinkled his dust. At Christmastime, Andy, my mother, and I stuffed grocery bags with old *Washington Posts* and made a papier mâché Santa and reindeer. Life in America was hunky-dory, like it was on *Lassie* or *Leave It to Beaver.*

~~

But then some things happened that didn't happen on TV. A girl in my class's mother and father got divorced, something that almost never happened in those years. The girl's name was Vanessa; her sister was Angelica—romantic English names like out of a book. I had Vanessa over a couple of times because my mother said I should. She lived in the ugly brick apartments on Bradley Boulevard. They were the opposite of romantic. I felt sorry for Vanessa. Sometimes I saw her chin wiggle in class as she tried to keep back her tears. I felt her shame and it made me look down. It made me feel too prim and lucky. Divorce was like a secret everyone knew—it made you live in a sad apartment with only your sad, frazzled mother who forgot to wear lipstick and whose clothes hung like sacks on her thin body.

~~

Missiles, lynchings, school buses to Mississippi: I had only a dim awareness of the world outside my school, but glimpses of the newspaper and snatches of grown-up talk drifted and rippled around me. The TV news showed crowds of shining-eyed black people singing "We Shall Overcome," a song that swayed like an insistent pulse in my body. My father told us that attorney general Bobby Kennedy had urged his brother, the president, to back the civil rights movement led by Reverend Martin Luther King Jr., a man with a voice like thunder.

One day at school I went to the bathroom during the middle of class when no one else was there. The bathroom had a strong, unpleasant smell. A big Negro lady was cleaning the floor with a mop and a bucket. I was shy of her like I was of everyone I didn't know. She stayed far from me and I stayed far from her. I tried to make my pee not make a noise.

~~

Despite my mother's begging him to refrain, at the end of summer, August 1963, my father insisted on going downtown to join in the civil rights march. Though I knew my mother agreed that all people should be treated the same, she was troubled by my father's participation in the civil rights movement.

Her voice trembled when she and my father were standing in the front hall, and my father was getting ready to go. "You've got to play the game. What if Smith and his mafia finds out? He's vindictive. You never know what those paramilitary types will use against you."

"By law, Lois, I have the right to my own private views, particularly when I'm in this country," he said, rolling up the sleeves of an old Oxford cloth shirt and setting out for the bus to the Mall.

"Don't be such a maverick," she yelled out the door. "You're a sitting duck for that man."

When we watched TV later that day, though, my mother said, "Oh my Lord, there's Charlie!" For a split second, we were sure we saw my father, in his baggy white shirt and his horn-rimmed glasses, in the crowd watching Dr. Martin Luther King Jr.'s speech. My mother's voice was excited and proud now, even though she had been worried and mad before. We all dropped to the floor and watched the speech. It was so powerful that it was like the ocean was roaring through your body. *"Let freedom ring from Stone Mountain of Georgia! Let freedom ring from Lookout Mountain of Tennessee! Let freedom ring from every hill and every molehill of Mississippi. From every mountainside let freedom ring."*

My father came home with his eyes full of stars. He seemed astonished, ebullient, and proud. I'd never seen him so lit up. America was a grand country, my father's squared shoulders and high-tilted head said. We won World War II and now we were fighting for freedom in our own country. "Look how we have struggled to defeat segregation and are finally doing it," my father said, sitting at the kitchen table, telling us about the 1954 ruling that made segregation unconstitutional, the 1956 bus boycott, and now Martin Luther King Jr.'s thrilling speech. "We still have a long way to go on civil rights," he said. "It is two steps forward and one step back, but we're making steady progress.

"We are a strong country," my father said, pointing to the pictures of marchers amassed at the Mall in the *Washington Post*, "because we can criticize ourselves. We can look at our problems and then do something about them. This is what makes America exceptional. . . . And we are such a rich country that, if we handle our wealth properly, we can end poverty and illiteracy throughout the world." My father's eyes were excited and sure.

"President Kennedy believes," my father said, "that helping to raise the standard of living in poorer countries is not only the best way to help the people of those countries, but the best method for influencing people in favor of our way of thinking, and the best way to prevent the spread of brutal Communist governments, and other undemocratic regimes around the world.

"It is a time of great hope," my father said. His words made my heart thrill.

~~

What turned my father, this Missouri boy, son of an irascible Baptist businessman, into a liberal, and a civil rights marcher? A couple of times, my father told me of the sole visit he had made, as a young boy, to see his father's father. That day, his father drove him to a street corner in Skid Row in St. Louis. There, surrounded by decrepit buildings and bedraggled people, his father introduced him to a bum standing at the curb: a grubby, scarily disheveled man—my great-grandfather. My father never knew the cause of his grandfather's degradation: alcoholism, mental illness, poverty, unemployment—he could only guess. But the incident was lodged in a prominent spot in my father's memory.

Another story my father told me just once. I was in my forties and my father stood close to me as he spoke in a quiet voice. One day when he was a boy, he said, one of his uncles had displayed for him his prize possession: a hanging noose from a lynching. My own body chilled at his words, and I could hear the horror in my father's unnaturally quiet voice, and see it in his trembling hands, holding the invisible circle of rope. Then and there, I knew how and why he had torn out his Missouri roots—and why he was a "yellow dog democrat," as he called himself.

Over the years my father would lean across a table in one country or another and fasten his eyes on ours. "Sara and Andy," he would say, passion charging the timbre of his voice, "remember this. The study of history is very important. It is only through knowledge of history that we prevent repetition of the mistakes of the past." In high school, my father had fallen in with a group of more affluent students from liberal families. He joined their more liberal church, had dinners with their families, learned of a different way of viewing the world—and cobbled his first new self. But still, what makes a man, or a boy, strike out on his own path, and seek to write his own history?

~~

My father would develop, during his college years, a passion for history and for liberal politics. To him, a liberal was a person who favored continual "progress and reform," protection of civil liberties, and who believed government should assume primary responsibility for the welfare of its citizenry as a matter of right. To him, men like Ben Franklin were not dead, but sitting beside him on a bench, striding beside him in the woods, instructing him from a lectern. From studying history, he gleaned three core ideas: First, that the rich should give to the poor. Often, he summoned the words of Franklin Roosevelt, his hero and the president of his youth: "The test of our progress is not whether we add more to the abundance of those who have much; it is whether we provide enough for those who have too little." Second, he believed that service was what life was for. He always said the most important work was service to country, and the noblest jobs were government jobs. And third, my father believed, like Thomas Jefferson, that a good patriot asked probing questions to help his country change for the better.

~~

I was in the ammonia-smelling bathroom at school on November 22, the day President Kennedy died. A teacher rushed in to notify all students to return immediately to their classrooms. Back in class, bold, strong Mrs. Levy was crying. All the other teachers who had come into the room were crying too. So many people were crying that you felt like crying no matter who you were. The girls in my class cried. I cried. The boys tried to be too tough to cry, but a lot of them did. No one acted like a brave marine.

That night, my father said, "President Kennedy was one of the best presidents we'll ever have." As he said it, his eyes looked bruised.

~~

It was a moment when the whole world was sobbing with America—when the whole world was one. Sometimes it seems to me that it is only through sorrow that people can come together. Though good fortune can make people generous, it often seems as if wealth and satisfaction too easily turn people greedy, smug, and self-protective. Can joy unite the way sorrow does? Is there such a thing as universal joy—or does one country's happiness necessarily cancel another's? Will envy always reign? As one of my father's favorites, Aeschylus, wrote, "It is in the character of very few men to honor without envy a friend who has prospered."

~~

Soon after President Kennedy's death, President Johnson asked Americans to help him build "The Great Society" in his inaugural address. He proposed a program of public welfare and medical, educational, and anti-poverty measures: "In a land of great wealth, families must not live in hopeless poverty. In a land rich in harvest, children must not go hungry. In a land of healing miracles, neighbors must not suffer and die unattended. In a great land of learning and scholars, young people must be taught to read and write."

While these lofty utterances lifted American spirits, the truth was that the war on poverty that Johnson proposed would be underfunded—unlike the military war that was being waged in Vietnam. By this time, sixteen thousand American military advisors were posted in the country. Johnson was determined not to lose Vietnam to the Communists, but the United States had little experience with this kind of war, in which the enemy suddenly popped out of and vanished into the jungle, and where the enemy was indistinguishable from the common villager.

~~

Despite momentous events in the world, my own life was happily ordinary. By the middle of fourth grade, I was a sloshing bucket of confidence. I knew my way around the world. Walking down the Bethesda streets, I popped a piece of gum in my mouth. I could blow the biggest bubble in the United States!

~~

It was after Christmas now, and there was one boy in my fourth-grade class whom I liked. It was an uncomfortable kind of liking that made me both fluttery and shy at one time. It was also a feeling like a sort of warm sap rising up in me as inside a tree. Liking Tristan was something different from liking a friend who was a girl. I liked how he looked; he had huge eyes the color of butterscotch and chocolate syrup blended together, dark eyebrows, and blond- and brown-streaked hair that made him handsome. When we were playing hide-and-seek in my yard and he found me next to the brick wall of the house, I imagined he might kiss me. These feelings embarrassed me—even though he invited me over and we ate Hostess cupcakes and looked at the boat in his neat, echoey garage, I never invited him over again. I did write about him sometimes, though, in a pink leather diary my father gave me, with its own lock and key.

These feelings about Tristan were a strange brush with teenagerdom that I quickly pushed away. Most of the time, the sap receded down my trunk, and stayed in my roots hidden under the soil, but it was as though, now that it had discovered the track up toward my branches, it was always there, ready to start pulsing at another embarrassing moment.

~~

On the early evening of February 9, I turned on the television to watch a show everyone had been talking about at school. It was the *Ed Sullivan Show*. Soon after I turned it on, Ed Sullivan, who was a stringy sort of man, introduced to a *dum-da-dum* drum roll four members of a band. The teenagers in the band had long hair like I had never seen before. Their dark bangs flopped down in their eyes, and the hair on the sides of their heads draped over their ears. When they started playing their guitars and singing a whiny song called "I Want to Hold Your Hand," all the girls in the audience started shrieking, jumping up and down, and looking like they were going to faint.

As the show went on and the girls got more and more shrieky, a strange, bubbly ginger ale–like fizz tingled through my body—and soon I felt myself wanting to shriek too. Again, like with Tristan, I felt like I was standing on a brink.

~~

The day I turned in something like my twenty-ninth book report, my father delivered some news while we were eating beef and green peppers over rice. It was one of those days that change everything—those days that became indentations in my life.

"I have some very exciting news," he said. "We are moving to Holland." He explained that even though he was a China specialist, he was being sent to Europe because the government liked people with expertise in one region to have familiarity with other places in the world so as not to get identified with any one country. This could endanger their loyalty and objectivity.

He got out the atlas and pointed to Holland on the map. It was a small, narrow strip, like a margin on the drawing of Europe. My father went on, "You're going to love it because Europe is a wonderful, wonderful place." My father's voice had joyful birds swooping around in it—like this assignment was a great accomplishment, maybe like being assigned to Normandy on D-Day.

He turned to my mother and said with that breathy lilt in his voice, "It's not London, but it's close. Ted says it's a great post."

Holland! I'd never thought of living in Holland. Immediately, a part of me was curious—I knew that in Holland they had windmills and beautiful red tulips—but in another part of me a rock was sinking.

~~

This would from now on be the pattern of my childhood: upon moving to a new place, I would spend a month of sheer grit-your-teeth survival; then I would spend several months establishing new footing in the new country; finally, through determination, I would win a place to stand and be; I would enjoy a year, two, or three of relative steadiness; and then—the minute I was beginning to feel as though I had conquered a whole world and it was now in my possession—the government would rip me away.

~~

My mother and father told us not to tell anyone that we were moving yet. My mother, especially, wanted us to keep it secret. We must hide good things, like hopes and plans, from other people. It was as if, if people knew, they might get the idea of having the good thing for themselves, and snatch it away from us. I didn't know, at this point, that my mother's caution was wise. Foreign assignments were tentative things—and *could* be snatched away, by people with more political clout or who suddenly sniffed an advantageous post, until the orders were signed.

For a week, Holland was our family's secret. At the end of the week, my father got official orders for The Hague, and we went to the State Department for physicals, and to another hulking building in Virginia for passports. My father knew his way around both buildings. At the giant white skyscraper in Virginia, there were even more security checks than at the State Department downtown. My father had to show his badge and my mother had to dig for her passport in her purse. Also, here, even more people came up and congratulated us and shook our hands. This made me feel important.

We ate lunch in the cafeteria where my father said he often ate lunch. Sitting in the huge room among what seemed like thousands of men in dark suits, my mother and my father seemed happy, like this was a big chance. As I ate my cafeteria Jell-O cubes with whipped cream, something we never got at home, I tried to picture Holland. In my mind, it was a place like in my book, *Tulips for Trina*, where there were thatched farmhouses, and where people skated down long, blue, frozen canals and wore wooden shoes. The picture in my mind was bright-colored. Later, though, secretly, in my bed, all I could think of was leaving Mrs. Levy, my tough-nice teacher, and Charlotte, and my Brownie troop, and Twinkies and American gum. I liked being Juicy Fruit, blend-in American.

The next morning, I didn't lock the sadness in a secret box. I set my eyes to look straight out into the air like the guard at the Tomb of the Unknown Soldier. Being a marine was almost automatic for me now.

~~

At school I was now allowed to tell people that I was moving. Telling people made me feel mighty because everyone else seemed so impressed, or scared. Charlotte told me she'd miss me and my throat started to thicken up, despite my telling myself not to be tender. I had wanted Charlotte to be my best friend for my whole life. Most of the girls, though, oohed and ahhed and flounced around me in a circle and said, "Too—lips! Too—lips!"; two girls said, "Oh I'd hate that!"; one girl who was often snotty said, "Too bad for you," and flounced off.

Even though some girls tried to exclude me from the jump-rope line, I was staying in Bethesda, in America, breathing the peppermint-sweet American air, until the very last minute. I stocked up on Wrigley's and Bazooka for the ship and the early days in Holland. I insisted on attending a Brownie meeting the morning of the day we left. The girls in my class gave me a lucky rabbit foot, and they signed a little autograph book, but I felt like I would be there again the next week.

~~

Soon, while my father flew ahead, my mother, brother, and I would board the SS *America* and head across the stormy, grey Atlantic. Standing on the topmost deck, looking back toward America, the building sea would mist my face with a fine, salty, obscuring spray.

In 1956, phone lines were laid across the Atlantic, making it theoretically possible that my stateside friends and I could keep in touch, but the price was so prohibitive all through my childhood that communication by telephone across seas was reserved for family emergencies only. The laying of the phone lines meant the world was getting smaller, and globalization—for all its good and bad—was underway, but we couldn't see it yet. For all intents and purposes, once I left the United States, save for letters, my friends and my Bethesda life would be gone. It was a degree of rupture and separation unimaginable now—not so different, in terms of communication, from heading west in a covered wagon.

The ripping-away of Bethesda, this loss of hard-won Charlotte, would make me into a person who treasured every note from a friend, every birthday card, like a starving orphan girl treasures a little lump of rice.

~~

This was the last week of my life that I would be an ordinary American. If I'd stayed in Bethesda now, I would have stood a chance. I might have eaten some tofu now and then, but I could have been the real McCoy. Forever afterward, my heart would swell with longing at the smell of fresh-cut grass, at the sight of young girls chatting in tight clutches, but the portal to an ordinary American childhood was closed to me now. My crystal coach had swept by.

Now, on a blustery March day in 1964, I left the United States as a simple and ordinary American girl—for the last time.

Book 3

RAINLIGHT
The Hague, The Netherlands,
1964–1968

9

klompen

Sometimes happiness slams into you like a freight train of love and you're knocked off your feet. Other times happiness is work—a painstaking trudge toward an appreciative state of mind. And sometimes it is a gradual accrual of which you're not even aware: with each passing day you feel more lighted up inside, as if your organs are being painted in pastels. As though each day is a second of the dawn, you absorb more and more light, like sunlight spreading over a damp, grey 5 a.m. landscape.

While my father was playing a murky game in a dim terrain, I was light-struck in one of the darker places on earth.

~~

My father met us at the dock in Le Havre with his beige Balmacaan raincoat over his arm. His dark eyes were reflecting the bouncing lights of the dim day; he grabbed us all into tight hugs and said, "You're going to love Holland!" I was so glad to see my father that I hung on to his arm, even though he was carrying heavy suitcases, all the way to the station.

We traveled by train to The Hague. Rain like white quill streaks on a flat, grey background gauzed the views of geometrically placed brick houses and green cow pastures the whole journey.

A taxi took us from the train station to the house that would be our home for the next six months: a yellow-brick row house in a sprawling new suburban development of identical houses at the raw edge of The Hague where the city petered out into farm fields. As I peered out the car windows at the gridded world of damp yellow brick so different from anywhere else I had ever been, my heart quickened. *What sort of life did people live in these houses?*

~~

The cab pulled up to a house at the end of a row on Anemoneweg—"Anemone Way." Tired and mussed, we shuffled out of the car. Out in the open, I looked up into a sky the bleached color of beach shells. Chilly, wet air hit my cheeks and eyes. Then, almost like it was a deliberate act, the sky flushed steel grey, and the lion's mouth of the sky widened to let rush a heavy fountain-stream of water. By the time we unloaded our eight suitcases from the taxi and made our way up through the doorway of our new home, my fingers felt as though they had been cased in ice and I was wet through to the skin. I had set my suitcase down in a land of rain.

~~

Our first week in the yellow-brick house was a blur of hand shaking. My mother had to make her calls, first to the ambassador's wife, and then to the homes of other officers, leaving her calling card if the lady wasn't in, according to protocol. My father took us to meet other embassy families and Dutch dignitaries. He was polite and formal in his dark suit, and introduced me as though I were an important adult. "Meneer Peereboom, this is my daughter, Sara," he said as I clasped the Dutchman's hand. I was living in a movie of the perfect, brave embassy girl; my mother, Andy, and I were Jackie, John-John, and Caroline, ornaments for my father doing his important job for the United States of America.

Most of the first days I was so absorbed with eating gorgeous Dutch cream puffs and crispy, mayonnaise-topped Dutch french fries called *patates frites*, and with arranging my room, that I didn't think about swinging in the park with Charlotte, or of the oatmeal cookies we had at Brownie meetings, or of the ferny smell of our Wilson Lane house. But one evening, at an embassy party, I was standing beside my mother with my braids plaited tight, when a lady asked her if she missed Bethesda, and my throat constricted. My mother had cried when she left Bethesda, but now, as the stalwart diplomat's wife, she said, "Oh, wherever I am is best." On the way home from the party, she sat up straight as a soldier and commented, about the weepy mother of another family who had just left her pregnant sister to come to Holland, "She should stop that nonsense. She knew what she was signing up for when her husband joined the Foreign Service." My mother's motto was, "We are Tabers. We can do anything."

~~

A couple of days later we heard a car drive up and we rushed outside. It was my father with our new, cream-colored Volkswagen Bug. The car was spit-spot; it even smelled new. But there was something else even more remarkable about it. My father pointed to the beginning two letters on the license plates: GN. "The GN stands for *geen Nederlander*," my father said. "That means 'not a Netherlander.'" Only representatives of foreign governments were issued these, he told us. I could feel an American flag waving inside me.

~~

Toward the end of our first week, we visited my father at work. My mother drove us—nervous at the wheel of a new car in a new country—from the recent-cut suburban sprawl into the city neighborhoods of cobbled streets lined with old brick row houses. The embassy was a white, blocky, modern building, an incongruity set on an old, gracious city square, with long horizontal windows across each of the four stories. We mounted the steps up to the wide glass doors, entered, and approached the platform from which the marine guard had an on-high view of everything outside. When I looked at him in his perfectly crisp navy-and-white uniform, my mind flashed back to the silent, stiff guardians at the Tomb of the Unknown Soldier, and a shiver trickled down my back.

The guard had met my mother, but still, he picked up the phone and said, "Mr. Taber, I have your family down here. Is it all right for them to go up?"

We climbed the broad, open stairway. My father's office was a big room on the second floor, with a large window looking out on the *plein* with the trees and benches down below. His office was bright with fluorescent light. My father was stacking papers as we arrived, as if there was a rule that he must conceal all his work from everyone, even my mother.

There were folders piled on his desk, and books everywhere. The books had titles like *From Lenin to Malenkov*, *Who's Who in Modern China*, *Brain-washing in Red China*, *Sun Yat Sen*, *The Finest Hours*, and *Mathews' Chinese-English Dictionary*.

My father had us sit down on chairs by the window, so he could tell us about his new portfolio. "As a political attaché here at the embassy, I do work to foster good relationships between countries," he said. I didn't know this, but this was his official line. Now he described something closer to the actual work he did. "Here in Holland, just like I was in Taiwan and in Bethesda, I'm a China watcher. My specific job is to work along with the Dutch, to keep an eye on China. Both countries are very concerned about what China is up to." I wondered, how did my father watch China from here in Holland? Through a peephole? Binoculars? Was he digging a secret tunnel to some Chinese place?

As I would know later, a large part of my father's job in The Hague was to act as liaison to the Dutch intelligence service. Both countries were tracking the activities of Mainland Chinese and Maoist groups in Holland and other parts of Europe, and recruiting spies. And they were, in fact, using gadgets like binoculars and other surveillance techniques to spy on the Communist Chinese. The Hague had one of the few Chinese missions in Europe—the Netherlands was one of the countries in Europe with which the Communist Chinese had formal relations—and the United States was there to glean information, by any means it could. Here in The Hague, like in Taipei, my father was serving as an intelligence officer under official cover. Once again, his basic work was masked, and he shrugged on and off different identities as he sought intelligence in the course of his daily activities.

~~

My father had studied Dutch at the Foreign Service Institute for six months before he came, and he was a natural linguist, so he spoke Dutch well already. The deep trouser pockets of his dark suits now, contained rubber-banded stacks of flash cards jotted with Dutch words instead of sketchy Chinese characters—as well as a little book in which, as he said, he "kept track of himself." When I was older, I learned that this was, literally, true. In the book, he kept notes of meeting places, names of agents, codes for the names he was using for particular contacts. It would have been handy to have owned a similar little identity notebook of my own in the trying weeks ahead.

My father took us down to the embassy auditorium where the ambassador was to address all the new embassy "dependents." Ambassador Tyler, a mustachioed man in a pinstriped suit, spoke to us from the podium.

"You should be very proud of your fathers," he told us. "They are representatives of the freest, most advanced country in the world. Their mission is to spread the great American way of life across the globe. . . .

"Now, the fact that your fathers are diplomats," he continued, "means you, too, have a job just as your father and I do. Your job, as a representative of the United States, is to behave like a little ambassador of your country. . . ." I sat up straighter when the ambassador said this. This was a rule I could latch on to.

As we left, my father picked up on what the ambassador had said. "Our duty in Holland is to learn the Dutch ways. As you know, whenever you're in another country it is your job to respect the customs of the people there and conform to them as much as you can." My father had shown me the State Department's *Post Report* on Holland, which explained Dutch customs, and I'd noticed that my mother had begun shaking people's hands, even in little shops, and taking flowers whenever we visited anyone. She taught me that, when you visited people in foreign countries, it was important to accept the food or little gifts they offered. It was crucial to ignore your own wishes, because to say no could offend people and we were guests in this country. My mother could play the embassy lady to a tee. She was an ardent patriot, a student of protocol, the ideal partner. And she loved the glory and the game.

~~

Soon after the ambassador's talk, my father wanted to show us around downtown *Den Haag*, as the Dutch refer to The Hague. The falling rain was turning to sleet, and the cold was sharp. Pulling our hoods over our heads, we followed my father toward the *centrum*.

As we walked along, trams screeched by on their tracks in the middle of the street and bikes spurted by us on the bike path. Dutch people rode bikes more than they rode in cars—just like in Taiwan, except here there were no pedicabs, water buffaloes, or chickens wandering among them, just more people on bikes: A father with a striped toque pulled down to his brows pumped heavily along with three children wearing wool hats on board, one on the rear, one on the cross spoke, and one on his lap, all of them squinting into the rain. A beautiful young couple—he the blondest of blond and she the blackest of black haired—rode along: he peddled and she perched on the rear fender with her hands around his waist, her cheek nestled against his back, happy as if it were a sunny day. A heavy lady about my mother's age, with a long thick scarf wadded around her neck, glided along, planted on the crossbar of her huffing husband's bike, like the figurehead of a ship. A man with a navy blue woolen cap charged by, a fishing pole sticking out of his rear basket.

My father stopped us to point out the odd-looking cars, all smaller and rounder than the cars in America. "That's an Opel," he said. "And that's a Citroën. That's a Peugeot, and that's a DAF. DAFs are made in Holland." As each car passed by, it sprayed water and whooshed like a small wave in the sea.

For an instant, a policeman raced by in a snazzy white Porsche sports car, weaving in and out among the other cars. A small, square white rescue truck blaring *eeh-aah, eeh-aah!* followed. Behind the ambulance came a mounted policeman on an immense chestnut horse. Then the traffic slowed and, best of all, a group of velvet-helmeted girls on ponies trotted through a main intersection.

After a brisk circle through the shopping district—past large department stores like Vroom en Dreesman and C & A, and tiny boutiques in narrow alleys—my father led us across the main street toward an open space. He said, "This is the best part. The Hofvijver."

Suddenly I saw what my father was hastening us toward. Beyond a small square I saw a shining, dark, open pond across which sat the brick façade of what looked like a fairy castle.

"That's the Binnenhof," my father said, pointing to the building, as we stopped by the pond, "the seat of the Dutch government."

I was gazing across the water at a picture from a storybook. The four- or five-story brick complex, the outer walls of which descended straight down into the pond, was studded with towers like witches' hats, chimneys, square towers, and turrets, and rows of narrow, darkened windows. I could imagine long, twisting corridors linking all the inner rooms that were sure to have wood-paneled walls, rich carpets on the floors, and immense hunting scenes and black-and-burgundy portraits of great men on the walls. I could picture myself in a long, velvet gown, seated on a prim velvet chair. . . . But then I came to my senses: the Binnenhof was a hundred times smaller than the Capitol in Washington. I remembered what Ambassador Tyler said about the United States of America being the most advanced country in the world and felt a stab of tight and cozy smugness.

~~

By Monday morning the smugness had evaporated. When I awakened, my room was dark, shadowy, and strange. My hands shook as I put on the new skirt my mother and I had picked out for my first day at school. My skirt was blue. My shirt was white. My sneakers were my old ones from Bethesda. The ones Charlotte and I had written "friends 4ever" on the bottoms of just before I got on the plane.

At breakfast I could hardly swallow my round of Dutch rusk toast even though it was topped with butter and *chocoladehagel*, chocolate sprinkles, my new favorite breakfast. My father smoothed his hand along my crown before he left for the tram. "Don't worry. You look very pretty," he said. *At least I have my long hair,* I thought. *The kids in Bethesda always liked my braids.*

Just before we left the house, I went up to my room and made sure the light was on—as if my mind was pretending that I'd actually be here all day, at home. At 7:30, while it was still dark, my mother drove us downtown to register at the American School of The Hague, located in the old heart of the city.

Now I was standing on the edge of the playground that surrounded my new school, a white Victorian mansion that looked like a rich merchant's villa or an embassy residence. It was set forward in a large, iron-fenced lot. It had a handkerchief front lawn, a playground to its left side, and a large blacktop and playing fields filling the huge back lot. Instantly I was, again, the sparrow in the cage. As at Radnor, I was in a place where I had no history and had to prove myself worthy. I no longer felt like an indomitable, superior American. I felt like throwing up.

I watched a knot of girls my age at the edge of the blacktop. Not one of the girls had long hair, and they were all wearing skirts, blouses, and sneakers that matched. The clothes I wore were all wrong. *Please Mom, come back, come and take me home.*

There was one particular girl—she looked American-pretty like Annette Funicello, only fair—who stood with her hip jutting out and tossed her head while making emphatic gestures with her hands. The girls leaned in toward her, cozy-tight like birds around a feeder, as if to peck up her every opinion. She kept pointing at one girl across the playground, saying something at which the other girls laughed. An uneasy feeling stirred deep in my stomach. To belong in this school seemed as if it would involve human sacrifice.

I felt my throat clutching up. I took a deep breath, trying to be a marine, but I felt more like a girl with a face wiggling to hold back tears. The bell rang.

In the fourth-grade classroom, on the second floor in what once must have been a bedroom, I began putting away my pencils and pens in my lift-top wood desk. I was looking under the lid when suddenly I heard a bustling. The teacher was standing at the head of the room and I was the only student sitting down. I felt my face turn red and hurried to rise. When the teacher said "Good morning, class," the students replied, "Good Morning, Ma'am," in unison as I stood there, sweating. I vowed to myself not to let down my guard for even a second, so I didn't make another mistake.

My head swirled trying to make heads and tails of this strange American School of The Hague. Though it purported to be American it was really a blend, in style and curriculum, of European, English, Irish, and southern American. In addition to rising when grown-ups came into a room, everyone called the teachers "Sir" and "Ma'am," instead of saying "Mr. Potts" or "Mrs. Webster." We had to write everything in notebooks, *cahiers*, and all our work had to be written neatly, in fountain pen, as they did in France. Because many of the teachers were British, we had to write *colour* for color, *theatre* for theater, and *centre* for center, and cross our sevens and z's, which they call *zeds*. "Doubl' up! Doubl' up!" our science teacher said, swallowing a syllable, when he wanted us to hurry. Before long, these teachers would spawn in me a sense of British-accented English as my sonic home.

Recess was also odd at this strange school. The kids played a game called English rounders—it was like baseball, except the ball was hit with a little flat bat. And the playground included a tether ball and a maypole, which I had never seen before. I watched as the kids dashed madly around the maypole holding onto the ropes. Every couple of minutes, they flew up into the air, laughing—but I knew I would never feel like I was flying, or even feel like laughing at this school where I knew no one in the world.

~~

When I arrived home from school, my mother had a snack of milk and Cheerios from the embassy welcome kit waiting, but my lip quivered and my throat stuck closed the minute she asked me how my day had gone.

Finally I said, "This is an American school, but the kids are really different from the kids at Radnor." It was true. The students at the school were a mixture of overseas oil company—Esso, Shell, and Aramco—military, and embassy families like mine. Also among the students were an Iranian princess and a sprinkling of half-Dutch and half-Belgian children, as well as the children of other Europeans who had American husbands or wives, or who wanted their children to speak English. The students had lived in Saudi Arabia, Japan, and Africa, and many other places. They were a mongrel, culturally mixed breed. I didn't yet realize that I actually was one of them. Or how "American" they were.

"Don't worry, Sara," she said, "You'll have friends soon. Just do your schoolwork and the friends will come." She patted my hand like she knew it was true, but I knew she was wrong.

After dinner, my father took me on his lap. "Don't worry, Sweetie, those kids will love you once they get to know you. It takes a little time. If you look straight at your fears, walk up to them and take them on, things usually come out right," but I cried for a long time anyway, feeling the wool lapel of his suit jacket grow wet against my cheek.

Tuesday, Wednesday, Thursday, and Friday, I tried to have courage, concentrate on my schoolwork, and be a marine, but mostly I stood off to the edge of the chummy girls in their matching skirts and Keds, pretending to be interested in my fingers and swallowing tears.

~~

Kicking Dutch puddles on Anemoneweg after school on Friday of this first week of school, it seemed as though Japan, Taiwan, and Bethesda—all my places— had been washed away and I couldn't see myself in the dark pools. I felt like a cloud, a ghost. I wondered, *Am I real? Do other people ever feel this way—invisible to themselves?*

What I needed now in Holland, more than anything, was for someone to stand outside me and tell me what they saw—to make me feel like I existed, like I was still myself. I ached for a twin. Trudging along, I said my name out loud. "SA-RA, SA-RA, SA-RA." It sounded odd, uttered into the air, but I could feel its hardness in my mouth. *I really am real,* I told myself.

In the dimming afternoon, I shook a basket of sugar cubes set on the empty windowsill. Each cube had a different wrapper from a different restaurant or cafeteria: from the Hot Shoppes on East-West Highway, from a motel in Indiana near Aunt Norma's, from the SS *America. I am a girl who collects sugar cubes,* I thought.

Just before the dimness turned to night, I unwrapped one of the cubes, and sucked it to nothingness. The sweetness made me feel strong and real. But, like the sugar, I was transitory in this new place, quickly melting away.

~~

In the bright of Monday morning, I was faced with an immediate, practical task: to figure out what kind of Sara would work best for this place, which kind of girl would fit in and find friends.

On the blacktop, in the face of the girls with their "we belong" coziness, I downed a sugar cube. I took out of my pocket the nicey-nice girl I used to be sometimes in Bethesda. As with Charlotte, I became a girl for the taking. I was a girl made of putty. I adopted the other girls' opinions. I asked them what *they* thought was the prettiest color, who *they* thought was the best teacher, what *they* thought was the most delicious candy, and then I said I thought so too. My father suggested that I follow Dutch people's lead in order to respect their culture and so as not to offend, so I did that here at school too.

~~

When you're new, one of two things happens: you're either befriended by another marginal girl, or an in-crowd girl decides to adopt you as her sidekick. It usually takes months to find true-blue friends. I found Charlotte thanks to a stroke of luck in Bethesda. Most of the time at the beginning, it's either kind or imperious, white or black. Fate decides which you get. At the American School of The Hague, I had one, and then the other.

First, the marginal girl came along. From the moment I stepped into Lucy's row house on one of the dignified old brick blocks of the city—her father was one of my father's embassy colleagues—she took me right to the heart in her prepubescent flat chest as a friend. A skinny sprite with flyaway blond hair, she was a girl thirsty for water, as thirsty as I.

We smoked chocolate cigarettes on her front stoop. We played World War Two among the scraggly trees in the park, with Lucy and me on one side and Jen, Lucy's younger sister, and Andy on the other, our bodies pumping with American swagger and war lust. We snuck up on each other's forts and stole each other's canteens and candy K-rations. We shot each other with bent sticks. We taught ourselves to blow through grass to make it croak, and to make perfect emergency-signal owl hoots.

At school, Lucy and I inched up the knotted ropes suspended from the swing set. From the rope-tops, together we looked down over the world. Perched up in the air with a friend, I felt a surge of confidence.

~~

But then came Candy, the larger-than-life girl who dazzled me and filled me with longing: longing to be as perfect an American girl as she was, and to belong effortlessly as she did at The American School of The Hague. I wanted to be her; it was simple as that.

Candy Ann Carlton, with her hank of dirty-blond hair hanging over one eye, and her ski jump nose—cute, smart (my mother would add, "alecky"), fearless, confident, saucy—was so American her head should have been on a quarter. She was like Shirley Temple, Annie Oakley, and Hayley Mills all combined into one blond, confident movie star.

One day at recess, we girls were watching two boys who were tossing a ball around. Jeff charged after the ball hurled by Mike, then caught it, skidding to a stop at Candy's feet. She put her hands on her hips and said, "And what do you think you're doing, Mister Jones?" He bopped her on the rear with his ball and she spun and stuck out her tongue at him, laughing with her eyes twinkling as he raced again across the field.

Candy, the queen of our fourteen-member fourth grade, knew how to play people like fish on hooks. I noticed right away that when Candy asked a girl over, the girl changed her other plans and went. When Candy decided to change her best friend, the old best friend was helpless, and had no choice but to join the rest of the girls in the pile of Candy's discarded old shoes. As for the boys, they all wanted to go steady with her, and Candy could have her pick.

Before I'd come to The American School of The Hague, I hadn't even known the word "popular," but now, suddenly, in this tiny school on a small cobbled street of The Hague, it was as though that word was written in purple block letters in the sky over the white school and was the only word in the whole English dictionary that mattered. I'd figured out the score at The American School of The Hague: popularity was everything and Candy was the only route to that goal. To me, this friendship was a *job*, and I had to accommodate to whatever the friendship required. So, over the next months, through abject subjugation and toil, I became Candy's vassal, and she my queen, my "best friend." If Lucy was my good twin, Candy was my bad.

~~

Another midmorning recess during my first month, I sat on the wall at one side of the front lawn, behind the wrought iron fence, with Candy, Stacy, Kathy, and other girls in fourth grade.

"Do you like Cindy's page boy?" Kathy asked.

"Yeah, she looks so cute," I said.

But Candy gave her shoulder-grazing curls a little shake and said, "Page boys are out. Flips are in." Her voice had the authority of the president of the United States, or of Louis the XV. "Off with her head."

Raised American, I licked my wound and seized, "Where there's a will there's a way."

~~

A week or so later, Candy was issuing her daily edicts to us girls, standing around her like monkeys waiting for tossed peanuts. She motioned with her shoulder toward Molly, over near the jungle gym. "Can you believe that hideous plaid skirt? And look at her hair. Her bangs are longer on one side than the other! She looks like a Dutchie!"

This was it: my moment.

I had heard from my mother that Molly's military parents didn't have much money, so her girls had to wear hand-me-downs from cousins in the States, and her mother cut the girls' hair. The girls in our clutch were all nodding, laughing, and straightening their miniskirts and plumping up their hair as they peeked over at Molly.

My thoughts had stopped. It was as though the part of me that had the capacity for independent thought and knew the golden rule had left my body and I was now solely want and need, and could only be Candy's echo.

I choked out, in a voice I didn't recognize, "Yeah, Molly's a hick."

Candy was a saucy gull who had stolen an egg from a sparrow's nest. She flew off, wheeling in the sky, laughing a raucous gull's laugh.

~~~

At home, when I reported, shakily, to my mother and father about Candy— "She's so cool, she has the nicest clothes, but she's also mean"—my mother said, "Just look at Tina Jones." She was an older embassy girl at school. "Tina doesn't care what other girls say. Just be confident in yourself."

My father took me on his lap. He told me, "What the other girls say isn't the thing to focus on. Look inside yourself for what you like and what you think is right, and then try not to think about what others think and do." I tried, but it was almost impossible. I had to be Candy's friend; craving has no shame or cease.

~~~

One day in late summer, Lucy and I went to the park together and stood by the huge old oak tree at its center. We took sharp sticks and jabbed and scratched them along our forearms until, finally, we raised tiny drops of blood. Rubbing our drops together, mixing our bloods, we became blood sisters. A few days later, Lucy left for the States on the SS *Rotterdam*. When skinny, flyaway-haired Lucy of the eager eyes sailed away on the ship, I was left with a hole inside me, into which—for better or worse, for good and for bad—Candy Carlton dropped like a stopper in a drain, or a gumdrop in a mouth.

~~~

Now that we knew where my father worked, and were established in school, the customary rhythms of our family life were slowly unpacked from our black and green footlockers. We ate pancakes for breakfast on Saturdays, as we had in Bethesda and Taipei, and on weekends we went for hikes—not on the Appalachian Trail in hiking boots, but beside cow fields in black Dutch rubber boots. Other elements of life were distinctly Dutch and we assimilated them easily into our American-style life. Marketing had a whole new meaning and rhythm: my mother hardly had to set foot into a shop. Every few days, the fish man, the meat man, the green grocer, the milk man, the bread man, and the flower lady magically appeared at our door and made deliveries to the yellow row house: of Menken Melk in wonderful plastic bags like water balloons; of paper wraps bulging with apples and tomatoes; of newspaper-triangles of fish; of bread that was still warm; and of bundles of tulips.

~~

Turned loose in the afternoons, Andy and I mounted our bikes and, under a felted grey sky, we charged off to fish in a canal with strung-up sticks and hunks of old bread; to feed yanked-up clumps of grass to wiggly-lipped ponies; to peer at the pots of red flowers and blue-and-white pitchers set in the large lace-curtained picture windows of the Dutch people's houses.

Days when we were not in the mood for cycling, Andy and his new neighborhood friend, Jan, dug holes to China in the kerchief-sized back garden, with my brother's turtle, Egbert, standing by. I zoomed up and down the sidewalk on my roller skates or clumped back and forth on my new Dutch stilts.

No day in our new country was complete without a dash to the neighborhood candy shop. By now we knew the Dutch names for our favorite sweets: *Kings* peppermints; *Mentos*, another kind of mint with a hard, white shell; candy necklaces; *Rangs*, which were like Life Savers; and strong *dubbelzout* licorice.

It was on one of our visits to the candy shop that I saw the thing that fastened me to Holland forever. If chewing gum symbolized America, what I saw at the shop distilled Holland to me.

This particular day, we had to wait to request our sweets until a magical farmer, who smelled of horses and cows, bought a box of cookies and a package of cigarettes. What was magical about this burly man was not his rich smell or his purchases, but his footwear. The farmer was standing in a mucky pair of wooden shoes, plastered with mud and straw—as were the two small, blond thatch-haired children in hand-knit, striped sweaters he had in tow. The moment I saw those shoes—then and there—I fell in love.

Clomp-plunk: that is the sound of Dutch wooden shoes. *Klompen.* I noticed them everywhere hereafter: on the feet of farmers, country children tromping in paddocks, and even some old fishermen walking around in the centrum.

We stopped one day in a village for pea soup. As we wandered down a lane, we came to an old wooden barn where a man was at work among blocks of wood. We watched as out of a block of blond-white wood set on a pedestal the man chiseled, with smooth, deft twists of his large hands, a shoe exactly like something out of a fairy tale—a smooth wooden slipper that fit my foot like a sock, with an upturned elfin toe.

When we got home, I put on my fairy-tale shoes and from then on, I wore them whenever I could. The Dutch shoe fit my parents and brother as well. My mother and father had by now taken to biking in the rain, their wheels splattering their coat tails as they pedaled. And they took great glee in reading the latest naughty Dutch novels. And as for Andy: rain just added to the richness of his dirt-digging. He was meant for a mud wallow.

By the end of the summer, six months after our arrival in The Hague, I could walk on stilts in my klompen, but even at this my patriotism held strong. Even a lot of Dutch kids, I reckoned, could hardly walk in their klompen this well.

~~

One night, on my way home from buying eggs for my mother at the candy shop, some neighborhood boys yelled, "Amerika! Amerika!" as I passed by, and tossed clumps of soil at me. While running away, I jolted the eggs.

Once I got home, with a basketful of broken eggs, I sobbed to my mother about the mean boys. "They're nothing but a bunch of dumb Dutchies," I said, mimicking the kids at school.

My mother patted me, in sympathy, and then she said, "But don't ever call Dutch people 'Dutchies' again. It's not respectful to our hosts." She then loped off herself, to buy another dozen eggs.

I sat stiffly on the couch during the time my mother was gone. While trying to focus on my book, I tasted, for the first time, the red-hot shame—the mixture of anger and chagrin—that would become one side of the split response I had to Holland for as long as we lived here. On the one hand, my chest burst with fierce pride in being an American—the unadulterated pride that only a grade school child can have—and, in my arrogance, I wanted to sic some big American boys on my tormenters to show them whose country was the stronger. On the other hand, a wonder had poised itself in my mind. What could the Dutch boys not like about America? This question was to be the porridge I ate each day for breakfast throughout my four and a half years in The Hague.

~~

Back in America, other kinds of eggs were being thrown. Cross-cultural conflict with another country was heating up.

One early August night, when we were sitting at dinner, my father said, "Something important has happened. Congress just signed the Tonkin Bay Resolution."

When we'd arrived at The Hague, just six months before, in March, the civil rights march on Washington had occurred, and America was full of people jumping up and down for joy on television. This summer, the American Ranger 7 space probe had sent back photographs of the moon, and Carnaby Street in London had become the coolest place on earth. I'd spent hours staring at magazine photos of English models in Mary Quant miniskirts. Now, over a dinner of mashed potatoes and wurst, my father said, "With the Tonkin Bay Resolution, President Johnson has been given a blank check for bombing North Vietnam, the Communist part of Vietnam."

My father pointed to Vietnam on the globe. He said more and more Americans were being sent there every month, to fight the Communists. It was a very difficult war, but it was important to stop the Communists in Vietnam, because our government thought if we didn't, the Communist Chinese might take over Vietnam—and then, like dominoes, one after another country would fall.

When I left Bethesda, I had left behind the possibility of being a pure and simple American girl. Now, just six months later, though I was unaware of it, my country, too, had lost its innocence and purity.

After this, more and more frequently, I heard my father talk about Saigon. "Bill said things in Saigon are hot . . . ," or "I heard from Tom yesterday. He said Saigon station is a messy place. . . ." I knew, deep in my bones, however, regardless of anything that went on in the world, that America was still the heroic country that won World War II, the most powerful country in the world—and I knew we could do no wrong.

When my father told us about the blank check, though, his eyes were very serious. I didn't realize it, but another war was gathering force, a war that would shape my life.

10
dutchies

One raw afternoon, my father took us to an exhibit of M. C. Escher's prints. The exhibit was housed in a vast, modern building stretching across a garden in a part of The Hague I had never seen before. Inside the immense rooms with large windows, I walked from print to print, captured by the artist's work. Each woodcut was a puzzle. One moment, all I saw inside the frame was black flocks of birds. The next, the picture held flows of white fish. One piece, titled *Day and Night*, showed a patchwork landscape of geometric shapes that gradually rose and changed into birds. Above the fields, white birds flew toward a black medieval town with church and windmill, and in the opposite direction, black birds winged toward a mirror image of the town, this time in white. It was impossible to hold both the black birds and the white birds, both night and day, in my eyes at once. One part of the picture rose up and trapped me every time.

Up until this point in my life, age ten, I had always had a clear picture in my mind of a world of white American knights in a castle on a hill fighting foreign enemy black knights from a castle below. But now, planted in a fresh and interesting country, I could no longer bring reliably into focus one clear, steady, white picture of America and the world.

My life became a nervous affair: of black and white doubles that flicked in and out of focus, white-then-black, black-then-white, as my ardent patriotism hit up against Dutch opinions about American foreign policy; as my efforts to act the confident, jocular American clashed with and faded into my private shyness; and as the tiny world of my American school was trespassed upon by, and warped into, the great world beyond. My life became a constant struggle to restore the white knights to their rightful place in the white castle on the hill.

~~

It was October now—my first Dutch autumn—and tinges of oranges and apples mixed with the green wetness of the trees and the damp red brick of the row houses. We had moved to an old, rambling brick row house on Duinweg, Dune Way, in the heart of the city near the sea.

Our new rented house with its seven bedrooms, five fireplaces, and four bathrooms; its old, heavy furniture; its dark, Dutch paintings; and its farm-style kitchen with a big rectangular wooden table in the middle, was dark and gloomy and the happiest house I'd lived in yet. Our housekeeper was usually in the kitchen with my mother, wiping the counters when we got home. Maria, who was stout and had ruddy cheeks that felt like sandpaper, gave me an enveloping hug against her broad bosom and said, "*Dag Lievert!*" Then she tickled Andy, who proceeded to flop on the floor. "*Andytje!*" Maria lovingly scolded, pulling him up with her gentle, chapped paw.

Maria was the reincarnation of Mary, our Taiwanese amah—but this amah was hazel-eyed, large, and sturdy. Maria was humus, an earthy woman putting forth delicate blooms. I've never seen a more beautiful face: radiant eyes shining from thick, wind-rouged cheeks—colors of red delicious apples and whipped cream.

One of the boons of living abroad is the way class differences dissolve. When you're in a foreign country, perhaps because you are so undeniably different and this cannot be changed and must be surmounted, love vaults the brick walls. I'd experience this years later, in my twenties on a job in Patagonia, where I was able to have friends as various as a member of one of the richest families in the land, a bush pilot, and a woman who lived from the proceeds of her tiny hotel in a two-bit whale-watching village. This forging of friendships across the frontiers of class is one of life's great pleasures—and now, here in The Hague, I adored a Dutch washerwoman.

My mother loved her too. Maria bustled around her, giving her pillowy hugs like she gave me, dispensing love like it was as cheap as Dutch tulips.

~~

I stepped out of the cozy warmth of the Duinweg house into the drizzle, my grey U.S. army surplus munitions bag slung over my left shoulder. I had swapped the Dutch leather satchel my mother loved for this bag, which was like that of every other child in my class at The American School of The Hague. I loved this bag. It was American. On its sturdy grey canvas I had inked slogans: "I Love Paul" (of the Beatles) and "Love Potion Number Nine." We lived only one long block from the school.

I looked both ways, crossed the street, turned left, and then set off down Parkstraat. The sidewalk was narrow and uneven with broken slabs. I had to watch for dog doo as I proceeded. Dutch people were dog-crazy and there was dog plop everywhere.

The cobbled street, a district of small institutions, was narrow, lined on both sides by villas and small mansions fronted by wrought-iron fences. There were a few spindly trees, and large, overarching willows. The rain misted down, making my face itch. Inside my wool jacket, I sweated. I loved my school, so I hastened along.

I hurried past the French and then the English school, bustling past the barretted and tailored French girls and then the chap-cheeked, bob-haired English girls in their uniforms, headed for my own species. Dutch children passed me with leather satchels in their hands on their way to somewhere also called "school," but with the "ch" pronounced in that globby Dutch way. I knew all Dutch children learned four languages at once—Dutch, English, German, and French. Besides languages, the Dutch were also good at sports. At my school, we hated them for that.

My heart racing like my piano metronome on its fastest setting, I passed three or four more villas and then came at last to *my* school—the school where I, deliciously, at last belonged.

I looked through the iron rungs along the street edge of the side playground: younger children were climbing on the jungle gym and jumping up to grasp the ropes of the maypole. Mr. Thomas, the dreamy British art teacher on playground patrol, was strolling with his head held loftily toward the sky. John and Jeff were hurling a ball across the blacktop as usual. They were wearing jeans, black loafers, and white socks. Both boys had slicked-back hair with little cowlick peaks in front, like Ricky Nelson's. A little nearer, over to the side, Candy and Lizzy were whispering together, sitting cozy as birds in a nest, on the brick wall. Both girls had brown loafers on their feet, the kind I coveted. Candy's hair was teased like Audrey Hepburn's so it poofed up on top and around her face in a perfect bubble, and flipped up on the ends.

As I stood at the fence I breathed in a rush of happiness. This was my school, and this was the way a school and children should look. These were Americans. It was a grand feeling. My father had his American world at the embassy and I had mine.

I turned in the gate and walked over toward Candy and Lizzy. Fighting an inner tug of shyness that was always with me like a pair of dog tags, I soldiered on, hurrying to join my kind.

~~

I'd become accustomed by now to the oddball collection of teachers that matched the motley crew of kids. Miss O'Malley, the Irish P.E. teacher who coached us in soccer and Irish dancing, was engaged to a Dutch hockey star. Mr. Leonard, the bearded eighth-grade teacher, was a San Francisco bohemian married to a Surinamese woman with creamy caramel skin and gorgeous eyes that glowed like lighted coals. Miss Bates was a glamorous, outspoken Native American lady who wore zebra-print tent dresses from *Vogue*. Mr. Thomas, the sixth-grade teacher as well as the art teacher for the whole school, was a tall, gaunt man who painted strange pictures of fruits with globby oil paint. The science teacher was another Brit, Wing Commander Potts, of the RAF. He taught us how to distinguish the elements, and to name all the parts of a Spitfire.

I was now in the hard work phase of establishing myself in the school that I'd attended for four months in the spring. The confusion alternating with euphoria of the first weeks had now been replaced by the hard reality of the struggle to find my place in the hierarchy. The kids at school had a pecking order, just like the chimp troop in the book about Jane Goodall my mother had read to us.

~~

My fifth-grade classroom, on the second floor of the Victorian manse, had French doors with a view out over the front lawn. Our desks, though, faced the wall toward the interior. Mrs. Van Gelderen was an American married to a Dutchman. Her main passion was riding; she sometimes wore jodhpurs to class. She started the day with a question, "So, class, I want to know what you think: What is America's role in the world?"

Billy said, "That's easy. We're the most powerful country on earth. We won World War II. Holland and all the European countries put together couldn't win without us. We kicked out Hitler."

"We also have the best researchers in the world," Tom said. "Our scientists took those pictures of the moon—those sure weren't Dutch scientists." A knowing snicker trickled around the room like a whisper in a game of telephone.

"And we're the best inventors. We invented rockets and hovercrafts and probably amphibious cars, and the atom bomb. . . ," Jimmy said, making up his facts.

"And what about Cassius Clay? He's the strongest man in the world and he's American," Billy said.

"And we have the most beautiful actresses. Katharine Hepburn is American, and so is Natalie Wood," Candy said.

President Kennedy was the best president, and we have Martin Luther King Jr. They are some of the greatest men in history. And we have the Peace Corps, they help people all over the earth. My parents often talked about these things at dinner, and this was what I would have said if I didn't get a pit in my stomach whenever I thought of talking in class, or of saying something that might be different from what others would say.

I'd felt different from the day I looked up into the pine fronds over my cradle back in Japan—and afterward, in Taipei and in Bethesda, too. I didn't like knowing something no one else knew—for instance, knowing about water buffaloes and sad Chinese eyes. I didn't know about gloating. I hated it when other people lorded it over me that they knew something I didn't know, and to think of knowing something all by myself made me feel alone. I hadn't yet got it that there wasn't going to be anyone just like me, ever—that we were all distinct stars in a galaxy.

"We're also about the biggest country in the world—except for Russia and China. And we're 225 times bigger than Holland. Holland fits in our pocket, that's what my dad says," Peggy was saying. She was another embassy kid.

We were building up our sacred argument, brick by brick.

"The White House is tons bigger than the president's house here."

"They don't have a president. They have a prime minister. But what about the queen's palace? That's big."

"Aw, that's just a palace. And the queen's just a figurehead anyway."

Margrite, who was half-Dutch, with taunting, sparking blue eyes and a beautiful, aquiline nose, tossed her straight-as-straw bangs out of her left eye. The traitor in our midst, she said, "The Netherlands was one of the most important naval powers in the world, way before America even had cities. Even now, we're way ahead in shipping. Rotterdam is about the biggest port in the world." None of us had known that.

"And," she continued, "in America, you don't have any barges. Our barges transport goods all over Europe."

"So? We have billions of super-fast trucks."

"Trucks are nothing to barges," she said. "Our friend has one and I've ridden on it." Having delivered these penetrating blows, she moved on without missing a beat. "We also have engineers that are better than any in the world. Our engineers can make land out of the sea!" she said, knowing she'd trumped just about anything.

The room was quiet for a minute and then Johnny said, "Anyone can build a dike."

"We also have some of the world's most famous artists," she went on as if she hadn't heard him. "Rembrandt, Van Dyke, Van Gogh." She said Van Gogh the proper Dutch way, with the gluck sounds both at the beginning and end of "gogh."

"You don't have artists *that* famous."

"Yeah, well did you hear what the Dutchies did yesterday?" Billy said, upping the ante. "They burned the American flag!"

"That's against the law!" Tommy said, his face growing red.

"Ja, well those protests are about the atom bomb. My mum told me about them," she said, revealing her ignorance by saying *mom* the British way. "My mum said America thinks it's great because it has the atom bomb. Well, the opposite is true. Who would want to come from a country that builds the most destructive thing in the world?" She paused a minute to let her point sink in.

"Just cuz Holland isn't smart enough to build one!"

"Life isn't about bigger and bigger weapons," she said, as though she was the pope, or God himself. "And what about what America is doing in Vietnam? Life is about being kind and letting other people rule themselves. That's what real democracy is."

We didn't know that at this juncture President Johnson was contemplating ways to intensify the war in Vietnam, or that the American public and Congress were paying little attention to the situation. It wouldn't have made a difference anyway—our country had been insulted.

"Yes, well, class," Mrs. Van Gelderen quickly dumped a bucket of water onto the flames that had erupted all around the little room, "Margrite has pointed us in an interesting direction. Let's talk about what democracy is. . . ."

We all fumed in silence as she droned on about Thomas Jefferson and the Declaration of Independence.

~~

How American you were was constantly being tested at school. I sensed I still had to prove myself worthy of the title.

The other fifth-grade girls and I were sprawled in the assembly room, making posters for a bake sale, eating our lunches, and gabbing. Our Keds were flung around the floor. Some of us had on the school sweatshirt. We'd campaigned mightily for this sweatshirt. At first the school had issued a Dutch-style velour pullover with a school patch. We all viewed it with disdain, thinking of our stateside cousins' big, baggy cotton shirts with their fathers' university seals on them, but we wore the sweater with the insignia anyway. When the school finally came up with a Golden mustard yellow sweatshirt with a huge crest of stars and stork blazing its front, we'd felt we could finally stand up for our school properly, the American way. Now, when we walked down the street, jacketless in our glaring, sun-glow shirts, no one could mistake us for Dutchies.

We saw Margrite out on the front lawn, yanking at Richard's jacket, flirting as usual. "She's probably never even lived in the States," Candy said. "Back in the States, we are *so much* cooler. Everyone imitates us. Look at all the Dutchies in blue jeans. Those are *our* jeans. They want to be like us, even if they say they don't." We were all swept up in the intoxicating thrill of jingoism.

"Yeah, we're the leaders of fashion, back in the States," Lizzy said.

"Back in the States": it was like those four words gave authority to any sentence that contained them. Though few of us had spent more than a couple of years on the American continent, when we referred to our native country, we all said it this way. Not "America"—that was too Dutch, and not "the United States"—that was too long, but "the States." We uttered our country's name with bravado—like little boys brandishing swords—as though we knew all about it, and privately owned it. And we would have defended this abstraction to the death.

"Back in the States, everything is better," Teri said. "I saw skirted bikinis when I was on home leave. They won't come out here for five years. My mom said they haven't even come out yet in London."

We lost momentum for a moment, as Carnaby Street and Kings Road spun into our minds, and then Kathy took up the banner again.

"I saw the cutest pants suit in the Montgomery Ward catalog. They don't have anything like it here."

"Yeah," I said, "and the poor boy T-shirts in the Sears catalog are so cute." My family had only just begun getting mail-order catalogs, at my insistence. My mother would never have bothered. She thought it was silly to buy clothes from the States when the Dutch had such nice things. But I talked like this with the girls and it was as though I was in a gentle sea, just swaying with the water currents. The girl who loved her housekeeper, Van Gogh, and thatched houses vanished, and I was bliss-fully a part of girl marine life. It never occurred to me that I might choose not to be in this particular school, or that I might follow my own nose through the ocean, or that I might even lead the school of fish. Only later would I think, *I shouldn't have said that*, or *I don't really think that way*. Then I would feel guilty and pricked by fear at my duplicity.

"And Dutchies don't even have sliced cheese," Kathy was saying. We were back to food, the refrain of our song.

I happily joined in, listing things Holland lacked: bologna, Fritos, good ice cream, chocolate chips, Oreos. . . . "And they don't even have Hershey's! All they have is dumb old Droste." I ignored the fact that I loved Droste chocolate coins.

"Yeah, well, you're lucky, Sara, you can get Hershey's at the PX."

"Yeah, but my mom won't buy me hardly any. . . ."

Scattered around the floor with our shoes were our lunch sacks. These held white–bread sandwiches, potato chips, and cookies—lunches as close to regula-tion Wonder Bread and bologna, Fritos, and Hershey's bars as our mothers could get on the Dutch market. In the daily lunch competition, the child who brought a fluffernutter to school (by definition a child whose mother had been smart enough to bring some peanut butter and marshmallow Fluff back from home leave, since they weren't available in Holland, or an even luckier embassy or military child whose mother could buy them any time at the PX at the American army base near Schiphol Airport) was immediately conferred five minutes of high status. Chocolate-chip cookies, Snickers bars, and Hostess Twinkies were also solidarity foods. I was dying for all these wonders. My mother could easily have gotten them, but instead she sent me to school with whole-wheat Dutch bread sandwiches, carrot sticks, and raisins.

This was what drove me crazy about my mother. She didn't realize that if she'd just buy all our food at the PX, I'd have kids admiring me all day long every day, but my mother had told me to lay low about our PX privileges. Almost every day there were debates on the playground over whether embassy and military kids had any more right than business kids to PX privileges. "We're as American as you are," the business kids said. "Well, your fathers make more money so you can afford to buy on the Dutch market," we embassy and Military Assistance and Advisory Group (MAAG) kids retorted, mimicking our mothers' words. Then they said, as if we owed it to them, "Well, next time you go to the PX, bring me five Tootsie Rolls."

I loved the PX—even if my mother groaned every time we talked her into going, which ended up being only about once a month. For me, to drive past the sentry at the guard post was to enter the one true church. There, inside the high walls of the base, were American soldiers with heart-stirring little American insignia on their clothes. I could find Wrangler jeans in the rumpled piles on the shelves of the shop. And on late Saturday afternoons, while my mother was shopping for Sara Lee cheesecake, frozen banana cream pie, and hot dogs, I could go to the little newsstand-cigarette kiosk just outside the commissary, buy something from the Juicy Fruit and M & M shelf, and nestle down with an *Archie and Veronica* comic. The *Stars & Stripes* and magazines like *Life* and *Newsweek*, with their headlines shouting out "Johnson Sends $400 Million to Saigon" and "Fifty American Advisors Killed in Last Four Years," were a subliminal, natural American-style backdrop. For fifteen minutes, I could slouch around with three pieces of Juicy Fruit in my mouth and flip the pages of the funnies. And for those delicious, transcendent moments, I could feel, deep down to my toes, what it was to be American.

~~

Back on the playground the debate never ceased.

"America's got the coolest stuff," said Katie, a kid who'd come at the beginning of the year. "Back in the States, there are troll dolls everywhere. I have one with purple, and one with pink hair. . . . It'll take about ten years for those to get to Holland." I didn't mention that troll dolls were Danish or that I'd just seen troll dolls with hair in ten different colors, and in every size up to the size of baby dolls, in the centrum.

"I love Dutch fishnet stockings," Gabrielle said, taking us back to clothes. Half-Belgian, she was the rare child among us who didn't care what other people thought. "They're wearing them all over Paris, and Paris is the center of fashion," Gabrielle said. "Maman said she'll get me some next spring, on my twelfth birthday. I'm so excited."

This threw us all for a loop.

But Candy was quick on her feet. "They'll fall apart in a month," she said with absolute authority. "My mom said Dutch stuff always disintegrates in the dryer. I'd never buy Dutch stockings in a million years."

"I wouldn't either," I said. These words just popped out of my mouth.

"And what about Dutch underwear," Teri said. "Can you believe they make a lot of it out of wool? It itches more than poison ivy. And even if it's not wool, it scratches. Dutch underpants come up to my arm pits, and they're so thick they show under everything, and the elastic stretches out in five minutes."

I squirmed quietly in my Dutch underwear, which came up higher than the American kind, but only to the waist. The American days-of-the-week undies I loved were getting holes in them, so my mother had bought me some Dutch pairs downtown just before school started. I hadn't given them a second thought until this minute.

"My mom orders all my underwear from Penneys," Teri finished. I took this in like an urgent cable from Washington.

"And what about Dutch toilet paper," Candy said, uttering the ultimate put-down in The Hague's expatriate American world. "It'll scrape off your rear!" Everyone laughed. I stayed quiet, remembering my mother's words about American ladies who complained about things like toilet paper. "Those ladies who moan about Kleenex and toilet paper are whiners. They should take a look at what the Dutch do offer—the churches, the pottery, the flowers, the traditions of helping other people."

Suddenly a disastrous thing occurred: a question popped out of my mouth. It was like an ugly duckling part of me—the undercover Dutch sympathizer—erupted out of the pond of white ducks where I had been quietly floating with the other white ducks, and soared into the air, betraying me. "What about paprika chips and patates?" I said. The second I uttered this, I knew I'd made a potentially fatal mistake and could feel my face beginning to burn.

Luckily, Candy was merciful; she corrected me relatively gently. "Yeah, they're okay, but American barbeque potato chips are even better, and McDonald's french fries are ten times better than patates, and we don't serve them with mayonnaise. That's just plain retarded."

I loved so many things about Holland, but when I was at school, I seldom thought of them, much less uttered any of them out loud. The minute I stepped within the gates of my school, I dunked the intriguingly different House of Orange in which I lived in order to pledge myself American. Whenever my America boasting got too far off track, though, Holland reliably reared its head like a whale from the sea, and challenged my position, in a loud, Dutch, guttural *hrummph*.

Along with my picture of the world, I, too, altered when I passed through the school gates. The girl who walked on stilts in her wooden shoes slipped away. Only the little ambassador, and most of all Sara-the-pleaser, remained. The American School of The Hague was, to me, a complete and buttoned world, a demanding, all-absorbing place that required the ultimate sacrifice.

~~

In one way, it was easy for me to meet all the basic qualifications of a real American. I could eat my brown sugar Pop Tarts from the PX, and wear my Wrangler jeans. I could put on my Keds, and carry my U.S. Army ammo bag swinging over my shoulder. And I could sneer at Dutchies and say "back in the States," as if it were home, and feel like I was the real McCoy. But there was something fishy in the hamburger.

Mrs. Van Gelderen tossed out a question: "Who is the U.S. secretary of defense?" I heard McNamara's name every night at the dinner table as my parents discussed the situation in Saigon, and I knew, like I knew that I had two big toes, that he was the secretary of defense. Nevertheless, in the fraction of a second after the question was shot into the air like a bullet, my mind fabricated doubt. "Oh no, maybe the secretary of defense has just changed, and that's why she's asking." Then, "It couldn't just be McNamara, could it?" To be wrong was too embarrassing to contemplate, and anyway, if I did answer, even if I answered right, everyone would look at me. My belly fluttered with anxiety. I squeezed my mind tight, and sent telepathic messages to Mrs. Van Gelderen, sinking down on my chair, looking hard at the paper on my desk, to prevent her from calling on me.

~~

Another day, Tommy Williams, a boy whose floppy blond hair and shirts with epaulettes I secretly daydreamed about, told me that I was a good soccer player. After he said it, my heart beat like the wings of an injured bird I'd seen flopping in the street. I was struck dumb. There was not one word in my head, much less a quick-fire, American-style, flirtatious retort. I went to the upper soccer field, where no one was, and hid around the corner until I could walk and breathe again, and I didn't look at Tommy the rest of the day.

~~

Like a fly in the ointment of my life, a shy girl kept displacing the sassy girl who ate peanut butter sandwiches and munched on Pop Tarts. I knew I was American. I possessed that most American of all things, an American *diplomatic* passport. But I had figured out something else, something that made my hold on the world waver: to be a real American, you had to be outgoing. Being a true-blue American meant being able to be light-hearted and josh around—and never, ever, to be tender. The Americans I'd seen on television and in movies—beyond those I noticed at school—all seemed to burst with confidence. To be a real American you had to be like Candy; you had to have that breezy, cowgirl air.

Could I be both all-American and the kind of person who shrinks in a crowd? This question haunted me. Being shy and being American seemed like two animals that couldn't marry. My equation of American and extroverted was a young person's overgeneralization, but it was perhaps an accurate perception of America's role in the world, and of America in the media. I had a Hollywood image of America, just like people all over the world did.

I couldn't see that the father I worshiped was shy, and I couldn't remember (and had I ever noticed?) that there were shy girls at Radnor, and there were even other shy American girls here. I didn't know that there were legions of quiet, successful American writers, doctors, and lawyers. I was incapable of picking out individuals from the loud, hearty, cheering crowd of American kids. Trapped in the big screen picture of American children joshing around, I pushed away the picture of the shy girl, but she kept popping back up in a corner of the screen.

It was Mr. Benton, the principal of the school, as much as anyone, who, unwittingly, had led me to this all-important conclusion. He was the quintessential American principal: stocky, with a blond crew cut, and blue-eyed. He wore Oxford cloth shirts and loafers. Hearty and funny, he was master of the quick comeback. He told us, at the opening assembly on the blacktop, that although "principal" could be spelled with an "le" he preferred the "pal" spelling, because that was the way he wanted us to think of him. Mr. Benton was our own private myth walking around. He was the way a person should be: all-American. I adored him. We all did.

My theory was further fortified by the way girls were treated at school. Girls who were cheeky and impulsive, and good at the immediate retort, received multiple rewards. Candy, who tossed her bangs and said "So?" with chilling authority whenever she pleased, was the first girl chosen at dances, always got the lead in the play, and held court on the playground like the queen of the largest ranch in Texas.

Even Mr. Potts, the harsh British science teacher, began to twinkle in her presence. "That's some kid," adults said, shaking their heads in admiration. If you were outgoing, you held all the promises of America—the apple pie, the pie in the sky—in the palms of your hands.

~~

My father and I had long talks about my shyness. "Be a leader," he said. "Don't worry if other people laugh. Speak out." "Don't be afraid to be different." "Be an Eleanor Roosevelt or a Harriet Tubman." "As [Ralph Waldo] Emerson said, 'Whoso would be a man, must be a nonconformist.'" Regarding my difficulty with speaking up in class, he gave me pep talks: "You know, Sara, other people like a person who can make a mistake and laugh at herself."

Tomorrow, I made stern vows to myself after a talk with my father; *I will speak up before anyone else when the teacher asks a question.* Determined to beat out my shyness, using all my willpower, I would force myself for several weeks to speak up, awkwardly, and with a squeaky voice—going cold like there was alcohol running through me when I did so—but the shakiness was always there.

During these days at The American School of The Hague, it would have been helpful to have had even a little glimmer of the European notion of "character" as something unalterable and inviolate and sacred that is given to each person, or to have someone acknowledge that you live in a different, but still legitimate world and have special qualities to offer, if you're shy, to balance my treasured American idea that a person could be anything she wanted to be if she put her mind to it—but this knowledge was many years in the distance, and for now I was American, desperately American.

~~

I took the only tack I knew. I made resolutions. "If at first you don't succeed . . ." In this land of thatched farms and windmills thrumping in the wind, I made vows to be breezy, to say "howdy" like Candy did, to boast about American power. I was sure that if I just tried hard enough I would receive the cornucopia the States had to offer: the chummy girlfriends, the boys in baseball hats, and most of all the do-or-die personality.

In the end, I could launch my campaigns, but my campaigns were those of a squadron set against battalions hidden in a teeming jungle. And my own brain kept calling my bluff. The cowgirl kept slipping out of my lasso. No matter how hard I tried to convince myself that I was one thing, the truth was otherwise.

~~

Nevertheless, there were moments of hope. One winter weekend, a bunch of us fifth and sixth graders were gathered at a skating rink in the suburban outskirts of The Hague. After skating to Beatles music for an hour or more, we stood at the edge of the ice, eating patates frites and sipping Fantas. As we were about to leave, a Dutch boy skated up, executed an expert twirl, and yelled "Amerika" as he sped across the circle of ice. A moment later, another boy appeared and did the same thing. By the time the third arrowed toward us and stopped just short, in a whoosh of ice shavings, all our bodies were pumping with adrenaline. I shrank with fear and wanted to just get away, but the boys with us were riled. To them, it seemed, all the mouthy crassness of our American identities had been summoned. Knowing they couldn't compete on skating skill, they began yelling back, "Dutchie! Dutchie!" as though it was the worst swear word in the language. The Dutch boys pooled on their side of the rink, laughing and pointing at us, and our boys did the same, on ours. It was as though we Dutch and American kids were giving voice to the welling antagonisms in the air of the world.

As time went on, the girls, too, filled up with a clean, murderous, white fury, and began yelling along with the boys. "Dutchies! Dutchies! Dutchies!" And before I was aware of it, I was yelling, too, and as I did I felt suddenly strong and free. The shy girl in the cage disappeared and a confident, outgoing Sara took over my body. As we American kids yelled, all the differences between us as individuals melted away as we united against a common enemy. We became one pulsating American army.

We finally left, us girls pulling the glowering boys along with us, but not without our hurling back that word—by now imbued with hate—over our shoulders time and again until we stepped out into the cold sunshine.

As we walked down the street, I felt like I was going to explode with happiness. For this half-hour flash in the stretch of time, I was all-American. I was exuberant and outgoing, and absolutely certain about the truth of the world.

~~

My life at The American School of The Hague was life in an Escher print. A trick picture, endlessly confusing, with seemingly contradictory truths flipping in and out of focus. I could be shy or I could be American. I could love America or I could love Holland. I could see the American point of view, or I could see the world's. I could never bring the black birds and the white birds into focus at once. I was not yet old enough to know that there could be two simultaneous truths about the world.

11
my father's bath

Ever since I was small, my mother had talked about fevers—tubercular fevers that killed children, fevers that felled whole villages in Taiwan and China. On a record of Rudyard Kipling stories that we had listened to time and again, I had heard about "the great, grey-green, greasy Limpopo River, all set about with fever-trees. . . ." Fevers were lush, black-green places, swamps of limbo and fear. Places of danger that sucked your spirit, where you dwelt—slopping through clutching weeds and swirling heat—until you finally stepped out onto new, clean, firm ground.

My father and I would each develop fevers in the next eighteen months—I would contract meningitis, my father another strain of illness, each serious and each an omen of more dire fevers to come.

~~

In the Duinweg front hall with its dark burgundy-black-and-brown two-story paintings looming overhead, my father put on his raincoat and tweed cap. His glove opened the front door. His head and then his desert boot disappeared. The door clicked closed. I hurried to the front of the house, to my window post. I put my face up close to the glass and watched my father stride past the front hedge, and on down the sidewalk. The rain descended in sheets, but his head held high did not bow even a quarter of a degree. His eyes stayed fixed somewhere way off—to a place out in the North Sea—and his swift pace held. I watched him walk over the brow of the little hill.

My father disappeared each day to the burnished, half-hidden world of the embassy. He vanished into his important, secret realm, but all day long, while I was at school, and after, while I was stenciling Bunsen burners into my lab report or reading the pages of my French text in the dimming light, a part of me was a girl at the window, waiting to be with my father again, for being with my father steadied and cooled me. He taught me about boys and men. More, he was my *Santa Maria*, my passage to other, grander worlds.

~~

At school I lived in a constricted, air-tight bell jar. Now in seventh grade I was not only obsessed with being plucky, all-American Candy, but with something else.

It had started back in the fourth grade, with my first boy-girl party. At that point, all the rules of the game had changed; the colors of my universe had flushed from those bright Crayola colors of kindergarten to the mauves and saffrons of nervous, mixed feelings. As of that moment of playing spin the bottle, I understood that all that really mattered, for a girl, was how pretty and saucy she was. That year I had cut all the "*Boys*" off the covers of my brother's *Boys' Life* magazines, and taped them, to his dismay, on my walls. The tenacious notion, that a boyfriend was the key to a girl's success, wouldn't be contradicted until I was exposed to feminism in college, and introduced to the startling notion that girls should not be rivals for men, but supportive sisters.

~~

During the fifth and sixth grades, the project had continued, and now, in seventh, boys were like a wildfire raging through my body.

While Madame Evans was pointing out places on a map, we girls were passing notes and keeping an eye on the boys. The boys, on the other hand, were all legs and arms and gawky bodies. In constant motion, they were hunching around at their desks, draping their arms down over the backs of their chairs, kicking their legs out into and down the aisle. Suave Jeff was leaning way back in his chair, and so was skinny Mike, who did everything Jeff did. (He was to Jeff as I was to Candy.) Roger was making a paper airplane out of a page of old math homework. Sandy-haired Billy, who most of the girls agreed was "Soooo cute!" was tossing a ball back and forth between his hands. He was interested only in balls, so we gazed at him in vain. Too-handsome Richard, whose mother looked like a movie star in her mink coat, was trying to listen to the teacher, but Kit was tempting him by pointing at pictures in the *Mad* magazine open in his lap.

Freckled, smart-alecky Roger was now softening wads of paper in his mouth and shooting them, whenever Madame Evans wasn't looking, at Jeff through a straw. With an expert, gentle puff, his spitballs hit their mark: Jeff's ear, his neck, his cheek. Jeff was raising his fist at Roger behind his chair. Link, who was cool and tall as a man, and wore mod, double-breasted pinstriped suits to school, was egging Roger on. Now Roger held a banana just below his desktop. He made sure Jeff was looking, and then squeezed so hard the banana pulp shot, whole, up out of the skin. Jeff was so choked by the laughs spazzing up from his belly, he had to put his head on his desk.

Meanwhile, dark-haired Kit had tossed his *Mad* on the floor and was whittling at the edge of his desk with a forbidden pen knife. Kit was like the handsome, dark-haired Artful Dodger in *Oliver*. You could smell the cigarettes and the motorcycle, imagine the shoplifting, feel the sharp-filed edge of the knife he was walking on.

~~

To us girls, boys were like promises. Because they had loose, straight legs and a jet-fired energy we couldn't match, and sped like a pack of cheetahs over the soccer field, they fed our imaginations. One day, we dreamed, one of them would emerge from out of the fray, and become ours. Kit with his gleaming-coal, straight flop of hair, Billy with his nonchalance, quiet Mike with his shy smile; who would it be, with his protective or possessive arm over our shoulders, in a few years, or just a month from now?

I assumed that all boys were like my father. When I finally had one, he would be quiet and dignified, and when he spoke, worth listening to. I would sit at his feet, and his sun would warm me as I absorbed his wisdom.

Later, in adulthood, I thought, *How strong the drive toward love is in a child.* It's an unstoppable force. There are the hormones, but there is also the raw sincerity of it.

~~

My friend Lizzy, who was one grade behind me, was my main source of advice on how to be with boys. She was the kind of friend you could slop around with and not worry about how your hair looked—a true friend.

Lizzy had sleek chestnut hair clipped in a blunt cut just below her chin, like Twiggy's, and big, wide, caramel eyes. She was very skinny (with weak ankles ending in thin, flat feet—her only endearing flaw) and very pretty: put together like the girl in an ankle-length coat and hair ribbon I'd seen one time going into the Ritz Hotel in Paris.

I knew, without knowing, that Lizzy was classy. She had a natural elegance, entirely different from Candy's cute, all-American, TV good looks. I didn't have a clue about this now, but Candy and Lizzy's differing styles of prettiness were the difference between New England and Texas. (Not for many years would it dawn on me that another thing that distinguished Lizzy was the natural confidence endowed by patrician wealth.) Lizzy told me her mother had been ABJ, which meant "Anyone But Johnson," in the last presidential election. Her family was pro-Goldwater. My father said Goldwater was a narrow-minded man. We were pro-Johnson, but Pop agreed that Lizzy was nice.

The best thing about Lizzy was that she was goofy. When she saw me at school, she said, "Hi, Gorgeous," and I said back, "Hi, Elegant," and then we hustled over to join the clutch of other girls, gossiping and nudging each other with our pointy elbows.

To be in Lizzy's female dominated home was to touch something as smooth as a silk slip, something feminine and fine. We were sitting together on her sixteen-year-old sister's bed. Lizzy was reporting to me all of Becca's secrets for attracting boys and I was listening eagerly.

"The only swear word she would ever use is 'Damn,'" Lizzy said. "It's the only one that is still okay for a lady."

I tried it out. "Oh, damn," I said. "Like that?"

"Not, '*Oh*, damn,' just 'Damn.'"

"And never say 'woman,'" Lizzy instructed. "That's coarse. Always say 'lady,' and sit with your legs like this," she said, holding her knees together and her feet—clad in flats—flat on the floor. Her sister had learned this at a Miss Somebody's Dancing School back in the States.

Now Lizzy was telling me about Becca's boyfriend. He was tall, handsome, and had a motorcycle. "Becca only rides side-saddle," she explained. "It's the elegant way. That way she can show off her legs and let her scarf flow out behind her."

Lizzy's two older sisters were attending Pembroke, the sister school to Brown University. "We'll all go there," she explained. I'd never heard of the school, but I could tell by the tone of Lizzy's voice that this was something to be impressed by, even though I was not even sure Lizzy knew what it meant. "Mother's a little afraid Becca won't get in if she doesn't start doing better in math. That's why she and Dick spend their afternoons curled up in the family room—doing Becca's math. Mother only lets them go out after Becca's homework is done."

In bed at night, I imagined being Becca: I was beautiful and sleek, with my waist-length hair hanging down like a walnut river. I sat gracefully, knees together, on the back of the motorcycle, remaining a lady even on a greasy machine. I imagined my hair flowing out in the air as I was sped off behind a tall, dark, and handsome boy who also possessed perfect chivalrous manners. As Becca, I was in possession of perfect knowledge. I knew the perfect thing to wear, had the perfect words for every social encounter, knew instinctively the perfect way to behave— the tiniest bit alluring but with perfect grace and loveliness. I almost swooned at the thought of being that perfect. Having all the mothers praise.

~~

We girls had strict rules for how to attract boys. Lizzy and I rehearsed them, primping against the toilet stalls, spinning around the maypole, and slouching around in our nightgowns on each other's beds. The rules were like commandments. If you didn't follow them you would be a slut, or even worse, boyfriendless.

Never be smarter than a boy.

When you're with a boy, never talk more than he does.

Your job, when you're with a boy, is to make him feel not only smarter than you, but stronger and better. Always build a boy up.

It's okay to break a plan with a girlfriend if you are asked for a date. Boys come first.

If you really love him, don't even tell your best friend about him.

It's better to be elegant and hard to get than cute and loose. You know which one he'll marry.

Be very attentive and then play hard to get; be charming and pretend you don't care.

Don't let a boy know you like him or he won't like you.

Take an interest in the boy's interests. Read up on football, if that is his passion.

Don't ever win if you're playing a game with a boy.

Never telephone a boy. It's too aggressive and boys hate aggressive girls. Let the boy be in control.

Never kiss on the first date.

Never let him feel you up; never let a boy use you.

And never, ever go all the way. That's being a slut and he's sure to drop you.

The most important question of all is: Does he respect you?

Lizzy and I, and the other girls, couldn't wait to do all these things. If only the boys would hurry up and get a little older. If they would just take their eyes off the ball, even for a minute, they might have seen that we were waiting for them, primped and armed with all of our rapt attention and our ardent hearts, ready to try out our new powers.

~~

The problem was, there were some flaws in the commandments about how girls should be with boys.

Mid-year, I won the recess ping-pong tournament for two days in a row, triumphing over one of the cool boys. I loved ping-pong, and I felt the wind of glory whipping inside me when I won, but when I went home each day, I felt engulfed by remorse. *I should have let him win,* I thought.

Another day I got a better grade on my science notebook than Richard, who everyone considered the smartest person at school. I told myself afterward that I should never do that again. *It's not that I'm smarter,* I reassured myself. *It's just that I work hard.*

Over and over, I came head to head with the same dilemma: how to be smart, how to be good at something, and still be liked by boys.

~~

The first dance of seventh grade, I stood near the door of the assembly room— the parlor of the Victorian home that our school used to be. The ceilings and walls were draped with crepe streamers and decorated with American flags. The lights were still on, the seventh and eighth graders just starting to assemble. I wore the new pink empire-waist dress my mother and I had selected. I had washed and set my hair, covered my pimples with Clearasil, and powdered my shiny clean nose (my mother would later refer to this period as my "gooky" stage), and I was brimming with a yearning so liquid-big it was about to burst the old plaster walls of the room and spurt into the yard.

As other students came in, they joined groups of two or three others across the room near the series of French doors leading out onto the veranda. "Yummy, Yummy, Yummy, I've Got Love in My Tummy" was put on the record player, the lights were doused, and I watched, across the room, the clutches of two or three girls and two or three boys (none of whom any longer had names) moving in and out and against each other like dolphins gobbling a school of tropical fish in a sea.

A Monkees song was on the record player now, and pairs of girls and boys had broken off from the flirting and jostling and begun to dance together. I stood in the doorway wishing so hard that a boy would ask me to dance that my arms and my legs and my body were like heavy, hooked-together stones hanging inside the cloth of my dress.

No one looked my way. For two hours, I leaned my heavy stones against the wall near the door, propping myself up against its hard strength, as the boys passed by back and forth, back and forth. When, toward the end of the dance, someone put on the single, "A Whiter Shade of Pale," I felt a welling like an ocean pushing up through and about to explode a mountain of rock.

I returned home saturated with disappointment. My new dress, too, was saturated; I never wore it again.

My mother stood beside me, patting me, helpless in the face of my crying. My father called me to him and took me on his lap, my legs—no longer able to fold up to join the rest of me in a lap-fitting bundle—dangling from his knees to the floor. "You're very pretty, you know," he said. "But, more important, you're kind and smart." This made me cry even harder: *Would any girl give up being pretty to be smart?* I cried on his shoulder in the big armchair in the living room until the heaving died down and I trudged upstairs.

But nothing could stop me. I was driven, driven by a possibility, a dream of which I couldn't let go. Driven to cling to the blade of a knife. I had enlisted in boot camp, and was going through the exercise where you crawl on your belly while people shoot over your head. I had to go forward, persist, or die. I sensed there was something I had to conquer, and the stakes were too high to give up. I couldn't see into the future and considered this my only chance.

~~

At night when I took my bath, I looked down at my body. I was twelve years old and now, when I looked, I was dismayed by what I saw. My body was growing fur, and there were apricots swelling up on my chest. Worst, the sides of my upper thighs had swelled. I hated this. Boys' jeans didn't fit right anymore. I felt ugly all the time.

One night after dinner, my father lifted my chin. "Girls are supposed to have hips, you know," he said. "That's a part boys like."

~~

Maria seemed to know best of anyone what a fever I was in. In her thick, chapped washerwoman's hands, she brought me tiny bunches of tulips—as if to say, "One day a boy will bring you these. And, until then, you are still my Saratje."

~~

Finally persistence paid off. In March I achieved the unachievable. I was going steady. Rusty, a boy in sixth grade, had given me a pin of a guitar. It wasn't an ID bracelet, but "what's the diff," as Candy would say: I could show it off to the other girls. I had only spoken to Rusty once or twice, but gazed at him a lot. He was tall, with unruly curls, and had a lopsided smile.

The weekend after he asked me to "go" with him, he invited me to a movie downtown. My mother, who said I was really too young to date, and to whom I replied "Oh Mo-om!" suggested that we go to the movie at the embassy. She would drop us off and pick us up.

Choosing a shirt to go with my Wranglers, I was nervous, but I knew I had to go. I was in a fever to get this first date under my belt.

But when we sat down again in the theater, after having stood up among all the little kids to sing "The Star-Spangled Banner" like you did at every embassy movie around the world, I suddenly realized going to this movie with this boy was nothing like going to see *The Sound of Music* with my family.

And when Rusty put his arm around me, I realized I found him repulsive. My stomach twisted. As the movie began, I tried to pretend his arm wasn't there. I'd thought going steady was something else, something else I had no knowledge of, but definitely not this feeling of being imprisoned by the grinning face of someone I didn't even know and a heavy arm across my shoulders. I wanted to run out of the theater.

When I got home, my shoulders, which had felt like stiff wings hunched on my back, fluffed back down into their settled position. My father was there, like a promise of something better to come, in his reassuring suit, and his talk of the Peace Conference.

The next day Rusty and I broke up by ignoring each other. Maybe my mother had been right about not being "ready."

~~

When my father finally returned of a late, dark afternoon, it was as though an extra lamp had been suddenly lit in the house. At the kitchen table, he listened to me tell him about my day, and then he said, like he was suddenly waking up, "Oh boy, I'd better take my shower." He and my mother were going out to an important event at a Dutch minister's mansion. They went out for cocktails or dinner parties, or hosted them at our house, three, four, or five nights a week. "Official functions" were a big part of their job.

Later, when my father entered the kitchen where Andy and I were sitting at the long, rectangular, wooden farm table, eating the yummy Swanson's fried chicken and Salisbury steak TV dinners that my mother had bought at the commissary, he was dazzling. Instead of his ordinary dark suit, he had on a tuxedo with a beautiful crimson-and-gold cummerbund. He looked as dashing as Prince Bernhard, Queen Juliana's husband. My mother wore a floor-length, turquoise silk dress and her pearls. I loved these romantic clothes. Looking at my parents made me shiver.

When my parents had a dinner party at our house, we had to put on nice clothes and descend the staircase during the cocktail hour to pass the crackers and cheese and peanuts and greet the guests. As I passed the peanuts, my father's eyes smiled at me, and he secretly patted my hand as I offered him the basket of nuts.

Fathers and daughters: an unmatched category of love. Of course, you, the daughter, want to marry your father when you're five, and you'll measure all boys—and then, men—against him. When childhood is as it should be, your relationship with your father is the foundation of exuberance and lust, but it's also something else: an experience of unfettered adoration, a sense of being loved without reserve, of having someone wild about you—a fundamental joy designed for every girl, every child.

It was elevenish on a Saturday morning as I watched my father walk down the street toward the sea. He was off to get the *Handelsblad* and *de Volkskrant*, the Dutch newspapers, and grab a bite of herring. I imagined what would happen. My father would sit on a bench in the wind on the promenade in Scheveningen, look out to sea, slurp his fish, and read his Dutch newspapers—and he would be perfectly happy.

When I was little, back in Taiwan, and in Japan, my father had gone away on weekends with his friends to climb mountains. He'd climbed all the biggest mountains on Formosa, and when I was a baby he'd climbed Fujiyama. He had special hiking boots and a cloth army rucksack in which he took his "provisions"—and when he returned his face was lit up. When I was five I thought of my father as "a man who climbs mountains." Here in Holland, and whenever we visited other places—farm villages or modern Dutch towns—my father took walks in the early morning. His walks were on flat land now, but the set of his eyes, the spring in the middle of his stride, as he moved toward the distance, were the same.

Most of the time when he wasn't at the embassy, my father was reading to me or Andy, racing through the paper, studying Dutch, or talking to my mother— doing things that helped others—but walking was the singular thing he did for himself alone. Sometimes he had an excuse—like today a need to buy a Dutch paper in Scheveningen, or the *Herald* or *Le Monde* at the newsstand downtown, or to check on something at the office—but mostly it was "I'm going to just go have a look around . . ." (Later I would learn that, on some of his walks, he had actually been working: doing things like checking out the territory; leaving a note written in invisible ink, under a stone in a forgotten churchyard; tucking a roll of money into a cone of frites or some other unlikely place; taking part in a clandestine meeting in the dunes.)

But mostly my father walked to walk. When I watched his body move down our brick street, or looked down at him from a high hotel window, he walked briskly, rain or shine, at his favorite pace. I could tell, from my perches at windows, that his walks were not only an exploration but a gathering. Pulling on his raincoat and setting out into rain, my father shrugged off his secrets and donned his truest self.

Like his secrets, he kept his dreams in hidden harbors—and on his walks, he went to visit them.

~~

As a young adult, I would soon discover how like my father I was. A devoted walker, I would love the anonymity of a big city: getting up in the cool damp of early morning as the concierges were sweeping the stoops and the garbage collectors and dogs were doing their rounds, faint whiffs of garbage and fresh bread in the cool air.

~~

It was a drizzly weekend. All of Holland was a green, soggy, foggy bog, but my father had decided to take us to a war museum he had heard about in a little village. Weekends, even if it was raining so hard it was like a machine gunner attacking our roof, his eyes always glinted miniature lighthouse beams as he thought about all the historical sites we could visit. It was as though he saw Europe as a sweet shop in which every little town offered a new kind of candy to sample. We were long past the early euphoria Foreign Service families usually experienced when they arrived in a new post— it had never gone away for my father in Holland.

After an hour or so, we reached the museum in a village with a main street of thatched, hunched-down farmhouses. The dingy cases of the exhibit were filled with helmets and guns. Andy and my father talked and pointed beside the displays, and my father struck up a conversation, in Dutch, with the curator. He was an old man, and while he talked to my father about World War II, he had to wipe his moist eyes like a lot of Dutch people did when they mentioned the war. After a while, I was bored with looking at bullets and maps. I felt like putting a piece of tape over Andy's mouth, so he would stop asking questions about the grenades and bunkers, so we could get out of the museum. Even when my father and Andy let us leave, we had to stay longer so that Andy could climb on the old cannons. Sitting on a cannon in the scruffy museum yard, his smile was so happy, I wanted to spit.

Soon after we visited the museum, we were wandering through a flea market in the village, and my father called to Andy. "Look at this!" he said. "An English helmet!" After that he and Andy started collecting helmets. Before long, they had several of the Allies' helmets: the English, the American, the Dutch, and also those of the Axis: the Italian and the German. One of them had a bullet hole through it, which Andy proudly showed his friends.

Another day, my father stopped the car by a mossy fence on an obscure lane in the countryside. He led us through a small graveyard full of mossy stones. The graveyard was quiet and still, and somehow different than those beside old Dutch churches. "This is a Jewish graveyard," my father said, a hush in his voice.

In Amsterdam, we visited Anne Frank's house. From the outside, it was just an ordinary Dutch house: narrow, brick, four stories high, on an ordinary street divided by a soupy green canal. The inside, though, was full of secrets. Walking around the tiny, grey-walled attic rooms hidden behind the bookcase—Anne's postcards were still on the wall—I could imagine being Anne, dreaming and thinking over her diary up near the sky, but the thought of the Nazis breaking through the wall and into the rooms was lightning mixed with frigid wind streaking through my insides.

Another day, we stopped along a country road and walked over a hump of land toward the purple-grey, foam-crashing sea. The wind was slamming in so hard from the ocean that I could barely stand. At a loose barbed-wire fence, my father, who was in the lead, put up his hand. "We aren't allowed any farther," he said.

"From here to the sea," he said, "the coast is full of mines from the war." Just seeing the innocent-looking dune, tufted with coarse blond grass, sent another streak
of cold lightning through me. I imagined taking one tiny misplaced step into the
fenced area and my body being blown to smithereens. Maybe this was why my
father's work was so important—to protect us all from being blown to smithereens.

When my father did these things—took us to war cemeteries and houses with
hidden rooms—it was as though the air parted around him and a quietness took
over his body, a quietness that radiated out and infected me too. My father had
told us many times that he had been eager to serve in World War II, but it had
turned out that he was a little too young. He was on a troop ship headed for Yokohama when the war ended. As he looked out over the Dutch landscape or tenderly
handled Dutch and English helmets in a flea market, it was as if he was looking for
the war he missed.

It was funny. By now, my father had taught us so much about the war, and
taken us so many places, it felt almost like I'd been alive in World War II. Because of
my father and his fascinations, my love of men would always be bound up with war,
horizons, and mined ground—and with men's potential for bravery and sacrifice—
as if I were a child of the last World War.

~~

I found it tiresome, though, when my father hauled us all to Normandy to look
over the cliffs at the sea from which the American soldiers, on D-Day, charged to
free Europe of the Nazis, and made us walk around huge graveyards of white stones
commemorating dead soldiers from many different countries. Only later, in my forties, when I revisited Omaha Beach, with its open, exposed sands and cliffs that had
to be surmounted to reach and liberate the farmlands of France, did I understand.
America—Americans—achieved a truly astonishing, brave, and noble triumph
back then in 1944, a triumph we've striven to match ever since.

~~

Andy, however, had the World War II bug in spades.

"Uuuuur!" "Eeeee!" "Kerblam!!!" "Shewwwwww-BAM." These were the
sounds that burst from Andy's room, every weekday afternoon and all weekend
long, as he exploded imaginary, plastic, or lead tanks and planes and aircraft carriers.
Sometimes Andy played with Lincoln Logs or LEGOS, but mostly he reconstructed
World War II battles. His room was often completely impenetrable, covered with

hundreds of small plastic army men set in position. At night he had to carefully remove the battalion set on his blanket and put it, piece by piece, on top of his chest of drawers. The battles raged for days, until one army took the right hill or village and the enemy surrendered.

Most things Andy did had to do with war. He did cannonballs whenever we went swimming in a pool. He wore swords and a wooden gun he'd made in Dutch carpentry class. He worshiped catapults. He had a dream of possessing one and shooting stones, like the medieval knights did, at everything he saw.

When he wasn't waging war, my brother read. He read *Moby Dick* when he was only eight, but mostly he read history books. He read and read and read, lying on his bed among the soldiers. Sometimes he read the encyclopedia. "I think I'll read B tonight," he'd announce as he headed up to bed.

Andy was dirty and funny (he told jokes about poop, toots, and elephants) and never brushed his teeth. Sometimes I liked him, and I laughed when he told silly jokes, but mostly he was dumb and boring. All he thought about was history and war. Sometimes I checked to see if he would do something useful like get me something I needed. "Andy," I'd say, pleading sugar-sweetly, "will you go get me a drink of water?" and, often, to my surprise and affording me a jolt of unexpected power, he did, like a puppy. If my mother caught me doing this bossy big sister stuff she said, "Sa-ra!" and I did feel a little guilty when my little brother brought me a cup with a guileless look on his face.

~~

World War II was America's great war. Now, unbeknown to me, my country was waging a new one. The U.S. Army now, in 1966 and 1967, was carrying out daily raids against the North Vietnamese, President Johnson was sending troops to Southeast Asia by the ten-thousand-fold, and all U.S. dependents, including some of my parents' friends, had been evacuated from the country.

~~

My father and I were walking along the strand in Scheveningen, on the North Sea. The sky was the color of pewter, the temperature was hovering around freezing, but the sea was calm. The grey-purple water was pulsing onto the wet slope of sand beside us. My father was keeping up his usual brisk pace and I was happy hurrying along to keep up. I had my father to myself so I took advantage of it.

"What do you think about God, Pop?"

He paused a moment, looked out at the sea, and breathed deeply, like the air was a supreme pleasure. Then he turned to me. "I believe that God is in all of us." I knew from his stories about his boyhood that he was raised Baptist, but as an adult he had become a Unitarian. "You'll have to decide what God is for you, but I believe human beings have all the qualities of God. I think human beings are basically good, rather than sinful as some others think, and we are capable of solving our own problems through thinking.

"I am a humanist, an idea that first took root in Holland. That means I don't think we need to rely on some greater being in the sky, outside of ourselves, to look after us or make us be good. If human beings just study hard enough and consult their hearts, and devote themselves to it, they can solve even the most terrible quagmires.

"I believe every human being should keep his own counsel," my father went on. "Every man is his own best advisor as he knows himself best. A man's own conscience is his best guide." I knew my father got these ideas from people he'd studied, like Immanuel Kant, Emerson, and Thomas Jefferson. As he said these things, I felt fortified, full of iron will—and certain that the world would one day be peaceful.

~~

The first day of summer vacation after seventh grade, my father told me, "You're smart and you need to stretch your brain. . . . I have only two requirements for you this summer," and he handed me *Jane Eyre* and *Silas Marner*. These two serious-looking British-published Penguin volumes, with fine print, were completely different from my steady diet of penny romance books. I read them on the beach on our family vacation at Lago Maggiore—and they showed me a depth of feeling, a wielding of language, that, like a moist leaven deposited deep, would rise up like yeasty dough in me later. But for now I was still more interested in how I looked in my new pink bikini than in reading good literature.

~~

On the weekend before Thanksgiving, at 3:30 when it was already black as crows, we drove to the church in Leiden from which the pilgrims set out for the New World. The American ambassador made a speech in a long, dark coat. Then a priest intoned from a dark wooden box up above the congregation. The words were all Dutch, but occasionally I picked out the word "Amerika." The church was dark and half-empty. It was so cramping-cold we were shuddering in our coats and hats by the end of the service. My father's step was light, though, as we left. "Just think of it," he said. "Setting out from this cold, dark church for the unknown!" His face shone with vision.

For the Thanksgiving vacation week, we went to London—via a very rocky overnight ferry from Hoek van Holland—and stayed in an American embassy hotel right in the wet, splashy bustle of the city. We paraded after my father as he led us, head high, to the Tower of London, Big Ben, and Westminster Abbey. I'd never seen him so happy. My father adored England, a place sunk deep and dripping with history. England, history—my father sucked them in like a man dying of thirst. For my father, holding one's counsel, a bit of beer and bread (or a box of K-rations), a history book, a moss-covered trench, a blanket on a heath: they were what he needed to quench him.

~~

It was springtime, and giddy like the Dutch at the sun, we set out for a hike. As we wended through the flat, green countryside, my father fired history questions at us. When did the Civil War begin? Who were the Union generals? When did Lewis and Clark cross the country? Where was the Battle of the Bulge? How many men were with Columbus? Where were they hoping to go? What do you think they ate on shipboard?

The questions about Columbus set my mind to making pictures. I saw men with ragged beards on ships holding their heads high in the blasting wind, chewing chunks of salt fish, heading to the New World: my country. This idea was enough to stun me forever: America was that grand.

My father—the way he talked, the way he looked toward the horizon—offered me glimmers of something else, another way to exist, another realm beyond that of my school: the possibility of walking out into all the hugeness of the world. He gave me a continent where people walked directly into rain, or straight up mountains.

~~

Following my father from country to country, from medieval cathedral to 1915 trench, led me to expect to follow a man from place to place. I would take to athletic, outdoorsy men who could light fires with wet sticks. And I would equate staying put with boredom. When I was twenty-four, sitting beside my boyfriend as he contentedly watched the sun strike a golden Santa Cruz field above the Pacific, I'd say, "Hey, I miss Europe. Why don't we get jobs in England?" While this freewheelingness might have had its charms, it would make me a hard woman to please. I'd marry a New Englander for his roots—that other, clamoring, contradictory part of me—and then expect him to sashay with me out into the world. I would constantly lust for the heath.

~~

I didn't know it, but this was the last perfect summer, the last summer to contain the shining perfection endowed only by the young child's happily blindered eyes. For this last summer, my world was still my family. I was the sandwich meat, plunked like a round of bologna, between the two different pieces of bread of my mother and my father. Everything was in balance: My mother was earth; my father was sky. My father was for the mind, my mother for the body. My father was the thinker, my mother the doer. My father was for outings, my mother for daily life. With my mother I had to be good; with my father, I could dream. My mother was the bread and my father was the ice cream.

~~

I watched my father take his bath in the long tub in the wide, open bathroom in our row house—as I had watched him from the time I could toddle. After he was naked, he waited for the tub to fill. He stood on the plain of white tile like a statue: tall, thin, and milk-white. Once in the tub, he was quick. Lying submerged with just his head up against the slope of porcelain, he splashed water over his chest and then ducked his whole head under, back of head down, with a sputtering, joyous gurgle-groan. He took a bar of Dial soap, lathered up his dark hair, and dunked again. In a moment he was standing in the water, swirling soap over his chest with the patches of black hair, and on down his frame. He ran the soap down each strong, thin leg, up and around his backside, and up his back in shoots, the soap held precariously at the tips of his fingers. In a final flourish, he soaped the fur above his penis. It got wonderfully sudsy and made squishing sounds. His penis, as he washed it, flopped and wobbled and dove playfully like a smooth-skinned mammal from the sea.

As I watched now, my father's body, which I had seen all my life, was like a reassuring assurance of something comfortable and real, something normal.

Watching my father's baths and receiving my father's thoughts bolstered me now through all the fumblings with boys—as they would years along, when my love of boys transformed from an attraction to arms, legs, and cowlicks to real people with prickable hearts and serious thoughts.

These were the gifts my father gave to me: the sense that a girl who was a thinker drew a man's gaze; the sense that a penis was a friendly thing; the sense that love between a lady and a man was as comfortable and natural as two deer on a hill. That love was a quiet stirring.

~~

Nights, in dreams, I was my father. I was striding alone up a mountain. I reached the crest. I gazed out over an infinity of rising and falling green-and-purple mounds to a sky so blue and deep I imagined that I could soar out into it forever. I took in chestfuls of the good wind. In a while, I took out my penis and peed over the side of the cliff. Then I ate my lunch of *leidsekaas* and chocolate. I read a paperback that fit into the pocket of my windbreaker, and snoozed under my cap.

12

the pistol

We spooned bowls of thick pea-and-ham soup for dinner, and then my mother drove us to the embassy where my father was serving as "duty officer" for the night. My father, whose straight, dignified posture and lean, pleasant face made him look like a diplomat in the movies, emerged from a room off the embassy's clean, milk-white entrance hall. The instant I took him in, my body flashed cold and a stone of fear thudded in my belly: my father was wearing a revolver strapped to his waist.

As though this was an everyday occurrence, Andy pointed and asked what kind of gun it was. "A Colt-45," my father said, patting the holster. "Just in case there's trouble.

"But don't worry," he said, looking at my mother, "there won't be any trouble. Sometimes a loony does something like climb over the fence or once in a blue moon, an embassy is attacked—but that would never happen in Holland. Mainly, the embassy just needs someone here in case an important cable comes in."

Then he showed us all the supplies that kept him safe and comfortable through the night: a store of canned food, a cot, and a mustard-colored sleeping bag made of soft, warm goose down. (Later, this setup would seem like a still life, the essence of America: Spam, fluffy sleeping bag, cold gun.)

My father hugged us all goodnight out by the marine guard's desk, and then he heard the cable machine and slipped away into the little cell.

As we stepped into the black rain that was beating like a tide, I felt stilled— startled and filled, like a vessel to the brim, with awe at seeing that cold, metal killing tool attached to my gentle father's thin frame. Disturbance fluttered inside me. *What does the pistol mean? What does it mean about Pop? What does his work require? Could he really shoot someone?*

~~

Another afternoon it was so dark, it was as if the grey-dark sea had taken to the air. My job was to help my mother get ready for an official dinner party she and my father were giving for some American and Dutch dignitaries.

My mother set down a beautiful centerpiece of orange and yellow tulips, and then she stood with a pile of plates against her bosom, sorting out who should sit where. Everything had to be perfect, in accord with protocol. "Let's see, Meneer Peereboom is the highest-ranking guest, so he should sit here on Pop's right. . . . And Mr. Klein, the highest-ranking American, should sit on Pop's left. . . ," she said, setting the plates down in a certain spot. "And Vrouw Peereboom should sit to my right, and Mrs. Wilson is a good conversationalist, so she should be seated next to her. . . ."

My mother had taught me all the rules for how to be a perfect diplomat, and a polite diplomat's daughter.

- The first rule was: *When you are invited to someone's house, never put people out; be accommodating.* Fold yourself into the ongoing activities, rather than imposing your own wishes. When people ask what you'd like to do, say, "Anything is fine with me. What would you like to do?" Also, eat whatever food is offered. Never ask for something special. Just ask for what the child before you asked for, so the hostess doesn't have to do anything extra just for you. The sin of all sins is that of imposing on someone else.
- The second rule had to do with conversation: *When you are talking with a Dutch person, or any person you don't know, always, always make the other person feel comfortable.* Be sensitive to the impact of your words on others. For instance, if you already have a gift someone gives you, don't let on. Just say, "Thank you so much. This is just what I have been wanting." (This would translate for me, in adulthood, into a wild, chilling sense of shame when I discovered I'd brought a replica of someone else's gift. The sign of a truly refined, well-mannered person was her unfailing, intuitive sixth sense for the perfect offering.)
- The third rule: *If you don't like the wet grilled eggplant, or anything else that is being served for dinner, eat it anyway, and furthermore, tell the hostess that*

it is delicious. The only time to tell someone something that might embarrass them is to save them further embarrassment. You might whisper to a friend, but not an acquaintance, that her slip was showing, for instance, though not so anyone else could hear.

- Fourth: *Take an interest in others and make them feel interesting.* At embassy parties, and in conversation in general, get the other person to talk about himself. Ask him questions about his work or his thoughts on topics such as politics or movies. Somehow the injunction to take an interest in others fit me like a dress made by the queen's tailor, and stayed with me for a long time. I seized the notion that everyone had a story and my duty was to find it. I loved sitting at people's feet, drinking in their tales.

All of these rules were connected to the effort not to be "an ugly American," which my parents considered very important. I had seen that book, *The Ugly American,* by William Lederer and Eugene Burdick, on my parents' bedroom bookshelf. An ugly American was someone who was loud, pushy, and bossy, and wanted his own way all the time, never cared how people in other cultures did things, and tromped on other people's feelings.

The truth was, these diplomatic rules made life manageable in different places. A kind of universal language, they gave me a recipe to follow anywhere I landed. By the end of my time in Holland, they would become a reflex that would stand me in good stead for a long time—until, one day many years on, it would come to me, like dawn in a brand new country, that not every human encounter merited a diplomat's unveering attention, that being a well-mannered diplomat could cramp and even offend.

Meanwhile, here in embassy circles in Holland, this approach worked like cream melting into tea. I studied my parents at dinner parties, talking to the Dutch. My mother was a warm, bubbly, American-style hostess; she charmed and entertained. She turned toward the man next to her, looked him in the eye, smiled, and said, "What do you think of the new exhibit at the Mauritshuis, Meneer Peereboom?" or "Your tulips are splendid." And my father was a master of diplomacy. With his elegant manners; his soft, intent gaze; and his shoulders bent toward the other person in a slight embrace, he could draw the quietest or the most bombastic person into earnest or freewheeling conversation. If my mother was a trumpeter in a marching band, my father played the wooing woodland pipes in a forest glen.

~~

My father's Dutch colleague, Meneer Wandersee, and his family were over for a visit. We kids—he had three girls—and the two mothers were drinking Coke at the table on the brick patio at the back of our house, while my father and Meneer Wandersee were drinking Grolsch beer and sitting on lawn chairs off to the side. I glanced at the fathers while the mothers tried to make us kids talk to each other.

The fathers talking shop (both were in the clandestine services of their respective countries) seemed not so much burdened, as puzzled and engrossed by their work. Their tone, as they spoke half in English and half in Dutch, was one of decoding befuddling happenings. They shook their heads and laughed aloud over their beer. They seemed content, glued to their chairs and rollicking inside their incessant conversation.

My father's laugh with Meneer Wandersee was happy. When he and Meneer Wandersee talked, there was an intimacy like that of my mother and her lady friends, only different. There was a sense of inside jokes, of the secrets of men who work together, but there was even something more. And for the first time, I detected a new strand in my father's laugh—a little streak of something I'd later be able to name: "irony."

I didn't know that there were two Charlie Tabers. The one I knew, the father-diplomat, was gentle, kind, thoughtful. I assumed the father at work was the same man, but was he? With Meneer Wandersee, and sometimes with other colleagues, I sensed he was some kind of different person.

~~

Into the deep pockets of his raincoat and his tweed jacket, my father was always slipping things: flash cards, newspaper articles, binoculars, radios, thick glasses, folded notes, secrets. The secrets had to do with his work at the embassy. All fathers, I assumed, had such secrets.

~~

During my fifth grade, sometime in 1965, Andy, my mother, and I had gone to see my father at the embassy. We went up to my father's office for a little while, the room with all the piles. My father had told me that his work at the embassy entailed reading and writing all day, and going to meetings. Some of his meetings were in restaurants, others in different cities. He also sent out cables. Sometimes he took a cab to Schiphol Airport, to meet the "courier," who was the man who carried the "top secret," "classified" embassy mail from Washington in a white ruck sack.

There was something stirring about this work my father did, about the way he and my mother talked about it. It was as if their voices suddenly had in them a quietness and an honoring. They stood nestled together in a way they didn't when they talked about grocery shopping or weekend plans; they stood close, as if they were each other's best and only friend. This hush and intimacy between my parents tinged all the work my father did with significance and mystery. Shivers trickled up my back when he mentioned the courier's arrival or a trip to an off-the-beaten-path koffiehuis in Haarlem on business.

After our stop in his office, my father shepherded us out for lunch at a restaurant in the centrum. "This looks like a good one," my father said, squinting at the posted menu in front of a small establishment through his fogged-up horn rims. The café was cozy as a bird's nest, with only ten tables, each covered with a deep-red patterned rug, lit by a candle, and with a tulip in a slim vase. It smelled pleasantly of patates and sweaty wool, coffee, and steam. We sat at a table positioned between the wall and the window.

I ordered a *broodtje mit leidsekaas*—a sandwich made up of a roll, butter, and a delicious hard cheese with little stick-like cumin spices in it. Andy ordered a *wurst*, a kind of hot dog that popped and spurted when bitten into. Andy got an *appelsap* and I got a big cup of hot chocolate—with whipped cream, of course. In Holland they topped everything with it. My parents ordered bottles of fizzy mineral water I found disgusting. They shared a bowl of pea soup "thick enough to hold a spoon sticking straight up" and an *appelkoeken*.

While we ate, my father updated us on world events. "China is in a new phase," he said. "Mao is now trying to export Chinese revolution to other countries. This is of concern to our government because we want countries to choose their own systems, and preferably to choose democracy. Our government is keeping a very close eye on Communist Chinese activities here in Europe because they are trying to push Communism here as well as in Asia, Latin America, and Africa. . . ."

Decades on, I'd read that, via the New China News Agency, a front for their intelligence service, the Chinese were using tenacious, rough methods all over the world to support subversive Communist groups, undermine foreign governments, and install Communist regimes.

~~

After lunch, with a whispery, intimate voice, as if he couldn't stop himself anymore from letting my mother in on a great secret, my father said, "Let's go for a drive." He drove us to a place in the centrum, and then he did an odd thing. He drove down a little street that was lined on the right side, where I was sitting, with a high brick wall. He turned right and the wall continued all down the next block. He turned right again, and the brick wall was still there. He turned again and the brick wall was still going—and we were back where we started. At nowhere in the circuit, it seemed to me, was there any way to see whatever it was that was inside the walls.

My father pulled up against the wall and put the clutch in neutral. In the resulting quiet, here in the middle of the city, the car engine hummed like a sea over a dune.

Then, his voice full of an import I didn't understand, my father said, "That's the Red Chinese Mission." I took this to be my father's work: circling walls, like our dog Gracie did when she was investigating, listening at cracks. In fact, as I would discover years hence, the United States had bugged the Chinese mission, and my father had listened in. I would also discover that my father had been involved in another operation that must have stayed with him throughout his life—but for now, all of this was hidden behind a curtain of Dutch rain.

~~

The summer of 1966, the summer between my sixth- and seventh-grade years, the bridge summer between childhood and the whirlwind of adolescence—had seemed the same as any other. I went shopping with Candy in the centrum, trailing behind her. The shops were full of Day-Glo colors: football sweaters with fluorescent stripes on the arms; ribbed, sleeveless turtlenecks in chartreuse and shocking pink; bright-colored bikinis draped with fishnet; and terry-cloth, miniskirted beach dresses. The streets were teeming with Dutch teenagers traipsing in all the latest hip rags, but to me, Candy—in her flippy, American miniskirts from Montgomery Ward—was far cooler than anyone.

When I was stuck at home not shopping, I ironed my thick hair, trying to make it more flaxen like Candy's, or—chucking my striving for a while—wandered with Andy and Gracie through the park. When she could break off from her Dutch-to-English translations for the embassy, my mother took us to the beach at Wassenaar to swim in the calmed-down North Sea and fling jellyfish at each other among the Dutch, flung-splayed on beach towels, who were gulping the sun like Arctic dwellers. This was all very normal for me—an average, lazy, 1960s childhood summer.

And it seemed that way for my father. He went to work as usual, and came home at the regular time, so far as I could tell. Of course, I was too self-absorbed to even notice a scrap of tension in my father—but for him, this was a summer of raging heat and high tension in his small corner of the Cold War. While I was worrying about my tan, the Chinese were feeling humiliated about not being able to protect the North Vietnamese from our bombings, which we were steadily ratcheting up, and my father was playing a perilous, high-stakes game with the Communist Chinese—a game with tragic consequences.

It was not until 2006, at a Washington Christmas party, that, by chance, while talking to a veteran *New York Times* reporter, I came across the story—an episode this newsman, Edward Cowan, recorded as a contributor to the 1967 book *The Espionage Establishment*. Cowan begins the story in this way:

Prins Mauritslaan is a street of drab row houses in The Hague, about seven minutes by car from the center of town. Number 17 is a three-story yellow brick house on the corner. On the afternoon of July 16, a neighbor observed a man lying on the sidewalk in front of No. 17, moaning in pain. He telephoned the police but by the time they arrived the sidewalk was clear. The injured man, forty-two-year-old Hsu Tzu-tsai, had been carried into the house, which served as the rented residence of the third secretary of Communist China's diplomatic mission. Hsu was a houseguest, together with eight other Chinese delegates to the Nineteenth Annual Assembly of the International Institute of Welding, which was concluding its meeting that day in nearby Delft.

At first the occupants of No. 17 refused to let the police enter, but after some discussion one officer and an ambulance attendant were admitted. Hsu was put into the ambulance, and accompanied by two Chinese, was driven to the Red Cross Hospital, a minute or two away. He was examined and x-rayed, the pictures showing a fractured skull, broken ribs and a spinal injury.

Cowan's account went on to describe the following unfolding events: While Mr. Hsu was being evaluated, a sedan full of Chinese pulled up at the hospital. During the time two of the Chinese spoke with the attending doctor and a pair of Dutch detectives, to request Hsu's release—a request they refused, due to the seriousness of the man's injuries—the other visiting Chinese hoisted Hsu onto a stretcher and absconded with him to the home of the Chinese chargé d'affaires.

The Dutch Foreign Ministry protested Hsu's abduction as a violation of law, and insisted that the injured man be returned to the hospital, but the Chinese refused. Finally, on July 18, the chargé d'affaires, claiming that the Chinese had wanted evaluation but not treatment from the hospital, informed the ministry that Hsu had died in his office during the afternoon of July 17. Immediately, the chargé was declared persona non grata and asked to leave the country within twenty-four hours.

The eight other technicians, who had moved along with Hsu, were now placed under guard in the home of the banished chargé d'affaires. In a retaliatory move, Communist China abducted the Dutch chargé d'affaires in Peking and held him hostage, declaring he would not be released until the technicians were set free.

The New China News Agency version of Hsu's death—quoted by Cowan—was that he, along with other Chinese delegates to the Welding Assembly had been hassled at the meeting by American government officials. "Secret U.S. agents, with the connivance of the Dutch government, used every sordid means to induce, illegally and repeatedly, members of the Chinese delegation to desert and betray their own country. . . . Hsu, incited by U.S. agents, jumped down from the building where he was lodged, in an attempt to run away, and injured himself."

A neighbor had noticed an open third-floor window at the time Hsu was lying in pain on the sidewalk—and also noticed that it was closed soon thereafter. The Dutch surmised that Hsu might have jumped or fallen in an attempt to defect—it would theoretically have been possible to have climbed onto the roof and from there to have escaped via the roofs of other houses—or been pushed after being accused of wanting to. When, at Dutch police insistence, Hsu's body was autopsied, the medical examiner determined that Hsu had fallen "from a considerable height."

For the next five months, the remaining eight technicians, holed up in the chargé d'affaires' house, refused to budge from the building or to speak to Dutch authorities. For this period, the Chinese were guarded twenty-four hours a day by a five-person police force, and surrounded by reporters and TV cameras as well as curious tourists and guitar-strumming young people planted along the street.

Finally, on December 29 a compromise was reached. The Chinese permitted Dutch foreign and justice ministry officials to speak with the technicians for an hour and a half—long enough to permit the Dutch to save face but not long enough to allow intensive questioning of the men. As the technicians left the country, the

Chinese diplomatic office reiterated its earlier claim, as Cowan writes, "that Hsu had been approached by American agents. A Yugoslav propaganda broadcast said they were CIA men."

During this period, Cowan reported, the Communist Chinese emphasis in its European missions was on counterespionage and prevention of defection. I know, as my father later revealed, that defections were his bailiwick while serving in The Hague. I also know that his portfolio included work as a liaison with the Dutch intelligence. When I asked my mother about the episode, she confirmed that he had been involved.

~~

My father adored Europe, and he thoroughly enjoyed his work with Meneer Wandersee and his other Dutch contacts, but sometimes he had a turbulent look and a hesitancy. Like a hidden-away part of him felt it was dangerous for him to get near people, like he, himself, was a kind of infection. In later years, once I'd learned of the Chinese defector's death, it would serve as an explanation for my girlhood half-sensed intuitions.

~~

In the seventh grade, about the time of the dismaying seventh-grade dance, my father hoisted the globe over to the dining table with one arm and updated us on world events. "The world is in a fever," he said.

"Back in August, Mao Tse-tung, China's leader, announced a new 'Cultural Revolution,'" my father said. "This is a crusade to wipe out what Mao and his people call 'the four olds': old ideas, old culture, old customs, and old habits. Specially trained recruits called Red Guards are now capturing good Chinese people, like thinkers and teachers, who Mao thinks have different ideas, or who are rich, and making them work like slaves on farms far away from their families.

"On the one hand, the Chinese are forcing their people to do things they don't want to do—and our government wants to take action to stop these dictatorial aspects of Chinese Communism. On the other hand, the Communists are trying to equalize life for all people in their country. This is a noble ideal. . . .

"The Chinese are trying to revolutionize their country to improve the lot of their citizens," he said. "This is not such a unique idea. Our Founding Fathers believed revolution was permissible in a democracy, when the system needed righting, when we needed to get back on track. The Black Power movement in the States is calling for revolution, for instance. . . . What's truly great about America is that we can have different opinions and change tacks, and no one kills each other or gets put in jail, like in Red China."

When my father told us these things, it was like a cool astringent washed over my face, my fevers cooled, and my world of American boys and girls at The American School of The Hague faded away—while at the same time the outside world suddenly expanded. For a few minutes I could see, in my mind, Chinese and Vietnamese children crying for their mothers and fathers. The raggedy Taiwanese girl flickered into my mind and I turned, for a moment, into my bold Columbus self.

~~

After work one day, my father looked upset. "What *do* you have to do to get a promotion in that place?"

"You know what everyone says," my mother said. "Out of sight, out of mind. You've got to be in Washington, talking to all the right people, like Terry does."

"You're right about 'Out of sight, out of mind.' But I refuse to flatter people I have no respect for."

"Well, you and I both know that's how you get ahead." Then my mother went and got a cigarette—she'd been smoking a lot lately.

My father believed other people would honor honesty. My mother saw things differently. She ranted over and over again to my father, "Charlie Taber, you're too good for this world. You're just not realistic; you're too trusting and too honest. There are a lot of son of a guns on this planet. You've got to be careful."

My mother said, "It is necessary to tell a little white lie sometimes, for your own good." "Always put your best foot forward," she said. "Don't air your dirty laundry in public," and "Guard your backside." As I looked at it, I had two mothers. The mother on the telephone who seemed cheery and told people "Things are grand," and the one who stood sentry at our door, like a fierce Chinese temple dog.

In the end, my father's scrupulous honesty would hurt him—my mother would be right—but to me, at twelve years old, his beliefs about honesty sounded clean, noble, correct. I didn't know, at this point, about my father's multiple selves. It was strange and puzzling: my mother believed in secrets. My father, on the other hand— the one who had real secrets to keep because of his "diplomatic" work—didn't believe in secrets. The truth was, he was becoming increasingly repelled by them.

~~

It was merely a requirement that duty officers wear guns, but all the same, there were tensions in the air. The Dutch were increasingly vehement in their protests against American actions in Vietnam and the embassy was a target. And at home, my father was tense. Work had been stressful of late—he had been meeting a lot with Meneer Wandersee about the Chinese—and now there was the question of his next assignment.

We were due to return to Washington at the end of the next school year. Just as Washington thought my father needed to get out of the Far East division to sample another part of the world, now—after close to five years—he needed to leave Holland to prevent the danger of "going native," of identifying *too* much with the country he was in. (This would puzzle me all through my childhood: My father was supposed to deeply understand every country he was sent to—but not to the point that he absorbed it, or sympathized with its concerns. To be American, this directive seemed to say, was to only care for the needs of people in one's own country.)

My parents would have loved to stay on in Holland, but my father had to mind his career, and play his cards in such a way that he could put off the inevitable assignment to Vietnam until his children were in college. This meant a return to Washington now. So my father was headed back to the China Desk at Headquarters.

"I don't know if I can stand being in Smith's shop again," he was telling my mother, standing in the kitchen, holding his last-minute cup of black coffee in his hand.

"That self-serving clique," my mother said this early morning, smoking, frowsy in her frayed yukata. "Just mind your Ps and Qs, Charles. I'll have Cherry over for coffee." Cherry was Mrs. Smith. "We can handle it. You can do anything for a year."

But my father's face didn't alter. His forehead was still ridged and his eyes still squinting with whatever was troubling him.

My mother said to me, when my father wasn't there, "Your father would be a lot better off at his work if he were less trusting." As she said it, her voice seemed to be smothering frustration. She seemed to be smoldering—about Mr. Smith and about Pop's situation, but also about Pop's job, and Pop.

Only years from now would I contemplate the toll that my father's work must have taken on my mother. We were all sympathetic to my father's fatigue and the unceasing demands of his job, while we took my mother's strength for granted. The tensions for CIA wives were enormous—and completely unacknowledged.

~~

We were in Heidelberg, a place of the darkest rain yet. It was January and the sky was black all day—now it was night and the sky was exactly the same. Today we'd visited the Heidelberg castle, a gloomy stone fortress on a high hill, in rain that descended in pencil lead sheets—and it was still pouring outside the window.

We were staying in a U.S. Army billet. There were American hotels all over Germany, left over from post–World War II operations, to provide R&R to American soldiers and embassy people. They had snack bars and mess halls where you could get scalloped potatoes, ham, biscuits, and ice cream sundaes. We had cheeseburgers and strawberry milkshakes in the mess with the military families, and then went up to the little room with khaki green blankets on the beds. It was the first warm place we'd been in all day. My mother immediately took a hot bath. My father said he wanted to see a film at the officers' club. My mother wanted to stay in—"It's too dreary," she said. "You go ahead."

We all laid around on the beds with the curtains closed against the rain, watching the droning German TV. After lazing around bored for what felt like ages, Andy and I were in bed and about to turn out the light when the door blew open.

My father was suddenly standing there, his coat sopping, water dripping off his tweed cap, his glasses fogged, with an enchanted look on his face. It was as if he were lit by warm, Italian sunshine.

He said to my mother, "The film was excellent. Very good—true to life!" He looked calm—like he had had a deep, confirming pleasure. "The film I saw," he explained to us kids, "is called *The Spy Who Came In from the Cold*. It's about a spy who sneaks into East Berlin through Checkpoint Charlie and does a very brave thing." He said this like it was a wondrous secret, and also like it was something deeply familiar to him.

Somehow the room seemed pregnant. It was like the movie, and my father's mood after it—the summer sunshine and the sense of moment that filled the little hotel room with the rain charging down outside in the black night—was a clue. But I didn't even know there was a mystery to be solved.

The night was black. The castle out there, cold stone in the rain on slippery, leafy hills—standing in the gloom and mystery.

~~

My mother patted my father's shoulder in the front hall, and he said, "Don't worry. I'll be back in an hour." He was going to meet a man somewhere. Just before he stepped out the door, he reached his hand down into his satchel and then tucked what looked like a packet of cigarettes into the inside pocket of his raincoat—but my father didn't smoke. As soon as he took one stride from the door, he disappeared into mist. (Later, I would picture my father and a Chinese man huddled over a Formica table in a fogged-up Scheveningen koffiehuis, with the smell of the sea whirling and the wind slamming through the panes, or on the soggy bank of a canal, exchanging cigarette packets, and my father patting the slender Chinese man on the back reassuringly as he turned to leave.)

~~~

Another clue: insinuation in the voices of some of my parents' embassy and business friends.

A man from Shell said to my father at cocktails one evening when I was greeting the guests, "Sure you don't work for some other outfit?" and my father chuckled breezily and said, "Oh sure, Dave."

And Mrs. Grant, the wife of another Foreign Service officer, always said, "Oh how's Charlie, the political attaché?" with a knowing look and a little sneer, when she greeted my mother, and my mother always laughed and pretended she didn't hear it, and then said afterward, "That idiot Mary," and my father laughed.

"It doesn't matter, Lois. She doesn't really know, or she wouldn't act like that," he said. And I could hear, in my father's voice, a little enjoyment of Mrs. Grant's uncertainty. (Years hence, I'd learn that this questioning of certain embassy officers by Foreign Service people, this sort of edgy, knowing-but-not-knowing questioning and denial, is a well-scripted act that takes place in every embassy in the world.)

~~~

Early winter, we were at a meeting about the eighth-grade class trip. Mr. Leonard, the San Francisco bohemian, was at the head of the room. He had proposed that our class go to Prague, in Czechoslovakia, a Communist country. He was so excited about the idea, he was bobbing up and down from his toes. He said he thought it would be fascinating and good for us American children to cross the Iron Curtain. There was buzzing in the room as the parents all discussed the trip.

At the end of the meeting, Mr. Leonard came up to say hello, and asked what we thought of going to Prague. My father said, "I'll have to check on whether Sara can go. The embassy may not permit an embassy child to go to Prague."

"But an embassy girl went to the Eastern Bloc last year," Mr. Leonard said.

My father said, "Yes, I know, but things may have changed."

Mr. Leonard said, "Hmm." A look almost like annoyance flashed across Mr. Leonard's face then—a look like he doubted what my father was saying and also knew more than my father thought he did. My father was nice, and he had an important job. I didn't know why Mr. Leonard acted this way around him.

It turned out that the embassy said my father was right: I couldn't go. It was weird, though. The embassy said Gabrielle Black, whose father also worked at the embassy, *could* go. *What was the difference*, I wondered. It must have been that my father was more important.

Mr. Leonard scowled when I told him, and then humphed, as if this confirmed something he'd known already. Because of me, Mr. Leonard had to change the class trip to Vienna.

~~

Without warning, my father was sick, with a high, high fever. Crawling with a raging infection, he was lying in bed with his eyes closed and his mouth open, making strange groggling sounds as he tried to breathe through his swollen throat. I stood in the doorway, peering in while my mother leaned over him, moving a wet washcloth over his face. "Oh Charlie, Charlie," she was saying.

Later, I stood at the banister, looking down to the ground floor. My mother was in the entryway with three tall men in identical tan balmacaan raincoats: my father's colleagues who had just been up to see him. The men huddled in the hush of the hall seemed like more than just a group of friends worried about one their chums. It was like they were members of a secret club, gathered like elephants around an ailing member of the herd, to keep my father safe. The huddle seemed important and charged with secrecy—like spies in a movie.

The men and my mother spoke in hushed tones for a while. Then my mother went to the telephone. She called for a cab that took my father away with one of the men.

"Mr. Rogers saved your father's life," my mother told me the next morning.

My father climbed mountains, he traversed cities, but there was something deeply vulnerable about him. I sensed rather than knew this: he was delicately made, like an artist or philosopher. It was as though, if the wrong person tapped his shoulder, or a particular germ found its way into his water, or a high wave caught him on the beach, he would be too skinny and trusting to fight back, or swim to shore. (If I'd known to ask, I would have questioned: *How can an artist or a philosopher—a person attuned to subtleties, however brave—engage in covert operations?*)

As he lay, weak and thinly dressed, in his bed, I felt shaken. It was like an important layer had been stripped away, and I could now see the naked body underneath everyone's clothes. I sensed the undertow pulling at my father, from under the surface of the sea. A deep and ominous chill ran through my own bare trunk and trickled down into my limbs.

~~

My father's dangerous fever and his weakened immune system would seem to me later—from the vantage of decades—linked to what must have been the enormous strain of the events of that year. What must it have been like to be involved—in any way—with the Chinese man's death? The events must have haunted him.

~~

I went upstairs for a while and sat on my bed, where I, myself, had lain in soaking meningitis fever a year and a half before. I shivered. I fiddled with a pencil, I looked at a hyacinth in a pot, trying not to think about my father's close call—about the giant squid of fear down in the deeps, lurking.

13
nicole

The tide was midway up the sand. We were trudging just below the mound of cracked fishing boots, caved-in baskets, broken planks, kelp, and shells cast at the tide's uppermost rim—the waves at Scheveningen rolling into the strand. In many parts of my life I felt as though I was, at last, on sturdy ground. I was in the eighth grade, the top grade at school—on Mount Olympus. On the other hand, it was like the sea was continually sucking the sand out from under my feet, and simultaneously like the horizon was widening in front of me. I was beginning to see new possibilities and new mysteries—and to lose my grip on past assumptions. With each thump and hiss of the sea, the cold mist hit my cheeks, calling "Wake up! Wake up! Open your eyes to the world!"

~~

I had just turned thirteen, and I had achieved one of my two big goals. Through desperation and grit, I had proven myself worthy: a red, white, and blue American. I could, by now, affect the blasé banter of a cowgirl, and I had gotten good at going against my grain, mustering my courage, and speaking out in class. When Mr. Leonard, our eighth-grade teacher, asked a question about current events these days, I could bomb back an answer with the speed of a B-52. There was always the shy, scarecrow part of me, and the embassy princess, but I had a cocky Sara Taber now well in hand.

~~

This year, 1967—as I'd learned from my father and current events at school—forty-three people had died in Detroit race riots, the first human heart transplant was accomplished, and the Beatles' *Sgt. Pepper's Lonely Hearts Club Band* album had come out.

My father said hundreds of thousands of American troops were fighting for Vietnam's freedom now, but a lot of the Europeans and even a lot of Americans thought this was wrong. In October, thousands of antiwar protestors massed at the Pentagon, and hundreds of them were arrested. The Netherlands was one of the countries at the helm of the antiwar movement. Holland was teeming with *provos*, provocateurs, people who held rallies and marches to protest governments' actions. When we'd first come to Holland, the provos were leading the Ban the Bomb movement; these days they were protesting the war in Vietnam. Everywhere we went now, there were rants about Amerika: hippies at the train station said to us as we passed them, "Amerika go to hell," in perfect English, and as casually as if they were saying "Good morning."

~~

In the face of this, I stolidly maintained my America-is-best stance, but some things occurred that rocked the simple cleanness of my patriotism.

We were in the auditorium again, eating lunch on a day of cold drizzle. Needing to move around, we went over to the front window so we could look out while we ate our identical sandwiches. To our surprise, the sidewalk beyond the ironwork fence was being patrolled by a handful of Dutch teenagers walking back and forth in the rain with peace signs over their shoulders. When they saw us, they stopped marching and put their noses up against the wrought iron rails and started yelling and raising their fists.

Back in class, like he'd had a burst of determination brought on by the provos, Mr. Leonard suddenly turned his chair backward in front of his desk, plopped down, straddled it, and faced us over the backrest. His face became serious. "It's time to talk about current events," he said.

Mr. Leonard had a beard and thin, scraggly poodle hair that curled around his ears. My father had commented that Mr. Leonard was a beatnik, like Joan Baez. I didn't really know what that meant, except that he was a little cool and a little weird. He used slang, was an actor, and slouched around and sometimes put his feet on the desk, like he was a teenager.

"I want to know what you students really think about the war in Vietnam," he said, leaning toward us.

Margrite jumped in, the girl with the Dutch mother. "Those were the provos on the walk. You guys know what they are, don't you?" she said with a tone implying that we were so dumb we probably didn't. "They're protesting the war America started in Vietnam."

Immediately, just like Gracie's fur when she sensed threat, our hackles went up. A clean martial urge surged in all of us pure Americans.

Billy said, "My dad's told me about them. They're really stupid. Our country is right to attack the North Vietnamese."

Margrite tossed her beautiful head and looked superior. "Mum said America is being a big bully in Asia. You think you're so great because you can push around a little tiny country like Vietnam. That's really impressive. . . ."

"Holland is probably more violent than we are," someone said.

"Holland is not violent," Margrite said. "We don't believe in imperialism. America might be big but you aren't gentlemanly. You're out for yourselves. My mum said what you're doing in Vietnam is criminal—killing all those mothers and children. You're just big bullies."

Candy said, "Why don't you just leave the school. You don't belong here if you're not on America's side."

"My father's American and he agrees." She winked her eye, flirting, to Richard, and tossed him her beautiful, knowing smile. Showing us *he* didn't think she should leave the school.

Then Mr. Leonard looked straight at me. At first, I assumed he thought I should have something special to say—maybe because my father had an important job at the American embassy. But no, as some more kids responded, and his eyes continued to flick back to me, a queer nervousness came over me. It was not, after all, like he thought I had some special knowledge because of my father's work. Instead, it was as though he was waiting for me to blurt out a secret—or for me to make a mistake.

Quickly, I considered: *What does Pop always say when Dutch people ask him about the war?*

I found it, and raised my hand. "I think we're doing the right thing," I said when Mr. Leonard called on me. "We're giving the Vietnamese help little by little, and seeing if it helps their cause."

Mr. Leonard scowled and shook his head and said, "That's what your father thinks. What do *you* think?" It was like he had suddenly yanked my chair out from

under me and I'd been plopped on a cold, hard floor of shame—and shock that my
teacher wasn't playing by the usual rules.

At dinner, I told my father about the provos and about what Mr. Leonard
had said.

"Was I right, Pop, in what I said about the war?"

"Yes, that's exactly what I say to Dutch people I meet. It's part of my duty to tell
Dutch people what our government thinks."

"Margrite said America is a big bully. Isn't that dumb, Pop?" I knew my father
would agree with me. But he said something I didn't expect.

"Well, sometimes we should listen to smaller countries," he said, looking at me
intently through his horn rims and leaning forward in his crisp suit. "Might doesn't
always make right. Sometimes we should take time to consider. . . ."

My father wasn't agreeing fully enough. I felt an urgency inside, like a fighter
jet lost in fog that needed to find its way back to base.

"But the provos are bad, right?"

"Well, our government thinks they are wrong, that we should aid the South
Vietnamese. But I can say privately, as an American citizen now, not as a Foreign
Service officer, that there might be something to what the protestors are saying."
He told me, "As a representative of the embassy I must take certain positions in
public and at official parties, but when I am with friends, even Dutch friends on the
weekend, I can say, 'Our government policy is such and such, but personally I don't
agree.' And, of course, I am allowed to speak my own views in private, and privately
I do have some questions.

"Next time he asks, you can tell him what *you* think," my father said. I was
confused. I thought what my father told Dutch people *was* what I thought. Now I
had another odd tweak. I suddenly had the sense that my father was expecting me
to think something he thought but couldn't say out loud. It was like I was supposed
to stand in for him—put on his Chinese cloth peasant shoes. But I didn't know what
he was groping for.

"But America *is* right, *right*, Pop?"

Looking at my face, he said, "Okay, basically . . . yes."

Back at base camp, restored to my job of being a patriotic American kid trying
to be like everyone else, I headed safely for bed.

But even though I tucked it away, like a spy, I had noticed my father's hesitancy;
the doubts had been sown. The grand white marble statue of America's greatness
had been nicked.

~~

In Amsterdam, having just come from a visit to the Rembrandts in the Rijksmuseum, we wound our way through the warren of narrow cobbled streets and then came to the plein in the center of the city. There, in a shouting, chanting mass, were thousands of Dutch provos demonstrating against the war in Vietnam. A lot of the provos, who hated our country, were wearing U.S. Army surplus jackets with the American soldiers' name badges still sewn on their chests. (Years down the road, I would note that this was often the case. People of warring countries commonly wear, on their person, some sort of emblem of the other side, of the enemy. It is as if inconsistency is the only consistency, and it is as if warriors can't help unconsciously acknowledging the humanity of the other side: the truth that we're all the same.)

Ignoring my mother's nervous protests, my father took each of our hands and led Andy and me straight into the thick of the crowd. We stood there among the long-haired, ragged hippies in loose Indian print clothes and saggy jackets for several minutes as my father translated the placards. There, among the demonstrators, a strong blended smell of bodies, marijuana, patates frites, and wurst filled the air—an aroma that opened my senses and lingered long after. Just before we left the horde, a tall, thin man in a shaggy, patchwork jacket, fixed a pair of fierce eyes on my father and said, "You dirty Americans, get out of Vietnam!"

Though he ignored me and focused on my father, I felt the Dutch man's anger like a blade slashing into me. More than I had before, I wondered what this was all about. *What is it about this war in Vietnam that makes people so mad at America; and why did Pop go stand there—almost like he wanted to be there—in the demo? Why doesn't Pop say the provos are all wrong?*

I didn't know that not only my father's actions, but many of his emotions were covert—and that I needed to read his feelings in his behavior, his gestures, the angle of his body. My father's wading into the demo was a message he had dead-dropped, waiting for me to find.

~~

One long weekend, we joined Meneer Wandersee, his wife Riet, and their three children on a canal boat they had rented. Meneer and Vrouw Wandersee liked us, I could tell, *because* we were American. I could tell that, from the outlook of their little country, our country offered a sense of exciting *possibility*, and my parents were full of praises for Holland. But it was different for us kids.

While our parents drank Heineken—and toward sundown, Dutch *jenever*—
and droned on and on, on the deck of the little red-and-blue boat, Andy and I and
the Wandersee girls charged across the lumpy, squishy fields to the neighboring farm.
Waving to the heavy-breasted farmer's wife, in her apron, we headed for the barn.

We clambered up the ladder to the hay loft and, at first, flopped down on the
quilted mattress of hay. Without our parents to smooth the way, we felt awkward—
and so we spent a few minutes grinning uncomfortably and picking at the hay as
the swallows swooped overhead. It wasn't clear who tossed the first handful of hay,
but before long we were in an exhilarating all-out, everyone-for-himself hay battle,
often falling down on top of our victims as we heaved our heaps of hay.

There in the barn, for hours, we hurled hay at each other, as though we were
American soldiers fighting provos—hurling and hurling, and laughing and thrusting so hard we eventually had to flop back onto the resilient hay to chase down our
breaths and calm the hearts that were jumping like tennis balls in our chests.

Mid-fray, at one point, Trina pointed at Andy and said, "Your nose is ugly!"
"Well yours is black," he retorted. We soon discovered that all of us—no matter
what country we were from—had nostrils blackened with hay dust. This led us to
another bout of hilarity as we blew our noses and showed the black smudges on
our white pocket handkerchiefs. We battled in the barn until we were ravenous as
starved wolves, and then raced back to the boat for rations of salami and cheese.
Once replenished, we sped for the barn again—back to the hay war.

~~

On the playground, too, things had gotten murky with regard to this matter of
the United States being superior to other places, and Americans being the coolest
people.

We were discussing the paper dresses that were in all the windows in the centrum this year. Candy seized the reins and led our wagon train in the direction
she wanted to go. "Paper dresses are dumb. The States is way better," she said with
absolute authority, "but I'd take the Dutch boy who lives near my house," she added,
laughing and flipping her bangs. Then, having delivered the gospel, she flounced off
to flirt with some boys across the blacktop.

I started to re-spout the gospel, but before I could . . .

"America's stupid," Barbie, a seventh grader, abruptly said. We were all stunned.

"Where I lived, in South Carolina," Barbie said, "there wasn't even a Sears. All
we had was a post office and a gas station. My mother had a cow about it all the

time, and I thought I was going to die of boredom. Have you seen those knee-high boots at the de Bijenkorf? I think Holland's ten times better than the States. The Dutch are much more mod."

At this, we subtly edged away from her, but our ears remained pricked.

Margrite jumped on Barbie's lead. "Holland's fashions are way ahead of anything in America." Her Dutch mother wore clothes from all the fashion magazines like *Vogue* and *Elle*. We heard the authority in Margrite's voice, but we pretended she hadn't said it.

Only—maybe because Candy had disappeared—we didn't.

Barbie continued her thought. "And a lot of American kids are delinquents. They shoplift and do stuff that's against the law."

I flashed to our last home leave, the summer between sixth and seventh grades, when, while my father checked in at the office—he wasn't supposed to work on home leave, but he had worked like fury—I had gotten to visit Lucy somewhere in Virginia for the day. While her mother sunbathed in just her bikini bottom on their back patio with a fan blowing on her, Lucy, Jen, and I wandered around their sprawling suburban neighborhood of ramblers and split-levels. When we reached the shopping center, Lucy had an inspiration. "Hey, Jen, let's go papering!"

Jen said, "Yeah!" and they led me straight into the five and dime, regaling me with tales of draping their classmates' trees with toilet paper. Each skinny, fly-away-haired girl tromped straight down a certain aisle, like she knew it by heart, and picked up a six-pack of toilet paper. As they walked—with me trailing them—back toward the front of the store, the store manager came barreling out of his office toward the back, saying "Oh no you don't," and took the pack of tissue out of Jen's hand.

"We have the money right here," Jen said, digging in her shorts pocket.

The man grimaced through a film of sweat and reluctantly let her go.

"He thinks he can get me," Jen said, smirking, as the man went back down the aisle.

As we proceeded by the cashier with the bundles, Jen slipped a candy bar off a rack and tucked it in her pocket, and then smiled merrily as she paid the older lady cashier for the toilet paper.

When we got out of the store, Jen fished out the candy bar, and took a defiant chomp. She offered me a bite, saying to Lucy, "You have ta get your own," but—wishing we were a lot farther from the store—I said, "No, thanks."

Next, the girls led me to a house up the street from theirs where, they said, a boy who had just papered their house lived, and started wrapping toilet paper around the tree and lightpost in the front yard. Pretty soon, though, a lady came running out of the house and yelled, "Cut that out, or I'm going to report you, young ladies!"

There was something too free about this life Jen and Lucy had, and I was glad when my mother picked me up right after we got back for the Oreos and root beer Jen and Lucy promised me as the crowning touch of the day.

~~

Back at recess, Peggy said, "I love all the historical things here—the castles, the cobbled streets."

Tammy said, "I like lots of things in Holland, like the dunes in Scheveningen."

When she said the word Scheveningen, my imagination took off. The beach formed in my mind. As the wind beat at us, Gracie and I raced to the water's edge, jubilant as the cold bit into our bodies and the sea hurled spray into our cheeks and eyes. . . .

All the Dutch things I liked began to stream past my mind's eye. The tulip fields in May that looked like blankets of apples, lemons, and oranges tossed over the earth. The tufted dunes in Wassenaar where Andy and I played King of the Mountain. The hyacinth-ringed, thatched farm houses that hunched on the rain-sodden pastures. The fat, fluffy ponies we rode on weekends. The Dutch rubber boots and wooly ribbed scarves we wrapped around us as we set out on wonderful, rainy hikes along canals. Our Dutch housekeeper, Maria, whose hugs felt as warm as those of Martha, the housemaid who looks after Sara in *The Secret Garden*. My beloved klompen. All the things I loved about Holland suddenly shone brighter than the sun, and flashed and whirled inside me. I tried to switch off the images in my head, but in those persistent mental pictures, the Keds on my feet kept turning into klompen.

I remembered how Peggy had said, "Holland fits in our pocket." I liked how that sounded. And that was what I liked about Holland: it was small and had beautiful little gardens and beautiful little houses and big, golden people.

In the logic of our junior-high brains, the inferiority of all other nationalities was essential, but try as I might, I couldn't hate the Dutch. Whenever I stepped outside the boundaries of the school gate on Parkstraat, I came face to face with a direct challenge to our American swagger. The Dutch—the provos and the hippies—were holding the court of cool. As my father said, "The Dutch can out-hippy anyone." The throngs of these tall, sturdy people in their long gowns and seaweed hair stirred me in spite of myself. The snarl-haired Dutch teenagers were more ragged than any Americans I'd seen, and their faces more careworn, in an exquisite, romantic, brooding way. The teenaged boys with filthy mops topping their tall, sturdy frames looked like bedraggled princes out of storybooks. I might swoon if one turned a blue eye on me.

By myself, up in my bedroom in our drafty row house, I sat and tried to fend off an insistent question: *If we are so cool, what about the Dutch?*

My father represented the U.S. government, and was a patriot, yet he too was drawn to the Dutch. Having grown up under Roosevelt, and educated on Norman Thomas, who believed in governments helping people, he was taken by the Dutch's liberal social policies. "America is a rich country," he said. "We can afford programs that meet people's basic needs, like inexpensive or free university education, a secure retirement, free medical care, and unemployment compensation. This is what government is for—to make sure people are secure, and to help them when times are tough like in the Depression." Even though he knew it bothered me, he said, "The Dutch do this better than we do. We have a lot to learn from them."

My mother loved all this about the Dutch too. She liked Dutch people's openness about naked bodies. She loved that Dutch doctors made house calls. She thought the Dutch had an excellent health care system. She admired the fact that the Dutch had motorized wheelchairs unlike anything in America, which let disabled people move around. She also liked it that the people in Holland selected their retirement homes—there was a lovely one down the block, an old, grand Victorian house with white-haired people drinking coffee from white cups and playing cards in the window—when they were young, and looked forward to entering it early with their friends. She thought Holland was a better place to grow old than America. She liked that the Dutch had apprenticeships for young people to learn trades. She liked that they learned many languages, which was good for children. She liked that they had hard schools. She liked that they ate meat slices for breakfast because it was good to have protein to start the day. The Dutch were practical, industrious people, like my mother.

I absorbed, like sponge cake, my parents' views on the Dutch. One day, in a graduate social work class on social policy in Seattle, I'd find myself delivering a fervent speech—with absolute conviction—about the importance of national health insurance. That a rich country such as ours should assure its citizens their basic needs would always be met, no matter what befell them, seemed obvious to me: I learned this while young, growing up in Holland.

~~

I was drawn to the Dutch, not only because they were cool and humane but also—I couldn't admit this to myself—because they offered me a salve for my failures on the American front. Dutch people often said to me, "You seem more Dutch than most Americans." I knew this meant they thought I was quieter, humbler, and more polite than some of my countrymen, and for a brief moment or two when they said these things, I felt my chest inflate with a thing like pride. With Americans I always felt too shy. It would take many years, and living in Japan as a teenager and in Spain as an adult, to discover that there were many people and cultures that viewed quiet, reflective people through another lens.

The Dutch dangled the exhilarating possibility that a person could be messy and earthy and not a sassy cowgirl, and still fine. The Dutch—I could tell—felt most themselves in the outdoors the way I did. In their rubber boots and big, baggy sweaters, with both their legs and their cheeks bare, flaming, and chapped all winter long, they seemed solid and basic, like primary colors.

Every week I experienced the alternation, the flip-flop. I went from my weekends of bike rides, feeding horses in the slop and rain, and mingling with the Dutch, to my little American weekdays of trying to be pretty, outgoing, and the same as everyone else. I didn't know enough about Dutch culture to know its inherent complexities and inner conflicts, but *to be Dutch*, I thought sometimes, tucked secret and safe in my room, *would be easier*.

~~

Without my awareness and through a stealthy, clandestine process, I had become part-Netherlander. There is some sort of essence of a culture—despite all the range and variety in its individuals—that is in the water, in the air—and you soak it up, through your six senses, when you live somewhere. Perhaps it is easy to caricature or idealize if you look at a culture from the outside, but an outsider also sees things those within the culture don't see—and if you live somewhere long enough, the habits and vistas of a culture seep into your muscles and blood. I didn't know many Dutch people save for the few at school—I mainly observed them from outside—but jostling them on the street, handing them coins in shops, bumping woolen shoulders with them in steamy koffiehuises, and tromping through their soggy paddocks, I had taken in something strong and real, though it had no name. It was similar to the way, within a decade, the whole world would, via television, have absorbed some tincture of Americanness. Something about the Dutch—their dike-consciousness, their practical way of stamping straight into the salty mud and mush of the world and shoveling it into farm fields—had become a kind of loam in my body.

Now dyed into my fibers, along with a longing for America, was a lust for the Netherlands, and, more broadly, for the worn stone of Europe. As the poet Czeslaw Milosz wrote, "Europe herself gathered me in her warm embrace, and her stones, chiseled by the hands of past generations, the swarm of her faces emerging from carved wood, from paintings, from the gilt of embroidered fabrics, soothed me. . . . Europe, after all, was home to me."

This was another one of those little packages—or Pandora's boxes—that life was tossing me, and would dare me, one day, to open.

~~

On the cusp of summer, a rare, blazing morning, my parents drove us to the beach in Wassenaar. Coming over the shoulder of the dune I looked down on a colony of Dutch mothers, children, and old people in various stages of undress. Mothers with smooth, athletic-looking legs stood, bare breasts hanging down like pendulums, wiggling into their bikinis. Their children had thrown off their clothes and were pouring sand over each other's heads. Babies sat, bare-bottomed, in the sand. Old men sat beside them, in white underwear, their splay-legged posture identical to that of the babies. The fathers stood, penises to the sea and bottoms toward me, as they donned their skin-tight bathing briefs. Unlike on Rehoboth Beach in Delaware where we once went from Bethesda, bare bodies were sprawled out everywhere on the beach, with not a whit of shame or modesty to diminish the caress of the salt breeze.

Everywhere, every which way, bare-bottomed tiny children and older children in just their white underpants were dashing. In the sea itself heads bobbed and bodies splashed and flashed merrily as sea lions. The summer beach in Wassenaar was a metamorphosis. With the reappearance of the sun, the Holland of wet navy wool had vanished. In its place was a land of toasted sand and calming sun sprinkled with tow-head children, royal blue and hot orange swim clothes, and curves of golden skin.

I hurtled myself down the dune, set down my knapsack with my *Seventeen* and my Droste bar, and staked out our encampment as the rest of my family approached. Once we were assembled, we got ready to swim. Andy only had to take off his T-shirt. He wore his knee-length army shorts every day, for both land and sea, so he had nothing to change, and my mother already had on her boxer-legged swimsuit from Montgomery Ward. My father matter-of-factly changed out of his khaki pants and into his swim trunks out in the open. He was calm, like a man after a war, when there was nothing to fear or lose. I mimicked the Dutch uninhibitedness my parents said was healthy, not bothering to cover myself with the towel as I put on my turquoise Dutch bikini, and as I did so, a little thrill of carefree Dutchness rippled through me.

At this juncture in my life, when I was so ardently patriotic, I was both as vehemently American as I'd ever be, and—though I didn't know it—at the end of any chaste Americanness.

~~~

Back at school, I still orbited Candy, but I'd begun hanging around a bit more with Gabrielle. She was the girl in my class who had a Belgian mother and American father, and was a little out of style, from the point of view of the rest of us full-blood Americans. Her knee-high black boots weren't quite high enough, and her corduroy skirts revealed too much of her thighs.

Gabrielle lived in a dark row house in an area of town my family seldom saw—on the outskirts of The Hague near where the old, three-story row houses dribbled into big, modern apartment buildings with a lot of vacant, not-yet-planted, rubbled space between them. The curtains were drawn in Gabrielle's house, making dark, shadowy shapes around the overstuffed furniture and obscuring the corners of the rooms. Her small, thin mother spoke in Belgian-accented English and Gabrielle spoke back in breezy, dismissive French. I imagined her mother to be horrified at having a daughter with such hearty American looks.

One Friday afternoon, Gabrielle had me over. She was excited to have me, and told me three times at school about the special dinner her mother would be cooking specially for us.

Gabrielle happily showed me around the house, to her strange dark room with—as I re-imagine it—a red curtain draped on the wall with art postcards on it. She was already an adolescent—she had older brothers to mimic—while I was just beginning to feel the first bubbles of that potent brew. With Gabrielle, I felt in the presence of an odd maturity. She viewed me as her peer, but I knew, via an inner tingling, that she was way ahead of me on the road: older boys and even men found reasons to tease her, though she seemed to pay them no heed. Maybe, it occurs to me now, she was simply European in her intimate femininity, but Gabrielle's doubleness—the simultaneous presence of both her adult and her child selves—made me shift a little on my feet, as if I were in the presence of a power greater than myself. There was an innocent lustiness about her. She was a person whom you sensed would take large portions in life.

When her mother set out dinner on the thick, dark-textured tablecloth, it was a large platter of pizza. "This is my favorite," Gabrielle said, dishing me up a large slice. And she kissed her mother on the cheek, a style of affection it never occurred to me to offer to my mother. "*Merci, Maman!*" she said. And her mother said, "*C'est bon, Cherie?*" Gabrielle gobbled down the pizza, drinking huge gulps of Fanta along her way, while I mincingly took bites of the strange dish. The pizza was topped with tuna fish—an experience too far out of my standard American repertoire of burgers and fries to tempt me, but, out of politeness, gagging a little, I got a piece down. (And later, after I left Holland, I would have given a lot for a slice of that pizza.)

The experience at the table with the pizza widened my eyes. Suddenly, for the first time, I could take in this girl before me. Somehow, at age thirteen, Gabrielle had accepted her foreignness and her odd American-Belgian ways, felt comfortable with her mother's strangeness, even if the rest of us did not—and wholeheartedly loved her own self and her own life. It was a lesson that would recur repeatedly during my life—these confident children with a foreign parent who had a strange taste, like a strain of soy sauce in the Jell-O.

At school, too, Gabrielle held her own, a goat happy among sheep. She could joke around with us, and yet she seemed happy to be alone too—doing twirls on the bars, not minding that she was showing the dark tops of her pantyhose. Funny and affectionate, she had nicknames for the people she liked. She called me "Tubby Tuber." She yelled across the side yard, "Hey Tubes, come climb on the ropes with me." And Gabrielle was, in equal measure, confident and jocular with the boys, over whom she towered by at least four inches. She had a loud, unselfconscious laugh, and would as readily kick a boy with a long leg as send him a love note. What was new and amazing to me, captured inside my bars of shyness, was the realization that Gabrielle, someone so odd as to eat tuna fish pizza, could be different and survive—and be happy.

~~

Back in seventh grade, during the first week of school, our French and home-room teacher, Madame Evans, a tiny, delicate Belgian woman with command-ing grace, had assigned us all French names. Almost everyone's name was turned French easily—with a shift in accent or by adding an "e"—but even though Sara was a name in France, Madame Evans said, "Sara, I think your French name should be Nicole."

Things people from other countries say sometimes stun you like car lights hit-ting you, a rabbit, on the road. In rebaptizing me Nicole, a romantic, sophisticated name as opposed to my, to me, old-fashioned one, it was as if Madame Evans had seen something about me that I didn't see. By renaming me, it was as if she were holding out to me another way to be: Some other cast of femininity something feathery, rich-hued, and confident. Something different from American-issue. Ever since then, and continuing now in eighth grade, this other femininity had fluttered around me as a possibility. Had I the courage to take it into my hand?

~~

One day my mother and I went to visit Madame Evans—Mr. Evans worked with my father—at her tidy brick row house. In her richly appointed antiques- and oriental rug–filled living room, Madame Evans asked me, in French, how my stud-ies were going. She was kind, but expected clear, honest answers—not just polite, cheery ones. This made me feel simultaneously challenged and comfortable. Ma-dame Evans's eyes scrunched just a tiny bit and twinkled softly as she listened—she was so pretty, with her soft fluff of ginger hair, in her angora sweater.

There was something about Madame Evans, and Vrouw Wandersee, and my mother's other European lady friends, that shot like an arrow into my bull's-eye. Eu-ropean ladies spoke the truth and knew things in a deep, eyes-wide-open way. Even their posture was different from that of my mother, Mrs. Grant, and Lizzy's Ameri-can mother in her Peter Pan collar and A-line skirt. Vrouw Wandersee was frank, almost strict—there was no evading in the blunt Dutch book of life, and Madame Evans seemed like she knew something about girls, and about boys—something having to do with delicate finger touches, up-tilted chins, and daring-eyed smiles— that was different from what American mothers knew. Madame Evans showed me a different kind of lady a girl could grow into, as she offered me a different kind of girl.

~~

My angle on boys was being shaken up too. American boys were sturdy Chevys and Fords. Boys from other countries, alternatively, were Peugeots and DAFS— different and interesting to daydream about and watch. French boys, for instance.

When Mrs. Evans first introduced me, at her home, to her son, Pascal, who was a grade ahead of me at the French School, he said, "So *you're* one of the girls from the American School." His eye had a twinkle, and his tone was a mix of mockery and teasing. I felt my cheeks grow hot with embarrassment. This made him beam and nod his head knowingly, which made one part of me want to flirt and slap him, and the other want to escape as fast as I could.

Pascal was taller than his mother, and while he uttered this troublesome sentence, his arm was around her tiny waist. No American boy I knew would kiss his mother, much less stand with his arm around her while flirting with a girl. And Pascal's whole manner was completely different as he assessed me, a girl.

After looking at me in his meaning-packed way for a while, Pascal winked and said, "*À bientôt*," and disappeared upstairs.

There was something troubling about French boys like Pascal Evans, something about their presuming ways that made me squirm. I was used to American boys who acted like cowboys, shrugging off their mother's shoulder pats with scowls on their faces. There was something I would only much later be able to label as intimate and seductive in Pascal's relationship with his mother, and it extended to all females. Pascal even kissed his sister, Sophie, hello, and to my half-discomfort and half-pleasure, he always kissed me when I was forced to go to his house. He loved to tug my hair and embarrass me. It was as though he wanted to break me down with his kisses and his taunting eyebrows—and though this half repelled me, it also magnetized me. It was as if he made me fancy him against my will.

~~

Dutch boys were simpler. They seemed more like American boys, but brighter colored in their orange and royal blue sweaters, wonderfully scruffy in their baggy pants and rubber boots, and made for the open air. Their cheeks were always blazing red from the cold, and they looked as if they'd just returned from eight hours of soccer, hay-raking, or constructing dikes. They seemed strong and open faced and their voices were loud and forthright as they yelled to one another across a school field. They sometimes kissed their mothers, but the kisses were hasty, matter-of-fact smacks, not lingering and tender like the French boys'. They and their moth-

BEFORE MY BIRTH

My patriotic young father, Charles (right), at army training, Fort Lewis, Washington.

My parents in front of their first Washington, D.C., apartment, shortly after my father was hired by the government.

My parents on the ferry at their early post in Hong Kong.

JAPAN

My parents cycling in the peaceful countryside of post-Occupation Japan.

My mother shopping near Kamakura.

My father and me.

My mother taking me
for a stroller ride.

The Taipei street scene. (David Collier)

A Taiwanese rice padi.
(David Collier)

My family, on our first tour in
Taipei, soon after my brother,
Andrew, was born.

During our second Taipei tour, the broken-glass-topped wall of our house, and the padi beyond.

With a broken arm, thinking hard during a spelling bee.

My father (left) on the summit of Yu Shan.

My father, "sampling the riches of China."

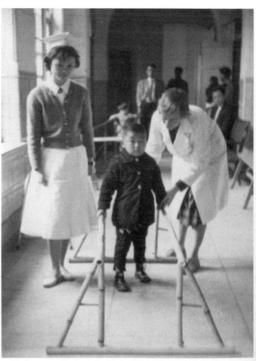

My mother (right) working at the Taipei polio clinic.

Andy and me with our adored amah, Mary, the morning of our departure from Taiwan, my first lost, beloved country.

BETHESDA

SS *President Cleveland*, the ship that took us "home" to America.

The (soon to be ordinary) princess entertaining passengers on the ship.

The miraculous visit to our Indiana cousins.

In our pajamas, with our father, at the time of the Cuban Missile Crisis.

The ardent American (front row, second from left) in her Brownie troop.

THE NETHERLANDS

Thrilled with my new Dutch stilts, falling in love with Holland in spite of myself.

Our wondrous
house in The
Hague (right
side of three-
house row).

My parents at an
embassy reception.

My parents enjoying an official
dinner with the Dutch (my
mother in front, father at back)

A trip to Bruges, Belgium.

The eighth grader (holding purse) on a class trip.
(Liza Webster)

My mother, Andy, and me with our dear Dutch housekeeper, Maria.

CHEVY CHASE

With a close Sidwell friend, in my disillusioned antiwar *provo*-poet phase.

BORNEO

Our house in Kuching, Malaysia.

Restored and happy in a new country.

A longhouse in the forest.

Andy, my father, and me eating with our missionary friend and his bible students in a remote hamlet.

A new life at Canadian Academy in Kobe, Japan, before the strange and frightening mishap that altered the course of my life.

The medical staff at Tachikawa Air Force Base (Dr. Cohen, front row, far left).

Our house in Tokyo

Waiting for a train to Mashiko, the remote village with exquisite pottery.

My father, gearing up for a return to Headquarters at the end of his Tokyo tour.

ers seemed to talk a lot, with loud, emphatic voices that also carried back and forth grins and good will. I liked the hay and chocolate look of Dutch boys.

~~

It was a perfect Dutch winter day. The air was sharp cold, the trees surrounding the pond were perfect black outlines against the creamy blue sky, and I was skating round and round. There were only a few people on the pond—just Andy, me, and six or so Dutch people. Suddenly a cute Dutch boy with a thatch of gold hair and a long maroon-and-yellow scarf skated by me, almost touching me. On his next circuit, he grabbed at my hat. The next, he took it and raced off with it across the ice, looking back at me, daring me, waving it, with a grin on his face. Without even thinking, I roared after him as fast as I could. For a breathless half an hour, the Dutch boy and I chased each other, grabbing at each other's scarves and hats, laughing and falling down, and then blasting after each other again. The feeling inside my pounding chest was not only an urgent need for breath but an almost unbearable pulsing of hilarity and attraction. This encounter with the Dutch boy adhered to no boy-girl rules. It was a pure draft of pleasure.

The boy and I kept racing until I heard a forceful Dutch woman's voice call from the top of the hill, at the edge of the park. The boy spun around me once, said "Dag!" and then left the ice.

For a long time afterward, I looked for him when I went skating. He seemed like both a boy of my daydreams and an honest-to-goodness, real boy I could like, a blend that would be just right, but our paths never crossed again.

14

home

If, in eighth grade, I had achieved the goal of proving myself an American cowgirl, I had also proven myself in the other important circus of my life.

Crepe paper streamers were drooping from the ceiling of the parlor-auditorium at school. Roger changed LP after LP on the record player: "Jumpin' Jack Flash," "We Gotta Get Out of This Place," "(I Can't Get No) Satisfaction" . . . It was like the music—no maybe all the world—was wooing me. Mike and I were dancing, then Link cut in and then Sam, the new boy, and then I was back with Mike again. We were slow dancing. Our bodies were wrapped together swaying to "Nights in White Satin," and it did feel like this bliss would last forever. With all these boys wanting their turn to dance with me, I was a bird soaring over the world.

~~

Now, in June, at an end-of-school beach party, all of us eighth graders were clumped in a circle on the Scheveningen sand, handing around a guitar. One by one, we each played "House of the Rising Sun"—the first song most of us had learned to play on the guitar, back in fifth or sixth grade—and all the rivalries of the last years melted into love. We nestled close, shoulder to shoulder, sprawled, jumbled, and intermingled every which way—interlapping with the sun and sand of the beach. As we played the sad song over and over again, it was as though we were both celebrating ourselves and grieving our soon-to-be-lost childhood.

The ecstasy of last days . . .

In a photo from that day of that final week of school during my last year in Holland, I was lying beside Candy on the sand. In the background, you can see the pier, with its spaceship-topped tower, and a calm sea with gentle, lolloping waves.

Candy and I were sprawled out on our stomachs on top of striped beach towels, our boyfriends lying beside us—Mike and I had been going steady for a couple of months now—and there were other boys and girls flopped on towels surrounding ours. All around us patriotic American kids, crumpled on the sand, were our Dutch miniskirts, our striped Dutch jerseys, and our bottles of Dutch suntan oil. I had on a pair of round hippy George Harrison sunglasses and my Dutch bikini, and there, on that beach, in that picture, looking straight into the camera, I seemed utterly happy.

~~

During this last year in Holland, I feasted on it: the glamour, glitter, and glow of sweet, smug self-satisfaction. I tasted the elixir, the feeling of being just right, popular, *enough*. Of emitting laughter into the air and not caring where it fell. (What is the name of the fairy godmother who appears and, with her wand, changes you from outcast to insider?)

My recently achieved steady relationship with Mike was just one more bit of evidence that I'd made it as a popular girl, but deep inside of me (that sense of truth slipping through my fingers again), I knew there was something wrong, *but what was it?* In some respects, Mike—by nature shy as I was—was simply a vehicle, a status symbol, like wearing a fraternity pin. Our pairing was mostly a stiff sort of affair—a marriage of convenience, like a French noble's. Even though it felt real in some ways—we were beginning to talk about how we felt rather than just gossiping and it *was* a kind of love—in another way, it was all acting something out. But this was murky to me now. For now, I just saw the sand, the sunshine, the boy.

The truth is, in these past few months, I had become the insider, popcorn-eating, all-American girl I'd aimed for. I was also perhaps the least myself that I would ever be—the shallow girl who edged up to the popular girls just to steal their glitter—and later, via a circuitous, painful road, I would have to find my way back, but this state tasted like some sort of melt-in-your-mouth cheesecake, very rare and rich. Maybe there is a kind of genius or triumph to be applauded in stretching as far as you can, like an actress, out of your natural character.

Years onward I would think, as I looked back on it, that this moment of such divine thrill may actually have been the nadir of my life. *Was the belonging more a constriction than a freedom? Was it, rather than a kind of sublime joining, a kind of voluntary self-disposal? Popularity sometimes seems awfully close to emptiness. And*

belonging seems to require excluding somebody else. And how many people did I tram-
ple or claw on my way up to the summit? How does a person atone for such things?

The crux was this: at this moment, this age of thirteen, I was sure I was at the
summit of my life. I had been cut loose from my prison of self-consciousness and I
was in with the in-crowd.

~~

Meanwhile, as I was wheeling, like a bald eagle, over the globe, something had
been happening between my mother and me. As our time to leave Holland drew
nearer—I had to suck down the urge to cry whenever I thought of how few days
I had left—a fury had built up in me. It wasn't as if my mother was doing things
she'd never done before. It was just that now, the same old things she'd always done,
whatever they were—the way she sneezed, the way she put on her nylons, the way
she breathed—made me want to get to the furthest corner of the house. Gone were
the days I absorbed her words like a good girl. My father could do no wrong, but
with regard to my mother, it was like I was a secretive Taiwanese krait, curled up, on
guard, poised, at any moment, to flick its deadly, forked tongue.

One Saturday afternoon, I wanted to go to the centrum with Candy but my
mother said, in her most commanding tone, "No, I want you at home today. I need
you to help me with some things." But I was equally determined. I was dying to see
the new summer dresses on display in the boutiques and I wasn't going to let my
mother stop me. This might be one of the last times I'd get to go downtown with
Candy before we both left Holland.

"You can't make me," I said, standing up straight, and looking right into her
pine needle–grey eyes. As I said the words, cocking my hip—even *I* could hear it—it
was as though I actually *was* Candy and *her* words were coming out of *my* mouth.

"You little brat," my mother said. "Well, you've cooked *your* goose, Young Lady.
That's the last time you'll be going downtown for a while," she called as I tore upstairs and crashed into my room.

Feeling like my fury would grenade all the windows in the house, I hurled myself down on my bedspread with a shriek of anger.

~~

While my mother held the fort and the line, my father struck out for cathedrals
and the sublime. One weekend toward the end of school, he took me to the Mauritshuis, the principal museum of The Hague. It was one of the places to which my

father took me that enabled me to expand bigger than my ordinary self. This was to be my last visit for many, many years.

We strolled through the rooms of paintings that looked like they'd been painted with crushed and liquefied ebony, rubies, and lapis lazuli. First, there were the still life paintings that seemed to burst: full of candy-striped tulips, berries, and caterpillars. Then there were the duskier ones with clocks or candles. These were *vanitas*, still lifes, my father explained: paintings that pointed to the fact that life on earth was temporary. The candles and the clocks, my father said, represented the idea that human existence could be blown out in a single puff. A single puff: I could only half-understand this. *Does my father mean we're all eventually going to die, or does he mean an atom bomb could go off?* I knew he was concerned about our competition with Russia over atomic weapons. In a flicker, the paintings suddenly expressed full-force my dread of leaving Holland and I had to squeeze my eyes to stop from welling.

Shifting to the next room, the art drawing me in, I suddenly recognized that many of these paintings were full of glee. Against the dark backgrounds of the sixteenth-century Dutch paintings, the darkened wood of Dutch farmhouses, and the landscapes of flat, wet land, ordinary people cavorted. The paintings showed jolly women drinking, men playing the pipes, children blowing bubbles, mothers cleaning baby bottoms, and ladies hitting their husbands with shoes. And scroungy dogs slinked around at the bottoms of the paintings. Way back, three hundred years ago even, Dutch people laughed at themselves.

There were the silly paintings of everyday life, and then there were the serious portraits that my father loved most. I watched his lit-up eyes as he took in the luminous faces against shining black walls. One of Van Dyke's portraits showed an elegant woman in pearls and black satin. Rembrandt's portrait of Homer and his straight-in-the-face, serious-eyed self-portraits had, my father said, "a haunting, stark elegance."

The Mauritshuis also had many portraits of girls and young ladies. These were the ones I loved most. Gerrit Dou painted *A Young Woman at a Casement with a Lamp*, a hardy-looking, pink-cheeked girl with light on her fingers. Then there was Michiel Sweerts's *Portrait of a Young Woman*, which showed a shy girl, almost beautiful, with direct eyes shining like the inside of a shell. I could only look at her sideways. It was almost like I was her and she was me. Beauty and liquid pain: they would always be together.

Most riveting of all was *The Girl with the Pearl Earring* by Vermeer. The girl in the saffron dress with the starched white collar, the girl with the soft, intent, unblinking eyes. It was like I could never get to the bottom of her look. The brochure said the painting was one of "ineffable beauty . . . blended from the dust of crushed pearls." I wanted to dive into its beauty, the truth of the girl. My father had to pat my back to lure me to leave the room when it was time to go home.

The Mauritshuis was like a tour of all the faces and places of Holland. I wanted to drink up its paintings—every last one. I wanted to eat the whole museum: every painting and the building, too, so that the beautiful pictures of sadness and happiness, ease and struggle, would become a part of my body.

~~

After the Mauritshuis visit, I had much to ponder. *I will be a painter when I grow up,* I decided—it was firm—*and I will paint everything I see. Then it will be there, and anyone whose eyes light upon it will see what I saw: There is a red bench. There is a pail in the sand. There is a man bowing his head before his wife. There is a boy kicking his feet in the air with tears rolling down his cheeks. There is a girl standing at the side, her back straight like her grandmother's. I will paint and paint and paint until the whole world is on canvas, and then I will die happy.*

~~

I crammed into my mouth three round rusks slathered with rich butter and dotted with chocolate sprinkles—eating as though I could never get enough. Then I went down to the little bakery shop around the corner and bought four boxes of sprinkles, ten Bounty bars, and a sackful of licorice. Later, I took the tram down to the centrum to stock up on other Dutch things I had to buy to take back to the States with me—the things I desperately needed in order to hold the world in place. Once I was downtown, though, in Vroom & Dreesmann, I froze. I couldn't decide what to buy. Nothing was all of Holland.

This moment of decision, in the middle of the department store, this moment of desperate loss and craving, left me greedy, insatiable, for all the countries of the world.

~~

From our years in the Netherlands, in a bucket from a Scheveningen kiosk, I took with me a toss of miscellaneous Dutchisms: a predilection for liberal social policy, a conviction that bicycles are the best way to get around, and an inveterate fondness for cream puffs. My years in the Netherlands left me fierce—almost too loyal—about friendship. And shaped me into, too, the ultimate sponge, the quintessential linguist, a confirmed chameleon, malleable as a spy. I'd been bred, in more ways than I knew, to take on any persona my country might require.

~~

At one of the going-away parties people at the embassy gave for us, the embassy wives presented my mother with a flute-edged silver plate. In the center of the plate were the engraved words, "Every Post Should Have a Lois Taber." In her little acceptance speech to the ladies, my mother joked that we were going home to "The Land of the Big PX." As she talked, holding her plate, sadness flushed through me. I was suddenly puffed with pride, even though a minute before I couldn't stand even the way she breathed. And when my mother came back to her chair, I hugged her so hard I might have broken her ribs. She welled up, said, "It's okay, Sweetie," and hugged me too.

My mother had her silver plate as a tribute to her service in Holland. What did my father feel he'd accomplished in his Dutch time?

"Well, there was a Chinese man I worked with in The Hague who defected after we left but after a time with us, he went back to the other side," my father said forty years later, sitting on the blue corduroy couch, whose ridges were now worn smooth. He always played these keys, these little one-notes of information, very softly. Of course, I didn't know if he was thinking of Mr. Hsu, who died at the foot of the row house, or of another. His tone implied that the defection was something beneficial from the Agency's point of view, but counted little to him.

Nevertheless, I think Holland was where my father found himself—if only to have to leave himself behind. Perhaps because he was sharing the weight with the Dutch, and because he was away from Mr. Smith, his work didn't seem to trouble him as much in Japan and Taiwan. Most of all, Holland seemed to nourish the historian–social philosopher he was meant to be.

~~

The tide was nearly high. It would not be long now before its missive would surface and spill from the sea. Within a year, my father would tell me the truth about his work—a truth so close I could have touched it any time, if I had just known, or been curious enough, to reach out my hand.

The long-held secret would simply slip out into the room, as I imagine my father slipped into and out of an obscure café or airport—and leave its salt, sprinkled, unobtrusive but glittery white, like a necklace at the high tide line.

The secret was wet, though—and would chill us all, in time, through our rocks and sands down to our deepest pits and tissues. The strain on my father, of assumed names, secrets, and unwise missions, would taint us all. It was one of those things that would take a lifetime to make add up.

~~

This June of 1968, my uniform was hippy bell-bottoms and hot-colored tank tops. I was growing my hair long, like Joan Baez and every other girl in Holland. My Villager dresses were long tucked away, and my childhood truths were wavering, like my country back home. I could feel the sap, all the hidden things of the world, pushing up from under the ground, like the tulips.

I was growing up and the world was heating up, as my father's dinner table talks had made plain. In February, the Viet Cong launched the Tet Offensive, attacking hundreds of South Vietnamese towns and American bases, and General Westmoreland, the American commander in Vietnam, had to call up 200,000 more American soldiers to fight. Now there were over 500,000 young American men detailed to the Vietnamese jungle. The war had become fierce, and many Americans were being killed. The Dutch were furious, and President Johnson had even stopped making public appearances in the face of massive antiwar demonstrations back in the States.

And other really terrible things had happened. In April, Rev. Martin Luther King Jr. was murdered. As a result, riots had erupted in 167 towns and cities all over America. And now, Sen. Bobby Kennedy had been assassinated.

~~

For a few more months, disturbing as these events were, they were far away and across an ocean. For a few more months—no more than three—I could continue to remain naïve, as though Santa Claus existed.

In short order, patriotism would no longer seem so simple as eating peanut butter and flinging out sassy comebacks. Soon, the truth—truths of many kinds, about my father, my country, myself—would stare me in the face. As my father had taught me, I would have a chance to prove myself: to look into the mess of the world, face my fears, and take a position.

~~

Meanwhile, as my country was being looted and firebombed across the Atlantic, I, oblivious, was spinning my own little world by the tail. As I joshed and slouched around with perfect embassy daughter confidence, I was sure I knew it all. Even though I had no real picture of America in my mind, I didn't even have to think about what life would be like back in the States. When we got back, people would be welcoming and nice, because, in the States, everyone was friendly. And, of course I would fit in. I would belong without trying. I didn't realize how quickly the princess's robe would slip off my shoulders, or how used I was to being special.

It was fortunate that I couldn't imagine the social challenges lying in wait for me at the elite private school I would be attending. Or how the reality of the war would burn into my heart. Or, for that matter, how soon Washington would spirit us off again—to a rainforest across the Pacific, complete with headhunters. Or how, most potent of all, the poison of my father's secret would concentrate in the years ahead.

~~

The last week that I was in The Hague, on a day of hippo-grey skies, we visited Maria's house for the first time. She had insisted we come for hot chocolate and *koeken*. We ate deep-fried apple balls, sitting in the overstuffed chairs of her living room, and then she said, "Saratje, Andytje, I want to show you something."

She took us up a squeezing, narrow staircase to the very top of the narrow row house. We emerged onto a terrace with a little room occupied by a set of cages set on a bench. Inside were twenty or thirty grey and white doves. She showed us how her husband, "*mijn man*," let them out to fly free, and how they returned for their food each day. As we watched, she let one fat dove out and it flew out over the city roofs.

For the first time, as I watched Maria's dove fly, I realized that Maria had her own life—separate from mine. It came to me that, all the time I had been here, I had been only partly in Holland. I had dwelt mostly in a Victorian house–sized world, serving as an actress in *The American School of The Hague*, a Hollywood movie. The whole world, it turned out, was separate from me. This was something to open my eyes to now, and to discover.

Maria gave us a basket of tulips and hyacinths, and chocolates, and then she began to sob, her big, heavy body sinking against my mother's. Then I began to cry too—looking at Maria's red eyes and red cheeks with the tears wetting them. Suddenly I was flooded by other eyes—Chinese-dark and glistening also—in a long-ago world. Seeing both pairs of eyes, I was nothing like a marine.

~~

Seated on a metal trunk, watching others like it be filled with our belongings, for the first time in my life, I didn't want to leave a place where we had lived. (Holland was the place I lived longest of all the countries of my childhood.) I despised the embassy, and all embassies that were ever created. My whole being collapsed at the thought of leaving my chocolate sprinkle at the edge of Europe, my land of rain-soaked farm fields, of windmills thrumping in the wind, of lumpy wool and apple cake, of Van Gogh, of frigid winter walks by the sea. My chest just would not bear the rupture of never again seeing my Victorian house school, or the best friends that existed in the whole world ever, ever again.

Leaving my land of rain brought on a drought that would last, in some ways, the rest of my life. Forever more, my soil would be cracked, for I was leaving my mud-wallow, the one place I had ever felt completely at home.

This ripping-away from The Hague would instill in me a keen sense of dying, of time ticking. I'd always now have a sense that, no matter how true the friendship, it would eventually vanish. And, as the poet Alison Townsend has written, "No one in our lives can ever really be replaced." From this time onward, I'd be a kind of pigeon that homes in on grief. I'd calm myself, always, with the Dutch word, "dag," the soft Dutch greeting that means both "hello" and "good-bye," the story of my life.

I would travel back with not only The Hague, but Bethesda, Taipei, and Yokosuka—whole countries—packed in my trunk. Can anyone imagine how hard it is to conquer, then embrace whole countries, and soon to have to unlock your arms from those places you have trained yourself to love, and let them go?

~~

My mother tugged out her tattered, old line, "You can do anything for a year," but, to me, it was a rag I wanted to tear apart. I yelled at her, running up to my room, "This is not 'just a year' or 'doing anything'! This is leaving Holland!"

I couldn't be a brave American soldier.

~~

I cried for nine and a half days—from the day the packers came to the day we left town. Then we loaded our thirteen pieces of luggage into our new tan Volkswagen squareback, and I wept all the way to Le Havre. And when my grief was finally spent, something in me was broken. It was the kind of fracture that hurts with the sharpest pain the first time around.

Holland was my first broken heart.

~~

My father held my hand as we looked back over Europe from the deck of the ocean liner, the SS *United States*. "We're going home," he said. "Another great adventure."

When we set sail, the captain blasted the foghorn, and my body started. It was like a pistol shot.

PART II. THE SHORE

Book 4

WAR
Washington, D.C.,
1968–1970

15

america the ugly

These next two years, my fourteenth and fifteenth, spent back in America, made a clean sweep of my sense of America and of myself—and took me on a journey into class and war, a journey I never expected.

A lot of young people have a year or two in their lives—full of emotional sticks and stones that do hurt them—that they somehow manage to erect into serviceable shelter.

~~

It was the summer of the assassinations, and the country was sweltering. The tenements of 14th Street, in Washington, D.C., had been burned into charred, hulking ruins from the riots following the killing of Rev. Martin Luther King Jr. Thirty thousand young Americans had died in the padis of Vietnam and there was no end to the war in sight. From California to the District of Columbia, the country was awash in marijuana-smoking hippies, shouting revolutionaries, and sign-toting peaceniks objecting to the war, and the rooms of the Capitol were a pitched battleground of confused and vociferous politicians. America was ready to boil—and the protected child of a "diplomat" was about to arrive on its shores.

~~

It was 5 a.m. America was a blur. I could just barely see the torch and draped silhouette of the Statue of Liberty through a cool fog as we sailed by on the SS *United States*, but still, my heart trilled.

We disembarked at the dock in New York into what looked like a huge warehouse. In this enormous, vacuous Quonset hut with a concrete floor, we waited, our good clothes wilting in the humidity, for our trunks to be trundled down from the stateroom. Then we waited again for our new VW squareback to be disgorged from what my father called "the bowels of the ship." By the time we loaded the car, it was 11 a.m., and five minutes after we got on our way, Andy said, "Okay Pop, time to stop at McDonald's."

"Yeah, you promised, Pop," I said.

My father heaved a big fake sigh and said, "Oh, all right," and he pulled into the first hamburger joint we came across: golden arches set deep in the grime of the city amid high-rising rusted girders and boarded-up buildings. Hamburgers, fries: *Ah! The glorious taste of America!* Then, bellies slopping with chocolate milkshakes, we began the long drive down the New Jersey Turnpike.

These were my first views of America: not beauteous waves of grain or a Bierstadt canvas of magnificent mountains, but the under-bridge of New York and the grim, endless, traffic-streaming asphalt aisle of the New Jersey Turnpike.

~~

We hauled our suitcases and trunks into the elevator at the Alban Towers, a dusty and dreary Gothic apartment hotel near the National Cathedral that reeked of cleaning fluids and seemed to be inhabited by old ladies in house dresses with odd smirks and twitches. When I read *Rosemary's Baby* later in the year, the Alban Towers would come to mind.

Soon after we settled into the grim billet, the *Washington Post,* which my father fetched from the desk each morning, had a big headline that said Richard Nixon had won the Republican nomination for president in Miami. Neither I nor the country had any clue as to what was in store.

While my parents went out house hunting, Andy and I stayed in the hotel with the large, dark rooms of brown scratchy furniture, a dim space inside Venetian blinds, as the window air conditioners grinded away. For the six weeks of waiting for my new life to begin, I watched *As the World Turns* and *Days of Our Lives.* I hadn't watched TV in five years—I'd lost a whole hunk of American culture forever—and I was magnetized. I'd never seen soap operas and was entranced by the unfailingly beautiful Americans engaged in crisscrossed loves, betrayals, unwanted pregnancies, and disastrous illnesses. People in my country seemed so good-looking, rich, and lucky, even with all their troubles.

When my programs were over, I wrote to Lizzy, Candy, and Mike, and ate heads of iceberg lettuce cut in half. This food, cool and the lightest of green—dolloped with ranch dressing—was safe and soothing to me.

Sometimes, between my soap operas, I checked different channels to see what was on. Often, shots of soldiers wading through swamps or shooting rifles from scrubby hills appeared on the screen, and even though Andy wanted to watch, I changed the channel to commercials. "War is dumb," I told him.

On August 20, between programs, I dialed the channels and again happened on the news. I watched, munching my lettuce wedge, as, on the screen, Soviet tanks rumbled into somewhere in Europe. Andy made me keep the news on, and in the evening, when he asked our father about it, he explained that there had been an uprising of liberals in Communist Czechoslovakia and the stricter Russian Communists had gone in to crush it. "Now the Soviet Communist party boss, Leonid Brezhnev, has warned that the USSR will attack any Communist government in the Eastern Bloc that doesn't conform to its way of doing things."

For a fleet instant, thinking of the liberals who had been killed or jailed, he had that haunted look again, that look of remembering things unutterably sad. But then, like he was dragging himself out of a faraway capsule, he gathered himself and said, "Prague Spring was a real bid for freedom."

The word "freedom" sent my blood tingling: that fine George Washington word.

~~

One day, my parents took us to see one of the houses they'd found. It was a small white bungalow in Chevy Chase. I pleaded with them to buy this one over the few others they'd shown us. I wanted this house because it had one bedroom with a pink carpet and a pink Princess phone, another bedroom with a powder blue rug and a powder blue Princess phone, and a tan living room with a tan rug and tan Princess phone. I didn't realize that the house wouldn't have the phones when we moved in and that my parents would choose one black rotary dial phone for the kitchen.

One sweltering August day, my parents took me for an interview at a private school, a Quaker school, a kind of school I'd never heard of before. The admissions office was situated in a stately brick house with beams of white light glancing off the clean windows. For the interview, I was ushered into a grand room with a fireplace at one end. I talked with a tall man in a tweed jacket and tie, with big hands. We sat in upright wing chairs and he leaned toward me slightly and listened closely as he asked me questions. I answered but barely knew what I said. I was still in a blur, half in Holland and half at the Alban Towers, not really in America at all.

When I was accepted into the private school, my mother asked me whether I'd prefer Sidwell Friends School or Bethesda–Chevy Chase High School, the big public school we'd peeked into the windows of—to see bare classrooms with desks pushed up against the walls. I didn't have any idea how to make such a decision. I couldn't conceive, really, of what difference it might make to go to either public or private school. "You decide," I said. Thus, the Fates chose for me one kind of America over another.

We moved into the little cottage on Ridgewood Avenue, and my parents enrolled us in the two different private schools where we'd been accepted. Andy wasn't accepted to my school and I was too old for his. I would attend the inside-the-beltway bastion of Capitol Hill politicos' children and Andy would be going to the Potomac School, a country day school with uniforms across the river in Virginia where Bobby Kennedy's children went—two different flavors of the liberal elite.

My mother and father believed education was the most important thing in life. My father treasured learning and "the life of the mind" above anything else. It might have looked crazy to other people that he and my mother, who lived on a government salary, would spend all their money on private school, but, to them, a fine education was the greatest gift you could give your children. It was a thing that would enrich their lives forever, and could never be taken away—unlike money or belongings.

Paying for private education was nothing to my parents; sacrificing for their children was second nature to them. They bought us new school clothes at Woodward & Lothrop while they ironed the old, frayed clothes they had had forever. My mother wore an old pair of British sandals from Hong Kong that she said she still loved even though the leather was so dry it was tearing, and my father wore his old Hong Kong desert boots run slanted at the crepe heels.

~~

August 29, at the new house, I was in the TV room, still cluttered with half-unpacked crates. Our new TV was unpacked, so I plopped down on a sealed box and looked for something good to watch. There was nothing on so I just settled on the news. My father had told us this was a critical day. The Democratic Convention, to choose the Democratic presidential nominee, was being held in Chicago. From my crate I watched as, outside the Hilton Hotel where the convention was being held, policemen were beating crowds of shouting, rock-throwing long-haired hippies with clubs and rifle butts, and loading them into vans. Someone on TV shouted, above the din, something about the police and the "Nazi Gestapo." What was all this? I'd seen lots of rowdy hippies in Holland but I didn't know they had them in America too. This was a different country than the Bermuda shorts–and–cowboys hats America in which I'd lived in 1963.

Over TV dinners from the A & P, my father explained that hundreds of young people and revolutionary groups had gathered in Chicago to protest the war in Vietnam and try to influence the Democrats. "The Chicago police tried to prevent the protestors from entering the amphitheater where the convention was being held, and the police got out of hand. Seven hundred people were injured. The hippies were throwing rocks and bottles at the police, but the police should not have retaliated so forcefully. It's a very complex situation, with fault on both sides."

When vice president Hubert Humphrey finally gained the Democratic nomination, amid the tumult, my father looked satisfied. "He's a good man, an old-fashioned, yellow dog Democrat," he said. My father's confident tone reassured me: America always righted itself and was always right in the end.

~~

My father was back at the State Department China Desk. He was gone late a lot at meetings and he heaved a sigh of relief when he walked in the door. When he was home, he seemed more preoccupied than he had when we were in Holland, and grimmer. He tiredly ran his hand through his thick hair and shook his head. "At the office it's just Saigon, Saigon," he told Mom.

To us, he said, "The poor Vietnamese are just tinder for the Cold War bonfire." I imagined two immense puppet figures, one of Chairman Mao and the other of Uncle Sam, heaving immense logs on a raging fire yelling, "Take that!" and "No, you take that!"

My mother was working as a physical therapist again. She was a missionary or a peace corps volunteer at heart, and, in some ways, she was happier here working with people with disabilities than she had been translating in Holland, though she'd loved The Hague. She said, "I know I've had a good day when someone's life was made better by my having touched it." While her patients told her stories of the Holocaust or society dinners, she forced them to lift their weak legs one more time, and this helped them become stronger. My father was a Rembrandt portrait of noble sacrifice and she was a Winslow Homer, depicting the triumph of hard work and willpower.

Andy, who was losing his puppy fat, gobbled up history book after history book, and cocked his head in thought as he asked my father about the Battle of the Somme, or the Normandy invasion, or Dien Bien Phu.

~~

So that my mother could keep the VW for her commute to her physical therapy job, my father bought a battered red tin-can Fiat with backward doors that had been advertised on the bulletin board at his office. The plan was this: my father would drive me to school first each morning. My school was closest to home—just down Wisconsin Avenue from Maryland into the District. Then he would drive across the Potomac, drop Andy at his school, and turn back across the river on the Roosevelt Bridge to the State Department.

Right up to the last moment before my father's astonishing revelation, it never occurred to me to question this morning routine. My father had always put himself out for me and I wasn't conscious of the great inconvenience this route would cause him. I certainly didn't consider that my father might be telling me a lie, nor did I have any clue that the Central Intelligence Agency was three blocks from Andy's school. My father's secret was tossing about in the waves that were now licking at the high tide line. I could have easily plucked it out of the water but I was oblivious. Only my little brother picked up the slips and asides, the telltale whispers in the tide.

~~

Late, empty summer, the cool, promising fog of New York harbor; the pleasant—if scratchy—limbo of the Alban Towers; and the green, open-ended hopefulness of house hunting paled. As I walked around our new leafy neighborhood beside the old frame bungalows with porches and stately brick colonials, I felt nervous about my new life in America, which hadn't yet taken any sort of shape. I told myself things like, "It'll be fine. I was popular in Holland. Why shouldn't it be like that here? After all, this is America, *my* country."

~~

Finally, to my relief and dread, the first day of school arrived. My mother gave us hugs at the door. Then she kissed my father and said, "Have a good day at the State Department, Honey." Her eyes twinkled with meaning as she said it, and her mouth smiled at him in a lopsided way.

As we drove the Fiat up to the school on busy Wisconsin Avenue, girls in white blouses and maroon tunics—with maroon bloomers that showed when their skirts flicked up as they dashed back and forth—were hitting balls with sticks on the front playing field. To me they looked like students of a British boarding school. A little shiver of interest ran through me. My father gave my shoulder a squeeze and said, "Just be yourself and they'll love you, Girl-child. This is a new, grand adventure. Just wait and see."

While I fumbled at my locker in the long building, the kids rushing past me in an endless river, I picked up snatches of conversation. A couple of boys wearing ties and jackets with hair flowing over their collars were whispering about "grass," and I heard a kid in pants that dragged on the floor exclaim to another, "that motherfucker," a nasty-sounding expression I'd never heard before. When the teachers—in beards or sacklike dresses—walked into the classroom, they stood at the front and opened the class with a moment of silence. The kids called some of the teachers by their first names, and the teachers put their feet up on their desks.

I blurred through my first two classes. As I stepped out into the hall after the second one, my English class, the river of kids eddied around a whirlpool of girls, one of whom had been in class with me. The girls' hair reached down to their derrières, as Gabrielle would have said, and they were a-shimmer with fluorescent colors in their minidresses. The girl from class moved over slightly to make room so I could edge into the circle. The girls were all talking about a program I had never heard of. Their sentences bumped up against and overlapped each other so fast that I could never have gotten a word in even if I had had something to say. One said, "Yeah, and remember when the fuzz cornered that dude . . . ," and another said, "Man, what a cool cat," and someone else said, "Yeah, and then the pig opened the door and that chick got arrested." I stood and nodded and laughed when the others did, but I was in the dark. I might just as well have been standing in a group of Russians or Egyptians, for all I could understand or contribute.

Late morning, I followed the crowd to Meeting for Worship, the Quaker religious service. My father told me I'd have "silent meeting," a time for reflection, once a week, and that it would be interesting. We all sat outside on the lawn behind Zartman House, the admissions building, and everyone was silent, except for two teachers who stood up toward the middle of the hour. One, a man, looked sad: "Like all of you, I am very preoccupied by what is happening in Southeast Asia. Today I am hoping for a lull in the fighting." A lady teacher said, "I'm deeply concerned about what our country has become. I hope we can work together this year to bring about change."

The kids shuffled around when the teachers spoke and then everyone looked down again and picked at the grass. I felt the hard, grassy earth under my legs and listened to what the teachers said, but I was too nervous among all these jazzy, hippie-ish kids to feel contemplative, and I didn't even know how to think about the war in Vietnam or about an America that needed to change.

~~

At a free period, I stepped into the Common Room, the space in the center of the building. I'd gathered it was the place people went between classes and where the students convened for assemblies or to make decisions about "the school community." I stepped through the doorway into a furniture-less, wall-to-wall expanse of carpet with pillows thrown around against which kids were sprawling every which way. Girls with hair like Rapunzel's were lounging against shaggy boys. Trios of handsome, lanky boys were caucusing on their bellies, their legs like the spokes of bicycles; a couple of boys were flopped out, asleep; pairs of girls were huddled together in deep, intimate whispering. At this sight of people engaged in intent conversation, a lightning jag of fear zigzagged through me. I edged backward out of the room. Safely in the hall, my heart slowed in my chest. I'd avoid setting foot in the Common Room for months, even when I didn't have class; the place was so pungent with intimidating cool.

The kids at Sidwell, with their Indian headbands, their moppy hair, and their high-lifted, laughing faces, seemed both the height of chic and remote as Indian braves—and worldly wise. When later in the month our biology teacher Mr. Pond demonstrated in the air, with a packet marked Trojan, how to open and put a condom on a penis, everyone acted nonchalant, like they already knew all about it.

Here, in this fancy school, everyone seemed self-contained and removed and, most of all, confident. Years later, I'd read Chilean poet Marjorie Agosín's comment on the people she met when she took up a professorship at Wellesley College. "Calm and indifference seemed the hallmarks of proper behavior in New England." At my new Quaker school, likewise, a cool, detached self-assurance seemed the required mien.

I traveled home on the city bus feeling small and drab in a world of the flashy and cool. I felt worn out, chastened by my American school.

~~

At seven o'clock, when my father came home in his work-rumpled khaki suit, he gave me a long hug that let me know he knew how hard it was to be new.

"It's not a good adventure," I said.

"It just takes time," he said. "Come tell me about it while I change my shirt."

When I explained how hard it was to talk to people, my father said, "Just be true to yourself. Be the good person you are. It will all work out."

At dinner, my father listened to my description of Meeting for Worship—"Really weird," Andy's report on school—"I hate having to keep my shirt tucked in," and my mother's day with her patients—"Mrs. Goldstein was cranky but I badgered her into taking three steps without her cane and she was proud of herself."

When my mother asked my father about the office, he said, "I like the contact with the Chinese, but it's life at Headquarters—you know what it's like." This meant the office was full of bureaucracy, territoriality, scheming, politics, cleaving to the current ideology, and watching your rear. My mother understood this, but I didn't have a clue.

Now my father said, skipping forward to the national political situation, "Things are really hot in Saigon. No one seems to have the answer. In The Hague I couldn't see how bad it was. I've never seen the place so divided between Hawks and Doves, and Ho seems to hold all the cards. Jackson, of course, is stomping around the office railing about Communists. All this, on top of the election . . ."

"And what do you think about it all, Charles?"

"I'm not sure yet."

Afterward, my father settled into the green wing chair and, as usual, read the paper. He sighed as he rattled the pages, and ran his hand through his bristly hair. I did my math homework and was too much a tight-rolled ball of yarn to wonder what he'd meant at dinner, and what it was he was reading that troubled him so.

I cried all night—for Lizzy, Mike, and Mr. Leonard.

~~

I was right to miss my past self and to be filled with loneliness and dread, for in the next few months, my new American school yanked out of the ground all the pegs to which I'd staked my little Army Surplus pup tent of confidence. In short order, Sidwell upheaved the store of surety I'd built up in my ability to express my-self through art, my ability to forge friendships with girls, and my attractiveness to boys—and my sense of belonging in my country.

I eventually found my footing—all transitions are toppling—but this, in my own country, was the most challenging of my childhood.

~~

In art class, on the second day of school, the teacher, a lady the shape of a short, stout vase, with snowy hair, flat bulbous shoes, and a commanding, pert look, looked at my drawing of a tree and announced, "You've never had any art training, have you?" I wouldn't take art again in high school until the last term of my senior year, when I was far away across the Pacific Ocean.

That was the first peg of my little pup tent expeditiously knocked out of the ground.

~~

The next peg: friendships with girls.

Over and over again through the coming weeks, as I walked down the long hallways, I passed closed circles: circles of maidens with long gold and brown tresses who shone with the buttery glow of belonging. Girls with a golden shine around them like around Jesus and Mary in a medieval painting. I dubbed them "The India Girls" because of their gorgeous dresses from South Asia.

~~

One day I was standing at the rim of the golden circle of the India Girls. Hedley, the queen of chic poverty, was gesturing expansively with her long, skinny arms. Her bangles tinkled with her enthusiasm. She was facing Alex, Francie, and Vita.

"My parents are out of town," she said, an excited hush in her voice. "James, Jonathan, Flynn, and Brian are coming. So it'll be four cats and four chicks. I've got the dope in my closet. It'll be a rush," she said.

I had heard that Hedley had a big house in the woods near Rock Creek Park, where kids went to play the guitar, smoke hash, and make love. In Holland we got together and ate popcorn.

After Hedley waved her arm like a golden wing that swept the three other girls within its protection, and said, "Let's split," the four girls disappeared down the hall, heads together, hair swinging like charms on the golden bracelet that was them. I could hear Hedley's laugh, trickling like a brook.

It was like I was born, back there at the beginning, at the foot of the Great Buddha of Kamakura, and dunked into a bath of envy for American kids who automatically belonged.

When I heard months later, via gossip, that Hedley was seeing a psychiatrist, I was filled with disdain. It seemed like a self-indulgence or an affectation of the wealthy. I didn't realize she could be suffering. I believed her devil-may-care air.

And I certainly couldn't imagine that I would, myself, be seeing a psychiatrist within a couple of years.

It was a mercy that Hedley hadn't invited me to her party as I'd have been swimming in water way over my head. At this point in my life, I'd have been far more comfortable in a party of foreign adult diplomats than in a room of my American peers, sprawling on couches, talking smooth, and sucking joints. But left here standing in the hall, watching the quartet flounce away, I wanted to hide in a dirt hole. What I'd suspected was true: I would never figure out how to make friends in America.

Two pegs yanked, my canvas started to luff.

~~

In the kitchen where we were doing the dishes, I heaved all my despair onto my mother: my frustration at being alone, at wanting to fit in and not fitting in, at girls who didn't acknowledge my presence.

"Don't worry, Sweetie," she said while I scraped the plates furiously into the sink where the disposal could roar them down. "The friends will come. . . . You can do anything for a year."

"Don't say that all the time! No, they won't. Not at this place!" and "No, I can't!" I hurled back.

I turned to my father, who was drying the frying pan.

"I hate it here," I said.

"Oh Girl, come here," he said, putting down the skillet to put his arms around me. "It'll get better. Give it time."

"I wish I were a different person," I said. "I wish my name was Sam."

The next evening, when he came in the door after work, he yelled out, "Hey Sam, where are you?" and I couldn't suppress the momentary delight. My father was the one star that was always visible in the sky.

~~

One more devastation to go.

While in Holland boys had taken an interest in me—and an afternoon with a Dutch boy on skates had spurted a charge of glory and hope through my body—in America it was as if boys had receded. In the face of Sidwell boys, seemingly so cool and indifferent, my dreams of romance had to go underground, all those exuberant "BOYS" signs I taped to the solid walls of my Dutch bedroom now attached to clouds.

But an event at school stirred my stifled yearning. It was time for the Sadie Hawkins Dance, and the India Girls were all aquiver. By the week of the dance, the popular boys were all doled out, except for one who had (how had that happened?) fallen through the cracks. Channing was one of the alpha boys, one of the kings. He was tall, he had shiny Beatle hair, and he strutted with the supreme confidence of the offspring of the wealthy. He had been at the school since birth. He was a portrait of cool—way too Washington-insider for the likes of me, a Foreign Service kid. But somehow—the Fates are playful—one of the India Girls decided that I should ask Channing to the dance, and the others chimed in.

This thoughtfulness on the part of one of the India girls, as it turned out, had inadvertent, unfortunate consequences.

Somehow—this was all a cloud—every part of me hesitant, but all my self-preservation instincts having flown in the whirl of the India Girls' certainty, I found the courage to ask Channing to the dance and somehow—Was he repelled? Was he being polite?—he said yes. Then came the agony of sitting on the wall in front of the school, eating the McDonald's burgers, and my tortured efforts at conversation. "What did you think of *Beowulf?*" There were about forty-five minutes when I felt naked and gagged, and also like I'd shown up in a tight, conservative suit at a hippie picnic—and then, when the dance was about to start, Channing vanished.

Like a naïf, I looked for him around the school for ten minutes and then, in the cream-walled hall outside my English class, a kind boy, Colin, told me, his eyes sorry, "Channing went home."

My tent flapping loose, anchored now to a single peg, I stumbled to the school telephone and my parents picked me up in the Fiat. I didn't tell them what happened, but I cried, heaving, on my father's lap, until I was limp-dry and could fall asleep.

~~

Exquisite shame. At school, I felt like that kid in the Chinese crowd again. Circled, plucked clean, mocked.

Cringe, slink, crawl. Humiliation is a burning inside, and then a squishiness. A frantic need to hide, a desperate need to disappear through a crack into a new world. Where was the quicksand—or the Foreign Service—when you needed it?

~~

After the smarting shame subsided, a thudding heaviness took up residence in my body. Often now, through my days at school, there was a sensation of cloudiness in my eyes. I could only look into the far distance, toward the sky. Or I could look down at my own hands. I couldn't and didn't want to see the middle distance where the people were. I could only be alone—inside this body, this autistic cage of myself. The outer world seemed too dangerous, too close, too judgmental.

And all day I felt so tired, so very tired. My limbs seemed weighted differently—like my bones were made of stone, my muscles gone lax. And it was as though there were cold pebbles rolling around in the cold, sour emptiness of my belly.

After an evening cry, cleaned out, sniffling the last of the tears, I spent hours looking at photos of Holland, caressing my gone-away life, the life where I was liked, where I was alive.

Depression had set up base camp in my body. It was a potent liqueur in my brain. All the dislocations and stretches of feeling marginal had been a slow drip that now, with these latest yanked moorings, became a steady flow. The losses had risen and finally filled the glass. I was receiving my first sip of concentrated melancholia, the nectar of tristesse. It had a lemon-sour taste, not entirely unpleasant.

With time I curled into it and depression became a sort of fascination, a romance, my partner in a dance. Any speck of sorrow became grist for my mill. I craved sad stories like chocolate-chip cookies. I read *Death Be Not Proud* and *A Separate Peace*, archetypal tales of teenage loss. Sad tales were my rice, my comfort food.

But out of darkness comes brightness. In a strange way, my new sadness opened up doors to the girls at school. It was fashionable to be depressed, to brood. The India Girls wailed on each other's shoulders, "I'm so depressed!" and now I could join in.

~~

Evenings, at home, my father tried to distract me. One night he handed me the *Washington Post*. "Just have a look at the front page," he said. I looked at a photo of sweat-faced young men in camouflage wading through a jungle stream with rifles cradled in their arms. I thought of some of the upperclassmen at school who were all whipped up, carrying around a *Life* magazine article that showed the photographs of 250 American soldiers killed in a week. They put up posters with slogans on them like "Make Love, Not War" or "Girls Say Yes to Boys Who Say No." They handed out flyers about conscientious objection, draft resistance, and Quaker conferences on peace.

I showed my father the picture of GIs. "What do you think about Vietnam, Pop?"

My father shook his head and said something that seemed off-topic. "I'm not sure we're spending our money the right way. With our resources and talents we could be an unstoppable force for good in the world. We could feed everyone on the planet, or end poverty if we put our minds to it."

My brooding self vanished; for an instant I was engaged. "Why doesn't America do that?"

"Our government has other priorities right now," he said. "But don't you worry. It'll be all right." But he didn't say it with conviction, and I was still confused.

"There's somethin' happening here. What it is ain't exactly clear. There's a man with a gun over there. Tellin' me I got to beware. . . ."

~~

It was strange. America was both too familiar and not familiar enough. Being here was like being with a cousin who shared some of your genes but from whom you had lived so far away that you didn't really know her at all. Though I looked American, I was not; I was a sort of clandestine foreigner. It was like the Canadians said, "You think we're just like you, but we don't feel like you."

This was supposed to be my culture, but I didn't know how to interact. Embassy kids were taught to be diplomatic, to make others feel comfortable by expressing interest in them, so I asked kids about themselves, but kids here didn't reciprocate. At Sidwell, when I told my classmates that I'd just come from Holland, they said, "Oh, really?" And that was the end of the conversation. Over time, I'd given up. I'd learned that Holland—my past, my self—could be and only was a private place.

The big hitch was, while most Americans were simply here in America, *being*, I was stuck comparing. I knew I could be in Japan or Taiwan, and that it would be different. Having lived abroad, I could *see* America from the outside—therefore, I couldn't just *be* American. I couldn't be *in* the movie.

~~

The kids at Sidwell had an unfamiliar ease, an offhand sophistication, a stance that said, "I deserve." They gave off a flitting scent, like a rare and faraway rose on the breeze. I couldn't identify it as such—elitism is something you sense beneath your epidermis, like an invisible river of liquid diamonds—but I was face to face with American privilege in concentrated form, the hidden American class system, for the first time in my life. Sidwell, it turned out, was a petri dish for the children of the elite. It was disarming and perplexing because these people appeared un-ostentatious, in their sloppy clothes and sloppy postures, but actually Sidwell was a castle of the powerful, ambitious, and status-conscious. I'd been around ambas-sadors, generals, foreign princes, and oil tycoons, but this was different. These were princes and princesses of a new stripe. My mother was confident in her work, my father had an important job, and I was proud of them, but these counted little in this sea of kids whose fathers were inside-the-Beltway TV journalists, lawyers, and politicians. Easier the brute, boasting wealth of Texan oil tycoons than the smooth, subtle exclusions of Washington insiders.

American wealth is hard to sink your teeth into. It doesn't look like European privilege. You know when an English person is wealthy—she speaks with a dis-tinctive crispness and wears cashmere and pearls, or when a Chinese person is wealthy—she wears rich navy or dark grey satin and sleek hair up in a bun, but in America it is hard to see. The differences are as infinitesimal and subtle as the hand of a watch—there is just something a little more exquisitely frayed about their jeans, a shift in the voice when they mention their cottage on Nantucket—and I wouldn't have a clue even that these giveaways existed, much less how to read them, until years later. I didn't have a clue that America was not the pure meritocracy it claimed to be. In graduate school, in the late 1980s, I would interview female tenured professors at Harvard and be told by each one her feelings of never being quite good enough—not being tall, male, or a Cabot or Lodge. And I couldn't have said I felt marginal at Sidwell. I just felt lesser, like I didn't have a right. I was just blundering along in the midst of them, wondering why I was feeling out of place: a bewildered middle-class kid struggling to stay afloat in a sea of privilege.

~~

It wouldn't be until twenty years later that I'd discover, at a gathering that in-cluded other Sidwell alums, that I hadn't been the only one. Other students, too—even some in the in-crowd—felt marginal and unintelligent in that subtly competi-tive world of burnished Washingtonians. And it wouldn't be until I entered social work school that I'd become acquainted with the concept of relative wealth: the notion that the sense of well-being is comparative. If you belong to social groups made up of people with your own economic status, you have a sense of well-being. If you are surrounded by those who are more wealthy, no matter how well off you might be relative to the whole of society, you feel poor.

~~

"There are no nice people at Sidwell," I announced to my father at home.

"Sure there are," he said. "There are good people everywhere." My father believed that people were basically good, that all human beings were the same inside, and, an idealist, he believed class shouldn't matter. He believed good people looked beyond upbringing and economic status to the person within.

But he also seemed to know, without my saying anything, what was going on—that while people are all the same inside, they can also be different, at least outside. (As I'd realize much later, he had an even steeper situation at his work: a clique of chummy Yalies to contend with, but he was better able to ignore than I.) He quoted Fitzgerald: "The rich are different," and he played for me his record of Carl Sandburg's *The People Yes* in which the poet quotes Iphicrates, the Athenian general and son of a shoemaker: "My family begins with me. Your family ends with you."

"You're as smart and kind and pretty as anyone there," he asserted, squeezing me tight. "The equal of anyone." I felt a little lighter, but I was still a lone leaf drifting in the fall air.

~~

I was walking down Maple Avenue by my new house. High, glorious trees were tipped with red, yellow, and orange, but each tree merely set the world afire with a Dutch memory. The huge oaks were golden like the Dutch sky just after a storm and the sun was blended with cloud, the maple leaves were the color of the wax on aged Gouda cheese. The leaves that were still green took me to the greenness of spring in the park up Duinweg where I took Gracie every afternoon. My whole body longed to be back in The Hague with a slanting rain coming down, hearing the snap of my boots on the cobbles.

If I closed my eyes I *could* be there. Shutting my eyes on the bed of my pink, closed bedroom, I was transported to my spacious Dutch room, sitting on my high bedstead, with the pineapple finials standing up, perky, like guards. The door of my wardrobe with the long mirror was a little bit open, displaying my history: the tiered skirt in the Indian wigwam print that I wore nearly everyday when I was ten, the candy-striped, empire-waist dress I wore to parties when I was eleven, the chartreuse miniskirt I bought in a boutique downtown when I was twelve, and the dress made of light blue eyelet that my mother had tailored for my eighth grade graduation. To my left, through the door into the bathroom, I could see the rounded edge and one of the rusted ball-and-claw feet of the tub where I soaked each night in a veil of steam. To the right were the French doors, looking out into the rainy grey.

I saw a zigzag of lightning in the sky. In a few minutes, a slit in the grey sky widened and down poured a lighthouse beam of yellowy-blue. In this beam, I lay like a lounging lioness. *I will just stay here*, I drowsed. *I will pretend Washington is not here, and will stay in Holland all day long.*

I was in a strange sea, holding on for dear life to something I loved so much that my fingers could not let it go. I was clinging to the wooden bowsprit of a bucking ship that was trying to shake me into the frigid waters. I *had* to hold on or everything that I had loved, everything that ever felt comfortable, that ever felt like home, would be gone.

All day long so many things made me want to cry: a lousy American pastry, a brick wall. Every time a European or Dutch place or person was mentioned—Van Gogh, Carnaby Street, Gouda cheese. I ached for black afternoons.

16
words

Things were tense at school, and in the country. Just before the election, my father showed me the headline: President Johnson had announced a halt to all bombing of North Vietnam. The Republican presidential nominee, Richard Nixon, claimed that he had a plan to "end the war and win the peace" in Vietnam. My father said he doubted the validity of the claim since Nixon wouldn't divulge any of its particulars. "He's a dangerous man—another virulent anti-Communist. His plan probably consists of threatening the Communists with more aggression." My father's lips were tight. For a moment, this made me halt in my self-centered tracks.

~~

Exclusion is a bruising you learn from. Like a good soldier, my job was to swallow reality and forge ahead. After Sadie Hawkins, I gave up for the time being. A tent becomes a dead flag if it has only one peg, so I struck my old shelter and fashioned a little hermit's hut of sticks and mud.

My father tried to tempt me out of my dejection with thoughts about the world while I dumped my bottled-up frustration on my mother's head.

~~

I'd just settled in to read my biology homework. My mother called up the stairs, "Sara, come set the table."

I was annoyed at being interrupted so I dawdled, knowing I was making my mother mad. The truth was, this gave me a cheap little shot of pleasure. I wanted her to feel angry. I couldn't stand any piece of her now that we were in America because she was glad we were here. Even though she made me tuna sandwiches with just the right amount of mayonnaise, like I liked them, and folded them lovingly in wax paper, she seemed to embody all that I hated in the world.

She came charging up the stairs. "Sara, when I say I need you, it means I need you right this minute."

"I'm busy. Why do I have to?"

"Because I told you to," she said, her eyes flaring.

~~

Now suddenly at home I was arguing all the time. At dinner I tried out the new ideas that were swirling around me at school and in the American ether—Sidwell was seeping into me in spite of myself—ideas I knew my mother would object to. Arguing with her made me feel alive and powerful, instead of like an ant skittering at the feet of the important.

"I believe in premarital sex," I announced one day as we ate soy sauce chicken, even though I was light years from even touching a Sidwell boy.

My mother took the bait. "Oh you do, do you?"

"If two people love each other, why shouldn't they get to know each other in every way to make sure they're right for each other before they commit for life? Look at all the divorces that result from the wrong people marrying each other," I said, as if I were a sociologist.

My mother was hot in the face. "Young girls should save themselves for marriage," she said. "Making love is sacred. And boys don't like used goods. . . . You watch out, Young Lady. Girls who sleep with their boyfriends live to regret it."

"I won't believe it even if you prove it," I said. This was my new favorite line.

My father laughed. "That's silly, Sara. But she might have a point, Lois. Look at the divorce rate."

This made my mother even madder. "She needs to treat me with respect."

Andy slipped out of his seat and went off to read his new American history book by the fireplace.

"It's okay for her to question," my father said. "She's fourteen," but his voice was almost inaudible. And my mother said, "Watch your mouth, Young Lady."

After the fight, when my mother was on the phone, my father came up to my room where I was furiously clutching my Delft wooden shoe, breathing hard, trying to find a ration of patience. He sat on the bed beside me. He said, "You need to be polite to Mom, but you keep on thinking for yourself. It's okay to explore ideas." But we knew he couldn't let on in front of my mother. It was almost like my connection to my father was secret, and he had to choose to defend either me or my mother.

~~

Another night, I tried out another idea.

"Marijuana should be legalized," I said, righteous as a right-wing hawk. "It's stupid to waste prison space on people who've just smoked a little pot." I acted like I knew all about drugs.

My mother left the table.

My father said, "You might like to think that through a little more."

~~

One evening, following a talk on American poverty at school, I fixed on my father. I knew he could withstand any amount of defiance I might summon. "Why is America like this? Why can't America be like Holland—doing things that are good simply because they are the right thing to do? Why can't we make our country the model of good things: the best schools, the best health care, the most leisure, the best research, the most kindness? . . . Or why can't we be like Sweden?" He had often told me about Dag Hammarskjöld and Gunnar Myrdal, and how in Sweden there were few differences between rich and poor.

"How can America be this way—spending all its money on defense when it makes no sense?" I said.

~~

I lay flat on my bed, thinking nonstop. *Why do I have to be here? Why do I have to go wherever the government wants Pop to go?*

The next night, as my mother was putting meatloaf on the table, I made my announcement. The moment she sat down, I blurted, "I hate America. I am going back to Holland. I am going to babysit to earn enough money, and then next summer I am going back." My voice was assertive and strong the way it never was at school. And my sentence sitting there in the air gave me hope, made me feel like I could accomplish anything in the world. My parents looked at each other, and my mother said, "All right. If you earn the money, you can go."

Immediately I started babysitting. My announcement gave me a heady surge of power, but the babysitting was hard work.

~~

On November 5, Richard Nixon was elected president. The next day at school, everyone was stomping around saying this was bad news for America. "He only won by one percent of the vote! The war is going downhill, and Nixon is going to make it worse." And their fathers should have known; many of them were Capitol Hill politicians and newsmen.

~~

A night after the election, my parents' friends, the Grays, came over to drink beer and eat Chinese hot pot. As they fished bits of beef, mushrooms, and Chinese cabbage out of the simmering broth, and dipped their loaded chopsticks in the sauces they'd mixed of mustard, soy sauce, peanut butter, and sesame oil, they talked first about the election, and then, as always, the conversation shifted to Vietnam. Everyone was concerned Nixon would bomb North Vietnam to smithereens.

Mr. Gray said, "The people at State are taking the position that there's a good chance of defeating Ho. Our guys on the ground think there's a snowball's chance in hell. . . ."

I didn't think anything of these words about "State" and "our guys," but I noticed Andy was listening carefully while reading his book on Vietnam over in his chair by the fireplace. The secret swirled like the mushrooms in the broth.

~~

In the barren world of my school, in spite of Mom's advice to do just this, I kept busy and focused on my studies. I was getting all As and would probably be on the Dean's List. Grades weren't a full meal, but at least they were some peanuts and crackers. And I turned to the printed word: books are hearty soup. Loneliness has its compensations.

~~

"She, suddenly pitiful, broke off a twig with three or four wan flowers and held them against her face. . . ."

My English teacher, Mr. Oates, was reading from D. H. Lawrence's short story, "Odour of Chrysanthemums." The protagonist of the story, Elizabeth Bates, was a desperate woman, straitjacketed in a coal-mining town with a drunken husband. The woman's only wisp of hope, at least as I interpreted the story, existed in the petals of the coal dust–blackened pink chrysanthemums she grew in her yard.

Mr. Oates had a gap between his front teeth, tousled sandy hair, and a flare for mod ties. He had a charmer's smile. Here, today in the classroom, Mr. Oates was at his passionate best, bringing to life in the classroom a lonely woman with a garden of struggling flowers.

With D. H. Lawrence's aid, Mr. Oates—one of those fine American teachers who fired young minds, who could point to a line in a story and paint a life—was teaching me far more than either he or I knew: that gingery, bitter scents, soft-flopping lobes, bright pinks or reds or whites—that literature and the application of the senses—could be a hedge. A protective wand of color and scent to wave at your own black moods. A hex to hold up later against a father's disillusionment, a father's future watery-wavering-slipping-away sadness.

~~

My father brought home to me one evening a book on Mahatma Gandhi. "Have a look at this," he said. "I think you'll like it." These late fall days he was encouraging me to look outward beyond the doors of the school into the sky, across the continent, across the seas toward Asia and the largesse of the world.

I took the fat volume upstairs, lay down on my bed, and as I read Gandhi's biography, it was as though a fresh wind was blowing into me. His creed of self-discipline, modesty, and humility suited a girl who was already on meager rations.

Gandhi's creed provided a counterpoint to the gluttonous America of overseas adventures and melded perfectly with the Quaker principles of nonviolence and simplicity that I was absorbing at school. I listened carefully now during Meeting for Worship. I liked the four "testimonies" of the Friends that the teachers referred to, listed in the pamphlet they handed out at school:

Equality: Friends believe all people are equal, and "there is that of God in everyone."

Integrity: Friends believe people should live their beliefs and strive to speak their truth at all times.

Peace: Friends are committed to nonviolent means of resolving conflict, and oppose war.

Simplicity: Friends are committed to "living simply so others may simply live."

In Sidwell's hallways, Herman Hesse's books were passed from student to student like forbidden bibles. Up on my pink bed, I opened the black cover of *Siddhartha* and I stepped back through a carved door to Asia. Reading about a country of gaunt people, stone gods, and prayer wheels, something was restored to me. Suddenly my veins were brimming with the elixir of the Orient. Dusty but familiar images reared up and flamed: gold-laced brocades, crenulated fans, dung, bamboo pipes, red lanterns . . .

Siddhartha led me to Buddhist and Hindu texts. In these books I discovered words that seemed both to be rooted in the earth and to sail on magic carpets. It was astonishing how a short word, in an instant, could change the color of the world. *Maya* was one of these. It referred to the transitory world of appearances—to the ephemerality of outer skins. This seemed an answer to the posturing I saw around me in America: so much of America seemed bluster and show. Another earth-shaking idea was the Buddhist notion that everything on this earth was transitory, in a constant state of flux. This was a concept cobbled for the Foreign Service child.

Seizing these words as holy writ—they complemented the current fashion for the "natural"—I cleaved to the idea of being real, of shunning veneers. I disdained makeup; I used only natural Herbal Essence shampoo. Increasingly I turned my mind toward worthier subjects: religion, philosophy, pacifism, war. My ideal now was to be a disciple to an Indian sage. More and more, Asia seemed the ultimate continent. I dreamed of going to India, of studying yoga, of joining an ashram. India was utopia. I lusted for it. I could feel Asia dancing in my blood.

Hungry for any instruction on life, I turned to the poets. When I discovered William Wordsworth my heart quickened to his delight in the smallest sprigs:

My heart leaps up when I behold
A Rainbow in the sky;
So it was when my life began;
So it is now I am a man;
So be it when I shall grow old,
Or let me die!

And my father suggested I study Emerson. His writings offered me clear and righting instruction on how to stand alone and cleave to your own truths:

Nothing is at last sacred but the integrity of your own mind. Absolve you to yourself and you shall have the suffrage of the world.

My life is for itself and not for a spectacle. I much prefer that it should be of a lower strain, so it be genuine and equal, than that it should be glittering and unsteady.

*It is easy in the world to live after the world's opinion; it is easy in solitude
to live after our own; but the great man is he who in the midst of the crowd
keeps with perfect sweetness the independence of solitude.*

I thrilled to his bracing, familiarly American advice. When I read these words,
I felt grand and noble, not low like the girls at school gossiping about who was making love to whom, and who had drugs hidden in his locker.

These pursuits took the edge off, but the darkness and frustration were always
washing just under my ephemeral skin, seeking a sluice.

~~

Relief comes at odd times, in unexpected forms.

My bookbag weighed a ton as I trudged home from Wisconsin Avenue after a
day of weaving around the India Girls. By the time I'd walked down Bradley, turned
left on East, turned right on Stanford, and turned left on Maple, I felt like the jumble
of books in my bag—like I was going every which way.

My mother was sitting on the couch when I got home—not fixing dinner; or
telephoning Joe Rock, her physical therapist colleague, in the kitchen; or neatening
up the living room; or writing up case notes at the dining room table. She was sitting and reading a mystery novel, like she used to do in Holland.

I fixed myself a glass of milk and a plate of Oreos and flopped down at the other
end of the navy blue corduroy sofa. I felt like a blob with bone-weary arms and legs.
As the chocolaty sugar and milk flowed into me I began to feel a little better.

"How was school?" my mother said.

"Okay," I said. "Not great. Some of the girls are . . . Kids in the States don't care."

"Some of the girls are pretty cool, aren't they?" my mother said. She meant they
were self-involved and distant, not that they were attractive and hip.

There was a note of sympathy in her voice. Her body was relaxed too, in her
shirtwaist dress. She wasn't rushing to get something done. She wasn't worrying;
she was considering.

"Like that Hedley or that Alex," she said, as though she, instead of me, had been
standing in the hall by the lockers and the recipient of Hedley's snub that afternoon.

"Maybe the best thing is to stay aloof, Sara."

Aloof. That was a word I hadn't thought of. Sometimes my mother had words
like that, words other people didn't use but were just right. She called my mood

these days "the mulligrubs," for instance, and it made sadness seem like a grumpy, quite overcome-able gnome sitting on a stump, instead of an impenetrable darkness.

I looked at the painting of a Taiwanese street over the mantel—it was all messy brush strokes of bright color and black accents that somehow caught the movement and stench of a Chinese street—and surveyed the artifacts of other places we'd lived. The old, hand-painted bellows and long-handled bed warmer, for hot coals, from Holland, and the rough-beautiful old stoneware plate from my babyhood in Japan. And I looked at Mom's blond-oak head bent toward her book, and I felt assembled again.

In my pink bedroom that night, darkness fogging down around me, I slipped into sleep thinking of Mom's word. *Aloof*, it was like a treasure, an answer.

The next day, I carried my word to school with me in my bookbag, and my bag felt lighter on my shoulder than it had in a long time. During the day, I fished out the word; I practiced being aloof. It worked. Hedley was laughing with Alex and Francie. I walked past her like she didn't exist, like I didn't care, like I hadn't seen her. It was a revengeful sort of sweetness to return her favor, to pretend she wasn't in the hallway like she did toward me, but oddly fortifying. A talisman. I'd crossed a rude bridge to greater freedom.

This credo of aloof was a new iteration of the Rawhide and marine guard version of me I'd decided to become back in the fourth grade at the Tomb of the Unknown Soldier. Here at Sidwell, I felt like an unknown soldier. I marched onward, trying to be as aloof and impervious and spit and polished as an American serviceman. It felt normal, I knew how to do it, but my back and shoulders were not relaxed; they were ramrods.

I will need no one, I declared, but of course I couldn't help but crave my fellows. Right now my solution was to be iron, even though my father said, "Stay open. Keep a lookout for the nice people who are often hidden."

~~

My mother gave me a silver word. My father gave me, a night after I'd had another lonely day and things were quiet in the house, one of those sentences that are driftwood planks onto which you can climb out of the sea.

From his green reading chair, he said, "Girl-child . . . Sam, rather . . . " He grinned. "You know, I've noticed that you aren't happy unless you're creating. Why don't you think about that. Maybe you should try poetry."

I took to writing down my thoughts in a small black notebook. I fell in love with certain words and made lists of them: hickory, apple, turf, sod, fecund, hock. Hard words with dirt in them, words you could chew on. I stringed them together: oak-fair hair. As I wrote my first tottering poem, I felt holy. Real.

~~

While a part of me was on the SS *United States* carrying me back to Holland to escape this America I didn't understand, the other part was a quick study. After a while, as I babysat furiously—babies crying, toddlers whining, older children refusing to go to bed unless I read them six Dr. Seuss books—my garb from The Hague began to seem all wrong, like it belonged to a much younger girl far, far away. There was something I couldn't fight going on. It is an almost impossible task, even for adults, to maintain two loyalties, and something in a young person craves loyalty. After a time, the here and now is irrefutable. You can't feed off "then" for too long.

One day, I folded up my polite Dutch embassy princess self and packed it away in a trunk in storage. With my deep sense of diplomatic obligation to blend into the culture where I was set down, I breathed a huge sigh, hoisted the heavily loaded pack of this 1968 Washington, D.C., private-school America and humped it onto my back. I jettisoned my old self. I let go of the bowsprit.

Mornings, I dressed myself in a new uniform: my Dutch desert boots like Pop's, Dutch knee socks, a fox-brown, hip-hugger corduroy miniskirt rugged like the woods, and a light blue chambray work shirt. These clothes felt right; they seemed to unite my old selves and my new Sidwell one. In them I could blend into America.

I now wore my long hair parted in the middle, hanging down on the sides of my face like a half-closed curtain; only the middle two inches of my face were visible. I worked to dissemble, to assume an alias, to be as American-cool as other kids, but an honest face afflicted me. I was so excruciatingly self-conscious I could hardly walk. I took things too deeply to heart. To be cool you have to be flit-hearted as well as hair-tossing confident.

~~

I was a mass of conflict and the world around me was too. In early December, Nixon appointed Henry Kissinger as his national security advisor. Kissinger was the ultimate ardent hawk. As I would learn twenty years later in retrospective tomes on Vietnam, this appointment of Kissinger was an unprecedented power grab by the executive branch. Nixon and Kissinger both disdained the expertise of the State Department and CIA officers, calling them effete Ivy League liberals too cowardly to support America's rightful dominant role on the world stage. Kissinger would admit to Italian journalist Oriana Fallaci, "What interests me is what you can do with power."

My father was reading aloud after dinner a description of Kissinger's views. "I don't think all this anti-Communist fervor is necessary," he said. "Neither the Chinese nor the Russians are wealthy or powerful enough to take over the world, and I doubt very much that they have the will to do so. They're poor countries; they have enough on their hands just trying to feed their people. I love *The Russians are Coming*, but the Russians aren't going to land on Cape Cod. And the Maoists are dangerous to the Chinese, but not that dangerous to us. I don't know what Nixon's men are doing. Neither we nor the people at State believe increased aggression is the right course."

I rose out of my brooding enough to catch a glimmer of the fact that my father was directly criticizing the government he was working for. I wondered: is he allowed to do that? But, again, I had missed my father's slip. Andy, though, was cocking his head, over there in the chair with his book, in the funny way he did when he was thinking.

~~

One rainy, cold day near to Christmas, my mother and father took Andy and me out of school. We drove to Baltimore, an hour away, to conduct some strange business. We entered a large courthouse building with broad steps across the front. We sat on benches like in a church, up near the front where there was a desk positioned high up on a platform. We were here in Baltimore to become naturalized U.S. citizens, to give up Andy's dual citizenship in Taiwan and mine in Japan—a detail of our national statuses to which we'd never paid any heed. My mother and father had always just told us the children of Americans were Americans no matter where they were born. My parents were concerned now, though, that if they kept Andy's Taiwanese citizenship he could be drafted into the Chinese army when he was fourteen. They'd decided to renounce my Japanese citizenship while they were at it.

Around us on the benches were poor-looking people hunched over books, with serious eyes and worried brows. The judge asked a woman who George Washington was. She faltered in broken English, but answered him correctly. Another woman with a foreign accent had to respond to a question about the Revolutionary War. A small man with tanned skin stuttered when the judge asked him something about his English. Seeing all the immigrants trying so hard to be American made me see that what Mom and Pop had said was right. This was the land of opportunity, no matter what. I felt smug since I knew the answers and could speak perfect American English.

The judge seemed to assume Andy and I needed little questioning—we were sitting here with our dignified, well dressed, very American-looking mother and father—though he perfunctorily asked me who Abe Lincoln was, and Andy what the Civil War was about. For a moment during the proceedings I had a flash that I'd like to keep my Japanese citizenship—to belong to two countries, to have an option, to keep that childhood part of myself—but the decision had already been made for me.

The judge's voice was continuing. He was talking about how lucky we all were to be Americans, and about freedom, democracy, and independence, and my questions evaporated at the sound of these high-flying, austere, exhilarating words. Suddenly I felt like waving a flag, and when, at the end—our red-ribboned certificates in our hands—he had us all stand and swear our allegiance to the United States of America, my heart cheered.

As I swore, I felt billowy and sure and happy as Betsy Ross. It was as though Sidwell and the turbulent political world that was slowly breaking its way into my consciousness had melted away. This was the most high-breasted and red-white-and-blue I had felt in months, and more than I would feel for years ahead. For the moment, in the thrall of high and glorious words, I was *American*.

17

raspberries

In the lull between Christmas and New Year's, still surrounded by the piles of books and scraps of wrapping paper, my father read from the *Post*. As of Christmas day, 540,000 American troops had been stationed in Vietnam; 30,610 had been killed in action, and 192,850 wounded.

Another day, in the clean, grey-branched freshness of the new year just before school started, over plates of my mother's fried rice, my father gave us a China update. "The Cultural Revolution is over now," he said. "Another disaster for the Chinese people. It's a terrible loss for China. A whole generation has essentially been denied an education. The only book they've been allowed to study for years has been Mao's *Little Red Book*."

"And what about Mao?" Andy asked.

My father explained that Mao had been sidelined now, and his wife and Premier Zhou Enlai were in charge. "They're vying for power while they try to get China back on its feet and rebuild the Communist party. . . .

"I've been meeting with the Chinese and they all say it's another rugged time for the common people in China." His eyes had that haunted look again as he said this.

My father's Washington job again entailed meeting with Chinese people to find out about the inside workings of the Communist administration. For this purpose, he met with Chinese dissidents and informants in obscure safe houses around Washington—always a dangerous undertaking for the Chinese. Decades later my mother told me, referring to his Chinese contacts, "Your father always worried a lot about his people."

~~

Andy and I were viewing the evening TV news with my father. We watched Soviet troops lining up in a wild countryside. "Things are extremely tense on the Soviet-Chinese border right now," my father explained. "Large numbers of Chinese are crossing into Russian territory, and the Russians have amassed a million troops along the frontier. Both sides are threatening invasion." A reporter announced the Chinese government was building underground shelters in Chinese cities in preparation for a nuclear attack.

Andy said, "Isn't this a powder keg, Pop?"

"Ironically," my father said, "this may promote peace. Because the Communist powers now fear each other, we may benefit. Our government may be able to exploit the tensions between them, and they may turn to us. Both the Chinese and Russians have made overtures toward our government recently." Indeed, this inter-Communist tension, I read later, led to a "mating dance" with the United States; both Communist powers would eventually seek reconciliation with the United States as protection against the other Communist power. "Nothing is ever straightforward," my father said.

"Russia and the U.S. are now spending $50 million a day on nuclear arms," my father told us over another dinner. "The burden is becoming intolerable. But something beneficial is finally coming out of this. Finally the two superpowers have agreed to meet in Helsinki for SALT, the Strategic Arms Limitation Talks, to try to halt the arms race."

"Why do we want the role of being the world's armory?" I said, getting warmer as I threw out questions. "Why can't we be leaders in nonproliferation? How can we think we have the right to the bomb while other people don't? And how can we accuse the Russians or Chinese of being belligerent when we are doing exactly the same thing?

"I can see how the Chinese and Russians see us: as people who want to take over the world. Why don't politicians see how our behavior looks to other people? How can they not care?"

My father listened to me carefully, as if I were an adult.

~~

Despite my reading and the words I held close as protection and exhilaration, my Sidwell days often seemed like wanders through a landscape as stark and empty as Siberia.

One day in the hall, a girl with silky walnut hair and blue eyes bounced up to me. She had a happy, chirpy voice. "I heard you came from Holland," she said. "I used to live in Geneva; my father worked for the UN.

"I'm pretty new too," she said. "This is a really hard place to fit in."

As if this wasn't enough, when she told me her name I trilled: it was the same as mine. She even spelled it the same: without an "h."

Soon I had Sara over for thick Dutch pea soup. Because she too had lived in Europe and visited Holland, she understood why pea soup was important. We soon were fast friends, going to each other's houses after school to do homework, flopped out on each other's beds or floors.

Sara's house on Albemarle Street was like a small castle, a high, solid brick manse set on top of a wooded hillside. I was entranced. With its slate mansard roof; small, lead-paned windows; its portal, set in the roof with a cast iron fleur de lys; and its tall, medieval-looking wooden door, I felt as though I was a Dutch princess approaching her secret hideaway. Tall, straight-trunked trees that surrounded the path were white like beams of light.

Sara's parents did the kind of meaningful work we at our Quaker school valued, jobs like the Peace Corps or VISTA that served humanity. Her father, a short man who had a fluffy mustache and merry Santa Claus eyes, was a botanist with the Environmental Protection Agency and her dark, wiry, tight-strung mother a staffer for California Democratic senator Alan Cranston.

Sara and I hung out in her third-floor turret room and commiserated like trapped Rapunzels. Perched at the peak of the high, dark house, halfway up the tall trees, it was like our own eagle's eyrie. Inspired by the peaceniks in *Life* magazine, we sprawled on Sara's rug and drew flower power signs. We studied books on wildflowers.

Listening to Bob Dylan, Crosby Stills & Nash, James Taylor, and Joni Mitchell, we discussed Hedley and the other India Girls.

"I heard Hedley is sleeping with Zeke."

"I heard she was smoking hash behind the gym during second period. . . ."

"I heard she got it from Clyde."

Then the conversation twisted to Sidwell in general. "Some of the kids at Sidwell are such utter snobs," Sara said. "So narrow-minded."

"And mean," I said.

~~

Meeting Sara primed the pump; gradually I began to kindle friendships with a handful of other girls: a girl with wild corkscrew hair who would become a community organizer and challenge the world; a quiet blond girl like someone in an A. A. Milne poem who memorized her favorite verses; her friend, Lolly, a brilliant artist; a girl with soft, fluffed hair and an independent stride who would become a sharp historian; a girl who wore pearl earrings and straight skirts like conservative society women wore, who asked me to her house for sundaes and laughed about people as if they were sweet trifles.

~~

Sara was making her mother's open-faced sandwiches: cheddar cheese and tomato slices on English muffins, toasted in her toaster oven. Everything tasted better when it was made at Sara's house. We sat on their patio made cozy by plants like in a European garden, and looked at the birds twittering at her father's feeder.

As the breeze tossed the red maple leaves around us and we chewed our little English muffin pizzas, we talked about how we hated our mothers. Sara thought her mother, who was really her stepmother, wished the worst for her. "She's jealous of me, and she thinks I'm a loose woman just because I went to a movie with Dirk." My mother drove me crazy because of her bossiness. She wanted everything her way. I hated how she took over when I helped her in the kitchen, and made me vacuum the house once a week, and thought Sidwell was a good school when it wasn't.

"I can't believe my mom," I said. "One minute she's yelling at me and the next she's talking in the sweetest voice to her friend Margaret on the phone."

Sara said, "You should see Linda. She's so fake. She just wants my dad's attention all the time."

The truth was, though, we liked each other's mothers. Sara's dark, skinny mother had a sharp intelligence I found interesting, and she kept a rock grinder in the library on one of the dark, built-in bookcases. Any mother who ground rocks down to beautiful polished stones was worth studying.

Sara said, "Your mom is full of good practical advice." I was secretly proud of that about my rounder mother in her stout oxfords and grey skirts.

We both agreed we had the best fathers in the world. Sara said about her father, "Isn't he cute, with his little bushy mustache?"

I loved my father so much I couldn't say a word.

~~

Andy was over on the couch, talking to my father about foreign affairs. "Aren't we doing something like President Eisenhower did in Iran or like President Kennedy did with Diem in Vietnam? Overthrowing people who are friendly to democratic ideas, dominating the affairs of other countries?" he said.

"Do you think the State Department and CIA are doing the right thing in Vietnam, Pop? Bobby Kennedy and a lot of people thought overthrowing Diem was wrong."

"Good analysis, *Jonge.*" My father always called Andy by the Dutch word for young lad. "Though each situation is different, you're posing some very valid questions.

"You're absolutely right to wonder about our stance in Vietnam. Ho Chi Minh was originally ardently pro-American. He looked to the American revolution and our constitution as his models. He only went over to Communism when we failed to support him in his struggle for his country's independence.

"And, as you know, I don't believe Communism is inherently evil," Pop said. "It's a bold social experiment. I'm sure Ho thinks he's doing right by his people. And he could be. Political systems have phases. This may be an important one that will ultimately bring greater well-being to the people of Vietnam."

Pop said he believed in giving other people the benefit of the doubt, in trusting them to come up with their own solutions, and in remaining open to the possibility of other governments' solutions. "Other people besides us in the U.S. have smarts and creativity," he said.

"And you're right about intrusion. We have a foreign policy right now that involves pushing our way into other countries' affairs. The war in Vietnam is a product of this doctrine. Vietnam is not about fairness. It's about domination. It's not about having an equal fight; it's about having more weapons than the other guy. We Americans like to dominate where we can. . . .

"And each American president has to have his war," he went on. "This is Nixon's."

Reading and thinking about Vietnam in 2005, I'd read Simon Schama, the cultural historian. Schama explained the audacity of imperialistic powers as a matter of perspective: force in the hands of others is viewed as an infringement on the laws of nature, while force in one's own hands is the definition of freedom. But these ideas were way down the road; my twelve-year-old history-buff brother was noticing things about which, at this juncture, I didn't have the dimmest notion.

~~

One day my mother took us on another duty visit to my father's boss's wife at their house in the woods in Bethesda. It was another awkward-feeling hour like we'd had back when I was eight, with Mom holding her back stiff and asking about Mrs. Smith's children.

Afterward, Andy said to me, "Did you notice Mrs. Smith kept saying 'the Agency' when she talked about Mr. Smith's and Pop's work?"

"What do you mean?"

"I dunno," he said. Then he trailed off, his mind wandering again, probably to dumb elephant jokes or something, I thought.

I didn't realize my brother was growing up.

~~

Looking up from my algebra homework another day, I saw my father, absorbed in the *Washington Post*. When he went into the TV room to watch Walter Cronkite, I wandered over and picked up the paper. I'd never before looked at the newspaper of my own accord in my life. On the front page was a photograph of a little Vietnamese girl in a village that had just been attacked by American soldiers. She was in ragged clothes, skinny as a wand. Her almond eyes were so frightened they were blank.

Suddenly the globe at the center of me rotated. I couldn't sit here and eat my hamburger while over there in the padi, girls were screaming, girls were sobbing, girls were shrieking in fear. I pictured the raggedy girl in Taiwan.

I studied the photographs of soldiers, rifles slung over their backs, wading through padi. Was to be American to be this? Killing Vietnamese people: silent old men and children, with beautiful, grinning eyes like the raggedy girl's? In Holland, we'd seemed all goodness. Now we seemed all bad. What was my country doing? What was I doing here, safe and breathing while innocent people in Asia were dying because of America?

My knee-jerk, self-centered, loneliness-spawned hatred of America spun, this instant, to a hatred based on political ideals. Perhaps this is how much political fervor is born. Emotion finds an ideological twin.

I charged into the TV room, pointing a finger at the front page of the *Post*. My mother left the room. She hated it when I criticized our government—or maybe, as she said, she just hated my tone of voice—so I railed to my father.

"Look, Pop, at what the CIA and our army is doing in Vietnam," I said, shaking the paper. "Pop, you've always said that America's strength is that we can be self-critical and self-corrective—unlike other countries. Well, Nixon is resisting all criticism about his nasty war, innocent people are being slaughtered by his soldiers, and draft protestors are being thrown in jail," I said, mimicking the kids at school. "How is what Nixon doing any different from any other bully-tyrant?"

I was like a machine gun that was pelting the whole room—until I noticed that my father had turned down the TV and was just quietly listening. This released me to keep going—to give full vent.

"Why can't we stand for peace instead of war? We could talk to the North Vietnamese, try to understand why they feel strongly about Communism." This was what a Quaker activist who spoke at school advocated.

"And why are we the world's bully? We are raining bombs down on these other people—'ordnance,' as Nixon falsely calls them—and none are raining down on us. We are big and they are small. What is the bigger one's responsibility? To take care of the smaller.

"Why can't we be antiwar like Holland? Or like Switzerland? Or like Japan?" My father had told me about Swiss neutrality and the Japanese refusal to maintain an army after the horrors of World War II.

"Let's emigrate, Pop," I said. "Let's move to Holland or one of the other small countries that can live by principles instead of power. Why can't we?"

Then, opening the paper, I jabbed at the picture of the girl. "Look, Pop. Look at who we're hurting!" I said. "What is our country doing?" My eyes started to spurt and my father, whose brown eyes looked deeply sad, opened his arms. "Oh Sweetie."

Suddenly now I understood that my father had questioned the war too. This fortified me since my father was a man who carefully weighed and qualified. Only in my forties, on a return visit to the Normandy beaches, would I see what a strain Vietnam was for World War II veterans—how to doubt their government's wisdom went against every fiber, how it *cost* them.

But, the product of my generation, I burned with hate toward America now. I burned to take a brave and serious stand: to protect Asia from America. My country was the enemy. Now I had an obligation to protect "my people," only "my people" was the world.

~~

As the daffodils held balls in the greening woods of Rock Creek Park, I read of eighteen-year-old boys from Kansas, Washington state, and Mississippi who'd died in the padis of Vietnam, and I clutched. While thirty thousand had been killed in all the previous years of the entanglement, in Nixon's first year in office, ten thousand more young men would have died.

For alive and dead soldiers now, I had opposite responses. Toward the uniformed soldiers I saw walking along the streets near the Bethesda Naval Hospital or in the caravans of jeeps that sometimes trundled through town—contrary to the way I felt as a young girl in Taiwan or Bethesda—I felt contempt. They seemed like automatons, with their shaven heads and erect postures. I didn't see them as the epitome of bravery as I saw those at the guard posts of the American embassy in The Hague. My mother said the young men were brave, but, to me, her words were thin. *How can they go along with this evil war?* I thought. *Why aren't they courageous enough to go to jail or to Canada?* Like for my father, it was hard for my mother, an old-fashioned, bobby-socked patriot who knitted scarves for soldiers through her high school years, to think soldiers could be doing something wrong.

When I saw the photographs of dead soldiers in the paper, though, I felt sucked in with pain. Why weren't people more involved, worried, protesting? Young, beautiful American boys were dying for no reason! I saw no contradiction in my reactions—or was there one?

~~

Then came the day I came across a photograph and article that clogged my heart. It reported on the death of a boy just my age, whose brother had recently died in Vietnam, who'd burned himself to death like a Buddhist monk, on the steps of the Capitol, in protest against the war.

I cut out his photograph and kept it on my bedside table. I looked at the boy's picture for hours. And every night afterward, I gazed at it with wonder and awe. What did it mean, this bravery? I felt his desperation so strongly, it was almost as if I was him. War was that important: the most important thing of all. We should all have been flinging ourselves at senators, burning ourselves on the Capitol steps, blocking the president's office—anything to stop the war. Those were the sacrifices for country that were needed.

One day my mother found the article while I was at school and was holding it in her hand when I walked in the door.

"Sara, what is this?" Her hand was trembling; her eyes were urgent and moist—fierce with fear.

"An article from the *Post*."

"Sara, I don't want you looking at things like this."

"It shows how bad this war is."

"And what good did his death do?"

"Maybe the government will pay attention."

Suddenly my mother's voice had a shriek in it. "Sara, his death did nothing. Do you think the government is going to pay attention to one boy's suicide? His death was a tragic waste. His poor family. Throw that thing away."

I heard her talking to my father in bed at night. My father was saying, "She's all right, Lois. She's all right."

~~

Depression made me focus on black and white patterns—in the air, in music, in newsprint.

In a way, this heavy mood felt holy—a link to my past. And true—in the face of Vietnam. As my father's child, I'd been trained to live inside world events. As a child raised in the diplomatic corps, and who took "when in Rome . . . " seriously, I had an emotional obligation to feel everything the Vietnamese felt. I was the one assigned to gaze straight into the eye of the monster. I was the sherpa of sadness.

And, true to my unwitting status as a spy's daughter, I was the carrier of the unseen, the unacknowledged truth. Ironically this was exactly the role of mid-level CIA officers like my father. As investigations would reveal again and again, it was the on-the-ground government officials who interviewed people and scoured the situation abroad who held the truth in their files, while their leaders refused to countenance the facts if they contradicted their worldview. It was as if they thought by ideologically based pronouncement they could jam the world into their image of it.

This was my modus operandi: If I didn't carry the truth of the world's horror, people might deny its existence. If you wanted the truth that the world was hiding, just ask Sara. She would tell you, "Yes, it happened."

I didn't realize that if I dared to be happy the sadness would still be there.

I felt helpless. The only way to make the war and the orchestras of spring daffodils add up was to eat plain bowls of rice, wear a flowered dress, and haul a pail of sadness.

~~

When you're very lucky, depression can dovetail with an issue that transforms it. As the psychologist Erik Erikson said, "The task of youth is to find an ideology that fits. Then he comes clear to himself."

The answer to my troubles in America came on the city bus.

One day on my morning commute down Wisconsin Avenue toward school, the bus was crammed with people carrying peace signs on their way to a march. I was grumpy about being pressed against all the people in the joggling bus, staring at the floor as usual, and then I noticed the hems of the corduroy jackets of the couple next to me. Following the cords of the cloth upward, I was suddenly struck with sunlight. This is how people should look, I thought: worn corduroy jackets, ribbed scarves doubled and pulled through themselves, just-out-of-bed blond hair. The people were holding signs. When I heard the couple exchange words in Dutch, I was slammed with happiness.

Suddenly, I was back on the cobblestones outside the Binnenhof in The Hague. Bear-sized provos were milling around, shouting, hoisting ban-the-bomb signs toward the castle-like government offices across the shining pond. A yellow ray beamed down on them like a spotlight. I breathed deep and the hunched wings of my gargoyle shoulders settled for the first time in weeks. I felt as though I was floating like an eagle abreast the top of a cathedral the whole rest of the bus ride.

That evening I scrubbed myself hard in the bath, and emerged clean and fierce, and with a brand new and saving notion: I would join the antiwar movement kids at school were always ranting about. I would be an American provo. I retrieved my pup tent and hammered in the stakes.

~~

Green of pines and hickory dabbed with persimmon and goldenrod. We were all flopped out on the lawn for Meeting for Worship in back of Zartman House.

Mr. Johnston, who was bent over and bearded like St. Peter in a Rembrandt painting, rose up into the silence and moved his large, hoary hand in an arc, like a circlet or halo covering us all. He said, "In this time of horror, with so many young men struggling in the jungles of Southeast Asia, I'm keenly aware of the light in each of you. How each of you is precious."

I pictured the soldiers, rifles on their backs, faces sweating under their helmets, threading through the Vietnamese brush, jumpy and twitchy as rabbits—bull's-eyes for the VC lying hidden in the sog. Then I looked around at all the students here sprawled, safe, on the lawn. Each face was like a face in a biblical painting—eyes downcast, oval shapes of cheek and chin, glinting cascades of straggled hair— backed by the piercing blue of the sky and the spring-tipped, keen-green of the trees. A sob rose in my throat—and suddenly tears were standing in my eyes.

For this split second, all these kids were beautiful, and I was one of the group, and each one of us was a precious being to be cherished.

I swept my eyes in a searchlight across all the boys. Some of them had low lottery numbers. What if they were . . . to go to war?

Another teacher rose to her feet and, standing in her baggy, African dress, spoke about the eloquent speech made by a Democrat in the house. She ended with the Quaker adage we heard all the time. "Speak truth to power." Each one of us can do it, she said. "Find the courage, and we'll change the world."

These moments are why I sent my own children to Sidwell, despite my ambivalence. With time I was able to reconcile the bad and the good.

~~

The war now became a funnel sucking in all my stray thoughts—and bringing them to a sharp point.

In May, the *New York Times* revealed the secret bombing of North Vietnamese camps in Cambodia. The bombing was meant to arrest North Vietnamese aggressions into the South, but it would fail. Vietnam specialists and CIA experts had apparently expressed doubts about Cambodia's significance, but Nixon had gone ahead with the campaign, theorizing that tanked-up aggression and the implied threat of nuclear intervention would force the Communists to negotiate a peace. All this while, "Vietnamization" of the war was supposedly in progress. Nixon was furious about the leak, and later investigations would reveal that at this time Nixon and Kissinger ordered wiretaps of journalists and Kissinger's own staff. The Cambodia attack caused an outcry all across the country, but Nixon persisted in seeing himself as a victim of the liberal Eastern elite.

I grabbed my father the minute he came in the door, galvanized by the arguments of kids at school. "What on earth are we doing in Cambodia, Pop? This is outrageous. We're expanding the war when Nixon and Defense Secretary Laird said we were pulling back!

"And why does our CIA and military think they have the right to change other countries' governments for them? What would we do if the Vietnamese decided to bring their soldiers here and control our government?" I was almost apoplectic now.

"These things are very complex," my father said. "Things aren't black and white. In war, morality gets murky. We aren't all good or bad and neither are the North Vietnamese. . . .

"Sara, the truth is we say we live in accord with principle or the rule of law, but it's really a case-by-case basis in foreign affairs. If we can win by force, we do it." My father sat back and looked at me squarely. "Sara, history shows we're one of the most violent and war-like peoples in the world."

"No we're not! We can't be." For a moment my mind flashed on a trip to Florida we'd once taken to visit Mom's sister. All along the way there were shacks selling bargain towels, firecrackers, and most of all: guns.

But my father kept looking at me with his steady eyes.

"Well then," I said. "We're the worst country in the world!"

The Sara in The Hague wouldn't have recognized this Sara, not even a year older, who was feeling a sensation close to revulsion about her own country. If to be American meant to be the warmonger of the world, I didn't want any part of being an American. Until now, I'd thought America was exceptional, that we did provide a model of freedom and opportunity, that we were able to correct our mistakes. What would my country be in this world? What would I be?

My father said, "It will be okay," as a father does to a child, but we both knew for a lot of people, Vietnamese and American, it wouldn't.

~~

One day I looked up from the war statistics in the paper and heard my parents talking about the pressures at my father's office. My father had just had to take the polygraph, to test his loyalty to the administration. As part of their work, CIA officers are required to do so periodically, as a kind of monitoring of their commitment and fealty. My mother told me years later that everyone lied about a thing or two. But this was more than a test.

"It's demeaning. I have a right to my views," my father said.

"We've got to get you away from that place," my mother said. "Why don't you put in for a post in Asia. India, anywhere, or Taipei again. I'd love Taipei."

"I'll keep an eye out for openings in Asia," he said.

"Is all this worth it?" my mother said into the air of the kitchen.

My father was stoic and my mother was upright and strong, working hard at her physical therapy practice, but she was more prone to upset than she ever had been before. One day I spied her sneaking a cigarette in the yard; she had promised to quit smoking when we left Holland. And my father was quietly, invisibly frustrated. His secret was hovering at the uttering point.

~~

Now every night I listened to Walter Cronkite and kept a count of the dead boys and followed the battles against the Vietnamese. Furious at the CIA and the army, I thought of the Vietnamese people dying in their villages. I saw young Americans dying, I heard bombs dropping, I saw children running, I saw helicopters dropping into crashing blazes. I saw the poor people on the street in Taipei. I saw almond eyes. I saw the raggedy girl. I choked up all the time for the young draftees and for the Vietnamese. I was like a crystal about to break.

~~

Sara and I climbed the 893 steps to the top of the Washington Monument. From here I could see all of Washington: the Capitol, the green swath of the Mall, the Lincoln Memorial. I could almost see the Tomb of the Unknown Soldier. It all seemed ostentatious and bloodthirsty. I knew now that soldiers really could die unknown. What did the monuments really represent? America, freedom, all the glorious words: a sham.

Sara and I sat in her tower room and wrote protest letters. The letters were white flowers scattered around us and we were flower children amid them. If only people would plant flowers and be kind to one another instead of making war. It seemed so easy, so obvious at fifteen—an age when a daisy is a discovery, newly born. Sometimes Sara and I went to Montrose Park and made buttercup and daisy chains for the whole world. And it seemed like we were doing the president's work—it was that important. There was a famous photo of a hippie putting a daisy in the barrel of a soldier's rifle. This was what should be happening all over the world. We could do it: if everyone would just join together.

While the war had crushed my apple-pie version of America, the counterculture was giving me a new vision of my country and its possibilities. If youth needs an ideology, this period was bulging with clear commandments to follow: *Make love, not war. Spurn material possessions. Be a nonconformist. Be true to your nature. Save the earth. Question authority. Be here now.* Each of these tenets felt like a blazing, pure, fresh discovery.

Through the lens of the sixties revolution, and my new-hatched abstract thinking, I could poke holes into anything now, and I suddenly saw flaws and hypocrisies everywhere. I thought about how everything in the world logically ought to be. Work should be done for its meaning and societal value, not its remunerative properties. Schools ought to be open and free like the British school Summerhill. We should live in communes where child care is shared by everyone. We should drive cars that don't pollute, or else bike or walk. We should wear our clothes two or three days in a row, to avoid polluting our rivers and seas. We should grow our own food and bake our own bread. People should be appreciated for their unique- ness, not their conformity—what notion could be more heaven-sent for a weird Foreign Service girl? Each of these ideas shone. During a course in psychological anthropology I'd take in my thirties I would learn that American adolescents, more than those of most other cultures, think they reinvent the world. As they recapitulate the history of thought, they feel like the great explorers.

The dictates of the counterculture offered me a way to be an American and feel good about it: I could be critical of the government but love my country, my father said. Dissent was American. Our country was founded on it.

~~

My family was riding through the West Virginia countryside—a realm of shag- gy blond fields and broken farmhouses, once upright, effortful, hardy structures sagged down into themselves like fallen soufflés, testaments to the back roads of the American dream. My parents loved this countryside. Each might have been happy living in an old farmhouse—he with a pile of books, she with a garden to cultivate— and perhaps be happier, life boiled down to its salts.

The tidy little car was rambling its way along an empty back road. The au- tumn sun was Achilles slashing swords of brilliant light into the crowns of the rus- set and lemon trees, and Demeter pouring a yellow of glory and goodness across the pastures. We curled around a copse of old deciduous trees and then the world suddenly seemed to flash open. On the left were the old, scruffy, bowing woods, and to the right was a meadow like a bolt of radiant cloth. It was an average West Virginia field—stretching to a creek bed where the trees lined up. But here, in the mid distance, it seemed like an early Christian tableau—with a beam of celestial yellow-blue casting a careless radiance over the world.

"Stop, Pop. I have to run in this meadow," I said. My father, understanding my urge—the draw of American beauty—pulled over, and as everyone slowly piled out, I darted out the door, stepped into the meadow as if into some sort of golden liquid, stretched out my arms, and ran into the grasses. I ran full-tilt toward the trees, then I curved like a hawk, my arms winged. Then I began to bound, eating the meadow in huge gulps. Chevy Chase vanished, the war nonexistent, Sidwell left in some long-ago past, I spun, like a top, free of self-consciousness, social life, and time. It was as if the beauty had shocked my mind into abeyance, knocked my heart onto an alternative beat—one that swallowed beauty like the finest, honeyed water—that sucked beauty, and beauty alone, from the array of the world.

I ran until my arms were cooled, tingling with sweat, my legs ached, and my heart was banging. I collapsed, sinking into the gold like a deer into its bed, and, swishing my fingers through the dry stalks, I looked up at the clear, watercolor-washed, Madonna-blue sky. My heart was thrumming like a lute; I'd never felt this happy. My body was fresh. I was beautiful, the world was beautiful—I was the meadow and the meadow was me—and everything was ever so fine.

~~

Through the natural world, I found my way to another America, an America I could love. Always the land had been at the heart of my father's love of country. Perhaps it is the particular lay of a landscape that holds a person fast to her country through, and despite, changing political weather.

~~

At Friends Meeting, Mr. Johnston described George Fox, the founder of Quakerism, standing on a storybook-green hill in rainy England—I imagined him shivering in worn moleskin trousers and a beat-up moss green hat, gazing into the trees and hills—and feeling a deep shiver of peace that flowed through his gaunt body and out of him into the world, uniting everything: the fount of Quaker worship. Just hearing the story, I felt confirmed. I knew about dissolving into the landscape. Human beings were simply mammals, offspring of nature: beautiful, green-white, tender shoots springing up out of the loam of the woods.

~~

Sara and I grabbed onto the Save the Earth Movement. Ecology had just been "discovered." This gave me more cairns to follow:

Move back to the land
Recycle envelopes
Build a dome
Heat with a woodstove
Do laundry by hand
Make candles and soap
Form a co-op
Chant
Grow a garden

~~

In my backyard, Sara and I read out passages of *Walden* to each other. Henry David Thoreau's masterpiece was our new bible.

December 24, 1841

I want to go soon and live away by the pond, where I shall hear only the wind whispering among the reeds. It will be success if I shall have left myself behind. But my friends ask what will I do when I get there? Will it not be employment enough to watch the progress of the seasons?

My new goal was to live in a cabin in the wilderness—to be a stalwart, self-sufficient inhabitant of the American woods. (I didn't know that Thoreau sent his laundry to town.)

~~

One early evening, Sara and I saw the film *Easy Rider* together. The film was a tour of American glory: a long, awe-inspiring motorcycle journey through a break-your-heart Western landscape. But it also was a bald and disturbing portrayal of intolerance: the two hippies—average practitioners of psychedelics and free love, a bit vapid but basically kind, harmless people—were sneered at along the road, and then blown away. This was an America that despised difference and wanted to kill freedom.

~~

Just as school was letting out, knowing his approval ratings were about to plummet, Nixon, and the Vietnamese president Thieu, announced the withdrawal of 25,000 U.S. troops. Kissinger, meanwhile, was flummoxed. He kept saying, "I can't believe that a fourth-rate power like North Vietnam doesn't have a breaking point."

This summer of 1969 would be the bloodiest of the Vietnam War—scores of American men would die each week—and the season I would learn how glorious a real American summertime could be.

In July, Mom, Andy, and I decamped and moved to a rambling wooden house overlooking the Patuxent River on the property of the Sotterley Plantation in Hollywood, Maryland. The rental house had been offered to us by other "State Department" friends, the Fitzgeralds, who, when they were in the States, spent their summers at the plantation in another shambling house on a bluff overlooking the water. The Fitzgeralds had three children still at home: Barb, two years older than I; Ted, a year younger; and Nan, a year younger than Andy. They were all lanky kids, with deep tans, lean salty legs, peeling noses, and hair the color of sun-bleached wheat. Mrs. Fitzgerald, with a puff of brown hair, pearl earrings, and a natural elegance, had a loud southern voice and a hearty laugh. She made wonderful pots of fish stew and delicious layered salads smothered in mayonnaise and dotted with bacon.

Weekends, when the fathers made the two-hour drive to join us, we ate Mrs. Fitzgerald's chili or my mother's soy sauce chicken out on the picnic table in the field overlooking the river, and the fathers drank beer and relaxed. My father was growing a mustache, and Mr. Fitzgerald, in a pair of baggy khaki shorts and a faded Ivy League T-shirt, fondled their big old Labrador while he and my father compared goings-on at FE and LA, the Far East and Latin American desks. Being around the Fitzgeralds and the other State Department people who dropped in on weekends, I felt like I was back with my own people.

We kids spent our days fishing for crabs with long nets jabbed off the long, rickety wood-slatted dock, jumping in and out of the square of the bay netted off from jellyfish, and scampering through the marshes and fields of the hot Maryland countryside, feeling like Tom Sawyer and Becky Thatcher. In the late afternoons and cool evenings, we took turns playing the guitar on the Fitzgeralds' porch, watching the sun cast rainbows on the water. How many times did the Maryland air, or the air of every state in the union, receive the notes of "Blowin' in the Wind" that summer?

It was American bliss, but the troubles of the world still managed to wend their way down to Sotterley and stir things up. One day, Barb and a visiting friend went off secretively to smoke behind the boathouse. None of us told the Moms. And when the Fitzgeralds' older brother Dan, who was brilliant and went to an Ivy League college, came down, he and Barb confronted their father one night at dinner. Usually we younger kids just half-listened to the fathers' shop talk, but this time we were alert as swamp foxes.

We were halfway through Mrs. Fitzgerald's crab and potato stew when Dan said, "So Dad, when are you going to really get us out of this immoral quagmire?" His tone was quiet and curious, but there was a slight thread of defiance.

Barb, who was the bubbly, passionate one, said, "Yeah Dad, you older generation are just a bunch of warmongering, establishment fat cats. . . ."

The two younger Fitzgerald kids stayed quiet, like this was a familiar dynamic and they knew to keep mum.

Mr. Fitzgerald, who had a dignity and an intelligent authority that made me both admire him and turn bashful when I was around him, just laughed and said, "That's one way to look at it. But we fat cats'll get it right one of these days. "

Dan and Barb exchanged meaningful looks. Mrs. Fitzgerald laughed and got up to fetch the salad, and the topic changed to the fine crop of tomatoes this summer.

After dinner, wandering around licking my ice cream cone, I heard Mr. Fitzgerald talking to my father on the porch.

My father had said, "What do you think about Saigon, Ed?"

Mr. Fitzgerald, who seemed to love Pop, said, "Bad stuff, Charlie."

Later I'd read about the atmosphere at the CIA and the State Department during this period of the war. Both arms of government were rent by division. "The best and the brightest," all those Ivy Leaguers and other smart young boys recruited into the government after World War II, had screwed up and everyone was blaming everyone else and no one knew what to do. Arguments reigned inside the walls of the giant buildings and protestors assailed them from without. Families of State Department and Agency employees, like mine and the Fitzgeralds, were being torn apart by the war.

I heard my father saying to my mother one evening on the porch, "What are we doing dropping eighteen-year-old boys into that God-forsaken mess?" My father's tone brought to me, out of the blue, a picture of Mr. Chu quaking with fear back in Taiwan.

But the warm tides of our red-white-and-blue summer resumed their soothing lapping when the fathers returned to Washington. One afternoon, we all scrunched into Barb's beat-up VW bug and she drove us, barefoot, to the carnival in Hollywood up the road, on Route 4. There, a nowhere spot along the highway, a traveling caravan had erected a small Ferris wheel, a rickety roller coaster, and a merry-go-round. We gorged on cotton candy, peanut brittle, and Cokes in between stomach-sickening twirls on the rides, again feeling like characters in a Mark Twain novel. On July 21, drinking lemonade in the sweltering heat, we watched, on a tiny black-and-white TV, a man walk on the moon.

The summer rolled on. As we hiked with our sticks in marshes and swam in a warm Maryland river, America's troubles faded into the background. Elsewhere, a coalition of antiwar groups planned a series of "moratoriums" on the war; the

Woodstock rock festival, a miracle of peaceful cooperation, sex, and music, took place in that soon-to-be-legendary field up in New York; and Henry Kissinger, true to his clandestine activities–loving self, met secretly with a North Vietnamese negotiator.

But the most miraculous day of that sun-kissed summer was that on which my mother led Andy and me along a little dirt road that traversed the plantation and showed us the raspberry bushes lining the path. We picked berries all afternoon, plunking them into beat-up saucepans from the rental house pantry. Back at the house, while the sea breeze sipped at our sunburned skins, she showed us how to make pie crust from scratch the way our Indiana grandma had, and to concoct the syrupy, delicious berry-glop for a raspberry pie. I didn't know my mother possessed such knowledge. This was the summer's miracle: my mother's raspberry pie, that homemade American dessert to eat for all our soldiers fighting in Vietnam. This was what they were fighting to get back to.

18
the secret

The month that school began, Ho Chi Minh died and the North Vietnamese vowed never to give up. They believed it was their "sacred duty" to defeat the United States and the South Vietnamese. Nixon, meanwhile, told the congressional leadership, "I will not be the first president of the United States to lose a war." From the outset of school that year, I felt part of the swirl. I knew how to do Sidwell now. The white halls were supercharged with antiwar fever.

~~

"I'm fed up, Lois," my father said.

He again hadn't gotten the promotion he'd expected.

"Don't worry about it, Charlie. Next round for sure," my mother said.

In a government job, a man and his career are subject to swinging political tides in the country at large and to the small, mean political tides within his particular agency, and his particular division of that agency. Promotions are a matter of political calculation, yes, but also random dumb luck. Who was at what helm at what hour. At a certain age, by wayward winds, men's careers rise or stagnate.

My father had more to say. "Smith and his gang are cooking up all sorts of crazy schemes to get the director's attention. I wish I could wash my hands of them."

"That mafia. I bet Terry's right in there with them. He's such a brownnoser he's sure to get the next plum post."

My father just stared out the window.

My father was trying to harden himself so as not to care, and my mother was trying to stay calm, but she was revving up instead. "That awful place," she said, her eyes flashing. "We've got to get out of here. Charlie, put in for a hardship post."

I didn't know what all this meant, but for the first time, moving sounded good to me. I could newly embrace my mother's motto, "You can do anything for a year." To get away from the States seemed like a delicious adventure. Besides, we were living in an occupied country. If America was ever good it was now in the hands of a tyrant: President Nixon.

~~

On October 14 there was an announcement at school about a big antiwar demonstration to take place the following day. It was going to be the biggest ever—and all the students were in a flurry. At home, I rushed into the kitchen to ask Mom if I could go.

"They gave out these." I showed my mother my armband, a strip of black cotton on which had been stamped in white the number of American soldiers killed in the war—something over thirty-five thousand. "We're excused from school if our parents say we can attend."

"I'm not sure, Sara. I'm not sure it's safe," she said. There had been reports that the Weather Underground and SDS, Students for a Democratic Society, were threatening violent actions and the riot police were gearing up, but I was determined. I believed the moratorium would be as peaceful as the organizers had guaranteed the police it would be. At Sidwell, we believed in Gandhian civil disobedience.

"But Mom, everyone's going!" I was not going to let Mom stop me from participating. This meant everything to me. But I could tell by my mother's face that she was in her worried, determined mode, and when she was like this she was an iron gate.

"Mom!" I was beginning to boil and she saw it.

"I'll talk to your father when he gets home," she said.

But at night I heard my mother in their bedroom saying to my father, "She could be raped, or, my God, Charlie, they could get caught in a riot and she could be killed!" Her voice was rising to a shriek now. I put the pillow over my head so I wouldn't hear her urgent wolf voice, to close out the contagion of her worry.

But my father won. He came into my room and said, "Your mother and I have discussed it. You can go to the demo as long as you stay with kids from school, avoid anyone holding an SDS sign, and steer away from any particularly vociferous groups like the Weathermen. Keep a watch out, and if anything starts to get out of hand, you get yourself out of there. Agreed?" I nodded and he said, smiling, "Okay, you can go," and gave me a hug.

I lay on my bed, thinking about how my father had fought for me to go to the "demo," a version of the word no American used. Ever since Holland, it had seemed like the word "demo" had magic sparkles around it for my father. Later, as an adult, I'd comprehend that that word had packed into its four letters all that my father loved about Holland, all that he had to smother in himself, and all that he believed about America. Without saying so, and without my knowing it—and probably without his awareness either—my father was setting me up to be his voice. By way of his daughter, by sending me off to the march, he was able to express the sprouting doubts, seeded in Japan and Taiwan, about his country's manner in the world.

As an officer in the CIA, it was dangerous to feel. To feel was weakness and turned you to prey for the powers that were. My father was not permitted emotion but I was, and he encouraged me to feel and speak out. My mother, on the other hand, needed me not to. I dumped my outrage on her head.

After my father retired, my parents demonstrated for every liberal cause. They were the fluffy white-haired couple in olive green jackets holding signs saying "Another Pro-Choice American," or "Equal Rights for All Women," or "Universal Health Care for All."

The next morning, my father patted me on the back and my mother sent me out the door with a desperately tight squeeze, as though she'd never see me again.

~~

As Sara and I and a clutch of other Sidwell kids traveled to the Mall, the bus was crammed with rumpled protestors wearing dove necklaces and carrying signs. Nearly everyone was holding or carrying a peace symbol; it was like we were all waving the passports of a brand new country. The morning news said a quarter of a million people had descended on the city; the turnout was massive.

From the gleaming Capitol to the Washington Monument and beyond, hand-painted VW campers lined the Mall, along with VW bugs, Karmann Ghias, jeeps, and beat-up Volvos. The air was pungent with the scents of wine, sweat, and marijuana. As far as I could see, the Mall was jammed thick with people flashing peace signs, hoisting hand-lettered peace symbols, "God loves America" signs, and "Fuck Nixon" signs, and everywhere there were people lighting joints, groups sharing loaves of French bread and cheese, and Hare Krishna devotees dancing, their spidery arms waving around.

Music was blasting from the loudspeakers on the multiple platforms: Richie Havens keening, "Marching to the Concors War, to Dunkirk, to Korea, Birmingham

. . . hydrogen bomb, guided missiles . . . Freedom! Freeeeedom" and "Sometimes I feel like a motherless child . . . a long way from my home. . . . Sometimes I feel like I'm almost gone. . . . Clap your hands, clap your hands. . . ." Joan Baez singing her mournful, "I dreamed I saw Joe Hill last night," and the Youngbloods' rousing "Come on people now . . . everybody get together, try to love one another right now. . . ."

And the Mall was chock-a-block with long-haired boys in bandanas, feather headdresses, and floppy Arlo Guthrie hats; boys with foot-tall Afros; boys in sheepskin vests or in loincloths; boys playing kazoos; and disturbing close-shorn boys in fatigue jackets with their names on the pockets. And long-haired girls: girls with feather earrings, girls hugging guitars, girls wearing silver rings on all their fingers or ten necklaces of love beads, girls in Mexican ponchos or army jackets or knee-high fringed moccasins.

It seemed as though I'd landed in Wonderland. . . . Everything I believed in was right here. I strained so hard to hear the speeches—by Benjamin Spock, Justice Arthur Goldberg, and others—blaring from the fuzzy microphones, my head throbbed. When Ambassador Averell Harriman repeated, "Nixon is going to have to pay attention," everyone roared. Nixon was reported to have said, "Under no circumstances will I be affected [by the demonstrations]."

Here on the National Mall it was all brought together: both the gigantic power and the deep flaws of America. Here, among thousands of other young people, I soaked into my bones one of America's basic lessons: the power of free protest.

As the sun went down, the peace marshals handed out candles and we all lined up. Sad and quiet, we followed Rev. Martin Luther King Jr.'s widow in a candlelight vigil to the Nation's Capitol. The city grew dark and hushed, even though thousands of people were gathered for the procession.

As we walked in quiet, I felt dissolved into the flow of people: just one pulse in a massive plea for goodness. In Holland, caught in the headiness of ethnocentrism, I had experienced the negative pull of the group. Here I felt its positive force.

The march was the most exhilarating experience I'd ever had, and seemed like the most important thing I'd ever done. Aside from being in the woods, this was the closest to God I'd ever felt. I was filled with righteous conviction. At last, I felt secure. I was part of something undeniably good. I was a balloon sailing above dark, peaceful, thronging Washington looking down on all the good people who wanted to save the world.

When I told my father about it, breathless, late in the evening, he said, "Bully for you!" I could tell he sort of wished he were me.

~~

The next day, the *Washington Post* reported that Nixon maintained that he had been "conducting business as usual" throughout the day of the moratorium.

At dinner, I said, "Nixon is a capitalist pig."

"Don't be disrespectful," my mother said, "you just control yourself, Young Lady."

"What good does control do?" I said, outraged.

I didn't know how dangerous emotions were in my parents' world. I didn't know the pressures on them, how my father's job was—surreptitiously, clandestinely—destroying parts of them. How my mother had to control her emotions all the time. How my father was going underground with his, and the submerging would turn into an undertow.

~~

I was seeing many things anew, however, even my brother.

I shambled down the powder-blue carpeted stairs in my nightie, feeling all clogged-up still with sleep, and turned the corner into the kitchen. I grabbed my granola and milk, barely seeing Mom and Andy who were in there too, and plopped down at the Formica table. As I began eating my regulation nuts and grains, I began to feel more awake. I felt the sun on my cheek and looked up. My mother was bent down getting sandwich cheese out of the fridge, and Andy was standing in the middle of the kitchen in a daze, like he sometimes did—probably dreaming about General Westmoreland, MacArthur, or someone.

But no! Suddenly the sun was playing in Andy's bed-tousled hair and on his nose, and I saw something new. *Plink!* went a new coin in the bank. My brother was beautiful! He was no longer a little boy with mossy teeth prattling about guns and making elephant jokes. He was almost as tall as I was, and he was handsome as heck standing there, all disheveled, in his navy blue Potomac School jacket and tie.

He ran his hand through his shaggy hair—I suddenly saw that his bangs hung charmingly down into his eyes and that the color was deep hickory-brown—saying, "Mom, where're the English muffins?" And I heard now a new, growly timbre in his voice, like the voice was coming from down deep in, what I saw now was, his broadening chest.

"I'll get 'em, Andy," I said. I'd never offered to do anything for him before in my life, except to get Brownie points with Mom.

As of this day, when Andy said something I listened. And new realizations came to me. As he talked to my father, comparing Vietnam to Guatemala, I saw that he had thought about it much more thoroughly than I had. He could name all the weapons being used in Southeast Asia, and he knew the generals' names and geographical positions. He talked about the Geneva Convention like he'd read it. This brother of mine, who I could suddenly see as a person, would be a key ally during the two blithe and tumultuous years that lay in wait across the globe.

~~

On November 3, Nixon gave a big speech in which he outlined his plan for gradually withdrawing the troops and ending the war. "And so tonight, to you, the great silent majority of my fellow Americans," he said, "I ask for your support." His ratings went up again as he and Vice President Agnew claimed they represented traditional American values. Agnew attacked the news media as a "small unelected elite that do not—I repeat not—represent the view of America."

~~

But on November 15, there was another massive antiwar demo in Washington. It was even bigger and more exhilarating than the last. Five hundred thousand gathered on the Mall.

Then, the next day, the My Lai massacre, which had taken place the year before, was revealed. Nixon's ratings plunged again as the country went into paroxysms of anguish. None of us at school could believe the photographs of the decimated village. We *were* those mothers and children. *And the outrage of this administration— keeping it secret for a year just to protect the Republicans!*

~~

Nixon reduced American troop strength by sixty thousand by December, and, in a bow to China, suspended patrols of the Taiwan Strait.

On February 21, Kissinger began secret talks with the North Vietnamese in Paris, cutting out the State Department and the Department of Defense. I had no idea about my government's fondness for secrecy. Nor had I any sense—despite all the clues—of the secret in my own house.

~~

The hints had been piling up into a tower like my father's Chinese flash cards. Now the tower was so high it was about to topple.

~~

Things were going along normally and then something big happened. My father arrived home one evening and announced he had just gotten his new assignment: Vice Consul in Kuching, East Malaysia, on the island of Borneo. Instantly my whole body bubbled with sparkling Seven-Up. Asia! Borneo, no less! A wild jungle island where headhunters dwelt, where tribal people lived in riverside longhouses on stilts, where hornbills squatted high in the trees—a realm untouched by the American paw. Kuching was a hardship post, so my father would earn extra pay, and it would afford him another grace period during which he didn't yet have to go to Vietnam.

Ironically, Vietnam, the post he was avoiding, was the place he would do the one thing of which he was proudest—the post where, in spite of the government and without government support, he would take a large, redemptive action. But we didn't know this at the time.

My father's friend, Terry, as my mother predicted, got his first-choice assignment: somewhere in Europe. Kuching was lower on my father's list. But my father refused to be defeated. "It's a pasture, but I think it'll be fun. The kids will love it." The strain of being with an agency he no longer fully respected and the repeated disappointments in his career progression were getting to him. Morale was guttering in Washington due to the faltering war. Like many, he simply wanted to get out of Dodge.

The only hitch about the new post was that there was no high school for us to attend in Kuching. After much family discussion, my parents chose Canadian Academy, a missionary school in Kobe, Japan. Out of pure reflex, the Foreign Service girl clicked into departure mode.

~~

But there was yet another bit of news to come, a bit of unsought truth that, without my knowledge, had been, and always would be, sculpting my life. The sea surged to the high tide line; the deeps divulged; the truth surfaced. Onto the sand rolled a murky grey pearl.

We were slouching around at the same old kitchen table, forking up ordinary meat loaf with ketchup and potato chips on an ordinary late-winter evening when my father looked at my mother.

"Sure, go ahead," she said.

Their exchange was strangely calm and offhand.

"I have something I want to tell you two before I go off to Kuching," my father said. He had to fly to Malaysia to take up his new post in a week and my mother and we would join him when school was out, in June. I didn't have a clue what to expect.

"I want you to know something about my work." He took a deep breath. "I don't really work for the State Department. I work for the Central Intelligence Agency."

The moment that should have sent a cold wind whistling through me and halted the world somehow didn't. I continued forking up meat loaf, and listening. I didn't quite get it yet.

"Normally officers aren't supposed to tell their children," my father was going on, "but I think you're both old enough and mature enough to handle it, and I don't want to mislead you any longer."

I still couldn't fathom what was going on.

Then Andy said, "Oh I knew that. You're a spy, aren't you, Pop?" My pipsqueak, bookworm brother explained he'd figured it out from his reading. He knew the euphemisms. *Agency, company:* he'd caught all the clues.

"Are you in intelligence gathering or the covert side?"

"I'm a covert operations officer," my father said.

Now, finally, I began to feel the smooth, dusky weight of my father's announcement. My father was a CIA agent, my brain told me.

Still, though, this chilling and shocking news was somehow not chilling or shocking at all. The news was not a tsunami. It was not even a storm. It was not an iron ball that took me to the bottom of the sea. My reaction surprised me: I was calm. The CIA was one of the prime enemies of the peace movement. I knew that, if I was doctrinaire antiwar, I should be outraged at Pop, but I was intrigued instead of aghast. Somehow the news made sense of things, gave the correct name to something that I'd just barely sensed. I searched and couldn't find fury anywhere in me.

I looked over at my father's face, the brown eyes now bright and eager with the pleasure of finally sharing this fundamental truth with his children. This was still my father, the same man he'd always been, the kindest person I knew, the man in the world I adored. My father never even went over the speed limit. It didn't add up for him to be engaged in anything immoral. I couldn't find even a strand of hate to tug on.

The secret didn't weigh me down, as people might have expected. On the contrary, I felt light and special, like I finally had a membership card—to a group to which I'd long unknowingly belonged.

Yet I had a keen inkling that my father wanted me to scream at him. Part of me sensed that he was getting frayed and he would almost have liked me to pitch a fit and insist that he quit so that he would be able to go into the office and say,

"My daughter is so upset I have to leave," and hand in his resignation letter. Other kids were doing this—fathers were leaving the government due to their children's outrage—but I couldn't help him out. I could do nothing but love him as before. Andy and I were young. We were intrigued. We liked James Bond movies. We were caught up in the glamour, the Hollywood of it all. Still, this was my first intuition that my father felt trapped.

Perilous though it may be, we make exceptions for the people we love. To me, now at sixteen, my father's choice to reveal his true work to his children, his willingness to break the Agency rule, showed his integrity rather than an unforgivable participation in the immoral actions of an immoral agency. How many nuances there are to this matter of honesty.

This matter was a marbled and many-layered cake. Even though they'd lived a large and stunning lie, neither of my parents were people who struck you as fake or deceitful—quite the opposite. My mother was baldly honest and my father the most transparent person I had ever known. He didn't pretend to know when he didn't; he considered every point. He looked at the government, he looked at the president, he looked at himself, and took on board even unpleasant and contradictory facts. He grappled with mixed and messy truths about the Communists, about Vietnam, about the CIA.

The only arena in which he was not open was about his own emotions. These he steadfastly denied having. "No, I'm not worried," he said about himself, his work, the world. "Everything will be fine." Was this simply a father's protectiveness toward his daughter? The self-soothing of a boy raised in a chaotic household? The smothering required to survive at his workplace or by the clandestine nature of his job? Or was it that this sensitive man had to crush himself to fit into a brutal world? In any case, I think he'd lost the ability to know what his feelings were. This is the effect on my father for which I would most blame the Agency: the murder of my father's access to the full repertoire of emotions due to any human being. So often, I heard fear in my mother's voice. "Did you hear what happened to Mr. Carson? He hid his depression, had a nervous breakdown, and lost his job."

Are you being dishonest if you have had your emotions kicked out of you and don't know they're there? Believing he ought to run his life according to principles rather than feelings, my father denied any emotion that might come up. To complicate things further, he didn't denigrate the emotions of others; he honored them. But he would have none himself. In all other realms, my father believed fiercely in seeking and cleaving to the truth. This might seem an odd position for a covert operations officer to hold, but if we accept that, no matter the means, the CIA's goal is to find the truth, it's not so hard. If we looked hard enough, he believed, we could find the truth, and then it was our duty to stand by it.

~~

"Why do we need a CIA at all?" I asked my father as my mother spooned mounds of chocolate-chip ice cream into dark blue Taiwanese stoneware bowls.

"Because there are always strongman regimes up to no good in this world. The world is messy and complicated and we need to collect information on these regimes in order to protect ourselves and others," he said. "Intelligence gathering is essential. A spy agency is necessary: a choice between evils. At its best it has a higher purpose, to stop people like Hitler. It is a kind of morality within amorality, a morality of thieves."

Also, he said, the spread of democracy was a worthy aim, it just depended on how you went about it. As long as it was supporting good causes, that was fine— but sometimes even that got murky. It was the operational division, the part of the Agency that sought to do away with people and governments, that was of questionable merit. Some of the things the Agency did were excellent; others were beyond redemption.

He told us he believed strongly, though, that a lot of the secrecy was unnecessary and many documents marked "top secret" should be open to the public. And a lot of the brazen spy schemes were ineffective and a colossal waste of money— even though the higher-ups often loved the showy, exciting cloak-and-dagger stuff. Much of the best intelligence could be obtained by listening to people closely at parties and in private meetings.

"If you don't believe in it all," I asked, "why do you stay there, Pop?"

"Because it does some good, along with the bad." Then he went on to give me the standard line I'd heard him give many people about why he stayed in government when he disliked the views of an administration. "I also stay with it because it's a good life for Mom and you kids, because it has a good pension, and it's a fascinating life. Learning languages, living abroad, it's vital."

Thirty-plus years later, burrowed into my house in Silver Spring, Maryland, with CIA men wrestling with the truth about Iraq, I would think hard about all that the lying entailed. When my father joined the CIA not long after World War II, he no doubt considered the ends justifying the means. He was lying for a good purpose: to discover the truth about untrustworthy foreign governments, to fight fascism around the world. But as the Agency overthrew Allende, blew Vietnam, and upped the arms race, his sense of the value of the enterprise, its tactics, its own honesty, and the trade-offs troubled him, and the lying became increasingly distasteful, and then unbearable.

The toll on my father was tremendous. Through the years, particularly after I left home, the dissembling, and the dark actions of the CIA, grew like a cancer within him. He grew to hate the Agency—to the point that he'd fight for his right to retire "open," and spend his retirement eaten up by depression. But by then, hiding himself had become a habit he couldn't break.

~~

We sat at the table for a while after our ice cream dishes were scraped clean and my parents were drinking their instant coffee.

Andy and I said, in unison, "Tell us more, Pop."

"It's a messy business," my father said. He shifted on his chair and his face turned serious. "In Chigasaki, when you were born, Sara, we were all doing some very secret work meant to undermine the Communist Chinese government. We were training Chinese to . . ."

"But Pop, what's it like to be a spy?" Andy broke in. "How do you leave secret messages?"

"Yeah, Pop, did you ever deliver secret messages or write in invisible ink?"

"Yes, tell them about *that*, Charlie," my mother said, with some sort of signal in her eyes, as if he shouldn't say too much.

My father's face flashed weariness. It was as though he was tucking away something he'd badly wanted to say. Then he reluctantly gathered himself up to join our mood.

"Yes, I have delivered lots of secret messages and written messages in invisible lemon juice. . . . What you do is write a note in regular ink and then write your secret message in lemon juice between the lines. When the note is heated with an iron, the lemon juice words turn brown and become legible. . . ." And then he showed us with hand motions how to make a chalk mark on a wall, and then leave a concealed message, or packet of crisp bills, in a designated spot at an airport, train station, or other public crowded places. It was just like on TV.

He was smiling his calm smile toward his children, but he told everything with that same sense of weariness. Like these weren't the words he wanted to be saying. There was no pride or lightness in them.

My mother was more able to join our spirits. She seemed a little giddy now that the cat was out of the bag. She began telling us about their days in Hong Kong before either of us were born. "Charlie, tell them about the Star Ferry," she said.

"Yes, well," he said, leaning forward to put himself in storytelling mode, "when we were in Hong Kong, the Communists found out about something we had done and they threatened to throw acid in the face of the man who'd done it when he next crossed on the Star Ferry."

"It was awful," my mother said. "We were scared to death."

Again my father's tired look.

"And I used to follow Pop when he was out on a mission, going to meet someone or leave something," my mother said. "I wasn't going to let anyone get my husband!" When my mother talked like this, I knew how much she loved my father. Her eyes sparked and her voice lilted.

"One time . . . Remember, Charlie? . . . I was trailing your father about a block away and something went wrong. . . . Pop got up too close to where he was going and saw that something was wrong, and he gave me a signal we'd prearranged. It was the sign to get out of there as fast as I could—and then he raced off in another direction."

"Those were exciting days—but they were frightening too."

My father was looking lighter now. The cat was safely curled back in the bag and he had recovered his usual equilibrium. The cat would be released at last a couple of years hence, but my father still had to wait.

My mother could play the game. Later I'd recognize she could do this because she didn't have to be around the crassness, the casual attitudes about non-American lives, the morally questionable schemes forty-plus hours a week.

When she finished, my mother said, "But you can't tell anyone any of this."

My father said, "Yes, I'd like you two to keep this a secret. Just keep telling people what you always have: that I work at the State Department."

This request may seem a heavy burden to put on a child, but it was exciting to me—and second nature, somehow. It was part of my duty as an American patriot. Here, on this strange night, I was not so much an antiwar protestor as a Foreign Service girl in a uniform, united to my past. I was here to serve my country—and most of all, my father.

My father's revelation came along at a time when I needed it. It gave me a boost, a secret society to belong to (even though I knew no one else who was in it), and a secret status (that no one else was aware of), within this secret society of America—and this bolstered me.

I was easily bought, perhaps. Spying and secrecy have a unique sheen and glamour. The movieness of it helped me get through the rest of Sidwell. The dusky pearl I slipped onto a chain and over my head, like a pair of dog tags, or my father's badge for work, restored to me my identity as someone worthy in a place where I often felt adrift. I would keep my father's secret for another fifteen years, and even then, I would only tell my closest friends. Without knowing it, I too was in the habit of secrets. Born under an assumed name, I cleaved to the disguise.

And as a spy's daughter, I inherited a distinct legacy: a penchant for complex and oblique truths, and a built-in, sensitive secret detector.

My father bought a special Sony Short Wave radio before leaving for Kuching—an expensive, compact radio unlike any I'd ever seen before, which I must tell no one about. Even though my father didn't say this directly, I figured out it was for listening in on Communist Chinese radio broadcasts.

When my father flew away to Borneo my stomach felt empty and raw.

After my father left, my mother tried her best, but she was at sea. My father wasn't there as a buffer between us.

On April 20, Nixon announced the withdrawal of 150,000 more troops by the end of the year. He said in a speech to the nation, "peace is in sight."

"Look," I said to Mom. I was the antiwar protestor again. "We caused Nixon to pull out more troops."

My mother sputtered. "You think *you* caused Nixon to pull out? *You kids*!?" She laughed—not knowing she was thrusting her knife into the crystal teardrop of me. To her, World War II was so much more important. She'd spent her teenage years collecting aluminum for the tanks that would save the world. Her heart thumped when she thought of her war, while mine ached for the Vietnamese and for the despair our soldiers were wreaking. Her war was drums booming; mine was a piccolo.

Then, on May 4, the students at Kent State, who were protesting the bombing in Cambodia, attacked the reserve officers' training building on campus. The Republican governor vowed to "eradicate" them and sent in the National Guard. Four students were shot dead.

At school we were staggered. At Meeting for Worship no one spoke.

~~

Toward the end of school, taking a break, Sara and I spent our last few times together working on our tans at the pool at the hotel on Van Ness near her house. I was beginning to feel wispy, like I was half gone. Foreign Service kids have a "quick release," and worn out from the war, I lay in the sun, trying—but failing—to capture in my darkening skin what these two years in America had meant.

In an essential sense, this Washington stay had been a moratorium for me, an in-between time—save for my engagement in the actual antiwar moratoria. Out of this bleak and stirring time, though, I was departing sturdier than I'd arrived. Pain had conferred some wisdom: I'd metamorphosed from a short-sighted teeny-bopper to a thinking teenager. I'd learned the value of quiet reflection, a legacy of my Quaker school that would stand me in good stead for years to come. And I'd learned, through trial by fire, to stand alone.

But socially, Washington had remained a way station for me, a movie set. Even though I spoke English, living in Washington had been like loving someone you could never understand, someone who could never love you back. Washington had never felt as real and alive a place as my other homes across the world. Because of my upbringing, a life that quickened the blood required living in another culture with an undecipherable language. This was an addiction I might never outgrow.

When I'd arrived from The Hague, I'd set foot into a benign place, a big PX, the best country on the planet. I was leaving a frightening, violent country, an evil menace to the world. *America is just a country full of hawks,* I thought, forgetting that I and all the other people at the marches were Americans too.

At school, I was devil-may-care. *I'm sick of this place,* I thought. *There are too many snobs.* I walked around quietly smug, like I had a chocolate cake all to myself: *I can leave all of you. I can just turn my back and fly across an ocean.* This intolerance is the luxury of the itinerant on the verge of departure. And it is easier to leave a place if you can find a way to hate it.

~~

I loved the sight of the packed boxes. Movement was in my blood. More than Sidwell ever had, they felt like home—and signaled adventure. The thought of a new culture stirred me: Asia! I was ready to kick this bucket over.

Book 5

ORCHIDS
Kuching, East Malaysia,
1970

19

colonial

Sarawak was the smell of heat, curry, incense, and gasoline: the perfect salve.

The thrall began the moment the door of the plane swung open and I stepped out onto the hot, bright rectangle of the tarmac. It was as if the tentacles of the jungle and its scarlet-persimmon ornaments reached out and pulled me in. I was translated. America was gone.

~~

My father had walked to the plane to meet us, and stood with open arms at the bottom of the gangplank. Tall, in a white, open-necked shirt, he squeezed all of us tight.

We walked through the moist heat toward a whitewashed building the size of an American gas station: the Kuching Airport. The heat was strong, but it was clean and lightly, florally fragrant. Just as we neared the double doors of the small terminal, five figures trailed out through the doors. Three caramel-skinned women, petite in beautiful sarongs, wisped out to Andy, Mom, and me and placed baskets of orchids in our hands. "Welcome to Kuching," they said in bright, British-accented English.

~~

My father had given us a rundown on Sarawak's history before he'd left America. The British had first arrived on the island of Borneo in the early sixteenth century. In 1839, Sarawak, the northern icing on the cake of Borneo, a river-rich land of swamps and mangrove forest populated by tribes such as Ibans, Land Dyaks, and Kayans, was acquired by James Brooke, the White Rajah. Brooke suppressed the prevalent headhunting and set up a social system of small holdings rather than the more typical European-held estates established in other British-ruled territories. In addition to its tribal peoples, Sarawak's population was made up of Malays and overseas Indians and Chinese. The Japanese occupied Sarawak for four years during World War II. Directly afterward, in 1946, it was ceded to the crown, and made a colony. Ten years later, in 1956, at the end of British rule, the Federation of Malaysia was formed. Sarawak was one of three Malaysian provinces on the island of Borneo.

~~

In the little VIP lounge, a sweet-eyed Malay official in a crisp yellow cotton shirt shook our hands. We also met other people, including cola-haired, handsome Mr. Taylor, the American consul. A man in a sarong and white coat served, from a silver tray, glasses of orange squash and triangular curry puffs—delicious melt-in-your-mouth pastries with spicy potatoes tucked inside. As these kind people from Kuching asked me about my flight, without effort I returned to my formal, diplomatic self. It felt delicious; I could be polite again! I felt set free.

We became part of an entourage of five small cars, jammed with ourselves and our luggage, and a driver whisked us for fifteen minutes down a white-asphalted avenue cut new, wide as a jetway, through the jungle, and then into the narrower, but still spacious streets of the tiny capital of Sarawak with a population of about ten thousand people. Trees lining the streets dripped with flowers beside half-hidden British-style bungalows and cottages. I thought I might have seen a monkey in a tree. I did see chickens dashing across the road, and men and women in straw hats moseying along on bicycles, and women on foot carrying baskets of vegetables. Along the way, my eyes struggled to adjust to the brightness.

Soon the cars ahead of us turned right into a drive that pushed up a green hill. The cars, including ours, stopped at the crest of the hill in front of a low, broad-roofed bungalow with a front veranda. This place reminded me of houses in which British people lived out on the plains of Kenya among lions and wildebeest, but here, instead of endless plain, there was an expanse of lawn dotted with blossoming trees and shrubs. Three slender people, a man in a checked sarong wearing a Muslim fez on his head, and two shy-looking pretty women with curly hair and flower-spattered sarongs, stood, hands clasped in front of them, lined up to greet us. They were our new cook—the man, and maids—his wife and sister, who lived at the back of the house. They beckoned us up one step into high-ceilinged, white rooms hung with broad-bladed, ivory ceiling fans. Bamboo furniture with batik-covered cushions was spaced apart in two large, airy living rooms that led, one following the other, to a formal dining room at the rear of the house, which, in turn, looked out onto a deep garden with a round, concrete fish pond. A small, rectangular building formed an "L" out one side of the back of the house. This was where the servants lived. Wings to the left and right off the second living room, the servants showed us, led to the spacious bedrooms and bathrooms.

My room was exotic, airy, and lovely—and spotless. It was beautifully decorated with objects from the surroundings. My mother had designed the room when she'd come out for a short visit in the spring. Her artistic side had emerged again— as it seemed to each time she was abroad, had household help, and was less rushed with work. Everything in the room was rattan: the tan, red, and black of Bornean basketry. A basket of orchids on the dresser, a round fan on the wall, a rattan-based lamp. She had placed a woven rattan mat over the bedspread on my high bed—to provide a cool place for napping at midday. The space had a restful purity different from the grabby mess of America.

Back in the front living room, I stood with my mouth slightly open—tasting the air of the house, taking in its low-stated beauty, its petit grandeur, its strangeness. Strange because, to my astonishment, I realized the front and rear walls of this spacious, tidy house did not exist. The house was simply open to the elements, like a jungle shelter. Delighted and amazed, I felt my entire body loosen and fill with light, fragrant air.

It was an extension of the sensation that had flown into me when I'd stepped into the bright doorway of the plane. For the instant that I'd stood there at the opening to a strange world, I'd felt the surge of contentment of being where I belonged: at the threshold of a new and fascinating country. I was charged: every pore open. My peripheral vision was restored, my blinders removed, my ears perked, my fingers itching to touch fabrics, thorns, pistils of plants. I was thirsty to drink in the new colors, the new choruses of sounds, the new blends of people. Assailed by the new and strange beauties and elixirs, I wanted to settle myself at a rattan table or pedal off on a bicycle and sample it all.

~~

The next day, I awakened to the sound of cocks and gibbon calls. From the whisper of light bedclothes, I watched geckos skitter up the wall. Seeing them, I curled up, snug and happy under my sheets, as I had years ago in Taipei, the geckos familiar miniature dragons overseeing me, like gargoyles, keeping out the demons.

Soon after breakfast served by Hipni in a sarong and white jacket, my mother, all bubbly with excitement, took us downtown to the market. "Sara, you're going to love it," she said.

The market was a kaleidoscope of colors, sounds, and smells. First I was a girl looking eagerly this way and that. I felt light on my feet, trying to direct my eyes up, down, and side to side all at once, in order to take in all the wares for sale in the jumbled shops wedged tight one after another: the gorgeous batiks with a strange and wonderful bitter fragrance, the intricately carved silver necklaces and earrings, the strange fruits and vegetables, the stalls of wild meats hung on strings, the crates of pirated records, the hand-stitched and embroidered clothing, the jumbles of buckets, oddly shaped rakes, plastic tubs, and bamboo tools. And to watch all the different shades of caramel and toffee people in wonderful, flower-strewn clothing: A woman in a hot pink sari embroidered in gold yelling at an Indian man seated on a pile of rugs. A pair of slight, graceful Malaysian men strolling down the street hand-in-hand. A group of children dressed in ragged shorts scrambling after a ball. A hawker of chicken satay sticks yelling from his makeshift grill. Women in fruit-color prints with baskets on their arms wandering from stall to stall. I tried to parse the sounds: the clacking of Malay, the jangle of Chinese, the whine of British English, the up-down rhythms of an Indian language, the shrieking of a different kind of music from every stall. The air smelled of crab, it smelled of bodies, it smelled of cumin, and of bitter fruits . . . In this sultry air, damp and heavy with moisture, my body slowed to the natural pace of the tropics. I could only walk languidly in the heat, the dress I'd made out of an Indian bedspread clinging to my back.

Then suddenly, while looking at a platter of shining fish, I felt woozy. The market turned in circles. Lumpy durian and surreal, spiky, rouge-colored rambutan fruits like something out of a sci-fi film; baskets of silver bangles; hangings of mango, bark, and lime batiks spun suddenly in a whirling, clashing jetstream of color around my head. The Indian, Chinese, and American rock music mixed together into a garbling blare. The odors of bodies, putrefying vegetables, diesel, and incense assaulted my nostrils. Now they were smothering me. My pores poured sweat. I was going to faint. I squatted, put my head down, and breathed fast until finally, my mother bending over me with concern, I still felt weak but no longer as though I would both throw up and black out. I clutched my mother's hand. She hailed a cab, and we went home. I lay in my bed in my new air-conditioned bedroom through the afternoon, ashamed by what seemed a clear case of culture shock.

I slept for two days. Maybe I'd gulped too fast.

On my second foray into town, restored, I was able to take in each facet of downtown Kuching with pleasure. I was taken by the little capital with its hubbub of people strolling among the hornbills, parrots, and birds of paradise like white tigers. I loved all the bare toes of the steamy place. There is a singular beauty to bare toes—sparkling, manicured toes in sandals; grubby working toes in zoris. I loved the shops of olive-colored urns painted with ochre dragons. I loved Kuching's blare: the incessant, full-blast din of mixed-up music, the twang of a sitar jamming with a Steppenwolf harangue. And the car and motorbike horns beeping and blasting as though their drivers had only that day discovered the joys of the internal combustion engine. I loved the clipped d's and r's of Malay and the long-lost but oddly familiar hard consonants of Chinese. I loved the men in white shirts and checked sarongs and the women in their sarongs of hot pink, mango, and lime flowers, all liquid grace. I loved the hot colors and the hot food to go with the hot, steamy air. The slow, watery movements of equatorial life enchanted me.

Watching the women moving like graceful swans across the rivers of the bazaar, gazing around at the oranges and silvers of the fish, at the extravaganza of colorful fabrics, at the tribal shields and woven baskets decorated with geometric frogs and snakes hanging from the stall poles, I fell in love.

Right away I adored batik cloth. I decided the sarong, after the sari, was the most beautiful kind of female dress: a simple tube of cloth doubled over in front, and cinched with a silver belt at the waist. It is partly the way a sarong feels—whispery, cool, and romantic around your legs. And you walk with shorter steps; you slow to tropical languidness. My mother and I were both taken by the colorful, spicy fabric that came in every tropical shade: the greens of pine and broad leaf palm; the reds of geranium, hibiscus, and fuschia; the oranges of mango, saffron, tangerine, and pineapple; the blues of sky, 1 a.m., and cobalt. The designs of orchids and snakes and dragons curling in and out of one another.

My mother bought me a piece of cloth for a sarong, pinkish-red on one half, white on the other, with saffron flowers scattered overall. After buying lengths of batik, my mother led me to a tailor who would make us simple dresses. I was fitted for one in lime and one in watermelon. Forever after it would seem to me that a batik shift was the perfect summer dress.

At one of the storefronts that offered pirated tapes, Andy and I ordered a three-hour tape made of our favorite singles: Steppenwolf, the Rolling Stones, the Doors.

With some of the money I earned babysitting in Chevy Chase when I was still plan-
ning to emigrate to Holland, I bought myself a silver ring.

"The amazing thing, Pop, is that there's no American influence at all," I said to
my father at dinner.

"Not a McDonald's on the whole of Borneo."

~~

Even though I had never been here in my life, walking around Kuching I had
a keen sense of return.

The feeling was of elation, of jail break. And I hadn't even realized I *had been*
in jail for the last couple of years. Ah, the wild happiness of being abroad. It was a
feeling deep inside—of light flooding. Colored lights. Pinwheels. The caramel lights
of whiskey. I was back in the gorgeous-glorious. This felt like the purest me. I was
toffee at the moment in cooking that it turned to itself. It was as though, after a long
hiatus, I'd recovered the file, the identity, the correct dossier.

~~

As for my father's dossier . . . Two fierce-looking Sikh men in turbans—instead
of the usual allotment of marines—stood guard at the entrance to the American
consulate, which occupied the second floor of a nondescript, concrete building on
the central plaza in downtown Kuching, just a few minutes from home.

The consulate consisted of the consul, Mr. Taylor; my father, the vice consul;
and Mr. Giddings, the communicator, a Vietnam veteran. In addition to being the
vice consul of East Malaysia, my father had been appointed consul of Brunei, a
British protectorate, by Queen Elizabeth II. I was "the vice consul's daughter"; it
sounded like something from a book. My father's primary job, as I would learn
after he retired, was to make contacts with the "overseas Chinese" in Kuching, in
hopes of finding some who traveled back and forth to China, had high or inside
contacts there, such as in the atomic bomb project or in the upper echelons of the
Communist Party, or in the jails, and could report juicy morsels back to him. He
was also to monitor the Communist insurgency from Kalimantan, the Indonesian
southern half of the island. He had regular consular duties as well.

This was the first tour abroad during which I was aware of the true nature of
my father's work. Knowing he was a spy strangely changed little. I acted the diplomat's daughter. There was just a tiny added shiver in all we did.

At the dinner table, my father regaled us with stories of his consular duties—
those he could talk about. Often, he was beset with an American twenty-year-old

hippie who'd been roaming around Borneo and, now that he was ready to head home, had been refused permission to enter Singapore, the only route back to the States and the world—due to the length of his hair. The Singaporean authorities arrested boys with locks. So, my father had turned into an appearance advisor.

"What do you think I should have done, Sara?" my father asked me one day after seeing in his office a young man with a passion for turtle biology who had just spent a month on the islands nearby, and had shoulder-length hair. I imagined a handsome boy I might see at an antiwar march in Washington.

"He told me the Singaporean authorities were unfair. I agreed and then I told him the best thing would be to go right to the barber and get a haircut."

Despite my own knee-jerk outrage at the Singaporean policy—*People should be free to dress and be any way they wish; it's a free world!*—I realized sometimes the practical was the only route. In the bold, equatorial light of Borneo I couldn't miss the truth that people in different cultures had fierce and varying outlooks, some of them too rigid for a twenty-year-old American to take on.

"I guess he has to if he doesn't want to go to jail. Unless he can find a freighter. . . ." Freighters figured large in my and Andy's images of wild, Asian romance.

"He came back today with a crew cut," my father reported the next day. There was a little start inside me; I envisioned the beautiful American hippie transformed to fuzz-topped soldier or scraped-bald prisoner.

My father seemed happy in Kuching. It was such a rare place, with mountains to drive over in the consulate Land Rover, with village chiefs to interview and Chinese to ferret out and meet. The job had taken my father out of the mainstream, which seemed both good and bad. It was a backwater, but a welcome reprieve from office politics and frustrations, and I thought my father relished the role of lone operative. The haunting that had sometimes lurked like a dark shadow in the backs of his eyes seemed to have slipped away, but there was both a "devil may care" and a "damned if I do and damned if I don't" quality to him. Years later he would evaluate his accomplishments in Kuching: "Did we think we were going to find a kingpin, a fount of information about China in Kuching? Nothing much came of all that. I didn't get much from those Chinese."

But while my father later pooh-poohed his posting in Kuching—by nature a humble man, he always downplayed the worth of his accomplishments—his good friend, another CIA operative, reflecting on it all, said, "I think it was a treat for your father, a bit of R & R. And what your father did in Kuching was a creditable contribution to our work. His opening up a station there was a feather in his cap."

~~

Kuching mornings I awakened in a cool, clean, muffled quiet, and to a rhythmic, soft shushing sound. *Swish, swish* went Ani's broom early mornings—and intermittently throughout the day. She moved, like other Malay ladies, with the graceful, slow movements of a swan. Her clothes, too, seemed to flow. With one hand, she whisked her broom of soft grass across the living room floor. She moved so silently and was so quiet in her being that she was barely perceptible, even to those a foot away—the ideal servant, or spy.

After I got dressed each morning, I wandered into the dining room where the long table was set with four places. Each place had a small plate on which was waiting a thick wedge of pineapple or a curve of papaya, with a slice of dewy lemon for squeezing on the sweet, orange flesh. After we ate our fruit, Hipni brought in homemade buttered toast and eggs on fresh white plates.

Hipni was a wonderful cook. From the moment we first set foot in the house, I hadn't entered the kitchen and almost never had my mother. The kitchen was Hipni's abode and he was such a master that it didn't make sense to interfere. Lunch began with British cream crackers sprinkled with spices—followed by club sandwiches or french fries and hamburgers. The Americans before us had been Italian, and so Hipni cooked excellent lasagna and spaghetti, as well as delicious Malaysian curries. For treats, he made us homemade potato chips or ice cream—out of powder from a can obtained with great difficulty from a special shop at the market.

Sometimes, on weekends, we went to the stinky, bustling market for dinner. My parents knew a special stall that served big spicy crabs that were pure—to use my mother's word—"delectamy."

One Saturday, my mother said, "I was at the Seventh Day Adventist Hospital today and made a discovery. Let's go over there after lunch!" She had an impish twinkle in her eye.

My father drove us in the consulate Land Rover to the Seventh Day Adventist compound, near a roundabout in the broad, empty airport road. There, from a little plywood booth set on the roadside, we bought what a sign advertised as "ice cream sandwiches": a scoop of soy milk ice cream placed between the two halves of a hamburger-like roll. That was how far we were from America.

And we were so ice cream starved that it tasted excellent.

~~

Steamy afternoons. Each day after lunch, a misting rain descended for an hour or so. Afterward, vapor rose over the streets to the height of our thighs. As my mother, Andy, and I walked down one of the residential streets designed by the British one day, white dampness rose around our legs and all around, under the high fronded canopy of green. At a large, open house, we played mahjong with a Canadian family—the father was a lumber expert—that had been planted in Kuching for decades. They had a sandy-haired son named Clive who was my age and had an appealing, offhand way of talking while he explained the game. I loved the feel of the ivory bricks, their clicking sound, and the flicked strokes of their intriguing characters.

My mother was all funny charm, talking with Clive's mother about the adorable children at the Cheshire Home for Crippled Children where she was now volunteering. "I want to take them all home," she said to this angular lady in a faded batik frock. My mother was giddy with happiness. She was inspired, like me, by the jungle air, the swirling batiks, and the sweet-eyed people.

~~~

Life in Sarawak constantly offered up the strange. An anteater lived in our sewer, and every twilight, Hipni made sure the dining room was clear of snakes before we went in. From some secret source, he appeared one day with a snake stick. It was a long pole of wood, itself twisty and long like a snake—to post over the entrance to the house.

Steamy-thick nights we sat on the veranda in the darkness, mosquito coils we called pucks glowing like dragon eyes, speaking only now and again, and then quietly, taking in the caress and insect hum of the silky night.

Life was too intriguing, absorbing, and complete in Kuching to miss America, though sometimes during my siesta, or while I was sunbathing outside on the orchid hill, I wished I could show Sara the batiks, the tapestries of jungle life.

I had been whisked into a limbo. It was a new kind of moratorium: a rest from worries about fitting in, a respite from worrying about my country's actions abroad.

~~

My mother was in her element in Kuching. Back to *her* double life: working at the Cheshire Home and at a leprosarium—and giving teas for Malaysian and Chinese ladies, along with hosting dinner parties, as part of her official duties. Within a week, it seemed, my mother became friends with everyone: a Chinese doctor, the museum director, nurses, missionaries, nuns. Happiness came easily to her here, unlike in Washington. Malaysia was a place barely retrieved from the jungle. It was perfect for her: she was always happiest with dirt under her fingernails. And she was living at her fullest, by her treasured creed: "At the end of the day, if I feel I helped someone, I can feel my presence on earth was worthwhile."

I was walking among small thatched houses down a small dirt street in a walled compound way outside of town. I was with my mother, and there was a man with us, an eager man, leading the way.

As we came abreast each dwelling, the man, my mother, and I squatted to greet the small occupant, a weaver who looked as old as the earth, seated, legs extended, in front of the doorway at a backstrap loom. Beautiful red, yellow, and black patterns rippled along each frame. Each time we squatted, my stomach clenched in revulsion and fear as I extended my hand in greeting. All the weavers had leprosy—we called them lepers then. Each weaver's hand was a palm studded with gnawed-off stumps for fingers. My mother, bringing her physical therapy skills to help the inmates, held each person's hand with almost reverential tenderness. As my hands met those of the villagers, their hands were rough, dry, and scaly, like I imagined an elephant's skin would be. But once I calmed myself, I lifted my eyes to smiles.

My mother's behavior spoke her values: that we were no better than anyone else, not better than a disabled orphan, not better than a Dyak, not better than a leper. In fact, people who were suffering might be more worthy. We should not dress in a superior way, and should treat everyone with equal respect.

My mother was back on her feed, treating leprosy victims, struggling children—as she would later treat napalm-burned children in Vietnam.

~~

My father, the refined and elegant covert officer; my mother, the half–embassy lady and half–peace corps volunteer: these were my parents. Andy, meanwhile, read about the White Rajah, the different Bornean tribes, and the hornbills and gibbons secreted deep in the jungle—an interest he would one day carve into a career as a wildlife biologist.

My family was expert at the twin requisites of good travelers: discomfort and curiosity. Our patron God should have been Ganesh, the elephant of overcoming obstacles. We had adventures in our family, instead of relatives. That was the trade-off.

~~

On the fourth of July, as took place in every American embassy around the globe, we went to the embassy party in Mr. Taylor, the consul's, walled garden. With the Malay and Chinese guests, we ate hot dogs and hamburgers. The buns had been flown in from the commissary in KL—that was the cool way to say Kuala Lumpur—along with Ripleys potato chips, Cokes, ice cream, and ginger ale. It seemed surreal to be eating burgers at the edge of a jungle inhabited by people who lived in houses roofed with leaves and didn't know what a television was.

Even though we were in faraway Borneo, we did the normal American things—though they all had a Bornean flair. I was of age to hold an American driver's permit, so my father taught us to drive in the consulate Land Rover, careening along the empty strips of gravel road that cut, like machetes, into the jungle.

Early on in the summer, a small occurrence startled me out of my diplomat's daughter complacency. My mother enrolled me in a swim team at the public pool, where an American Peace Corps volunteer whom she had met was teaching Malaysian kids to swim. I was not interested in competing, and soon quit. What was striking to me, though, was that this lanky American gave me no special attention. In fact, I was of less interest to him than the Malay kids in his charge, and I was taken aback. I found this both discombobulating and bracing. I was not the center of the world—and maybe the world *was* more interesting than I was. This little upset was the first jog onto a new path.

~~

My mother had structured my day. Borneo was a time of calm, of liking my mother. In our eagerness to sample Borneo, we were in sync—and she had arranged my day, like pieces of furniture, into a lovely whole. Each day I awakened to the sound of the rooster who lived in the compound at the rear of our house. I slipped on a shift, brushed my long hair loose, and then proceeded into the cool, open dining room. I ate my gracious breakfast with a glass of powdered skim milk. Then I mounted my bicycle and rode down the hill and into the neighborhoods of walled houses in the Kuching outskirts, to my batik teacher's house.

Riding to batik, along the padi and then winding through the humble, shacky houses, I was humming. I was not thinking about anything, even myself. I was just a girl on a bicycle, her legs pumping, her arms strong with steering, the damp breeze on her brow, passing by the houses with eaves, the children running in slapping shoes, and the mothers chattering in their clangy language—just experiencing the deliciousness of hearing, seeing, and smelling, without thinking.

Ramsay Ong was a brilliant batik artist who had agreed to take on Clive, the Canadian boy, and me, for art lessons. For three hours each morning, we sat on the concrete floor of the veranda at the front of his elegant, antique-filled, low-bowing house beside a fish pond and a garden of fecund tropical plants, and painted large pieces of muslin with wax. After each waxing we scrubbed our paintings with dye, in darker and darker colors, until, with the last dying, they were finished pieces in four or five crackled colors.

Painting with my waxy brush in the sun of Ramsay's patio, my life seemed like a batik painting: I came into the world with a fresh, clean piece of muslin. Each time I moved, that piece of cloth had been dunked into a new, distinctive, vibrant color, and as I lived along in that place, portions of that color had been waxed permanently into the cloth. In transit between countries, the cloth had been crumpled and wadded and the wax had cracked so that the dyes of the ensuing places had bled into and mingled with the previous, to make the rich, multicolored picture that was my unfolding life. Wax and dye, wax and dye: that is life.

I painted a turtle, an owl, a castle—and then, later in the summer after trips into the jungle, I painted a woman in a straw hat with a plow, an Iban *kampong*.

Clive was the gifted artist of the two of us. He painted graceful men carrying bows through the jungle, and women in bright, ornate sarongs. We quickly became fast friends. This was my first experience of having a boy as a real friend. It was as though I was tuning up for real romance, for there were sweet rhythms in the air between us as I told him about the kids at Sidwell and he talked about how his father hated his artistic bent. "I hate my boarding school in BC," he said.

"I'm a little nervous about going to mine in Japan. Who knows what it'll be like," I told him. With Clive, I felt at ease. My shyness loosened. Unlike the earlier rehearsals with boys, Clive and I knew each other as real people rather than images in books or characters of our imaginations.

These mornings on Ramsay's veranda were a time of utter peace—the peace of doing, creating while surrounded by other quiet creators, a circumstance I would cherish throughout my life. We chatted, but mostly we painted, and Ramsay painted alongside us, spinning out stunning painting after stunning painting of willowy women on the planks of longhouses, small houses on stilts above rivers, chickens and roosters being fed by slender lads, men laboring in padi. Midway through the morning, Ramsay's servant brought us lemonade on a hand-wrought silver tray.

On the beat of twelve, I biked back home through the curtain of sweltering heat, to the coolness of the house, where my mother, Andy, and I ate one of
Hipni's simple, delicious meals. My father sometimes joined us, the consulate was
that close by. After lunch, everyone rested. Sometimes I lay in my room, under the
whisking cool of the fan, and dozed or read, or I went outside and sunbathed. After
our siesta or "kip," and after the usual brief afternoon shower, we went to "the club"
for a dip. At five or so, we returned home and got ready for dinner and my father's
arrival. We dined on lasagna or veal scallopini, and then slipped into our cool beds.
It was a perfectly balanced, luxurious life.

~~

"The club," set up decades before by the British, was a white building with low
eaves and verandas set high on a hill in the middle of a rolling golf course. A swimming pool sat on the crest of the hill beside the club building. Set as it was on the
highest rise in Kuching, the club truly lorded over the town.

The club dining room smelled of tea and cakes. Like in Taiwan, white-jacketed
waiters brought Andy and me sweating glasses of ginger ale and hamburgers, and
our parents toddies and cups of tea, even when the air was steamy and soggy.

The many British and other colonial—Australian and Canadian—women wore
shirtdresses and batik shifts. The men wore loose trousers and open-collared, loose
batik shirts or safari shirts with epaulettes. Talking to all the Anglophone people
at the club, I again felt a rushing back of my old diplomatic self. I plied my formal
manners.

The luxury of the British colonial way of life is impossible to resist—the ironed
white table cloths; the food and drink brought at your whim (just sign the chit, no
money involved); the serene, dustless, gracious houses; the club life. It is almost like
living in a book—and offers both a sense of the absurd and a sense of dabbling in
moral trouble. The inequities glare, but if you're on the lucky side of it, it's seductive.

One afternoon, my father—who was game but laughing and shaking his head
at the ludicrousness of it all—joined the British men and a sprinkling of Canadians and Australians for their game of Hounds and Harriers. This was a crazy
routine in which one man took off from the top of the golf course in the heat of
the day, and broke a path through the jungle, leaving signs and way markers as he
ran along. After a time, the herd of other players left the top of the hill, raced off
into the jungle, following the signs, until they returned, five miles later, sweaty as
rags and puffing with exhaustion. My mother, Andy, and I waited at the pool until

the first man was spied. Looking like bedraggled shipwreck survivors—oh, how the British love tests of endurance—the men straggled up the hill and fell in piles before a table of shandies, and slowly revived as they downed the lemonade-beer, puffing and snorting about what a good run it had been. "Only mad dogs and Englishmen . . ."

I watched Mrs. Clement, wife of the British consul, beside the turquoise sparkling pool. She had deep breasts and wore a royal blue swimsuit that showed them off. She was very pretty, and very polite, but the politeness was a kind that made you feel dismissed and small. When she said hello to me it also felt like good-bye.

She treated the waiter similarly; sitting at her customary table, she summoned him with two disdainful fingers and issued her order without looking up. "Yes, Missee," the deferential waiter said, and slipped soundlessly off to fulfill her command.

"These Malays," she commented to Mom in passing. "They're nothing like the Chinese. They don't know how to work."

Mrs. Clement's comment made me cringe. I loved the delicious leisure of the club, but all this luxurious graciousness—all this distilled beauty—depended on servants, on a human caste system. St. Peter's, European castles, Asian palaces, British clubs: all built on the backs of peasants.

~~

One day we were eating curry puffs and taking drinks at the club—orange squash for Andy and me and shandies for my parents—in the coolness of the rattan-furnished dining room with the big-winged fans rotating, leisurely, overhead. I felt as though I was living in an E. M. Forster novel.

Andy wanted another orange squash. With an expert flick of his finger, my father signaled the white-jacketed waiter, a quiet, straight-postured Malaysian man in his ubiquitous spotless white jacket.

When the waiter brought the drink on a small silver tray and placed it before my brother, my father, looking crisp in his pressed white shirt, just kept listening to my mother and didn't seem to notice. Later, when we were about to leave, and my father signed the chit, he scribbled his name in his illegible, offhand chicken scratch, and handed the note back to the waiter with the same casual ease.

That's when it hit me like an invisible blow inside my chest. We were just like Mrs. Clement. Maybe we felt guiltier—and my father was a deeply fair man—but our actions were the same as hers. Our good manners and easy life depended on viewing others as if they didn't exist. This was the rub: Elegance and sophistication equaled seeing through people. Beauty was cold and exploitative. It was suddenly upsetting to see my father treating the quiet-moving waiter as though he barely existed. It didn't match my image of my father, or of us.

That evening when my mother asked me to ring the bell, as she sometimes did, to summon Hipni so that our dinner plates could be removed and dessert brought, I said, "No. I don't believe in having servants. I'm not going to ring a bell for a human being."

My mother said, "Please ring the bell, Sara."

"No, I won't. I can't." I both felt my mother's words pushing at me like a command and a clutching inside. I felt tears rising. Maybe it was all the poverty I'd been absorbing, or maybe it was the complexity of trying to be a sophisticated diplomat's daughter and also be a good and fair human being, or maybe it was the legacy of Sidwell, of feeling invisible myself, but I suddenly felt chaotic and rampant.

My father understood that this was not about defiance. "Sara, the world is not a fair place. I know you don't feel comfortable having servants do things for you, but the truth is, we are offering Hipni something very valuable to him. We offer Hipni, his wife, and sister a much better job than they would have otherwise—an easy job at a much higher salary than they would get on the local market."

This didn't convince me.

Then my mother added another facet to the complexity of this crystal globe I was trying to balance. "You know," she said, "Hipni has his own servant at his home by the river."

How do I put all this together—the snooty British, our polite but exploitative manners, Hipni's servants? Does feeling guilty make you any less culpable for the inequalities in the world?

Propriety, custom, rules, and roles were reassuring; everyone knew what to do, jobs needed to be done. All my life I'd heard embassy mothers debate whether or not a lady should be friends with her servants. "If you give them an inch they'll take a mile. If you're too intimate with your maid, it'll be harder to give her instructions. It's good to have clear boundaries," the argument went, but there were always people who wanted to *know* the people who worked for them as people.

This concern about servants was more common among Americans. The people I'd known from other, older cultures seemed more comfortable with inequity, with people's "stations in life," with subsets of people serving other subsets.

I'd come across a similar debate when I'd live among the sheep ranchers of Patagonia as a young adult. The peons would discuss the pros and cons while eating mutton barbeque under the enormous open skies of Argentina's southern steppe. "Spanish landowners are like *compañeros*," they'd say. "They don't pay as much and they're always late, but they're like you and me." British landowners, on the other hand, they'd say, "pay better and your check is always on time, but they'd never come and eat *asado* with us. They keep us here and them over there." That was the dilemma: rules kept relations straight, exchanges fair, and roles clear, but they always had demeaning class divisions built into them. On the other hand, the colonial way of life was delicious. Who *wouldn't* like it? Hipni, our cook, liked having a servant. And wouldn't it be a more gracious and inviting world if everyone had someone to serve them once in a while? So I roiled.

In my twenties, I would read Paul Scott, Rumer Godden, and Penelope Lively, and I would think, *I have lived in the American Raj.*

~~

Sarawak is a land of waterways: broad, narrow, shallow, and impassable, deep rivers along with rapid, narrow streams. There are few roads. Settlement followed the river system, as my father explained, and rivers provide the main communication system. On the lower reaches of the large rivers, Chinese, Malays, and Melanaus are mixed with Ibans. Villages of Malay and Melanau fishermen live in houses high on piles along the river banks. The people earn their lives through fishing, planting padi, and working timber and sago. A few run Chinese shops and bazaars. On rivers farther inland live the Ibans, Land Dyaks, and other tribes. The rivers—and lands—to the south and east, toward the Indonesian border, are virtually uninhabited. Tea-colored waterways lace in and out through the jungle, revealing a rubber plantation here, a square of padi there, but mostly miles and miles of impenetrable, dripping, fecund rainforest.

We traveled upriver by boat to a river kampong. Here the river was fetid, overhung with crowded, dilapidated shacks. Crude, slender houseboats, and straw thatch-tented canoes hung with laundry and fishing poles, crowded the water along the banks. Rickety houses on stilts perched over the water. We disembarked at a drooping wooden dock and walked along the main dirt street of a village. We passed women carrying broad, flat baskets of durian fruit. We passed men bent over under the weight of huge bundles. We passed skinny-legged and skinny-armed children. Squatting beside a ramshackle house was an old woman with a filthy piece of cloth wrapped around her head, her lips red from betel nut.

In a little cantina, we drank soft drinks from enamel cups. Below us, down a muddy alleyway to the river, I watched two women, hair tied up in old cloths, washing clothes in the stream.

I pondered the poverty around me: the chattering of poor people and their quiet dignity; their dark, soft, strange eyes. I sat drinking my soda, worrying. Should I pity them, honor them, help them, observe them, or should I keep away? These questions would send me to work with the underclass after college.

As a transient, a foreigner, as a diplomat's daughter, I possessed perhaps the world's greatest luxury: the freedom to leave. Whatever problems the natives had to face I would never have to grapple with.

~~

We took a boat to a riverine island where the British established a resort, a Robinson Crusoe isle of clean thatch-and-reed huts set around a central canteen, and spent three days on its sandy shores, swimming and eating delicious trout and clams cooked for us by a man in a loose white shirt and sarong over a smoky open grill. This was the quintessential colonialist's weekend.

Another weekend, we drove for an hour and then walked for half an hour to make one of my father's official calls. We passed through the flourishing stubble of slash-and-burn agriculture to an Iban longhouse: a multifamily house made of bamboo, set high on stilts above a dark brown, peat-flavored stream. The house was a rambling platform, one side of which was partitioned into family compartments. Along the other side was a veranda, the common gathering and working place. At one end was a round chamber for important meetings. A man with two teeth and a shallow bowl haircut identical to every other man's guided us into this chamber, where we were asked to sit down. Ladies with their breasts bare, in sarongs, brought us cups of a cloudy liquid and offered us plates of mushed vegetables. The longhouse dwellers sat all around us in a circle, watching us drink and eat. Women with betel nut–stained teeth squatted, and children stood at the edges. All of their faces were shining with sweat. There was a strong smell of bitter nuts, bodies, and flowers. We couldn't communicate except through our interpreter. Just before we went outside again, two girls about my age, with red teeth and silver rings around their legs, were pushed in front of my father. The interpreter said the chief of the longhouse, in a gesture of honor, was offering them to my father: two virgins. My father, serious-eyed, thanked the chief, but shook his hand politely, no.

Afterward, the chief led us to a little hut perched off the edge of the veranda. Inside the dark dome we saw small brown orbs hanging: the community's collection of shrunken human heads.

On our way back to Kuching, my father shrugged off the offering of virgins. "He was just showing me respect," he said. My mother said, "Did you see the maggots in the bottom of our glasses? Ughh!" Andy said, "Where do they pee?" My mother said, "Mrs. Cassell told me that the jungle people are so intrigued with modern inventions that they name their children Helicopter and Brassiere!" Andy asked, "Are you sure they don't shrink heads anymore?" It was goofy, creepy, intriguing, and strange. I didn't know where in my own head to put this longhouse with its collection of heads.

~~

The longhouse gave me a sniff of the just-out-of-the-jungleness of human nature—and the precariousness of civilization. With one wisp of the wind, one little nudge, we'd be tipped back into vengeful, fury-and-blood tribal warfare: hand-bent bows and poisonous, blood-dipped, feather-swathed arrows.

Back in Kuching, Borneo seemed riotous. Neither careful nor neat, it was a place of clutter and clash, a realm of multiple angrily and pacifically cohabiting cultures, with a mismatched jumble aesthetic. Choose what you want from among shouting parrot and peacock colors: brown with red, with yellow, with pink; black and fuschia; or screaming green. Unlike France or Holland, or messy chambray shirt and jeans America, Borneo opened my eyes to the world's fecundity, its extravagances, its generous, infinitely fruiting nature. Like Antoine de Saint-Exupéry's Little Prince, I walked around in wonder. It seemed a kingdom of excess, multitudinous, anything-goes freedom. "If it's worth doing, its worth overdoing."

~~

Sarawak yielded up two experiences that changed my life.

The first was a trek.

My father drove Andy and me in the Land Rover for three hours over mushy ruts cut through the jungle to a little outpost of three small buildings. There, we parked. In front of one of the buildings, we met Father Downey, a round American, a slim guide, and another local man. We'd come to accompany Father Downey on one of his missionary rounds. We slathered our legs with insect spray, hoisted our rucksacks, and the six of us started down a narrow path leading straight into the jungle. We carried U.S. Army canteens and we wore green khaki jungle boots with rubber soles we'd bought at the market. We wore hats, but still, in ten minutes, we were already dripping with sweat.

Soon we got our stride. The path was narrow and wet. The jungle was close and claustrophobic. We crossed tiny rivulets and brooks on felled logs. There was cawing overhead, and the drone of insects. We spied a gibbon hanging from a long vine, and a hornbill. Otters slooped through the currents of a stream.

At one point, when our spirits were drooping, the guide had us sit down on the path, while he plunged off to the right. Soon he returned with what looked like six long staffs. They were not staffs, but lengths of cane. He showed us how to rip off a hunk of the stalk with our teeth, suck and chew the fiber until all the sweet was gone, and then spit out the remaining wad of plant. The cane was lightly sweet, and utterly refreshing—a new discovery. We didn't have to suck on stones here: we could chew cane.

Finally, at the end of three hours, we saw a bright opening in the forest. All around was scrub, interspersed with fruit and rubber trees, and vegetable and pepper gardens. Ahead was an open green, and behind it hills of padi. Walking ahead we found on the green a tiny hamlet of bamboo huts on stilts, surrounded by palm trees. Red hibiscus flowers laced their way up the stilts. Beneath the tiny houses chickens skittered.

On our approach, we passed a line of six or eight upright stones, animist figures like ancient beings, being licked by some scruffy goats. I stopped a minute to circle the stones. The figures seemed open-faced, small, and friendly.

Up a rude ladder, in one of the houses, a woman in a faded sarong served us tea. She smiled at me and listened intently to the priest. A boy led us to the hut on stilts where we'd spend the night.

After simple plates of brown rice and vegetables served by the woman, four young men appeared at the ladder of our hut. Father Downey greeted them with open arms and beckoned them up, then got busy with what he was here to do. My father, Andy, and I sat with our backs against the bamboo walls as Father Downey read for an hour from the Bible. As he read on with the drone of an insect, I thought of the collection of small stone figures outside in the pasture. It seemed so violently wrong to me. I thought about imposition—about the priest's imposition of his beliefs on people with their own perfectly serviceable religion. I thought about missionaries and about the U.S. government: how both imposed their ways on others with a sense of righteousness. To a fault, I'd be wary of imposition always—that of others and my own.

At night, we slept fitfully, slapping mosquitoes, sticky with heat, on mats placed over the bamboo-slat floor. Accompanying us, all through the jungle-black hours, was a chorus of crickets and chickens and insects.

The next day, with Father Downey tapping his Bible and clapping his young protégés on the back, we set back through the jungle.

On the return trek, Andy and I were exhilarated. We fancied ourselves explorers, discoverers of new monkey species. How quickly the explorer took us over. The more mosquitoes and disasters, the better the heroism, the better the story.

On the way back through the swampy forest, I longed to go more deeply into cultures than the embassy life allowed or promoted. I was burning to understand what the stone figures meant to the villagers. I wanted to understand as an insider, not just as a watcher against a backdrop.

~~

The second happening was this. One afternoon, when I returned from batik, I found my mother sitting with two guests in the rattan chairs in the first living room overlooking the garden. The woman had long straight hair like mine and was dressed in a plain jean skirt and a tucked white blouse. The man, tall and burly, had a full, scruffy beard. The two looked American, but there was something unkempt, vaguely wild, and totally intriguing about them. My mother patted the seat beside her and offered me some lemonade from a tray.

She introduced the couple as two anthropologists from the University of Michigan who were studying the jungle Dyaks. I spent the next two hours listening, rapt, to stories of thirty-day river trips through the jungle, afternoons passed eating fish and talking to toothless women in longhouses, and of weeks devoted to helping out with the slash-and-burn rice harvest. The couple explained that they had only as many possessions as they could carry on their backs and fit into a dugout, and otherwise lived from the jungle. Gibbons and orangutans swung from the trees outside their tiny jungle hut.

I listened, mesmerized, as the couple gobbled up the tuna fish sandwiches, spicy crackers, pineapple, and homemade ice cream my mother offered them. I had never heard of a life so romantic or fascinating. Their tales reminded me of sitting in my amah Mary's house, back in Taiwan. Even back then, perhaps, eating red rice with Mary's bent parents looking on, the quest of my life had been laid down.

Living somewhere, having a house, and establishing a routine of life, is different from just visiting. But it is an in-between existence. It is neither like being a tourist, nor the same as being "of" the place, living "on the local market" as the embassy people say. Being with an embassy was like peering in a window—tasting only the appetizer of the other culture.

As an embassy person you're not a visitor, you're something else. You have access to the local people, and to experiences a visitor does not, but you are mainly a kid with your own kind against a foreign backdrop. Still, backdrops are significant. They penetrate deep.

I resolved, here and now, to become an anthropologist so as to study other cultures. And I did, in the end, do just that. My twin passions—to discover cultures and figure out what made people tick—led me first to study psychology in college, then to earn a master's in social work, and finally to complete a doctoral program that let me explore to my heart's content the interplay of personality and culture. First as a psychiatric social worker, then as an academic, and finally as a literary journalist, always following my nose, I immersed myself in the lives of Mexican and Vietnamese immigrants, Patagonian sheep ranchers, Spanish dairy farmers, and French bakers.

~~

Kuching renewed in me a thirst for adventure, a taste for the foreign, a draw to places with strange milk. Our treks through the jungle gave me an instinct for the pleasures of grubbing—and for wooly places. In Asia you're already on the fringe. Disappearing into Mongolia or Tibet is a real and tantalizing possibility.

In just three months, Borneo had left me a large bequest: a sense of the world as a fruit tree for the plucking. This outlook made me do unwise things like enroll in graduate school in Washington state where I knew no one, and live in a dismal basement apartment in the rain. You can be too intrepid for your own good. But it would also make me game for a move to the stubby outlands of Patagonia, a couple of years I'd trade for none in the world.

Another bequest of Kuching: a sense of acceptability. The great gift of an ex-pat community is that you can always belong—because no one does. Belonging is easiest abroad—there you automatically belong to the human race.

As things would turn out, I'd always feel best abroad. It would always feel right to me to carry out daily life among people who lived in a different way, and where there were curious icons to puzzle over. It is far easier to struggle with another culture than to struggle with your own.

In Kuching, I felt like my most natural self. Some people like to be at the center of things, to put their stamp on all that takes place. I, instead, was hungry to gather the many ways of the world.

Here in Kuching, all my longing was transformed to fascination. The urge for security and belonging was replaced by the quickening of curiosity. And Borneo was a banquet for the curious.

~~

Late summer, my father received an old copy of the *Post*. He read aloud to us over dinner. "America is so polarized," he said. "Some are afraid it will explode. A commission assigned to study the situation stated the divisions were 'as deep as any since the Civil War,' and might 'jeopardize the very survival of the nation.' Nixon had ordered secret surveillance of his critics. One senator described the Nixon crowd as having a 'Gestapo mentality.'"

Washington seemed so far away.

~~

Several times with an English family—Mr. Sanderson was the head accountant for the East Malaysian government—we took trips to Giam, a spot by a jungle stream about an hour from Kuching, where there was a lovely waterfall cascading through the deeps of green. While the Sanderson girls, Moira and Daphne, and Andy and I took turns shrieking under the waterfall, the mothers prepared the picnic. Mrs. Sanderson opened a huge wicker hamper. Inside, to our astonishment, were porcelain plates and silver flatware. Next, Mrs. Sanderson opened up a huge thermos. Inside was a delicious curry made by the family's cook. With flowered plates in our laps and silver spoons in our hands, we sat sweltering in the heat under an umbrella of singing green, eating a curry made of all the spices of the world.

Like Clive, brown-eyed, short curly-haired Daphne welcomed me into her life as another English speaker her age. Clive, Daphne, and I made a threesome.

Daphne and Moira had been sent from Borneo to England to boarding school from the age of six and it so happened they would be leaving for England on the same day (in a couple of weeks) that Andy and I would be leaving for Japan. Mrs. Sanderson said to my mother, "I apologize in advance for Moira. She may well make a scene at the airport," she said. Moira was eleven, and would not see her mother until the next summer.

My mother replied, "Don't apologize for Moira. When I send Sara and Andy off, you're going to see me bawling! Moira and I can bawl together."

~~

Time slid toward the end of August—and our departure. A part of me wished I could stay in Kuching for the year, study by correspondence, take treks on the weekends, but another part of me was excited about boarding school and seeing Japan—my birthplace. I had the romantic notion that boarding school would be wonderful—like Putney School in Vermont, a free school I'd read about at Sidwell where teenagers built barns, created their own government, and learned by following their noses.

My mother welled up at the drop of a hat these days, even though she was delivering us to school, while my father kept pooh-poohing our dread. "Oh, I envy you," he said. "You're going to love Japan." My father had always spoken of Japan with a dreamy hush in his voice—as if Japan held a secret that could be found nowhere else—something to do with Japanese block prints, with Mt. Fuji, with monks holding gnarled staffs. It was the place where he fell in love with the world.

In the moist, orchid-blooming warmth, my father sat us down in the corner of the living room a couple of days before we left. He looked at us square. "This is very unlikely to happen," he said, "but I want you to know what to do if you were to be kidnapped." He had told us that there was an almost infinitesimally small possibility that a CIA officer's child might be abducted in order to obtain information or money from the officer, or to pressure the officer's government.

"If you were to be taken captive just tell your captors everything you know. I haven't told you anything of value, so, pretty soon they should figure out you're of no worth to them and set you free." My father presented this as though it was simple fact, a mooring for him and us to tie up to. (Only three decades later, with teenage children of my own, would I be able to imagine what it must have been like for my parents to fear for their children's safety in this way.)

He shifted again, reaching out his arms. "Now, don't be afraid at the new school, Girl. Just be yourself. They'll love you. You conquered Sidwell. You can conquer Canadian Academy too. And you too, Jonge," he said, hugging Andy on his other side. As always, my father's words were gifts of freedom and release.

~~

As we drove down the wide, empty, jungle-lined swath to the airport, my stomach jittered. I was leaving my Kuching home as a marine guard with a lump in my throat and a stone in my pocket—stiffened with the knowledge that the Clement and other British children in Kuching had gone off to boarding school across the world since they were six. Within the hour, my mother, Andy, and I would board the Fokker Friendship for Singapore. From there we would fly to Hong Kong, switch planes, and then fly to Tokyo. From Tokyo we'd take the bullet train, an amazing train that could go two hundred miles an hour, to Kobe.

On the tarmac, my chest started to heave when I looked up at my father's face—so handsome and serious—to say good-bye. He put his hand on my cheek and started to say it. "You're going to love Japan. This is another great adven—" And then he choked up.

I hugged my father as tightly as I possibly could. He smelled so clean, his body strong and sinewy, this man: my father. Smothering my face into his chest, I gulped in the feel of his arms wrapped around me.

When we unclasped, he picked Andy up in a big bear grapple, and I shouldered my marine corps gear. Turning away from him, as I would so many times, I felt a plunging sadness—and a fortification as I assumed his independent, jaunty stride. I fixed my eyes ahead toward the horizon and walked toward the Fokker Friendship purring on the airfield.

Book 6

MOSS
Kobe and Tokyo, Japan,
1970–1972

20
gaijin

Japan was where I found my truth—which was buoying, and where my father found his—which was devastating. Neither of us had been looking for the information that came to hand. Mine landed out of the blue and his chased him down.

~~

At Kobe train station, we took a taxi to Canadian Academy (CA), trying to pronounce the school's name to the cabbie as a Japanese person would: *Cah-nah-dee-anu Ah-cah-day-mee*. The car beeped and twisted its way through the tight-packed streets, and then up onto the ridge that flanks the city. From this elevation we could behold the wide, modern urban jumble below.

Abruptly, the cab swerved to the left off the main boulevard, and started climbing a road so steep it felt as though we were going to fall off backward. The cab driver swore and rubbed one hand up and down his head. He ground the car into the lowest gear, and my mother, Andy, and I looked at each other and crossed our fingers. Finally, about a mile up, the cab turned right and passed through a pair of stone pillars and onto a campus perched on a terrace partway up the still-rising mountain, where the buildings stopped. Beyond, I could see an intriguing graveyard rambling up the slope, and then scattered trees mounting toward the summit. But ahead was a beautiful half-timbered building that looked like a Swiss hotel, with a modern wing built out one side; an old, haunted-looking house like something out of *The Addams Family*; a prefabricated gym; and a modern-looking building that looked like it could be a dormitory; along with playing fields. We checked in with a Japanese woman sitting at the front desk of the hotel-like edifice. This was the main classroom building, and it turned out that the girls' dorm was the modern one while Andy's was the moody house.

At the *genkan* entry hall of the girls' dorm—beckoned in by the house matron, a Mrs. Elliot—we placed our shoes in little cubbyholes, chose flip-flop slippers from a shelf, then proceeded into the dormitory proper. Double rooms ran along one side of the building, one after the other, with bathrooms on the opposite side.

My room was on the third and top floor of the dorm. The room was just big enough to accommodate two twin beds, two dresser-closets, and a big window looking out onto a strip of woods headed down the mountain. The room was plain and functional, and a big question mark: my roommate had not yet arrived.

We stayed in a hotel the first night, and then wandered around downtown Kobe—bombed to rubble during World War II and now a gleaming ultramodern skyscape of immense department stores; shimmering boutiques sporting bizarre shoes, chic frocks, and U.S. Army jackets; restaurants with frontal display cases of plastic food; and tucked-between, tiny tea shops.

In the corner of one of these tea shops with eight or so tables, where we stopped in for a snack, was a recessed alcove in one wall in which hung a beautiful calligraphied scroll. Below it, a low, rectangular vase supported a single spray of flowering cherry. "A *tokonoma*," my mother said. "A lot of Japanese homes have them too. They're one of the ways the Japanese honor beauty." The arrangement was like a Dutch still life, only not rough and wild, but exquisitely refined: a single, pristine apple as set beside a tumble of worm-eaten Dutch ones. "*Shibui*," my mother said. "That's the word in Japan for 'simple elegance.'" This quiet, arresting nook, easy to overlook at the back of the shop, sent a ripple through me. I sensed this was a sip of the nectar my father associated with Japan.

We bought sheets, towels, and cotton yukatas at a super-modern multistoried department store. My mother also bought me a plaid thermos—I couldn't figure out why. Later I'd see her purchase was incantatory: if she could prevent me from going thirsty, I would be protected from all dangers.

When the dreaded moment arrived, at the genkan my mother said, "Oh Sara!" gripped me madly, then, forcing herself to be a good soldier, left me, mopping at her eyes. The lump in my throat was the size of an egg.

Girding myself, I mounted the steps to my room. Seeing the daisies my mother had given me as a last gift, I fetched some water from the bathroom down the hall and placed them, one by one, into the thermos. Then I organized my desk. I put my pens at the top, placed the thermos of daisies just right of center at the back, put my copy of *Siddhartha* on the left-hand side, and a notebook in the middle.

I am ready, I thought. *I can do it. Everything is fine.* There was no reason this shouldn't have been true.

~~

Half an hour or so later, a blue-eyed girl with straight blond hair hanging to her shoulders appeared at the door with a disheveled pile of sacks and cases. My roommate, Gretel, as it would turn out, was sweet like grass and honey, slow-calm, and a dispenser of simple truths—the one surety on which I would be able to depend during a year when lightning struck.

Dumping her luggage and plopping down on the bed across from mine, she opened a crackly cellophane sack and offered me what looked like a snag of shaggy yellow string. "Want to try some dried squid?" she asked. "I love it. I eat it like potato chips." She giggled. A waft of fishy sweetness flowed into the room.

In the evening, after dinner in a building next to the boys' dorm, Gretel and I went down to Mrs. Elliot's lounge for evening snack. The room, furnished with a couch and a jumble of stray chairs, quickly filled up with an exuberance of yukata-clad girls—who flopped on the chairs and the clean but spotted carpet. Mrs. Elliot was seated in an overstuffed chair like a presiding Humpty Dumpty, and some of the girls fluttered over to her and hugged her hello, saying they had missed her during the summer recess.

Mrs. Elliot was out of an English novel: one of those strayed, solitary English-women who fashion for themselves good, solid lives far from their original homes in Dorset or East Anglia. She was short and round, and wore faded flowered dresses, and, as I'd soon sense, she was fierce.

"Okay, girls." She clapped her chubby hands. "Time for introductions. We have some new girls. One of us has come all the way from Borneo!" she said. The girls all looked at me and smiled. In a blur, they introduced themselves. "Hi, I'm Charity. Hi, I'm Jane. . . ." They waved their fingers or giggled.

I looked around the room at the mélange: a gorgeous Asian American girl with pool-deep, dark eyes like the raggedy girl's; a blond and chap-nosed girl, with a voice as sweet and quiet as that of a wood thrush; a tall girl with chestnut hair who carried herself like a Masai queen. . . . The other girls were a tumble of messy hair and nighties with legs and feet sticking out. At this point, I couldn't sort them but, in the dorm, just before lights out and on weekend afternoons, their hidden secrets, worries, and delights would tumble out like junk and treasure from beat-up steamer trunks.

After one of the girls handed out cookies—still, in my experience, the best oatmeal cookies in the world—everyone flopped out on the floor, perched on the arms of each other's chairs, and the room filled with chatter. I heard, in a mix of Japanese and English, breathless boys' names, shrieks of laughter, and over and over again, the word *gaijin*. For ten minutes or so, it was as though we *were* one big family of girls, like in an English book.

On the way back upstairs, I asked my roommate what the word, gaijin, meant. Gretel said, in her blithe way, "Oh that's the Japanese word that means 'foreigner.' We're all gaijin," she said, like this was a basic fact of life. Japan, as I'd soon discover, was not an assimilative culture, and even these missionary kids, brought up in Japanese villages and towns, who were for all intents and purposes Japanese, lived in a separate category. Japan had a long history of eschewing foreigners as uncultivated people who didn't bathe often enough. Living as a gaijin here would afford me much food for thought as to the nature of my own country as well as that of Japan itself.

~~

The teachers at CA were another motley crew like those at The American School of The Hague. My French teacher was a fastidious man with impeccable clothing from which he brushed off invisible bits of lint with his manicured fingernails. My chemistry teacher was an elegant, eloquent African man. He wore a white lab coat and had a twinkling smile with a glint of mischief in it. My English teacher was a hearty Canadian in old tweed. And my history and religion teachers were the two halves of a couple: the Meads from the University of Chicago.

Plunked at CA, I felt far from America, from Borneo, from everywhere. It was as though I'd stepped through a crack in the atmosphere—but into a surprisingly welcoming and homey world. Thirty years on, from the safety of greater age, I would reflect on the fact that this school was not an American school, and how that had made a difference.

~~

A girl named Nancy and I wandered down a twisting-narrow street in the heart of ancient Kyoto. Nancy, a five-day boarder at CA, had graciously invited me to her missionary parents' home for the first weekend. The doors to the shops along our way were diminutive and narrow to match the street, and made of aged, dark, beautiful wood. Tiny signs with elegant brush characters invited us into tea shops with twiggy teas in a variety of green-grey hues displayed in wooden canisters; shops with hand-woven obis and bolts of exquisite kimono brocade in watermelon, sherry, and iris; shops with strange, geometrical arrays of bean paste sweets in pale rose, lime, and lavender; shops with triple-size strawberries and apples nestled in the crackly straw of beautiful handmade boxes; shops with window displays of carved folk gods with high, bald heads erupting out of tree stumps. I was enthralled: I seemed to be strolling in a village that had been transported to earth from some faraway Tolkien place in the clouds: a village, it seemed, of people who possessed sensitive, nimble fingers; myopic eyes able to examine cloth and wood with the closeness of a microscope; and a sense of color so subtle as to almost slip away into the air. I would only find anything near its match decades later, as I gazed into Parisian shop windows. Deep in my body, I felt a slowing down in the face of such a sublime sense of detail, such fineness, such perfection.

As a shopkeeper wrapped the beautiful, lopsided *raku* pot with which I'd fallen in love—making an exquisite piece of art out of precisely folded brown paper and rope tassels—I could sense the Japanese reverence for taking time and care, their worship of craft. "Japanese potters," Nancy told me, "have to apprentice for seven years before they are allowed to make a pot."

In this dusky shop filled with subtly beautiful teapots and plates I was being infused with the power of another culture. Culture enters through the pores, and foreign places where you don't speak the language are even more powerful than those where you do because all you have are your senses—and the senses register a place more viscerally than cognition. My appetite was whetted. I wanted to know more of this place of my birth; I sensed that important secrets were to be had, if I could just discover them. Gradually, Japan would reveal itself to me, like a fan, fold by fold.

Nancy and I ducked now into a tiny, dark tea house. At our tiny table, Nancy ordered our snack: bowls of sweet red beans cradled on crushed ice.

~~

At CA, for the first time in my life, I was in a school where the majority of the students were not wealthy. There was a sprinkling of kids from the Kobe consulate, a kid or two whose parents worked at Vicks and Kodak, and at Iranian oil concerns, but the majority were the offspring of American and Canadian missionary parents. The school had been founded to educate these children and they hailed from small villages all over Japan, and beyond. They came from the little island of Shikoku, the big island of Kyushu, and the snow monkey island of Hokkaido, and included among them Southern Baptists, Lutherans from the Midwest, Episcopalians from New England, Methodists from Toronto, as well as representatives from multiple other denominations and locales.

Perhaps something tilted when I changed hemispheres, for the world was different, or maybe my perspective had altered. In any case, among these missionary kids, I perceived no monolithic culture. There were lots of little twosomes and threesomes but I didn't pick out a shiny clutch to be envious of. For some reason, perhaps because I *lived* with them in the dorm, here I could see those not in the limelight. Rather than an indistinguishable mass, they seemed, rather, a hodgepodge of approachable, quirky kids—some boarders and some day students—each of whom seemed to me unique, beautiful, and fascinating, like a character in a fairy tale. A boy, for example, with the beginnings of a soon-to-be full beard wore a Japanese-sleeved cotton jacket and a cloth band of cotton, like a sumo wrestler's, around his head every day. A girl with gleaming, bottom-grazing black hair carried a large milk can for a purse. Another girl, blue-eyed and fluffy blond, wore the red and white sweaters of a Norwegian travel poster.

In contrast to Sidwell, where the kids seemed burnished and fast, these kids were of an innocent and natural bent. For fun they went to Japanese temples and ate noodles in little shops. Even the rule-defying behavior that took place seemed more wholesome, unglazed by sophisticated double-talk. The kids who acted out were transparently troubled, searching for something obvious, like love. As with anything, I'd discover, there were squabbles between the various denominations and a missionary upbringing had heavy baggage, but there was still, to me, something refreshingly unpretentious about this batch of people. And among them— released from the noose of privilege—I felt both comfortable and unique. Elitism is seductive like an expensive meal in a fine restaurant, but this felt nourishing in a daily way like chicken and mashed potatoes.

Maybe because I couldn't possibly belong—I couldn't metamorphose into a missionary kid raised on a Japanese island—I felt freed. No one here was like me. Few of them were impassioned like I was about the Vietnam War, but I felt like I could be myself. How odd that here, among these half-American, half-Japanese missionary kids I was among my kind. Or perhaps it was no mystery at all.

~~

One day during the first month, I was sitting in English class in the middle of the school day when one of the school's administrative staff summoned me from the doorway. Andy was standing by his side. The staff member muttered something to us about "registration," and we were shuffled into a car containing two uniformed policemen who spoke only Japanese, and whisked down the hill away from the school. Andy and I looked at each other and raised our eyebrows. Neither of us had a clue what was going on.

At police headquarters half an hour from the school, we were seated in an interrogation room when three Japanese policemen came in. They bowed to us and we bowed back, but they did not have kind looks on their faces. The three men sat around the big desk and, for what seemed like hours and could well have been three, asked, over and over again, the same two incomprehensible Japanese sentences, within which the word "gaijin" kept being uttered, emphatically, again and again.

The men were increasingly annoyed at our lack of comprehension, and I began to feel worried. Why were they keeping us—a couple of kids—talking to us like this for so long about being foreigners? Did they think we were spies or something?

At one point, a lady in a kimono came in with a tray of tea.

Andy whispered to me, "You know in Japan, I've heard, they always serve you tea before they send you to jail." I really wished our father were here. He could have cleared this all up in a trice.

Finally, when a Japanese man named Mr. Fukuda was called from the school to translate and help out, it became clear that, although the dependents of U.S. embassy employees stationed in Japan did not need to have alien registration cards like other gaijin, which was what the embassy had told my father, we needed them since our parents did not reside in the country. Once this was understood—that we must get our cards immediately—there were many more bows and head nods all around, and we escaped.

But now the driver took us across town in another direction, again on an unspecified mission. In a district of low apartment buildings and shop fronts, he double parked, got out, and directed us into one of the buildings. He issued a few words at the woman who greeted us, pushed us into her inner chamber, and removed himself to wait in the car. The woman, hunched down in a kimono, bowing and with exquisite politeness, beckoned us into what looked like her living room, and then into a little room beyond where a camera was set up. Finally we understood that we were there to have our photos taken. We smiled to the woman and she nodded and said a lot of Japanese back, and the job was soon done.

At this point, Mr. Fukuda rejoined us in the shop—but now he had a look of annoyance on his face. He pointed to our shoes and said, "You know, here in Japan, we don't wear shoes in the house." We looked down at our feet in mortal embarrassment.

We had known about this custom from the time we were weaned—we'd always prided ourselves on our cultural sensitivity—but somehow that inbred knowledge had been lost in the afternoon's shuffle. So the chagrin and mortification of the day were now complete. Not only had we broken the Japanese immigration law, but we had also literally trod on one of the most basic of Japanese rules of decorum.

Now I felt not only a status-less and distinctly unsuperior American, but like a bona fide dumb gaijin. One of Japan's first lessons, that of humility, had been conferred.

~~

Outside the dorm, I said good-bye to Andy—in his old, baggy corduroy sportcoat that had been our father's. Thank goodness he was here with me. He was my reflection.

~~

On the mid-September eleventh-grade bus trip to a beach called Tottori, I wound up sitting next to a girl named Annie, with hair the color of wet wheat and heavy as a bolt of velvet, from Rochester, New York, who'd been at CA for a year. Immediately we realized we had a lot in common, partly because, unlike most of the other kids, our parents were not missionaries, and because we had recently arrived. Since Annie had participated in the antiwar movement too, with her I felt like I could make assumptions, express my provo self.

Annie was funny and all the kids flocked around her as she tossed sand at them, teased the boys, and raced people into the water. After a while, we went off together to pee behind a dune and suddenly a man rose up from a hillock of sand, pulling down his pants. He had pink polish on his fingernails. We dashed away, bonded by breathless, giddy laughter.

After that Annie and I were fast friends. We were very different—I was a shy poet and she, an outgoing artist and an actress—but there was a mutual feeling that we were complements. Annie was inimitable. With her large personality and her instinctive inclusiveness, she enfolded everyone in class in her embrace. A party girl and a clown, she could be sad and funny at once.

Sitting in her living room in a vast, modern apartment a few train stops from school, eating her mother's brown-sugar cake, we talked about Vietnam—and then Japan. Annie had lots to say. "America is a warmongering heap . . . and it's so plastic. Japan has much better values. The Japanese have a highly developed sense of beauty and the arts. Japan is outasight. . . . Have you seen a temple yet?" Annie said. Thus, my new friend floated out to me the idea that Japan, rather than America, might be the country to admire.

~~

We were a mixed herd of antelopes, buffalo, and zebras galloping toward the station. A bunch of kids from school, led by Annie, were going this Saturday to visit a Shinto temple a couple of train stops down the line. Buoyant and boisterous, we clambered onto the train and plopped into seats. Japanese ladies in kimonos wagged their heads and shushed us for our noisiness, but we were irrepressible tickle and bounce and high spirits.

Once at our destination, and having passed under the temple torii gates onto the raked gravel path, my Japan-bred companions turned quiet and reverent. At the broad temple entry, they met the monk with prayerful hands and soft murmurs. I folded my hands and bowed in imitation. Like birds, we sprinkled ourselves through the dark, hallowed space.

Monks in brown robes were gathered before the altar, chanting droning prayers. The sound filled the entire quarter—a soothing, deep-pitched humming only broken once in a while when a designated monk clacked two pieces of wood or rang a wooden bell.

After a time, the monks stopped chanting and filed out, and silence resounded through the high, wood-timbered building. Now I felt flowing into me something utterly new, a sense of peacefulness unique to Japan I dubbed "the hush."

I had begun to notice this hush in many places in Japan. In the ubiquitous tokonomas I'd by now glimpsed in odd walls and corners, in the graveyard behind school, in tea shops shadowed by soft, white paper *shoji* walls. It was there, lingering, a possibility, everywhere I went: the Japanese penchant for places of repose, for the soft voice, for reticence. Into my veins was trickling the power of a quiet country.

Japan's implicit support for inwardness—something natural to me—ironically let me open outward. Or perhaps it was not ironic: a clinical supervisor I would have as a budding social worker would teach me that if you wanted a client to develop a particular side of herself, you should emphasize and support the opposite trait.

Some Americans I would come across would seem impervious to the Japanese hush, to the whispering beauty of Japan. They would feel restrained by the quiet, straitjacketed by the ritualized, stiff politesse. Some of them would ram themselves down the Japanese streets, talking loudly and devil-may-care, blasting out to the Japanese what freedom was. I would sometimes feel this urge too. Instead of bowing, or being tactful and polite, I would long to yell and misbehave. But mostly, Japan suited me. Something in me sang to the crisp formalities. The rules and boundaries were clear. There was a rail to hold on to if the ship pitched.

With the temple visited, we kids transformed in the sunshine into our gay American-Japanese-Canadian-gaijin selves and began to sing "Hey Jude."

A miracle had occurred: I belonged.

～～

Something else had occurred: my assumptions had been shaken. I'd thought Christian missionary kids would rigidly disdain all other religions, but these kids delighted in Shinto and Buddhist ideas. Zen Buddhism was the spiritual practice most revered by the kids at school. It was as though Christianity was assumed—and then there was this other possibility—nearly unattainable, set up on a pedestal above everything else. To be able to withstand the rigors of Zen training—to sit for hours in motionless postures, to empty the mind and dissolve the self, to achieve enlightenment or *satori*: *that* was the greatest attainment.

Over the two years ahead, these kids and their families would shake up my sense of the missionary endeavor. Such fine people—offspring of educators, farming experts, translators—they would broaden the knee-jerk sense of missionaries I'd hardened up in Borneo. I'd sneered at the Mormons on the Kuching streets; the Catholic priest in the jungle hamlet had turned me cold. They'd seemed to me to be committing sacrileges themselves, violating the culture of another people. (And what was my father doing?) A couple of years from now, when a friend's missionary father would take a gang of us skinny-dipping in a Hokkaido river, I would gain an even more acute sense of how variegated and unpredictable the world was. I added to my repertoire a new kind of Christian: those who were open-minded, embracing, and curious.

～～

We tend to repeat ourselves, and I had done so in place after place, but here something different happened. This move to Canadian Academy taught me that schools *were* very different—each from the next—that place really *did* make a difference, and that moving could be beneficial.

Because I had been to the States recently, here at CA I was like a messenger from the old country, the bearer of special knowledge. Also, I was unique because I lived in faraway, exotic Borneo. Suddenly—magically—I had status. Here, where I didn't expect to fit in, I felt in the running.

Filled up on Bornean sun, fecundity, and excess, I felt potent, full of seeds like a pomegranate. And in a reversal of my normal approach, here in Japan I didn't relinquish the self I'd had across the sea. Instead, I added to it. And I called upon the Foreign Service child's specialty: instant intimacy. This time, faced with the question, "Who am I?" it wasn't such a fraught affair.

~~

I trudged up the stairs to my room on the third floor and the girls were in an uproar. The other girls on the floor were standing in their doorways rooting, and Agnes, Pippa, and Ginny were in a scrunching race. These were three of the girls in the rooms next to Gretel's and mine. Ginny, with flying feathers of mango-colored hair, strong, freckled legs, and a sergeant's commanding voice, was a girl who, despite her basic solidity, played a little too freely in the fires of drugs. Scrawny, electric-haired Pippa was sure she had a brain tumor, went wild with worry about her boyfriend's faithfulness, and alternated between escapes into hilarity and deep, hair-twisting desperation to go home to Hong Kong. And Agnes was a beauty with cheeks as pink, cream, and perfect as porcelain, and a matching perfect figure, who, despite her breath-stealing beauty and the shrieking delight she showered on those around her, viewed herself as a sinner and treated herself as though she were a piece of chewed gum to discard in the nearest barrel, her self-image tattered by a frantic despair of some unknown origin.

Agnes had heard that if you sat on the floor with your legs straight in front of you and scrunched along on your bottom, you'd lose weight in your thighs and derriere. She was speeding down the hall on her tiny rear, yelling out "I'M SO FAT! GO FAT, GO!"

It so happened that Pippa had had chicken pox and was covered with scabs. She could only stand to live in her body if she went around naked these days, so she was racing down the hall on her naked, skinny, spotted bum. Ginny was way out ahead of Agnes and Pippa, athletic even in this kooky sport. It was hilarious: these three skinny girls absurdly scooching down the hall, laughing hysterically, all of them troubled and delightful in different ways. I rode on the magic carpet of my new friends' high spirits.

~~

But the girls' troubles often rode roughshod over their native exuberance. The graveyard behind school was a hallowed, mysterious place—a ramble of grey, lichened Shinto and Buddhist headstones leading up the mountain slope. I escaped there to think, to write poetry, and to experience quiet. For some kids, though, it was a place of the illicit, a place for drugs, kissing, and the forbidden.

One day Agnes appeared and plopped herself on my bed. She was tearful, looking down. "You'd be ashamed of me if you knew what I just did," she said. "I let Greg feel me up in the graveyard." Then she was hysterical, crying and laughing at once.

"Are you okay?" I asked, patting her back.

"The problem is, I liked it," she said, sniffling. "Oh Sara, what am I going to do?"

Another girl, Dottie, an eighth grader, did the same thing: plopped down on Gretel's bed and said, "I'm bad, Sara. I'm bad. I got a D on my math test and my dad will kill me. Anyway, I went out in the graveyard with Davy and we smoked—not cigarettes. I couldn't help it."

Some of these missionary girls had been taught that playing cards and dancing were forbidden; kissing was not even in the realm of possibility and drugs grounds for excommunication. They were so self-flagellating, so never good enough, that they seemed to have a headlong need to go to extremes in order to obtain even a sip of self-determination. If only some of these missionary parents could have realized a little leash went a long way.

Agnes was the one whose being expressed the most conflict. Though she was all fair and pink beauty—eyes as blue as forget-me-nots, hair an unruly, playful bob—she was constantly wailing, "Oh God, I'm so ugly." Though she was a warm and giving friend, she was always telling me she was bad. She shrieked with gay pleasure when she saw a friend, but there was another shriek in her that you sensed would shatter one day.

Somehow I had quickly become a kind of mother-confidante to some of the younger girls. They seemed to see me as a standard-bearer. While I had grown up in an institution with strictures and rules—to be unfailingly polite and diplomatic— their institution made an even greater, more nebulous, and basically impossible demand—to be everlastingly "good." In any case, some of them sought me out for common sense, for self-respect.

~~

Then there were boys—or one, in particular.

The first week of school, I had peeked at all the new boys from behind my hair. There was one, a tall Japanese American guy who was always talking to one girl or another. A boy named Will—with a smile like a movie star's. He was naturally friendly and nice, so he smiled at everyone. The thing was, when it hit, that smile beamed out and rayed into my body in a spreading warmth that melted my entire insides.

I tried not to look at him—his beauty hurt. His shining, black-rain hair framed a face so open and genuine—and he had those Asian almond eyes, like two melted chocolate kisses, the eyes of my earliest childhood.

I gave myself lectures. "Don't even look at him, Sara. He'd never like you. He can have any girl he wants. . . ." But I couldn't not peek at him.

Annie and I laughed at him from our table in the dining hall. He was across the room, slouching against the wall, talking to one of the twins who'd started the year late. While he was talking to one he tossed a wadded-up napkin at the other.

"What a flirt," Annie said.

"You're not kidding," I said.

~~

At sixteen now, I didn't just obsess about cute boys. In Kobe I was finally old enough to deliberately take in a culture—to study it and seek to absorb it. I asked questions about Japan of my peers who had Japan in their bones. The other students taught me about their country, and thereby my sense of the world deepened and complexified.

~~

A girl in a bath taught me about Japanese subtlety. One night early in the year, I followed the girls who were rushing about in their yukatas with towels on their arms, and buckets of shampoo and soap dangling from their arm-crooks. "*Ofuro! Ofuro!*" they called out as they trooped down to the first floor.

The downstairs bathroom, I discovered now, was literally that: a room for the bath. And the bathtub, it turned out, was a square, tiled box set against the back wall, big enough for six girls to fit in, with water up to their chins. From the doorway I beheld a half dozen or so girls squatting on the expanse of tile before the tub, shoving plastic buckets under low faucets, swishing themselves with water from their pails, soaping themselves and rinsing off with more water from the buckets. Once they were done with this peculiar washing *outside* the tub, they clambered into the steaming bath.

I tried it—awkwardly washing myself beside a faucet and then lowering myself into the water, which was alarmingly hot. Even though the other girls were chattering in the tub like it was a party, I was so overheated after one minute that I felt as thought I was going to faint, and had to hurry out and splash myself with a bucket of cold water. Ofuro-bathing was an acquired taste that I wouldn't comprehend until later, when, at a small bathhouse in a seaside village, I would discover the delightful companionableness of communal nakedness, a Japanese comfort with the body to match my earlier experience of the Dutch strand.

But now, in the outer dressing room, putting on my yukata, I talked to Sachi, the beautiful Asian girl I'd noticed the first day, who lived on the first floor. She said she had a Japanese mother and a Chinese father and invited me to her room to talk about Japan. I looked at her lovely collection of Japanese obis and teacups, and then she offered me a slim volume from her shelf. "Here's my favorite book of haiku," she said.

In my room, just before lights out, I read poems like these:

The Little Valley in Spring
A mountain stream:
even the stones make songs—
wild cherry trees
—ONITSURA

Symphony in White
Blossoms on the pear—
and a woman in the moonlight
reads a letter there.
—BUSON

I adored the half-hidden, torn-leafness of the poems, the light brushstrokes, so different from thick, hard-painted American sentences. They seemed more profound for their minimalism—the way they left the reader to conjure a whole garment from a shred of cloth. And they seemed to not just respect, but to revere the infinite range and infinite delicacy of human feelings—to hold the human spirit, like a cloud, in a gentle cup of leaves.

Through the poems I gleaned a sense of the Japanese preference for the suggestive and the shadowy, for the subtle and the hidden. Tanizaki's words, which I would read years later, express this. "If everything is depicted, the flavor is lost."

The interrogatory view of life in haiku affirmed my own penchant for questing—it implied that it was permissible to have wonders rather than answers, to have fragmented or multicolored truths, unlike in America, where you were supposed to have a ready, firm, black or white answer at all times. It also seemed to confirm the existence of the mysterious, unrevealed, secretive side of life so slippery-familiar to me.

~~

One late afternoon, a girl named Alice—the russet-haired, queenly senior—invited me to her room, the sole, coveted, *tatami*-matted room on our dormitory floor. She and her roommate, Bea, slept on futons, which they rolled away each morning, in the Japanese custom.

As the city out the window pinked with dusk, Alice, Bea, and I sat on zabutons at a low table, our feet curled under our bottoms, and ate rice crackers and sipped green tea from small, gnome-size cups.

As we ate and sipped, Alice explained honorifics to me—why it was "O-cha," rather than just "cha," the word for "tea," and "O-furo" rather than just "furo," the word for "bath." The "O," she said, was added to honor the object and its associated activity. I was reminded of the American Indian custom of offering prayers of honor to elk or deer hunted for food.

As the conversation drifted from Buddhist philosophy to Graham Greene—Alice was perhaps my first intellectual—I sipped in a glimmering sense of the Japaneseness of these two Japan-bred girls. They had a calm reverence about them—reverence for the ritual of tea, for the ritual of talk, for the ritual of friendship. They lived the honorific. Their Japanese attention to honoring, and to courtesy and ritual, offered a comforting structure as contrasted to the free-wheeling, sink-or-swim whirl of American teenage social life. Once again, I found here a station for my proclivities.

As I set about to leave, like Sachi, Alice handed me a book. Her fingers were slender twigs extending from the baggy sleeve of her Shetland sweater. (She was one of the few students from the East Coast American Episcopalian missionary set. There were classes within missionaries too.)

The book was *The Quiet American*. I read the book, and was compelled by the portraits of American violent innocence and British fatalistic cynicism. Greene seemed to view a change from one to the other as the inevitable change of age—that of a man or of a country. How true this would turn out to be. I would return to the book with profit, over the years, and it would seem to me that my father's life had patterned itself sequentially on the two figures in the book—at first the idealistic American and later the saddened, almost too worldly-wise Englishman. But I wondered, as I read the book now, *Does Alice* know *about Pop?* My stomach fluttered as I thought about this. I had never said those words to anyone.

At the end of the first month of school, Dean Kent asked me if I would represent America as one of the year's Flower Princesses at the annual international festival in Kobe. I didn't have a clue what he was talking about. The idea of being a princess of any kind had no attraction to me now, much as I would have leapt at the opportunity when I was seven. It turned out this was a kind of international social service and goodwill tour. Flower princesses walked in a parade in downtown Kobe and then, over the next months, visited gardens, children's schools, and old people's homes. The dean asked me in such a way that I didn't really have a choice, so I agreed to serve. It turned out Annie and a younger student from Texas would also be representing America.

My first dilemma was what to wear for the parade. What should I wear to represent Americanness? Should I represent the show-offy America of the movies, the America of the Wild West, or what? I was so ambivalent about my warmongering country I was probably not the right one to stand for it, I thought.

I dragged a bunch of clothes out of my narrow little dorm closet and for days couldn't figure out what costume to wear in the parade. In the end, I chose the flowered skirt my mother and I had sewn out of black cloth sprinkled with pink and yellow and blue flowers, and a Mexican peasant blouse Sara had given me. Annie wore something similar, while the sophomore who was going along wore a spangled, fringed cowgirl outfit complete with pointed cowgirl boots and a tall Stetson.

The parade was tolerable because Annie was there and she and I could joke as we waved like movie stars to the Japanese crowds gathered at the roadsides. When we trailed through the city gardens and stood on stages at the old age homes, I felt foolish with ladies in kimonos pointing at me, whispering behind their hands, and showering gifts on me. How had I gone from antiwar protestor to this? Over time, though, I began to see that we were actually bringing pleasure to the old people and children and the Japanese people who didn't often get a close-up look at gaijin. What must it have been like for these old people who'd been through World War II to look at American girls spot-lit on the stage?

~~

Before she'd left, my mother had taken us to see a man named Mr. Tilman, who worked at the American consulate downtown. He was a young man with a wife and a little baby—and lived in a tiny apartment on the side of a hill, perched over the busy street.

One Friday night Mr. Tilman invited Andy and me for dinner. It was a little strange to have this young family invite us over, but we were used to people being polite to us, to being looked after, to being special when we were abroad.

The evening was fun; it was great to be in a real home, with real American adults, for a few minutes. Mr. Tilman served us delicious Kobe steaks. "I figure you don't get these at the dorm," he said.

"We sure don't," we said.

Mr. Tilman seemed to like having us there, having a chance to talk to teenagers. As I remember him, I have an impression of fierce brightness, a flirtatiousness, and a coyness. Something had changed. I didn't have words for it, but I was suddenly under the eyes of men. Only half knowing it, I suddenly had a sense that I was attractive to Mr. Tilman, that I'd be an adult soon.

Mr. Tilman asked what music I liked. He laughed when I said Steppenwolf and The Doors. He said, "Let me play this for you," and he put on a Beethoven record. As we went out the door, he said, "When you're older, come back and I'll play Mozart for you."

Only years later would I realize the reason Mr. Tilman had had us over: he was one of us, perhaps the only spy in Kobe. My mother had asked him to look after us as one of the clan.

~~

Unlike the missionary kids who'd had plenty of religion and hated it, my favorite class was religion class. I had never really gone to church, so when we discussed Christianity I was fascinated. While my father had raised me to think people didn't need an external guide in order to be good, some of the Christian kids thought they couldn't be good without an external, dictating, finger-wagging, and punishing God. This struck me as a crutch or an addiction.

When Dr. Mead, a University of Chicago–educated minister, asked us to write a paper about an Asian religion, I told him about my love of Thoreau and he introduced me to Taoism. I got the *Tao Te Ching* out of the library and it was like a door opened. "The Way" became my creed: everything that came to pass was natural, the way of the world—and everything contradicted everything else and was part of the "one." Taoism was a bit like an Escher print.

Twenty-Two
Yield and overcome;
Bend and be straight,
Empty and be full;
Wear out and be new;
Have little and gain;
Have much and be confused.

Therefore wise men embrace the one
And set an example to all.
Not putting on a display,
They shine forth.
Not justifying themselves,
They are distinguished.
Not boasting,
They receive recognition.
Not bragging,
They never falter.
They do not quarrel,
So no one quarrels with them.
Therefore the ancients say, "Yield and overcome."
Is that an empty saying?
Be really whole,
And all things will come to you.
—Lao Tsu, *Tao Te Ching*

Lily, the thrush-voiced girl from the dorm, and Annie and I, Will and his brother, and some other students—most of us had come from the United States recently—had been talking in the cafeteria about the Vietnam War and American consumerism and America's aggressive stance in the world, and we wanted to awaken our, to us apathetic, fellow students to these threats. With Dr. Mead as advisor, we inaugurated the Social Change Workshop. We started designing a slide show that would reveal to the students all the contradictions at play in the world. We began collecting photographs of Vietnamese children whose homes had been blown up, of American soldiers, of huge gas-guzzling American cars, of peaceful Japanese streams. In the structured context of these meetings, I found I could talk comfortably with Will, and successfully hide my feelings from myself as well as from him.

~~

Andy was also in the workshop. My brother had come into his own. He had a good friend named Ian. Andy wore an Arlo Guthrie hat, the brown velvety corduroys my mother had made for us in Kuching, and a loop of sailing rope around his neck above his open-collared chambray shirt. At dinner, we sometimes sat together and traded our parents' letters. We even shared friends, and sometimes gallivanted out for noodles together on the weekends. Alone in this foreign country, with our shared heritage as offspring of an American "diplomat," we were knitted together. Some secrets make you strong.

~~

Annie and I were downtown shopping on a Saturday afternoon. We browsed in Sogo Department Store and then wandered through the dingy open market stalls under the train tracks. Walking in the semi-darkness, trains rattling overhead, we fingered knock-off Levi jeans, tie-dyed T-shirts, tooled leather belts: coolness that could as easily be found in The Hague or Washington as here in the bottomlands of Kobe, one of the Japanese cities we Americans had firebombed with B-29s during the war. I bought a pair of imitation Lee jeans at half the American price. It was the same everywhere: Japanese Irish sweaters, Japanese Clarks desert boots, Japanese American University t-shirts. Blasting American music.

And everywhere we went, Japanese schoolgirls, in uniforms and rolled-down white bobby socks over their buckle shoes, came up to us, wanting to practice their English. "Will you speak Ing-rish with me? Will you speak Ing-rish with me?" They seemed so young and eager, even though they were probably our age. Annie and I rolled our eyes to each other when we saw them coming, but we patiently talked to them, indulging their adoration of our country. It would take me another year to see the Japanese girls' curiosity in a different light.

Along with the schoolgirls, men with sophisticated Nikons frequently stopped us on the street, wanting to photograph us: against a brick wall, against a temple backdrop, with their arms lightly around our shoulders. They'd send us the photos later, showing themselves proudly at our sides. I wondered what they told their families about the gaijin girls in the photographs. Sometimes Annie and I were asked to model for shops and magazine ads. Once Annie decided to take one of the offered modeling jobs. Pantyhose packets appeared with her long legs positioned fetchingly on the shiny cellophane.

At times when these men approached us I put on the blinders I'd learned to use in Taiwan and pretended I didn't see them. I told Annie, "Let's hurry before they catch us." The attention made me uneasy. There was something uncomfortable— and uncomfortably flattering—about the way the Japanese men admired gaijin looks, about how all these Japanese men wanted Caucasian girlfriends when there were plenty of pretty and sweet Japanese girls around. On the other hand, perhaps it is natural to admire different sorts of faces—for the GIs to be taken by the exotic beauty of Vietnamese women, for instance.

Though I loved Japan, and hated American foreign policy, I was secretly proud. All this admiration and imitation proved, despite our mistakes, American worth. We were the country everyone wanted to be like. And it's easy to reject your country when it's a given that you're on top.

~~~

Mid-fall, Annie and I were talking in her family's kitchen, baking banana bread, and listening to James Taylor's "Fire and Rain." As we listened, Annie told me about James Taylor's hospitalization at McLean Mental Hospital outside Boston. I was intrigued by this story of someone who'd turned so sad at losing his beloved that he'd wound up needing special care. Perhaps because I had lost so many people and had felt the frayed hems of depression, the romance of emotional illness once again stole into me—but I never imagined it, really, touching me. I was still the marine, and psychiatry was for weak people.

~~~

All autumn, I wrote lots of letters on onion skin paper—to Clive, to Daphne, to Sara—trying to hold on to people, to prevent them from wisping away. In November I received a blue aerogram, a tri-fold of Oxford cloth blue, with gummed fold-over flaps, another cheap way to post letters abroad. The return address on the letter read Albemarle Street. Sara wrote that Lt. William Calley had gone on trial in Georgia for the My Lai massacre. She said the war was still horrific. . . . But her biggest news was that she had a new boyfriend. "We made out in Hedley's rec room. It was wonderful. I got home all flushed and my mother, said, as usual, 'Have you been smoking marijuana?'"

I felt suddenly very alone—as though I'd been left at the top of the slide at the salt mines in Berchtesgaden. My friends were disappearing down a chute into the deep unknown and I was still standing exposed in the open air, holding childhood in my hands.

~~

Deep in the night, in the pool of light from the small goose-necked lamp on my desk, Gretel asleep two feet away, I suddenly saw a cool, winter light flicking upon the cresting waves of the North Sea. I was standing on the beach at Scheveningen looking out over the ocean, my parents nearby on the strand. Suddenly I missed my parents with my whole body. They were two figures who had always been there whenever I needed them. I yearned for one of my mother's Chinese meals. I longed for a walk with my father—to talk about the Japanese hush.

At the intimacy of my dusky desk, as I did three or four nights a week, I wrote to my mother and father. ". . . Annie and I are collecting *Life* magazine photos of the war and this guy is making them into slides. It's going to be really cool. . . . I'm reading *The Tao Te Ching.* Have you ever read it, Pop? . . . How is Hipni, Mom? Have you had curry puffs lately? . . . What do you think I should do when kids tell me they're taking drugs? Some of these missionary kids are really messed up. . . . I love Japan. You were right. It's so beautiful. . . ."

My mother wrote letters every day or two. About the adorable children she worked with at the Cheshire Home, and about her and my father's adventures. "We went down the river to a longhouse. We had to drink that awful rice wine with maggots in the bottom. And then the chief offered Pop the oldest virgin. Her lips were colored red from all the betel nut. . . . We went to Capit and our room was infested with flies. . . ." She loved all these semi-miserable, fascinating adventures. My mother said she and my father listened to the pirated tape we had had made of Steppenwolf, Jefferson Airplane, and Crosby Stills & Nash in the evenings, and cried.

My father wrote to me of meals with Chinese men, and the trips he took to find out about the Communist insurgents. I pictured him eating dumplings in a dirty café near the market, gesturing with his chopsticks to a slick-haired Chinese man—or I imagined him with his staff, hiking briskly down a jungle path with his white tennis hat on his head, and then conversing with the village chief in a hut. I envisioned him listening intently to the Chinese growling from the shortwave radio in the bedroom, and leaving money for an informant in a rattan basket of orchids. Busy in my life, I conveniently forgot about the man, Lee, and Mr. Smith.

To my questions, my father always wrote back, "Trust yourself, Girl. Look inside yourself. You'll always know what's right." He seemed happy; Borneo was always tossing adventures in front of a person. He told me not to worry about the war. Nixon was winding it down.

My parents' letters made me feel strong.

~~

Life was good.

One Saturday, Andy, Dottie (the girl who'd smoked marijuana to escape the thought of her father's wrath), and I, all of us in a silly mood and inspired by the health-food craze, collected pine cones in the strip of woods bordering the grave yard, washed them in the girls' dorm kitchen sink, and then set them to boil with ramen in a pot. The broth tasted disgusting, but the noodles were fine. Giddy as eight-year-olds, we sang a made-up song about pine cone soup.

~~

Arriving home to Kuching for Christmas, I felt stalwart as a Brit. My father was brown and relaxed. Mostly he seemed contented, taking each day as it came, drinking Chinese beer. My mother too was invigorated. She was in her element, working with children with disabilities and adults with leprosy.

They regaled us with tales of their adventures and mishaps. One week, they had traveled in a raft of dugouts toward Kalimantan deep into the jungle, where the Communist insurgency was thickening. My father had received instructions to find out what he could about this Communist force deep in the rainforest. My mother said, "The oarsmen of our boats were trembling with their guns, Sara. We had no idea where the insurgents might appear. They were hidden with guns all along both sides of the river. It was really scary." My father did not contradict her. Perhaps this was one of the incidents to which my mother was referring when, years later, she would draw her hand across her face tiredly and comment that their life in the Agency had too often been frightening.

One day we visited one of my father's colleagues, a Chinese man. While we sat as ornaments to my father's work, the man's servants offered us a delicious sixteen-course Chinese dinner. For Christmas, we decorated a potted palm tree with tiny Iban baskets my mother had collected. On Christmas Day, which coincided this year with Eid, the end of Ramadan, we sat in the front room in good clothes among the orchids, and received visits from my parents' friends and Malaysian officials. Hipni had made all kinds of goodies—curry puffs, herb crackers, spicy beef, which he served on a silver tray. He looked sharp in his starched white jacket. The people stayed for a punctual twenty minutes. They all had many rounds to make to friends and colleagues. The formal, familiar rounds of diplomacy were *home*.

My father rattled an old *Washington Post*. He read aloud an article on Vietnam. The article reported that the troops in Southeast Asia were plagued with loneliness, frustration, and a sense of futility. Some GIs had begun "fragging" their officers; some had killed them with "accidentally" thrown hand grenades. And the drug situation was out of control. The Army estimated that 65,000 GIs were on drugs; entire units were on heroin. The number of soldiers in combat was down to 280,000. As of now, 44,245 Americans had been killed in action, and 293,439 wounded. Little did I know how soon and how relevant these figures would be to my life.

I left Kuching strong and tanned, and fortified with love. I didn't even have to clutch a sucking stone this time. I was a clear-eyed and indomitable soldier. I liked CA and I knew the drill.

21
tachikawa

You expect a boat to capsize once in a blue moon, but it's unusual to pitch-pole, stern over bow, in flat calm, in the daylight.

~~

The moment I was at my zenith, the crisis came.

Maybe I was more tortured than I'd known. People have a way of enduring, of weaving mantles that fend off worry and stress. But then sometimes the valve releases when a person is in an upswing, at her happiest and most thriving—like when a cold hits on the weekend.

Maybe sucking stones, marine-ing around, wasn't going to work forever.

Maybe it was that I needed a new, more encompassing solution: some new way. Life delivers what you need. . . .

Maybe all the pieces—my country's aggressions, the Vietnamese dying, the young GIs dying, the separation from my parents, my father's secret, his worries, the places loved and lost, the years of marginality and the endless trying, the shyness, the perfectionism, the strain of being a marine, and James Taylor—all got poured into a big cauldron at once and began to boil.

Maybe everything was too fine, too perfect—and unbeknown to me, there was a thread in the cloth that was too tight. Quietly pulling, tugging, gathering. . . .

Or maybe it was simply a case of Deus ex Machina.

Whatever it was, I was suddenly fey. One morning I awakened out of fever, and was someone else.

~~

Since Christmas, I had been burning the candle at both ends—literally—except my candle was a flashlight. I liked everything I was doing but I was burning too brightly. I went to play rehearsal until late five nights a week; we were doing a play called *Man and the Masses,* about a woman trying to start a peaceful revolution among working people. Annie was the star, and I was one of the supporting witches. Despite a dragging fatigue, I stayed up past lights out, flashlight in hand, every night to study.

~~

One night, I got a splitting headache and a raging fever. I sweated and shivered until dawn. Mrs. Elliot telephoned the missionary doctor in downtown Kobe, called me a taxi, and dispatched me off to his office. No one knew it, but I was entering an unknown country.

~~

Riding in the small, black taxi, I was being whisked along the city streets, and the music on the driver's screeching radio suddenly blasted James Taylor's "Fire and Rain." Still feverish, I felt as though I was floating inside the song.

We were in a neighborhood now of tiny, narrow twisting streets lined with tight-packed walled houses. The driver pulled up at a small, mossy-looking home with a tile roof. The waiting room was like a living room, with, as I see it, old overstuffed chairs in dim mossy-brick patterns like the streets outside.

The doctor was short and grey-colored, in a white coat. In the examining room, I could tell he didn't like me. Perhaps he was solely used to serving missionary or Japanese children. Maybe the school didn't call on him very often, and the sudden appearance of this embassy child was out of order. Or maybe he didn't like the way I was dressed in my hurriedly flung-on Indian print dress with blue jeans underneath. In any case, he seemed rattled or in a hurry.

But I was woozy and aflame. He gave my body a quick runover—stethoscope, ear pokes, a peering into my eyes—and allowed that I was sick. He gave me a vial of medicine. He rushed me out, as if I were dust he wanted to sweep out the door of his examining room and then out the door of his house. He told me to look for the cab outside, down the street.

Back at the dorm, I took the pills and lay on my bed. My Singapore Airlines poster with the willowy Malay women batiked in scarlets and hot pinks was at first reassuring, but then began to waver. I looked at the small batik Ramsay gave to me, and I wanted to cry.

By the second morning, though, I was tough. I was also gone. The fever had broken—and I was a girl I didn't know.

I took my pill, walked through my school day, did all the usual things, but everything had changed. The classrooms slanted, I could barely stay awake.

It was as if I was encased in gauze, and now, instead of being the person who inhabited my own body, I was a watching spirit, a couple of feet distant, watching my body and my mouth—now strangely charged up and vehement—do and say things that had nothing to do with me. I was also like some wise old man, stroking his chin, following myself, watching this other antic me do strange things. Inside my gauze, I was philosophical about this turn of events, oddly calm—the sense of disturbance was faint like the palest pink in a morning sky. I mused to myself throughout the hours as I watched that other me speak, "That isn't true," but I had a strange detachment, a sort of wait-and-see attitude about it all. None of it mattered all that much, and it was kind of interesting to watch, to see what this other Sara did. She was giddy, she was outspoken and forthright in a way I'd never been. She had a loud voice, and strode around like a pirate, all confidence and purpose and devil-may-care. She did not hesitate. But what a mess she left—for me to clean up afterward.

Things began to roll like I was in a movie. After English class, I cornered Annie and whispered, "I took acid." Later I told her, "I got drunk in the graveyard." It was also like watching a silent movie because the old, normal Sara was silent. She couldn't speak. She was just watching this new one do things.

I was now the producer, the director, and the actress in my own movie, a movie of a foggy world in which I was the only salient actor.

The night of the first day I was back in school, I had play practice. Somehow, in a confused blur, I got through it. I didn't have many lines, or maybe I didn't have to perform—we weren't very far along in rehearsals. I loved being one of the witches stirring the Macbeth pot, but I had a roaring headache the whole evening. I insisted on staying late even though people told me I looked tired and overwrought and should go back to the dorm. I was a fever of fatigue, restlessness, and agitation. When I finally left, the hallway out of the gym was dark. I was all alone. This was when I began to act strangely. I suddenly felt light, elated. I reached into my pocket and took out a pack of gum I had been keeping there. With a bolt of glee, I scattered the slices along the hallway. I fancied people finding them there the next day, treats waiting for them. They'd think fairies put them there.

The next day at school was even more slanted and blurred and feverish. One five-minute stretch was crystal clear, though. I can still feel myself doing it, see the messy piles of papers on the desk, see the packed, disordered bookshelf to the back of the desk chair, feel the hard wood of the chair under my bottom, see through the large window the gravestones I loved straggling up the mountainside. Then the chair was suddenly full of a man. A man I disliked, disliked fiercely—Dean Kent, the one who had asked me to be a flower princess when I first arrived. And now I was a Sara who acted on her impulses. The dean, very tall in a tweed jacket, with a large, looming face and strict brown eyes, settled in his chair, started to take me to task, "Now Sara, what's all this I hear about . . ." But I didn't let him. I was belligerence and I would stop him. My anger was deep and it quietly crept out into the short space between the man and me. Quiet and sure, my hand darted out, picked up his coffee cup, and poured the coffee onto the messy paper piles on his desk. Just as quietly then, I walked out and, even though it was the middle of the day, I went back to the dorm and up to my room, and lay down. I was satisfied, but so, so tired.

Whispering. Anger like electrified pink fluff.

~~

"How about an arm?" he said. It felt comforting to have an arm lightly across my shoulder. Dr. Mead was walking me down the steep hill to his apartment near the bottom of the mountain. I didn't know why we were going there; he was just ushering me there and I trusted him. I vaguely knew I was sick, and that something not right had happened. I felt calmer with him, away from the school. He was tall and kind. He was going to take care of me.

The apartment was tiny, a room of only eight mats: a tiny sleeping/living room, a closet kitchen, a bathroom. Mrs. Mead came soon after. She knelt down beside me like a Japanese lady, with her feet curled under her, on the mat where I was curled on a futon under a puffy quilt. She said, "Sara, we are going to try to call your mother. Okay? Do you hear me, Sara?" I rustled under the covers. I didn't know why they were going to call my mother, but okay, whatever they did was fine. I just wanted to sleep.

Before this, before we'd come to the apartment, I'd had a conversation; maybe it was with several teachers. I was wild, I watched myself. I was chuckling inside, I felt evil. I was also lost in a swirling-groping-grasping for what was true. The real, the old me, was trapped behind bars. She wasn't unhappy; she was calm there behind the bars. She was just watching this other Sara move and say things she—that Sara—thought were true, but weren't true.

"Did you drink some alcohol, Sara?" the teachers said. "Yes. Whiskey," I rustled, I nodded and grinned inside. I was giddy; I would say yes to anything.

"Did you smoke some marijuana?"

"Yes," I said.

"Did you take any drugs?"

"Yes," I nodded. It must be so. It was probably so. I did it all, I said, I did all of them. I did all those prohibited and dangerous things. I must have. That must be why I was like this, why the world was like this. Maybe I was like James Taylor. Their eyes darkened with concern as my mouth put out words. My mouth put out words, but I couldn't reach the teachers. I couldn't give them the right answer. I didn't know. I nodded and nodded and nodded, and then I lay back down—tired, so tired.

~~

The Meads had to go back to school. I didn't know if this was the same day that I had come to their apartment, or three days later. My mother, they said, was due to arrive in a few hours. Mrs. Mead squatted down beside me again, and gently patted me. Her face was tiny, narrow like a pixie's, with large, kind eyes. She said, "Will you be all right here alone?" I nodded. She opened the refrigerator. "There's yogurt, and some cheese, and bread. And there's some chicken stew. Heat that up if you want to. Anything, Sara," she said. I told her I would be all right. I still could be polite some moments, even though most of me seemed gone.

I slept awhile and then I woke up. I thought, *Maybe if I eat it will help.* I was beginning to feel some panic about all the strangeness now. I went to the refrigerator and I got out the pot of stew. I was watching myself now. *Maybe this will do it*, I thought. I ate some of the cold, congealed stew out of the pot. Then I got out the bread and cut some slices. I spread the stew on the bread: big lumps of chicken, the cold, sticky soup sogging through. I forced myself to eat. At first it was good, and then it was too much. But I forced myself, even after my stomach was too full. I chewed and chewed, big blobs in my cheeks, until I couldn't anymore. *Maybe this will do it.* Then I lay down again, my stomach too too full, but I had done my job.

In a blur, my mother's figure appeared in the apartment. Dr. Mead was behind her. Why is Mom here? It's not right. I am in school. It isn't vacation. (Later I would hear over and over again my mother's story of getting to Kobe. Frantic after Dr. Mead's phone call, she dashed to the Kuching airport and got the first plane to

Singapore. In Singapore there was no flight to Tokyo so she boarded a flight via Okinawa and rode in the cargo bay. In Tokyo, someone from the office met her and put her on the bullet train. She was thin and wavering there in the doorway. She was speaking but I could barely hear her. She was saying my name and bending down and hugging me. I was indifferent. It was wrong. Why was she here?

We were in a modern hotel room now, a luxurious room like our family would never normally have. It was creamy and modern, with a big window looking out onto the broad streets of downtown Kobe. Way below I saw people walking briskly with shopping bags and satchels in their hands, a whole city down there going about its day's business. I liked my mother now, but I still didn't know why she was here. She took me to a department store. I liked this. I liked shopping. We passed a make-up counter. I was against makeup, but this new Sara was daring and she liked it. Even though my mother was moving ahead, I stopped and started putting on the lipstick. I picked up one tube, slathered it on, and then I picked up another. I was trying them out to see how I looked—but something was wrong. In the mirror I had lipstick on my lips but also smeared all around my lips into my cheeks. I was pleased with myself but my mother came hurrying back. She was apologizing to the clerk. I was frustrated. Annie and I had done this for silly fun before, but this time, even I knew, something was not quite as it should have been. My mother was hurrying now. We passed along the glittery underground corridors of a fluorescent-lit mall. When we came to a pastry shop, she said, "Why don't we get some pastries for your friends?"

I had talked to Annie on the phone and she'd said she would bring some people to see me. It was so strange that I was not at school with them, that I was staying in a hotel with my mother, but I had to go along. People told me I was sick, that I was going to see a doctor in Tokyo who would help me. I knew that the world was slanted now, that I was saying things that were not true, that I was giddy and my arms were hanging too free, but I didn't really understand all of this.

We bought eight pastries—beautiful ones. My mother let me pick out all the different kinds.

Back in the room high in the air, I was alone. My mother had to go do something for a minute or two, probably call my father, which she was doing a lot. I nodded. I was fine. I was sitting on the bed and the pastries were sitting in a pristine white box, tied beautifully with ribbon. I opened the box and ate a pastry. I needed sweets right now. These were just the thing. I sat on the arm of the tan-upholstered desk chair and ate. I finished one pastry and then I started on another. By the time my mother got back there were only two left, and crumbs sprinkled all over the desk and the chair and the floor by the chair. There was a blob of whipped cream on the desk. My mother said, "Oh Sara," but she cleaned it all up as I sat there, full but feeling sure I'd done the right thing. As she squatted down there, cleaning, tears were running down her cheeks. I was hard though. I just watched. What was this nonsense?

Very soon there was a knock on the door and Annie came in with Matthew and Zack in tow. My mother went out, to let us be alone. I felt like a princess in her boudoir, holding court. It was as if I had on one of those long satiny gowns, and I was receiving intimates. But it was ephemeral. They talked to me, asked me how I was. It was awkward for some reason. Now I was a sixteen-year-old girl again. But I was still not the right Sara. Annie and Matthew were sitting on the edge of one of the beds. Zack was sitting in the desk chair. I went to him and lay my cheek against his chest. I reached my arm up around his shoulder. I held on to him, lightly hugging. I nestled my face there against this boy who I must have thought about, must have wanted to be close to, must have thought was handsome. He cocked his head a certain way; he had dark hair flopping by his eyes, a lopsided smile. But who was this Sara who would do this thing of going right up to a boy and hug him, who would sit there with her face against him, silent, embracing? It was all wrong, but the Sara I was watching was happy. She thought she was fine. She just did what she wanted. Flick, flick—I want that, I want that. Soon, the awkwardness strange and surreal, they were leaving. Annie told me she hoped I felt better. The boys said "Bye."

Soon after, my mother appeared again. With her, though, was my father—my father now!—and Andy behind him. What was this? But I liked having the family there. I was a small girl now, confused and tired mostly. I could tell even Andy was worried. He hugged me several times. He kept shaking his head to my parents and saying, "I don't know."

Now we were in a taxi again—all four of us. "Fire and Rain" was playing again, at least in my mind—as I went toward this next future.

Next we were on the train, the bullet train, to Tokyo. My mother was across from me—we had seats facing each other. My mother and my father were on one side, me on the other. Andy was back at school. A Japanese woman and two little children sat across the aisle from us. They were eating mikans from a mesh sack. I asked Pop for some mikan, and at the next station, he got off the train fast and bought me a bagful. I was happy now, eating tangerines. But one thing was so un-comfortable. My mother was acting weird. She was wearing sunglasses even though we were inside the train and it was not a bright day. She was crying behind the glasses, or not crying, but hiding past crying. I was angry at first. I was defiant, a girl composed of iron pipes, looking at my mother. Why is she crying? My mother is so dumb. She's such a worrier. Then, where are they taking me? Why will no one explain, no one speak to me, or really talk to me? Why is she crying, acting like things are so bad? And then the blackness of the glasses got to me. Maybe I was dy-ing of some disease, and that was why they were taking me to a hospital. That must be it. They must have explained why we were going, but maybe they had not, and it was that I was dying of some disease. Why won't Mom just talk to me normally? For a moment my whole torso flashed with fear. My father was quiet. He patted her on the knee, he reached over and held my hand. I noticed a slight tremble in his hand. He was being infinitely gentle with me. I squeezed back and felt comforted. I ate mikan, looking at the Japanese countryside whipping by out the window.

Later, when I looked back, I knew my father had been deliberately calm on the train that day, that he had been holding back his grief—keeping it on his lap in his old leather satchel, held close to his chest, his heart. I was a soft, thin girl of flesh, eating from the string bag of mikans, when I looked at my father, and he had been a thin father in love, in anguish for his daughter.

Taxi, taxi for a long time through streets deep and thick with honking cars. Then we were at the gates of "an Air Force base," my father said. We showed our passports and my father handed the guard the paper with his orders out of his breast pocket, and we were let in the gate.

And suddenly we were in a kind of America. A flat grid of streets lined with small, ticky-tacky one-story houses on checkerboard green lawns. No walls or moss or crumbling stone like in Japan. The cab dropped us off at what my father called our billet, a little motel, one story and modest, like the cookie cutter houses we passed. The billet was small and simple, with regulation Air Force blankets tucked into metal beds with spic-and-span hospital corners.

Now we were at an office in a long, rectangular, two-story building. Everyone spoke American English and wore uniforms, some with white jackets over them. I was in some kind of medical office. There was a desk and across from it, three fold-ing chairs. We were sitting on the folding chairs. My mother was wiping her eyes, my father was sitting with his hands resting on his knees. I was squirming. Why the heck were we here? I hated army people. I was against the war. And there was nothing much wrong with me—nothing I could put my finger on, anyway.

A doctor in a white coat came in. Tall, dark-haired, with glasses, he shook my mother and my father's hands, talked to them. Dr. Thompkins. I turned my head away and pretended I didn't hear what they said. I was astonished when I heard my father say, "Actually, I work for the Central Intelligence Agency." I had never ever heard my father say this out loud to anyone except Andy and me before. The doctor hesitated for half a second and then said, "I see."

A psychiatrist with an active mind might have thought, one could imagine, "This daughter is a stand-in for the father. The covert agent's hidden self steps into the open. The daughter's fugue, and the outpouring of truth, could be his."

After a little while, the doctor told my parents he wanted to talk to me alone. I felt defiant. I was not going to talk to a psychiatrist. I didn't believe in them. I put my feet up on the coffee table and aimed them at him while he talked to me. I watched myself do this while thinking, in the voiceless part of me, "Sara, that's not right."

The doctor asked me strange questions about the date and he had me add up numbers, and he asked me stuff about school, questions that I didn't remember and didn't know the answers to. He also asked me if I knew where I was.

"On some base."

"Tachikawa Air Force Base, outside Tokyo."

He called my parents back in. I mostly ignored them, but heard him say, "It's a good sign that she's angry."

As he led us out, another doctor came up. He was blond and young, and had a kind face. "This is Doctor Cohen," the dark-haired doctor said. I didn't know why he was telling me this. Why was it important to me? But it would be so important. I didn't know, either, that I had gotten lucky: Dr. Cohen was the only U.S. military child psychiatrist in the whole Pacific.

It became clear that I was going to stay in the hospital and my mother and my father would stay in the billet without me. They could visit. I was a little nervous, but—a man nurse had me take some pills with a glass of water—I just did what they said.

A year later, my mother would tell me how my father had wept when they'd walked out of the hospital.

~~

This was how it looked. You were walking down a typical hospital hallway: scrubbed floors smelling faintly of disinfectant, wide enough for a golf cart plus two people abreast to walk down, lit by small windows. There were sets of double doors at intervals that opened into the wards—doors that swung on their hinges, like entrances to saloons. The doors to Ward 3 looked deceptively the same as the others: that blue-mixed-with-grey favored by the Air Force. The doors opened into another wide hall, with three doors into patient rooms on the right side, and two or three doors into smaller staff rooms on the left: a therapy room, a staff meeting room, and finally the nurses' station behind glass from which they had a wide-angle view of the ward. At the nurses' station, and the third patient room, the hallway opened out into a wide, spacious community room with chairs, set in a disarrayed circle in the foreground, and five beds, hospital-cornered in white sheets and blue-grey blankets, at the back wall. A door to the left of the back wall led into a boarding school–type dormitory, with beds lined up on either side. At the end of that room, a door was posted with a sign that said NO EXIT.

I was in a room off the entry hall now, with another girl, Binny. She was happy I was there, and showed me the bathroom and helped me put my clothes in the drawers, while she bounced on the bed and talked about her boyfriend. She said, as though it was a matter of course, that she had just been in overnight for a drug overdose. She acted like this was a normal place to be. This made me feel like maybe it was. Maybe I could get some rest.

But no. An orderly came in and told me to put on the Air Force pajamas and robe that were lying on the bed, and then "Come out to group." I felt so tired I could hardly move. I lay down on the bed.

But the man came back and said, "Come on, out you come. Dr. Cohen's orders." We entered the big room at the end of the hall. A bunch of people in Air Force pajamas and robes like mine were slumped around on the folding chairs—pulled into an approximate circle. Everyone in the room except for Binny and a tall, worn-looking woman, was a close-shorn man. The orderly pointed me to one of the chairs. I thought, *Why am I here, surrounded by GIs, the thing I hate most about America?*

Pretty soon the doctors came in and sat on other chairs in the circle for "Check in." One of the doctors was Dr. Thompkins. Dr. Cohen was the second, and the third was a burly man with warm, brown eyes. He introduced himself, extending his hand. "Hi, I'm Dirk. I'm the psych tech."

Dr. Cohen began the group. "So how's it going for you today, Chet?"

"Pretty bad, Doc, I've still got the jitters."

"Let's talk after group," he said. "And you, Blair?" he said to the next man in the circle.

"I'm working at controlling my temper—talking about my feelings instead of hitting out, like you said."

"Great." They talked a little.

"And Steve?" Dr. Thompkins said.

"When do I get shipped out? I want out of here NOW."

"We're working on it as fast as we can."

I felt fogged up, bewildered. *What am I doing here?*

In the fog, an older man with dark brows and eyes like a basset hound's said to Dr. Cohen, "I'm still fighting the daymares."

The only teenager other than Binny and me had a Bible in his lap. It had a million bookmarks in it. When it was his turn, he said, "Jesus said . . ." I noticed Dr. Cohen frowning. Excessive religiosity can be associated with psychosis.

"How're the voices?" Dr. Thompkins asked a man named George.

"They're still telling me to do very bad things." Again, there was a lot of talk about what George could do to help himself.

The tall woman who had a crackled face and a rattly voice laughed a throaty smoker's laugh when it was her turn. "Come on, Doc. Let's all go have a drink."

To his question, a man named Brad said, "I'm okay. I've just gotta get back to my wife."

"What are you here for?" Brad turned to me.

"I don't know. I don't want to be here. I want to go back to my school in Kobe."

Dr. Cohen said, "Sara and I met last night. We'll be meeting tomorrow morning, Sara. Until then, I want you to just go to group and let the others help you settle in. They all know what to do." He looked straight at me in such a soft way that I felt cared for.

The orderlies told a man named Jim to come sit with us, but he just perched on his chair for an instant before he flitted off again, like he was chasing butterflies.

"And how are you, Sam?" Dr. Cohen said to the man next to me.

"I'm just glad to be outta Nam."

"You'll probably be transited tomorrow."

"Where'll I be stationed?"

"You'll go to Bethesda first."

"Oh Doc, can't I just go home?" And he began to weep.

I felt completely bewildered. I'd never been anywhere like this before. And yet, everyone assumed I was where I should be.

~~

In the late afternoon, they let me go to my room. My parents visited and sat on chairs by my bed. My father read to me from *Walden*. I watched his familiar, bent fingers play at the foxed pages of the book. I couldn't listen too well, but his voice made me feel calmer than I had in a long time.

It was the next morning. I was tired, but things seemed clearer. The floor didn't slant. The people weren't nearly as blurred. The air outside the window was clear, clear as nothingness and clear as brightness. Pristine, crisp, each cloud distinct. I wrote a little in my journal.

After Dirk told me to get dressed, the men and I went to what they called "the Mess" and ate in our bathrobes. I was beginning to figure things out. We weren't allowed to wear our clothes in case we tried to run away. Earlier Dirk had been scolding a man who had run away during the night and had been picked up barefoot, in his pajamas, in someone's backyard on the base. "You're a pain in the rear. That really pissed me off," Dirk said. People talked plain here.

After breakfast, we had to clean our rooms until they were in Air Force order. Then there was group therapy. After group, Dr. Cohen came up to me and took me to one of the little rooms off the entry hall to the ward. He asked me how I was doing and how I felt about being on the ward.

"It's awful," I said.

"It's really tough to be torn out of your school, and to suddenly be in Tachi, in this strange hospital, I bet."

His tone was so empathic that I felt less like hissing, and my body calmed.

He said, "When you got here, you really weren't quite like yourself. Today you seem like you're doing a lot better. We gave you some medicine to help, and I think it's helping. I'm glad you're back. Your parents and I were really worried about you."

He went on, "Your and my job now is to figure out what happened so that we can work to make sure it doesn't happen again."

"When can I go back to school?" I asked.

"I promise to get you back as soon as we can." He sounded like he could be trusted.

"Why don't you tell me something about how school's been going and what things were like in the week or so before you came here. That may help us get started on this job of figuring out what happened."

I began to tell him about school, about the dorm and about the play, and he was so interested that I just kept talking—telling him about how hard I'd been working, how I loved haiku and . . .

He smiled and then he asked me how it had been to leave my parents to go off to boarding school. I was just sixteen and we'd been a pretty close family, he'd heard.

"Oh, it was fine," I said, wanting to convince him nothing fazed me.

He just said, "You know, any feeling you have is okay." Soon, we finished. When he said, "We'll talk again tomorrow," I felt happy.

~~

After lunch we got a tiny rest, then we had to do our jobs. They had assigned me the task of neatening up the community room, which made me mad because it was such a girly kind of work. I was sure they'd never assign it to one of the men. Then, in the late afternoon, we had group again.

The psych ward at Tachikawa was a revolutionary new program in the military. Not long before my sojourn there, there had been race riots on the ward, and Dr. Thompkins, Dr. Cohen, a junior psychiatrist, a career military nurse, Dirk, the psych tech, and a few others, had come in and created a warm therapeutic community that quickly welcomed and integrated evacuees, and set a standard of talking about feelings rather than acting them out.

By the evening group, the men were beginning to emerge from the fog. Vaguely, I realized the other patients were almost all soldiers on their way back from Vietnam; Tachikawa Air Base was one of the main evacuation way stations. A few were enlisted men from bases in Japan, Okinawa, or Korea, but the majority on the ward were Vietnam med-evacs with PTSD, overwhelming grief, suicidal depression, and/or flagrant psychoses. In group, their stories began to come out. Many of them were angry. They swore and yelled at the doctors.

One man jumped up when a plane went overhead.

Another one, who had been sitting with his face in his hand, finally spoke in response to Dr. Cohen's coaxing. He said, "I just can't take it," and his body started shuddering and sobs began to wrench out of him. Through the sobs, he said, "My buddy. We lost him to the VC in a fucking swamp." And then he screeched like a wild animal.

Dr. Cohen went over to him and put his arm around him and he collapsed against his chest, sobbing.

I felt my eyes begin to prick with tears.

~~

Several of the men seemed haunted, unreachable across some horrible mystery. They'd crossed a frontier that was only theirs. And they saw sights belonging only to them, the unchosen. I was on one side of a chasm and they were on the other. They'd been forced across. I could only watch them. Their minds were inaccessible.

But I took it in—all their terror and sadness. I began to listen to helicopters as they did.

In the evening the staff set up a projector in the community room and we sat on the folding chairs and watched a Humphrey Bogart movie.

~~

The next morning, Dr. Cohen said, "How did you feel about what happened in group yesterday afternoon?"

"Sad," I said, and I couldn't help beginning to swell.

"Stan's been through something really tough. . . . And what about you? How are you feeling about being here?"

I started to say, "I'm doing fine," and to put my best foot forward as I would have at an embassy dinner party, but that didn't fit here, so I said, "Bummed out."

He said, "You know, Sara, feelings are not right or wrong. They just *are*. And you have a right to every single feeling you have."

Time didn't stop, but this was the single most revolutionary thing anyone had said to me in my life—or perhaps ever would.

"And I'll bet you *are* bummed out. This must seem like a pretty weird place. All these men have been through some tough times. . . . You've been through a lot in your life too. You've had a lot of experiences, and I'll bet you've had a lot of feelings to go with them.

"Caring, loving, missing: none of these are anything to be ashamed of," Dr. Cohen said. "In fact, they show you're a full human being. . . . Anger, disappointment, sadness, they're all part of being human. Loving and missing people—and even being angry at the people you love most—is completely natural," he said. Years from now Dr. Cohen's words would resurface when I read Terry Tempest Williams's words, "Suffering shows what we're attached to."

Suddenly I was crying, and then I was crying harder. I was missing my mother and my father, and Sara, and Holland, and I was feeling all alone in a hallway. . . . All of it came rushing out of me in a flood. Sara the marine dissolved and my whole bucket of pent-up sadness just tipped out.

Dr. Cohen just sat calmly and said to tell him what thoughts had caused the tears. And when I did, he didn't think I'd failed, he thought it was fine.

~~

One day while I was sitting on the bed writing in my journal, one of the young men came in and stood just inside the door to my room, his back against the wall. He was agitated, twitching all over, and looking at me with possessed dark eyes. He started to move now, to wander around my bed, saying nothing, eyes serious and black and full of intent.

Just as fear began to ripple inside me, Dirk came by the room and called the man out of my room.

The next day, Dr. Cohen told me, "I heard about Tank going into your room. If he or anyone else goes into your room, you come get us. Shout if you need to."

His concerned eyes made me melt.

"Now, how are you doing today?"

"Okay, except I'm mad about missing the play at school. . . ." I found myself then telling him about *Man and the Masses*, and Annie, and even Will.

"Sounds like you're angry about missing out on things at CA. There are a lot of things you love about it."

I had never had anyone listen to me so carefully before. My father listened closely, but it was different.

With Dr. Cohen, I learned to name the emotions. It was like learning an alphabet of feelings. Every day, I felt amazement. To let go of the marine was easier each day. "You mean it's okay to be disgusted? To feel dismal? To feel frustrated enough to kick a wall?" Each feeling, Dr. Cohen taught me, had a worthy and valid name— like the different birds in the woods. My father had empathized with my feelings, and my mother had intuited them, but Dr. Cohen gave them words. In his little office, I examined them like a blind girl catching sea gulls and robins in her hands.

~~

Each morning, noon, and evening, the nurses came around with our pills. I was taking Stelazine and Artane—what I'd later know were major tranquilizers used to treat schizophrenia.

Dr. Cohen had said he was trying these medicines with me, but—"We're puzzled about you," he said. "It doesn't quite add up."

~~

On the ward I had become very aware of a particular soldier named Ken. Gaunt-cheeked and stick-bodied, he walked like a zombie in a white t-shirt and Air Force bathrobe—with hollow, haunted eyes, eyes that had seen horrors. He wandered, and then he plopped down to sleep on the linoleum. Lying there, he was concave. A lens, his whole being an eye, he was a window into war.

The orderlies found him under beds, in corners, anywhere he could curl and hide, get away from the rank smell, the screeching of bombs, the shrieking, the scrambled green-black, brown-crimson scenes.

He saw something the rest of us couldn't see. It was too private. Nothing should ever be that private.

In Vietnam, where I would live for a summer during college, while my father was posted there, I would watch the beautiful women on the Saigon streets. They had a hardness to them, something impenetrable and determined. Hardened-up desperation, terror petrified into its opposite: ferocity. In Ken, terror had turned to limpness. The human spirit can go either way.

One afternoon, Ken was curled asleep on a pile of dirty sheets. I was sitting nearby. He looked serene there and then Dirk and a nurse named Alvin started poking him to get him to move. Afterward, he stood, like always, at the edge of the room, saying and doing nothing, just staring ahead of him as though nothing was happening in the room around him, like he was a ghost. "Ken is catatonic," Dirk told me. "We need to keep him active." I wanted to give Ken a hug; he looked so frail and lost. And, even though it was for a purpose, I hated it that they were so mean to him.

One mid-morning, Dirk said to Alvin, "Ken's still in there." This meant he was in the dormitory room at the back of the common room where he and all the rest of the young men slept. I watched Dirk and Alvin go into the room, and I went to the doorway to peer in. There were ten beds on each side of the room. They were all made up, the strip of white sheet folded down over the grey-blue blanket. Everyone else was out of the room, but Ken was there, standing beside the bed near the door on the right aisle. Slender, with a tousle of sandy hair, he was like a waif trying to hide himself.

He stood utterly still, staring straight ahead. Dirk ripped apart Ken's made bed and then said, in a loud angry voice, "Ken, make your bed." Ken moved like he was sleepwalking, like he was walking inside a wave of water. Slowly, slowly, he picked up with his slender hand the sheet that Dirk had thrown on the floor, and tried to put it on the bed. It was like it was slippery, like a drapery, though, and he couldn't get it to do anything. He got it pointed in an arrow toward the head of the bed, but then he let it drift off his hand, and collapsed. Dirk yelled again, "Make your bed, Ken!"

I shuddered and moved back into the common room.

~~

I talked to Dr. Cohen about Ken.

"He saw some terrible things during the war and he wants to curl into a ball and shut out the world. Catatonia can be very serious. The best thing for him is to get him to feel and to act."

"It's so awful," I said. Then I couldn't keep it back any longer. I told Dr. Cohen I hated the war and I told him about the antiwar marches. "I hate what America is doing in the world."

He said, "I do too. I was drafted when I was in medical school. I chose to serve rather than go to jail, but I know a lot of servicemen agree with you."

Suddenly I got it, a blasting truth: most of the servicemen didn't *want* to be in Vietnam.

~~

I hated OT, but it was something to do out of the ward. Sitting on stools around a table with a couple of the men, the teacher fetching us supplies and helping us, I made my father a leather key wallet from a kit of pre-cut leather pieces and gimp. I made my mother a copper-embossed picture of a pointing Labrador. Annie and the kids at CA seemed far away.

~~

One day, despite my resistance, the techs insisted that I go bowling with the guys. It was mortifying because we had to wear our PJs and robes, so everyone at the bowling alley would know exactly which ward we were from. It was an exercise like a cognitive therapist might design in 2005 to help someone overcome an anxiety disorder. If you can survive this embarrassment, you can do anything.

The hall leading to the hospital exit was scrubbed clean, American clean. It was long, stretching ahead to a rectangle of light far away. As we walked, gurneys whizzed by us: men with bandages around their heads, men whimpering like baby kittens. We passed doors to the other wards—for treating men with shrapnel wounds, for treating head injuries, for stabilizing soldiers with massive internal injuries. Tachikawa was one of the main medical bases where fighters were steadied before shipping home.

There were six of us trailing along the pale, white-green hall. Our regulation blue-grey robes were our signature. Some of us had them tied at the waist, like me—trying to conceal the pajamas underneath—and others were disheveled and just let them hang off their shoulders and drape around any which way. I felt like a bedraggled hobo in my man-size robe.

Most of us walked with the shuffling, listless Ward 3 walk. We'd been thoroughly medicated, so there was a wanderingness to us, a dullness that turned us compliant and sleepy, some of us with idiot smiles on our faces. Bonded through knowledge of each other's stories and wildest emotions, and with our matching robes (I finally had thirty twins), we were a clan.

There was Elmer, who must have been in his fifties. He was balding and had the saddest eyes I'd ever seen. I didn't know what he was doing here. George was sandy-haired and had blue eyes that flashed out like pistol shot. He'd have been handsome if he had been normal, but he talked to himself all the time. Sometimes he raved and shouted and then they took him into the nurses' office. They were trying to get him to do normal things—like they were trying to get the rest of us to do—but it seemed like a long shot for George. He seemed way gone, into another world full of beasts and sorcerors. And there was wild-eyed frantic Steve, bright blond and skinny like a string bean, for whom this trip was an advance because he had tried to run away so many times. Up until now he had had no access to shoes or even a robe, and had been watched like a hawk. Blair was with us too—young, dark, handsome, and angry. He spit out his words, held his shoulders straight back, and stood fiery, vigilant, and cocked, as if he was ready to blast the head off anything that even brushed past the corner of one eye. He was striding, instead of walking, down the hall. Jim was looking vacant-eyed and oh-too-happy, like this was an outing of his own devising, like he was back at home just trucking off to meet his girlfriend at the local movie house instead of in a holding tank here at Tachi, like his life had not been altered forever. And then there was Brad, pacing along beside me, truly looking forward to getting a breath of fresh air, hoping it would be the kind of fresh air he would breathe when he got back home. And then there was me—feeling foggy and mad about having to wear my dumb robe and go to a place and do an activity that only old, square people in Florida did.

The medics had assigned us each a buddy. Brad had been assigned to me, and me to him, maybe because we were both very young—though he was three years my senior and had a wife and had been to war—and they wanted us to feel springy hope. We walked along chatting about group, his eyes, with their background coloring of worry, glinting with play.

As we exited the door at the end of the long hall, the bright light of the real world shocked. Shading our eyes, we trundled across the wide, empty street of the base, and turned right up the far sidewalk. There were little one-story bungalows and offices set down on the flat, green lawns. The air was fresh and cool—I felt almost happy, through my medicated cloud. The orderlies shooed us along the next block and a half.

At the bowling alley I suddenly felt embarrassed about my robe and the company I was keeping. There weren't many people inside, but the heavyset man at the soda fountain and the three or four other young men wandering around looked at me. I felt like I was, well, in my pajamas in a public place, and so I pretended I didn't see them, and tried to hold my head high, allied to my kindred.

The bowling was a joke. I could barely lift the balls, I felt so tired and weak. And I was hampered by my prejudice against bowling. Elmer had to be prodded to take the ball each time. His eyes were constantly full of tears. He could barely look down the alley, and he just squatted down and sort of gently let the ball roll out of his hands like you would a little child setting out to walk on its own.

George had to be reined in constantly. He didn't know what he was doing or where he was. He trotted across the alleys talking to himself, he bumped into the little desks at the head of the alleys, and finally Bruce, the orderly, had to stay by him every minute, walking with him up to the place you got the ball, and directing him to toss it down the right alley. He did so, jerkily, like it was not a ball but a nasty piece of sticky garbage he was trying to get off his hand.

Steve's eyes darted all around, looking for escape routes, but then when it was his turn, it was like another person suddenly slipped into him. He strolled up to the alley like he was the alpha in a pride of lions and gracefully swooped the ball down to the pins, deftly making strikes almost every time.

Blair picked up the balls like they were rightfully his, and hurled them down the alley, as if they were bazooka rounds and he was making a clean massacre of the enemy.

Jim sort of danced around with the ball and when he let it go, it zigzagged down the chute.

Brad was impatient, and so sometimes his balls were well aimed while other times his thoughts were back in Montana and he didn't care and it just wandered, unowned, along the gleaming wood slats.

Mad that I had had to come here, and feeling very weak in my stomach and arms, I made halfhearted attempts to hit the pins. I really didn't care where the ball went, though sometimes I did have a spurt of mild pleasure when more than two or three pins fell. At regular intervals, I thought of Will, Annie, and Matthew, and everyone back at CA, and everything seemed strange beyond strange. *What am I doing here? Let me out of here.*

We were all in our own worlds. Even so, our orbits seemed to overlap, and we were a team. We all clapped when anyone knocked down any pins, and when Steve came up to the plate, we all held our breaths and watched, stunned, talent in vivo. Blair exuded anger but even he got a little quirk of a smile on the corners of his lips when we clapped for him. Brad and he shook hands. Brad whistled when I managed to get a strike.

I'd lived in a lot of cultures, and this one, in a way, was at once the most rigid and the most caring. Somehow the doctors and the other staff, none of them older than thirty-five—had put hard thought to it and cobbled together a community that worked. The rules were clear, we each had a role and a job; there was no choice but to attend group and go to meals and go to OT. And the doctors asserted both a sense of challenge that we perform at our best, and a deep kind of caring that rippled around the meeting room and scooped us into its embrace. Even blazing Blair, who stood during most meetings, moving constantly like a leopard at the zoo, snapped out "Way to go, man!" to George when he managed to pull himself together and pass out the popcorn before the lights went out on movie night. Probably even for the doctors what they'd accomplished was startling. Fate, or the draft, had conspired to bring together some guys who could work together, and out of the mess of ingredients, even though some of the inmates would no doubt have disagreed, concocted a nourishing stew.

All the men seemed to me infinitely old, even though the majority of them were no more than ten years my senior. Brad treated me like an equal, a best friend. I didn't realize that to him I looked grown. After the bowling, he sought me out. One day, looking out the window, he told me, "I faked depression so I could get back to my wife. She's trying to divorce me," he said, his eyes tearing up.

I asked about where he lived and what he wanted to do before the army. "Maybe things will change when you're there in person," I said. "I bet they will." The murky look in his eyes lifted and he gave me a hug. His cheek was both hard and soft against mine.

Suddenly I knew I was attractive, at least to this man.

~~

One day, in group, the men focused in on me. "How's it going for you, Sara," Dirk asked.

"I'm a little pissed off to still be here," I said, showing off my new Ward 3 lingo.

"So you got your eye on anyone back at the school in Kobe?" Steve, the escape artist, asked. He was actually focused on me rather than unguarded doors.

I blushed. "I'm worried about what everyone will think when I get back." This whole experience was so weird and such a strange mixture: I hated it and yet it was also a kind of miracle.

Brad said, "They won't even think about it. You're great."

"We're gonna miss you, kid," Blair said.

Elmer gave a huge, heaving sigh and I started to cry. And they all just let me, sitting there with kindness in their wounded eyes.

~~

Each day at group I got the hang of it more. I had never heard men talk like this: of feeling pissed off, of feeling murderous, of feeling like "offing" themselves. One man started crying uncontrollably as he told of a little child he thought he might have killed by accident. Another tore up a Kleenex as he described putting his dead friend in a helicopter. Another one refused to talk about Nam at all, though his body shook when others talked about it. Ken, though forced to come to group, usually collapsed in a heap and had to be forced to sit, with Dirk holding his arm.

As I listened, I was taking in a new view of both stoicism and emotion. I saw now that stoicism—being a blind and blinkered, unseeing marine—could be, for the GIs in Vietnam facing horror, or for a girl plopping down year after year in a new place, a necessity. Also, I saw that, with stoicism, anger, sadness, and disappointment would poke out sideways if they weren't at least acknowledged. It was better to respect them as guideposts, rather than as black cats to be avoided at all costs. These bruised-eyed airmen had taught me it was safe to be tender.

I had always thought the world must be set up so that we all had an equal proportion of joy and sorrow or it would be too hard to bear. Now I saw, looking at Blair and Ken, that the world was not fair and was never going to be. The airmen taught me both not to be a soldier and what true bravery was. Bravery was taking in and feeling and acknowledging it all—and marching on. As the Buddhists I'd read counseled, "The only way is through." And group made me see that openness, rather than restriction and secretiveness, brought joy. Our shared vulnerability made us human. Our armor didn't.

It was a new and better world I was walking into. It was huger than ever: blue-skyed and towering and broad and lightly canopied, an infinite curve of bright-shining possibility.

~~

American GIs weren't what I'd thought they were. Up until Tachi, they'd been stereotypes to me: a mass of unfeeling, brute, crew cut rednecks who lacked the courage to oppose the government. Blindered automatons who didn't think, but merely shot at what they were told to shoot—the worst interpretation of the marine at the Tomb of the Unknown Soldier.

The men on Ward 3 weren't a mass at all. Each was as different from the other as scrambled eggs and blackberry pie and beef stew. Or twigs and rocks and ocean. And they were not unfeeling, brute cowboys. They seemed a world older than I felt, but they were simply young men, fragile as any: with hearts that could be seared and punched, and violently and desperately wounded. At last, I'd lost my ability, facile during the antiwar demos, to lump all soldiers together with a sneering dismissal.

With Dr. Cohen, I'd learned a new, more honest way to interact and I had added a new mode to my repertoire. I could be the chirpy embassy girl, making a brave, good show of things, and I could also be emotionally honest and open. And either was true-blue American.

~~

I met with Dr. Cohen and we troubleshot about my return to school. "What if it happens again?" I said.

Dr. Cohen said, "You know, Sara, we don't exactly know what happened to you. It doesn't fit any common pattern. I don't think it will happen again, but we should

be careful." I loved that "we." "What we do know is that when you became disori-
ented, you had an excruciating headache and a very high fever. If you get either of
those again I want you to immediately take a high dose of aspirin. Start with two
and then if it continues, take two more."

Next worry: What would I do if the kids asked me where I'd been? It was so
embarrassing.

"It'll be five minutes of embarrassment and then everyone will forget about
it. Why not try honesty? Tell them you were burned out and spent some time in a
military hospital." I thought of my father's words from long ago: "Sara, you must
face into your fears."

Then we talked a little bit about the kids at school I liked and what I wanted to
be involved in when I got back. Dr. Cohen said, "Remember, if you like someone,
take a chance. You have nothing to lose."

Then Dr. Cohen gave me a big hug. He was sending me back to CA refreshed.
Like a spy, I'd been handed a new identity: a portfolio to a new land, a new language,
a fresh passport with a new photograph in which my hair framed, rather than covered, my face. But this identity was real.

A balloon, if squeezed enough, will burst its skin. This February in 1971 was
one of those points in life when an external event squeezes you, and you break
open. Before Tachikawa, I had had a false identity, an identity too tight to encom-
pass all of me or allow me to thrive. Now I had space to breathe and feel and move.
The ordeal I had just come through—my loss of identity, hospitalization, and
reassembly—presaged a parallel slippage of identity, upending, and transformation
that my father would soon undergo. Both my father and I, sooner or later, had to
face the miasma of our secrets, stoicism, and false identities. And beyond the obvious secrets and fake identities, we'd long harbored deeper ones with which we had
to come to grips: the secret of our human needs and vulnerability, and the mask of
invincibility we wore. This was the year of reckoning.

As I left the ward, Ken was lying crumpled by the nurses' station. Walking out
the double doors at the end of the hall—Dirk was holding the door for me, saying
"Good-bye, Princess. We'll miss you"—I suddenly understood why Dirk and the
other techs had talked to people leaving about the likelihood that they'd miss the
hospital.

~~

In two weeks, I'd gained a decade's worth of experience.

In Japan, I was born in one U.S. Air Force hospital; in a U.S. Air Force hospital, I'd made my second beginning.

~~

During my hospitalization in Tachikawa, Lieutenant Calley was being tried for premeditated murder of the South Vietnamese civilians at My Lai. At the base snack bar, my father showed me a copy of the *Post* he'd gotten at the Tokyo embassy, where he had been going for talks. While I'd been living with shell-shocked men, South Vietnamese troops had made incursions into Laos, trying to disrupt the supply lines of the Ho Chi Minh trail. This first action that the South Vietnamese had taken on their own had failed miserably. Furthermore, the regime was now acknowledged to be a Swiss cheese of corruption. As the American forces withdrew, the South Vietnamese were beginning to feel like the sacrificial lambs of American power. Anti-American protests were springing up in Saigon. One of President Thieu's inner circle had made a bitter pronouncement: "The Americans are businessmen. They'll sell you out if you can no longer assure them of a profit."

22

tea and bean cakes

I was in a medicated blur again, back at CA, but it was a different kind of fog when I'd left. This time, even though I was so groggy I slept through American history class, I was tracking the world. And there was no second Sara in operation.

The first day back, Andy was solicitous and protective, his eyes concerned, his floppy hat askew. He checked on me between classes. And my friends were quietly helpful. They didn't quite know how to behave with me and tried to act like nothing had happened. I told Annie and a few others that I'd been in an Air Force hospital but was better now. Gretel didn't even need to know; she was her same old, reliable sweet self.

At the end of the first day back, I lay down on my bed and placed my hands on my belly. I could feel my hip bones just under the rim of my hip-hugger jeans. Touching my own hard bones, I felt calm. I had within me, under my skin, what it took: the strength to name and hold pain until it subsided, to protect and express myself as I moved through a day.

~~

My mother rented a tiny apartment halfway down the CA hill to be near me. Every couple of days, I went there and she cooked me some Kobe beef, fortifying me with protein. In her wanders around the city she had also discovered a German bakery, and she fed me excellent thick black bread slathered with butter, to fatten me up.

My father had had to return to Kuching. He called my mother and me at her flat every few days to check on me, even though it was prohibitively expensive.

"Just go slow and take it a day at a time. I know you can do it," he said, his voice gentle and worried, and saturated with love.

Each week, and then every two weeks, I went by bullet train back to Tokyo, to Tachi, to see Dr. Cohen. Little by little, he tapered off my medications so I could walk around without squinting, the air was clear, and I could hear clearly and focus again. Gradually, I re-entered the stream. And one day, I was jabbering with Agnes and Annie like nothing had ever happened. With one big difference: I was strong, but no longer a stiff marine. Instead of saying "I had a great day," I would say, "I'm a little pissed off about the math homework. . . ."

~~

Upon my return, I befriended some new people. A girl named Ruth, who wore a bun and was one of those girls who looks twenty-five and possesses a forty-year-old's wisdom at seventeen, invited me to meet her in Rokko, the village at the foot of the CA hill, one afternoon. She led me into a small doorway in a row of shops in the tiny village center. The realm into which we entered was carpeted with tatami mats and a handful of low tables. We sat down on zabutons at one of the intimate tables and Ruth ordered tea.

A lady in a kimono brought us our *cha*.

"It's your karma," Ruth said about my time in the hospital. "We all have our own fates, our own natures. . . . You just have to respect who you are. Each person is meant to be here. We're all waves in the ocean."

Ruth recommended I read a beautiful book by the literary giant Yukio Mishima, *The Sound of Waves*. When, a few days later, I opened Mishima's paean to young love—gorgeous in its simplicity—it seemed as though the words and feelings, rather than my taking them in, were issuing from me. This tale of a young fisherman and his sweetheart was suffused with an honoring of the nonverbal.

"There you see Mishima's capacity for subtlety and tenderness," Ruth said. She then explained to me the Japanese preference for the indirect, the nuanced, the unsaid. "The Japanese ideal," she said, "is to understand through the pores instead of the ears. Words not spoken are considered deepest. The smartest and most developed people can read each other between the lines. In Japan, we believe the innermost self is kept hidden—except with a true love, when it is understood intuitively." I set Ruth's observation beside the American's propensity for saying out loud, and loudly, exactly what he thought, forever drawing attention to himself.

"We could spend hours together without talking. We understood without words." To my friends and me, this would be the ideal in romance. In college, two of my friends would be driven crazy by their Japanese boyfriends' propensity for silence and by their assumption that their girlfriends should understand them without words. But for now, I harbored a new dream of a boy who would understand me even from far away through the skin.

~~

At the boys' dorm one evening, we watched the U.S.-Chinese table tennis match. Everyone was talking about ping-pong diplomacy. My father wrote that this thaw in U.S.-Chinese relations was a huge event. The Chinese had stopped calling us "running dog imperialists" and had invited the American ping-pong team to China.

Sara's recent letter said that American support for the war in Vietnam was down to 34 percent. Half believed it had been morally wrong to get involved in the conflict. The protests, she said, were now led by Vietnam vets. I imagined Brad back there, marching, and a warming syrup flowed through me.

~~

Suddenly at school I was no longer confined to looking. It was like I'd broken out of the cage. I was a talker and a runner, active now. I'd taken onboard a little of the nutty Sara, and laughed and opined out loud.

~~

Annie and I were watching Will Suzuki dribbling a basketball with Jim.

Will was Japanese American, but as all-American as all get out. He'd spent most of his life in the American west. He was so good-looking—shaggy black hair, perfect build—and so affable and easygoing that almost every girl at CA had had a crush on him this year and he had playfully met the flirtations with an easy grace. Maybe because he was so naturally sweet, he could be generous with himself. A Mormon boy who incongruously rode a red Kawasaki (another missionary stereotype bites the dust), it seemed preordained that he would be a beloved doctor and boys' coach, with at least five children later in life, but for now he was an overgrown boy besieged by girls.

"Just watch him," Annie said, an ace flirt herself.

"Yeah," I said. "God."

But everything he did was appealing—Will making a basket in the gym, Will carrying a pile of books under one arm, Will talking over there, gesturing to Jim with his right, basketball-tossing arm. How is it that a starry mishmash of genes can roil around and then suddenly produce—maybe this is the true mystery of God—a constellation of features so pleasing to a beholder that it is like ultimate beauty?

~~

In the clean spring air, we were all out on the baseball field, which was suspended out on a terrace perched over the city far below. We girls were in our skirted gym togs, cheering the boys, who were playing a Japanese team. I watched as Will, the golden one, walloped the ball across the field.

At halftime, Will did something incongruous. I had to check behind me, just to make sure. But no. He was smiling like that at me—not at Agnes, not at Christy, not at Annie—at me! It had been ten seconds and he was still smiling in my direction. Frantic, I darted my eyes to the front and back, and tried to look out of the back of my head—without losing my lock on his gaze—but there was no one else here.

It was like the *plink* of a raindrop. A quick intake that stops you to the quick, drops like a tear of gold to the exact center of you.

And suddenly now, the world as I'd known it had vanished. The sounds of the baseball hubbub were gone. It was like Will Suzuki and I were standing in the emptied world alone, in air that had been scrubbed to a pure fineness. We did nothing, but our bodies seemed to float closer, without us and without anyone noticing (and somehow this seemed critical—as though if we made one false move the whole glass world we were in would shatter), and soon we were standing, in our gym clothes—me in my little black skirt and he in his shorts with the one-inch slits at the sides of his thighs—chatting idly about the game with our arms lightly brushing each other's.

Something startling had occurred: everything was shining.

As the game rejoined, we cheered, Will yelled to his teammates, I waved to Annie, but each thing we did had one sole purpose—to return to that position where we were two marble statues with their arms ever so slightly touching.

~~

When he said good-bye, I vanished. I was nothing but Shakespearean fairy fluff: gossamer light, ethereal, a mere bubble rafting on the breeze. I left the ground, gyred upward, surged, mounted, gushed up the air. Now I was larking: springing, escalading, spouting from cumulus to cumulus. Now I broke through the prism into pure whiteness. The air and me.

~~

At dinnertime, weak as a spring willow branch, I wisped into the dining room, but I couldn't possibly eat—not two grains of rice, not a piece of Sara Lee cheesecake, not one of Sara's toaster-oven tuna melts, not *ma po dofu*, not even a single patate. I was, instead, a hollow husk. I didn't need food or water or shelter—just the air I shared with him.

When I got back to my dorm room, it was the same. All I could do was look out into the night sky. He was out there in this same air somewhere. This moon was his moon. Oh, just transport him to me!

Can it really be true? God must exist. He likes me! He likes me. Will Suzuki likes me!

This feeling was so intoxicating I was terrified. The sensation too tender to bear, too precious to touch. Like a tissue, it would disintegrate if I even brushed it with a fingertip.

~~

The next morning, I was trying to pull my jeans up my legs, but I was trembling so badly I could barely do it. My hands and arms were weak and tingling, and no longer belonged to my body. It was like this about everything, suddenly. I'd dropped my pencil three times while I was doing my math the night before, and now, putting on my shirt, I had to stab a couple of times before I could get my arm in the hole.

I went down to breakfast in the dining hall and my fork clattered awkwardly against my plate as I tried to pierce a scrambled egg. I managed to take two bites, but I could eat no more.

I half-listened to Dottie and Agnes talking about Zack's messy hair—he never combed it—but it was like my whole being, not just my head, but my arms, my belly, and my legs were all thinking about Will: thinking about Will's being in the world, and his inching closer to me, by the minute, as he rode through the Kobe streets toward school.

After I brushed my teeth with my shaky hands, and checked the way my hair was tucked behind my ears, I picked up my books and set out for the classroom building.

The air was spring-cool on my arms, and I was able to take one deep breath before the shallow breaths took over as I walked down the little road beside the boys' dorm, toward the main building. And then, across by the gym, I saw him. He was sitting astride his red motorcycle—just poised there like glory, an arm dangled over the handlebars, a shoulder slanted, talking to Jack. His hand went up to brush a flop of hair out of his eye, and he tossed his gleaming head.

Should I die, or should I try to keep these legs moving forward, and see if he sees me? I was forcing my legs forward, but I felt like I might throw up. Everything was in slow motion, like in a movie. It was like I was a cresting wave that was trying to spend itself on the beach, but couldn't.

And then, in the middle of his joking around with Jack, he turned his glinting head, and saw me walking, throwing up my heart. Next, as if everything was normal and it was just a normal cool spring day, raising his arm in a wave, he gestured to Jack to hold on a second, and walked toward me.

As he got closer, I could see his face. It was smiling in that gentle way, his face beautiful as sunrise, his chocolate-kiss eyes . . . And as he touched my hair, the wave crashed. I was no longer twigs and twitches, but liquid gold.

I lit up all over—each little twig of me, like some kind of Christmas tree who didn't even know it had lights.

~~

"You and Suzuki the lady killer, huh?" Annie said at lunch, as if she'd never have guessed it. And then she put her arm around me. "There he is—comin' out the door." And there he was, that six-plus bundle of sinewy maleness, waving the minute he spotted me. And as he ambled over like some kind of easy-loping majesty, there went my stomach again, doing the flip-flop that in the last few days had come to seem its most natural rhythm.

~~

Until now, I'd always feared that if people really knew me, they couldn't possibly like me. These days, I no longer wondered this. It didn't seem to occur to Will that I was weird. He didn't even ask about the hospital. Being with someone so normal made me feel normal myself. Perhaps for the first time in my life, I could relax. I had passed some test and would never go back to that girl hidden between two hanging-down hanks of hair—and I had Will and Dr. Cohen to thank for this gift of all gifts. Will was a gift my life gave me.

~~

I was in forest green batik. Will was in black. The whole evening of the prom was the two of us floating through a shimmer of phosphorescent darkness and twinkling lights. From time to time, between slow dances, we stood and chatted with other couples or got a drink of ginger ale from the refreshment table. . . . It was like all of Japan descended and folded its dark, velvet kimono-sleeved arms around us in tender, *sakura* cherry blossom protection.

~~

School was almost over and I was moving to Tokyo. My father had been transferred there, so that I could keep seeing Dr. Cohen. For my senior year, I would go to the American School in Japan, just outside of Tokyo near Tachikawa.

I talked to Dr. Cohen about how sad it was to leave my friends at CA. In a year, all of us juniors would be dispersed across the world. Who knew what we'd all become. Some of the missionary kids reminded me of army kids I'd met in Europe. They had the same restless-eyed quality. Like migratory birds who'd lost their way, many of these kids would spend their twenties restless—zigzagging across the Pacific, trying to choose between the two shores. Back "home," they, like I, would stand too close or too far, be too formal or too oddly spoken, always "too" something.

But the agony was parting from Will. He was moving back to Colorado.

Before he flew back to America, he came to visit me at our new house in the Shibuya district of Tokyo. We went to visit the Meiji Shrine, then a sea of iris in full bloom. Each iris was as crisp and individual as a person, sticking straight up as if making a speech to the sky. On a patch of grass outside the shrine, he lay with his head in my lap, drowsing in the sun. While his eyes were shut, I tried to memorize his face.

On our way back to the house, we got our photos taken in a photo booth— hoping to fix time forever.

When I saw him off, I was sure I would die. My heart was broken. There is losing one's physical virginity but first there's the first broken heart—another kind of broken hymen. Ever afterward, sense plays its hand. Reason messes with passion.

~~

I wrote to Will regularly throughout my senior year, and wore the medallion he'd given me until it slipped off my neck one day in a coffeehouse swirling with milling teenagers. I would only see him once again—when we stopped in Denver on our way back to Washington at the end of the year. We exchanged ardent embraces on a neighborhood sidewalk, but by then two other young men claimed pieces of my heart. My love for Will, however, had the pliant tenderness of spring's first buds.

~~

Tokyo, decimated by firebombing during World War II, was all ultramodern glitter: high-rise department stores with thirty-foot flashing neon signs; mobs of sleek, long-tressed teenagers; elegant, mincing ladies in intricate kimonos; trim-suited businessmen; transvestites as thin as telephone poles, tottering in heels and gold lamé skirts. There were cozy tea shops and intriguing, high-fashion boutiques every few yards.

The Tokyo house, hidden behind a stone wall on a back street only minutes from a main train station, was a beauty. An old-style Japanese abode, it was half-Western, half-Japanese style inside, with old, dark timbers and white walls. Andy's and my rooms were tatami floored with shoji doors, and we slept on futons my mother purchased at Takashimaya. The house had both a Western and a Japanese living room. The latter was huge, with what seemed like an acre of mats and a beautiful, shadowy tokonoma at the back wall. The house had the hush.

My father's new job was to work in collaboration with the Japanese media to produce programs that supported U.S. positions in the world. He met with editors, newspapermen, and translators, informing them about what the United States was doing and why, and trying to influence them to give these activities a positive slant. "It's fascinating," he said, "because I have to be up on the very latest American actions and translate them to the Japanese." My father was delighted to be back in his most favorite of all Asian countries—the place where it all began for him. The bounce was back in his step, as he gobbled up ancient Japan like he had old Europe.

~~

To distract me from mooning over Will, my mother arranged private Japanese lessons into which I poured myself. She and I took the family housing allowance and went out shopping for furniture for the new house.

~~

My father brought home *Washington Post*s and read from them as we ate the dinner our new cook Toshiasan had prepared in the small, Western-style dining room.

The *New York Times* had recently published *The Pentagon Papers*, exposing secret discussions that had taken place during the Johnson administration. "President Nixon has become obsessed with leaks and exposure of 'state secrets,'" my father said. "I hear from Headquarters that he's begun to distrust not only us, but State, the courts, and congress." Time would reveal that Nixon began to keep tabs on people he believed to be his enemies, and created a secret policing operation.

In September, the "Plumbers" would break into Daniel Ellsberg's psychiatrist's office (Ellsberg had found the Pentagon Paper). Nixon saw him as part of a Communist conspiracy. A White House assistant would say, "Anyone who opposes us we'll destroy. As a matter of fact, anyone who doesn't support us, we'll destroy."

One day my father showed us a headline: Nixon had announced that Henry Kissinger had made a secret trip to China. He was the first U.S. official to visit China since 1949. "Twenty-two years is a long time to not have relations," my father, the China watcher, said. "This is good news. But Nixon and Kissinger are absurdly secretive. They love this kind of operation—back channels, secret meetings, surprising the world."

~~~

The American School in Japan, ASIJ, had a large and sprawling campus, like an American public school. Abroad, only American schools have these huge plants: Americans stake claim to vast open spaces and playing fields for their schools as well as their bases.

After so many moves, I'd got it down. I knew how to be a stranger, a new girl, and I was not deferring anymore. In fact, during free periods, when I sat down outside on the grass, people seemed to gather around. Perhaps because I had Dr. Cohen, I no longer needed one, exclusive friend. Quickly I had a motley and lovely collection· a brilliant Japanese diplomat's daughter with a British accent who could expound on Plato and Marx; a Norwegian diplomat's daughter who sang like an angel; a missionary boy with strawberry-gold hair and dreams of blueberry and dairy farming in Hokkaido; a girl who'd renamed herself a bird; a lanky boy with a cooler-than-cool Indian fringed bag with whom I shared long, intense conversations about the lives we would lead after the Revolution . . . the list went on and I was intrigued by them all.

I sat on the grass behind the school and wrote poetry. I reveled in how the words you used could cause meaning to slant: *fierce* versus *stubborn*, *light-hearted* versus *shallow*, *delighted* versus *intense*—and in the pure pleasure of a beautiful or thorny word: *clandestine*, *bristled*.

This was a school influenced by the progressive education movement—for better and worse. We studied in modules and were allowed to do a certain portion of our work in independent studies. In an inspiring independent study with my English teacher, I wrote poetry. In a dubious one for biology, I read books on weather: the sky, the clouds.

On the way home—it took three trains and an hour and a half to get there—I stopped with friends at tea shops where we listened to Beethoven or The Doors, depending on the shop's theme, and drank mixed juice, a delicious blend of bananas and other fruits, or green tea. In these tiny, intimate realms, we leaned in close, discussing parents, term papers, and moods. These Japanese tea houses afforded an inviting niche for friendship and conversation like the pubs I'd discover in my twenties in Britain. In its headlong race for prosperity, American society had forgotten about the need for pause—there were no Starbucks then, even on the horizon—so these shops were a revelation.

~~

My whole family flung itself into Japan. My father's passion drew us along. Inspired by the tastes I had had at CA, I thrust myself deeper into my apprentice-ship in Japanese culture—an effort that would bear fruit. Japan would clarify for me who I was, what I believed, and how to live, supplying needed correctives to my American schooling—and completing the lessons on perfectionism, stoicism, and intimacy I'd begun with Dr. Cohen.

Over the fall, as we explored our new metropolis, China and Russia were seek-ing rapprochement with the United States. My father brought home newspapers sent from Washington, and kept us abreast of the unfolding events. The troop withdrawal from Vietnam was continuing. By December, American troop strength would be down to 140,000. "Nixon's approval ratings have spiked. Even if he's the worst American president we've had in decades, I guess he is due some credit."

~~

For a time, America faded; Japan's curiosities were rampant. Around every cor-ner crouched beguiling arts, symbols, and stories: blue-faced Kabuki ghosts; wild ginger festivals; brush paintings of "Fish, Birds, and Peach Blossoms"; sumo wres-tling; full moon viewing; eggplants that symbolized an auspicious new year. . . .

~~

The train was rattling through gorgeous, vast padi lands dotted with faraway thatched farmhouses. Three hours of this, changing trains at smaller and smaller stations, and we dismounted at a post along the track and a small wooden bench—in the middle of brush-edged padi. We threaded our way on a slender path through rice fields toward a cluster of houses set along the dirt street that comprised the village of Mashiko. We selected one of the tile-roofed dwellings that rose like topsy to their rears in similarly tiled, stacked additions up the hillside. Upon entering we faced a potter bent over a wheel. Around him and in all the ascending rooms beyond were piled hand-thrown pots of all sizes: three-foot vases, teapots, and minuscule sake cups. One pile was the hue of moss darkened by rain, the next the autumn russet of persimmon, the next the brown of dewy chestnuts.

I could taste refinement on my tongue, in the air, and sense it in the treasuring gestures of the potter's hands on the wet mounds of clay.

We bought a set of ten cups the color of deep forest moss—the potter rolled each meticulously in rough paper—and carried them home on our backs, taking turns, in a basket pack made down the lane by another artisan.

At home, my father held up a cup for me to examine. "Look at the tiny imperfections in the glaze," he said. I saw a sliver of raw grey clay showing at the skirt of the cup, like a shoreline at which the sea flowed. "See how the catches and ripples and indentations—the mistakes—in the pot are part of its beauty? This is what makes it exquisite," he said.

Often, my father and I had talked about the importance of not being so afraid of making mistakes that you don't learn or take chances. Ben Franklin had made a chart of virtues and whenever he made a mistake, he recorded it. Tracking my mistakes had long been my forte. Perhaps my urge for perfection had contributed to my hospitalization. In any case, since I was small, I'd been the queen of self-correction and second-guessing. But now, as my father talked, it seemed this American perspective was only half the formula.

"To be human is to be flawed," my father went on. "The Japanese believe it is right to forgive and embrace human imperfection. Each pot has its flaw; the mark of the maker. The flaw is integral to the beauty, *is* the beauty."

Mistakes that aren't mistakes, flaws that aren't flaws. Could it really be that we were all perfect in our imperfection?

Years on, in my forties, confronted with another culture, in Paris, I'd be struck further by the complexity of the desire for perfection. While the Japanese embrace imperfection, at the same time they seek perfection, and they can, while gifted at beauty, be fastidious and finicky in its pursuit, like the French. And while Americans boast of perfection, they are also masters of the shoddy: building houses that begin to crumble in a year, purposely propping foreign policy, despite accurate intelligence, on posts of clay. Everything veers toward its opposite.

~~

Soaking in Japanese ways through my eyes and ears and nose, I wandered through an exhibit of prints hidden away on a fashionable street in the Roppongi district. In the shrewd-eyed dragons and swirling-fingered demons of the prints, the scary, mysterious, and difficult portions of life danced. This was a relief to me. From what I'd seen, from my sojourn at Tachi, life didn't seem to me as exclusively light-hearted and bold as Americans sometimes seemed to insist.

~~

On another weekend, I walked along the shoji door–lined outer veranda of an ancient Japanese farmhouse, its roof thatched and its body hunkered close to the ground. Inside, its ceilings were an exquisite lace of dark, aged beams. In stocking feet, I tiptoed along the time-smoothed wood floors, trying not to make a sound to infect the elegant quiet.

Much later, I'd read in Tanizaki's essay, "In Praise of Shadows" of the Japanese love of "worn beauty." Unlike Americans, who favored the shiny, new, and bright, he wrote, the Japanese chimed to the loveliness that dwelt in the chiselings of wind and age. Further, Tanizaki wrote that his countrymen preferred "colors compounded of darkness." "The Japanese accept darkness as inevitable," he said, "while people in the West are always after bettering their lot." According to him, the Japanese liked their tools, furnishings, and utensils to bear the marks of grime, soot, and weather —rather than bluffing, pushing away, blustering, or denying the effects of time and pain. The Japanese have a word for life's intertwining of pain and beauty: *aware*.

Older cultures, like Japan and the countries of Europe, who had attacks on their own soil, seemed to include in their view of life a sense of the tragic—a perspective that seemed truer to me than American bluster. America's lopsided penchant for boundless, entrepreneurial—and only apparently innocent—optimism was what had led to disastrous wars, and to the needless sacrificing of our friends.

Japan had once strived to dominate Asia as we were doing now. Each person, each country, was capable of both positive and negative acts, treated in both happiness and sorrow. People's and countries' stories tended to accent one or the other, some the glory, some the tragedy. To feel true, as in Japan, my story would always have to include both the bitter and the sweet. The terror-struck eyes of a Vietnamese girl or an American soldier, the bright orb of a tulip, the love and pain in my father's eyes.

~~

One day I took tea with my friend, Sakiko, the Japanese diplomat's daughter. Sakiko ordered us tea and bean cakes. When the kimono-clad waitress arrived with her small tray, the bean cakes were beautiful, delicate, sugary-looking mounds in pale pink and green. I nibbled one. It had a mushy texture and was far too sweet. Sakiko must have read my face. She said, "Try drinking some tea with it. It cuts the sweet." The excellent tea did diminish the sweetness, and after a few bites, I could fully appreciate the mix of bitter tea and sweet cake.

~~

More revelations lay in store. One day a couple of girls came up to me near Shinjuku station and said, "May we speak Ing-rish with you?" They were identically dressed in their school uniforms: ankle-length plaid skirts, white blouses, and bobby socks. They giggled behind their hands as they asked, but they were intent.

They asked me my name and how old I was and where I was from, question after question . . . and then they looked at their watches and said, "We are sorry but we must be going now. Thank you very much. 'Until soon!,' as you say in America."

Then, like Malaysian men, they linked hands as they went off together toward the train. Suddenly I was struck by one peculiarity of this. These Japanese girls were comfortable with being the same, and unafraid of intimacy. It wouldn't have occurred to them to be cowboys or marines.

But even comfort with conformity has its extreme. Japan is a fad culture—as we are, but, perhaps because of the country's homogeneity, even more so. That year there was a Mona Lisa craze. There were Mona Lisa tea cups, hats, socks, sunglasses, blue jeans, frocks, and even sneakers. There was a rush among girls on Mona Lisa nose jobs. Then it was Mickey Mouse. What had happened to Buddhism, to the Middle Path, everything in moderation?

The obvious faddishness of the Japanese makes an American marvel. We, after all, believe in individuality. We Americans take great pride in standing alone—even though it's illusory. As a child, I'd gobbled this impossible ideal—and been disappointed in myself. All through my life, I had been unable to sing rounds. Every time I tried, I'd inevitably ended up singing what the person next to me was singing. I couldn't hold independent and sing my own tune. The surrounding culture was too strong for me—and I had always criticized myself for this. I would finally, thirty years hence, become fully reconciled to culture's compelling, shaping power—and forgive myself its hold. The truth is, we are a gregarious species. The English— whether compliant or not—are shaped by the English belief in the stiff upper lip.

The Japanese—whether they wish to be or not—are influenced by their country's belief in interdependency.

~~

Perhaps the most important idea Japan held out to me was the lightning-bolt notion that to be sensitive could be positive. I saw this outlook in the solicitous tea shop hostesses, in the deferential girls on the streets, in the ever-considerate Japanese people I met. The Japanese seemed to have a special respect and radar for others' feelings. To intrude or tread on another's sentiments unwittingly was the greatest faux pas. Japanese ways were diplomats' ways. In this aspect of Japanese culture I found confirmation. Why is it, in American eyes, that being sensitive is so much worse than its opposite?

Japan was a salve for my past humiliations. Deep engagement was my nature, and this culture where I was born helped me come to terms with it. Years later, I'd discover a passage in the American book-of-all-books that further confirmed what I'd begun to digest in Japan—and what my father had always tried to convey to me, despite the overt messages of my culture: that it was acceptable to be downcast sometimes, to ripple with the wind: Aunt Alexandra has just admonished Scout that she ought to be "a ray of sunshine" in her "father's lonely life . . . but," Scout reports, "when I asked Atticus about it, he said there were already enough sunbeams in the family and to go on about my business, he didn't mind me much the way I was." Harper Lee's hero believed in authentic feeling; she didn't put up with false bluster.

~~

Different cultures validate different parts of you. They seep into you if you're porous enough. Just as Japan validated subtle, nonverbal communication, Argentina and Spain, I would learn in my twenties and thirties, embraced people's need for one another, and allowed free expression of a wide range of emotion, including difficult emotions like grief and jealousy, with an ease my culture did not. And while England shared, or was the fount of, our American emphasis on denying emotion and soldiering on—a quality both beneficial and problematic—that island offered a literary life and a delight in words I could find nowhere else. Being in another culture is protective, affirming. If you could become aware of and gather the permissions of every culture, you would probably feel most fully human of all.

~~

I had yet another puzzle to solve. What of my mental health? What *was* it that had sent me to Tachikawa and Dr. Cohen? In April, I came down with a fever and sore throat, and a doctor at the embassy dispensary gave me some medicine for my congestion. The next day, I was in PE class at school, doing gymnastics. I stood waiting my turn at the horse, and at once the room and people around me started to look fuzzy. Then, as I began my run toward the jump, I began to waver. There was the running me and then there was the removed one watching the runner. I could feel myself beginning to slip. Instead of flying over the hurdle, as I usually did, I jolted onto the leather top of the jump, and hung there, wobbling.

I was afraid. Without asking questions or notifying anyone, I left school, walked to the local train station, and took the train to Tachikawa.

In Dr. Cohen's office—they had called him out of a meeting—I said, "It's happening again, and I'm really anxious." That was a word I had never used before the hospital.

After just a couple of minutes of my telling him what was going on, Dr. Cohen said, "I think we have our culprit. Ephedrin. I think we can say you have an allergy to ephedrin. I'll check out the medicine you were taking before you came to the hospital just to make sure, but I'd put a million dollars on it." Once this was confirmed, he went on to say that my case had puzzled everyone. My symptoms had never added up to schizophrenia, the dreaded psychotic illness that often launched itself at just my age, but they'd still been nervous about the possibility.

By the time I left his office it was as though my world had turned from black to lemon. I felt bouncy even through the fuzziness. I was not inherently flawed after all. My sickness had been a fluke. Deus ex machinas occur in real life.

Over the next weeks, Dr. Cohen coached me on how to handle this new information. "I don't think I have to tell you that it would be best if you never take mind-altering drugs of any kind. Your brain is sensitive, and you'd be taking a risk.

"Avoid ephedrin," he said. "Check all medicine labels and I think you'll be fine. I think the mystery of *What Happened to Sara Taber?* is solved."

This meeting with Dr. Cohen was a profound relief: my mental confusion had been caused by an external, physical influence, not an organic, mental one. Not only did this confirm that I didn't have anything inherently wrong with me, but showed me that the American idea, that we should be unaffected by circumstances, was the true straitjacket. My whole life I'd thought I should be able to be unaffected by things outside myself, if I just exerted enough willpower or kept a stiff enough upper lip. Now I knew that to be affected by circumstances outside my control—whether a chemical change or a change of culture—was unavoidable and human. I didn't have to castigate myself for feeling more comfortable in one place than another.

This conversation also made me wonder: If a drug could transform me into another person, how stable was identity, or personality? We Americans are supposed to have selves as solid as the granite presidents at Mount Rushmore but, in fact, who we are might be a pin's prick from crumbling. I was also struck by how a particular piece of information could alter your whole outlook, your whole sense of things. By resolving a conflict I'd been struggling with my whole life, this information about ephedrin gave me power. A sense of confidence replaced my long-standing feeling of inadequacy. I would soon see that the influx of information could work both ways. My father would shortly come by a piece of knowledge that would lead to a decline only ended by his death.

How odd life is. What would I have missed if the lightning bolt had not hit and sent me to Dr. Cohen? Who would I have been?

~~

One afternoon toward the end of school, a ballerina friend of mine took me to her tea ceremony lesson. First, we sat in the sublime, impeccable hush of a small, tatami-matted room furnished only with a tiny, footed tray. We two American girls waited, completely quiet, and watched as the teacher—a beautiful seagull of a woman in a fine kimono, her eyes downcast—swirled the powdery green tea in an elegant earthen cup, in that pristine and lovely Japanese ritual.

Afterward, exchanging formal bows and warm thanks with the suddenly spunky-eyed teacher, Tammy took me to the next room: the teacher's workroom. Just adjacent to the elegant, Spartan tea ceremony chamber was a garage-sized atelier crammed with *stuff*: toppling piles of *ikebana* vases, buckets, tumbles of cloth, canned food, books, plants, parasols, bicycles, baskets: all the jumble of the world. Restraint and extravagance—both—mingled in this nondescript, revelatory Japanese house. This refined Japanese woman grabbed all the best of the world.

~~

Here and now, seventeen, in Japan, I kicked away the artificial notion of belonging to one country and insisted on being more than one thing: *I can be American and I can be Japanese. I can be an outgoing American girl who wears ripped jeans and runs, shouting, with her friends down the street, devil-may-care. And I can be demure and Japanese, shawled in mauve, attuned to the sounds of brooks and breezes, slipping out in the silky dark to view the fingernail moon. I can be both.*

Taiwan jangled and clanged, America boomed, Holland plashed, Borneo twanged, Japan shushed and tinkled. I could love all these sounds. As for my aesthetic, I could love Dutch cozy clutter, Japanese worn beauty, Taiwanese dragon-fire garishness, wild Malaysian color and fecundity. I could be sophisticated and intellectual, and earthy and casual.

~~

Japan had given me myself: I could be both American and Japanese—and Dutch and Chinese. I could have my cake and eat it too.

My creed could be curiosity about the world.

23

the emissary

Almost exactly a year after my hospitalization, my father, my mother, Andy, and I watched Nixon's arrival in China on television. A momentous event, Nixon's handshake with Zhou Enlai bridged twenty-two years of hostility. Chipmunk-cheeked Nixon and thick-browed Zhou announced a "long march together" for peace. That handshake must surely have provoked in my father and his CIA colleagues some consternation about their careers. What did this concord mean about the way they had spent the last twenty years? Had all the effort devoted to frustrating the Chinese, all the sturm und drang, been worthwhile?

Nixon proclaimed this "the week that changed the world." He promised to reduce American military presence in Taiwan in exchange for peace in Vietnam. My father said, "I agree with Nixon on one point: this new warming of U.S.-Chinese relations does alter the world balance of power."

The thaw in China-America relations was radical, but there was small change on the ground in Southeast Asia. Both the USSR and China were supporting the North Vietnamese, and a big offensive was building. By March 30, the North Vietnamese had launched a huge offensive across the DMZ and were trying to seize as much territory as possible. My father reported to us that enormous losses had been incurred on both sides. The North had lost many thousands of men, but they had occupied large portions of the South (and thus successfully laid the groundwork for the final push yet to come). Defense Secretary Laird claimed success, but the North presciently announced that the South was not sufficiently willing to sacrifice in order to win the war.

At these two sets of events, I rejoiced and grieved, holding in my breast these unruly emotions that seemed like the heart and lungs of the earth.

~~

While relations were opening up in foreign affairs, there remained in the Taber household mysteries unsolved. What had my parents' hushed and fervent discussions of Mr. Smith amounted to? What of Lee, the man whose mention flashed a dark wash through my father's eyes?

~~

My father had been enjoying Japan—grabbing print shows at his lunch hour, walking temple grounds, gazing at Mount Fuji rising godlike through the clouds. As usual, every day, he swallowed his dogged career frustrations and silenced himself like a good soldier, as his job and country required. By this point, he felt he deserved, at least, a promotion to a GS-16 if not an appointment as CIA station chief somewhere in the world. He put on a brave face—like most American children were taught to do as they ate their Rice Krispies and drank their orange juice in the morning—although the frustration at not properly advancing in his career, which had trailed him since I was small, must have been supreme.

In the face of the CIA's brutalities and his anguish about his own, to me very fuzzy, participation in dubious acts, and diminished by the Agency's lackluster treatment of him, my father had, nevertheless, made his best effort to be one of those who can transcend unfairness and destruction. At this point, I might have said of my father what the nurse of *The English Patient* noted about the dying man in her charge.

> *She knows this man beside her is one of the charmed, who has grown up an outsider and so can switch allegiances, can replace loss. There are those who are destroyed by unfairness and those who are not. If she asks him he will say he has had a good life—his brother in jail, his comrades blown up, and he risking himself daily in this war.*

But constantly swallowing foulness and moral frustration is not sufficient nourishment. Eventually the empty belly insists. How little we acknowledge the man in the middle—the man crushing his disappointments, tamping down his careful judgments, smothering his true feelings, disguising his true self for some greater cause, or the man stuck in the wrong job—perhaps the story of most men, not just those locked inside secrets.

But that middleman role, at the world's most secret organization, must be particularly suffocating. It wouldn't be until I read about life at the Agency in my fifth
decade that I'd realize how crass, ruthless, and demeaning the Agency could be—
depending on the executive branch of the moment. Under authority-loving presidents, agents and officers alike are used and cast off like plastic sacks. When useful
for the American policy, they are pumped full of pure oxygen. When their ideas
differ from the current ideology, they object to a dirty scheme or a certain set of lies
or another man's shaky but career-enhancing ploy, they are muzzled or disposed of.

For his family's sake, my father had sucked in his frustrations about his career
and his boss's aggressions and diminishments, and soldiered on, making the best.
Where did my father belong? Probably at a college somewhere, in an old wooden
office.

~~

But here was my father, going along, as I imagine him, meeting Japanese men
in out-of-the-way tea shops, conducting briefcase exchanges in tiny art galleries,
fairly serenely doing his duty at his post. There wasn't much to trouble him about
trying to influence the Japanese media. It could be justified.

Then this happened. Another truth knocked at the door, identified the thorn.
It was April, around the time Nixon authorized bombing by B-52s near Hanoi, and
intensified bombing of the North. The American president kept up his false, optimistic front in the failing war, pronouncing that only by bombing could we achieve
"peace with honor."

My father returned from the embassy this dark night, and his face was a wreck.
He hugged me as usual, but something had shifted. I could feel it in his body: a
wound, a tremor. Later, from behind the dining room wall, I heard him and my
mother talking in the narrow, dark, wood-paneled back hallway that divided the
dining and living room side of the house from the kitchen and maid's quarters. It
was a secret passage in which spies would hide or down which prisoners would
escape.

My father was saying, "Damn him. After all these years . . . explains everything." His voice was choked. In it was lodged a burr of anger and a shriek of hyste-
ria—and a dangerous calm.

Then I heard these terrifying, hissed words: "I can't go on prostituting myself,
Lois. Working for that man, I might as well go work for the other side. . . ."

"Charlie, don't be ridiculous." My mother's response was instant, harsh and
afraid. "You should fight back. He's a goddamned son of a bitch. You should . . ."

I couldn't hear any more, except the silence of my father's stiffening. Then a dark, hard sentence.

"That man's beneath me, Lois."

For years my mother had sputtered and raged—and now would continue to sputter and rage—about "that man," that man, Mr. Smith. It wasn't until just before my father died that I would learn the story that brought all to light—the episode that had flicked the switch in my father's eyes from hope to despair, and a pernicious, slow, and fatal yielding.

That day in Tokyo, an officer from Langley, an emissary from Headquarters—I picture a floppy-bereted messenger dressed in Shakespearean tights and bloomers galloping up on a horse and skidding to a stop outside the embassy gates—had flown into Tokyo especially to speak with my father. In an obscure tea shop where he was sure they would have privacy—or perhaps one of the safe houses where my father met his Japanese contacts—the man informed my father of a recent investigation at Headquarters. Due to mounting complaints, there had been an inquiry into the promotion of officers in the Agency; in particular there had been a study of the progress of officers who had worked for Mr. Smith. A pattern had come to light: certain officers with excellent efficiency reports had not been given the promotions their fine records would dictate. The visiting officer, one of the investigators, had traveled across the American continent and across the Pacific Ocean to tell my father in person that his had been one of the records of note. My father's efficiency report, comprised of excellent evaluations in post after post, showed that, while he *had* been given minimal promotions, he had time and again been denied the rightful, steady, and greater advancement his work merited. The investigator had been impressed: the unfairness was blatant. He'd been determined to tell my father in person.

He then went on to open my father's dossier and show him an evaluation, from his posting in Taipei back when I was seven, wherein my father's boss had written, in effect, the following damning six words: "This officer should advance no further." Those black words—doubtless resulting, as my father explained to me, from a disagreement Smith and my father had had about an operation, and about which my father's predictions had turned out to be right—and Smith's subsequent, repeated blockages of my father's promotions, had indelibly altered my father's career, and, like water subtly eroding stone, or acid attacking skin, eaten away at his spirit. How does a person stay buoyant if all his steady, bright efforts, which he knows are of high quality, are deemed inferior?

My hospitalization had been an existential turning, a jolt into another way of being. Similarly, this news from Washington shunted my father onto a new track. But while my ordeal gave me a bigger world in which to live, his delivered him a more constricted one.

A dimming spread through my father's eyes that day, and was never cleared. He knew that, even if Smith retired soon (and he would be pink-slipped shortly), the damage had been done and there was no redress. He knew the Agency culture. Nothing would change, the Far East desk was dug in. And—it was too late to leave now. My father was trapped. He had a child entering college, and another right behind. Years of discouragement now furled into a situation where he couldn't sink or escape; he had to swim.

~~

The name Smith was one source of my father's conflict. Another was Lee and all he symbolized.

When I wrote to the Central Intelligence Agency in 2005 to request information regarding Chigasaki, the site of my father's first assignment, at the time of my birth, in Japan, I received the following response.

Central Intelligence Agency
Washington, D.C., 20505

7 March 2005
Reference: F-2005-00833

Dear Ms. Taber:
The office of Information and Privacy Coordinator has received your 25 February 2005 Freedom of Information Act (FOIA) request for:

> **"information or records on the secret CIA**
> **base at Chigasaki, Japan . . . from 1950-1958."**

We assigned your request the number referenced above. Please use this number when corresponding with us so that we can easily identify it.
The CIA can neither confirm nor deny the existence or nonexistence of records responsive to your request. Such information—unless it has been

officially acknowledged—would be classified for reasons of national security under Executive Order 12958. The fact of the existence or nonexistence of such records would also relate directly to information concerning intelligence sources and methods. The Director of Central Intelligence has the responsibility and authority to protect such information from unauthorized disclosure in accordance with Section 103 (c) (6) of the National Security Act of 1947 and Section 6 of the CIA Act of 1949. Therefore, your request is denied under FOIA exemptions (b)(1) and (b)(3); an explanation of these exemptions is enclosed. . . .

The letter gave me the creeps. Reading it, I sensed I was experiencing, to a minute degree, the withholding, arbitrary, authoritarian culture of the organization to which my father had devoted his best years.

~~

One long weekend, we went to a hotel near where we used to live when I was a baby, and where my mother and my father had once stayed before I was born. It was a famous ancient, weathered inn on the Tokaido Highway perched above a rushing stream. Our room, a large rectangular tatami room with a view across the brook and into the woods beyond, had the gorgeous hush. My father adored this place more than maybe any other in the world—it recalled a time when he and the world were young and beautiful.

I will imagine the scene taking place here. My father's story evoked such a searing sense of his pain that where exactly it occurred is a blur in my memory.

We all took an ofuro together in the quiet, spotless, white-walled and wood-trimmed bathing room off our suite. This was the first time we had all been naked together in years. It was as if Andy and I were adults now—and we had all taken on Japanese notions of nudity.

After we were all fresh, warm, and moist, wrapped in the hotel yukatas, we sat down at the *kotatsu*, a low, square, quilt-covered table with a heater beneath it, for tea, brought in by a *tabi*-footed lady in a beautiful gold-threaded kimono. It was as though, now that his body was clean, my father wanted also to clean his mind.

Around the *kotatsu*, while we sipped, the Chigasaki story tumbled out.

My father started to tell us a little about his work in the hinterlands of Japan when I was born. "The whole goal of the Chigasaki operation was to train penetration agents to parachute into China." He explained that, in Chigasaki, he and the other Americans had developed a comprehensive program to teach their pro-American Chinese recruits how to use various firearms, how to carry out demolition actions, how to engineer evasions, how to use radios and send out secret radio signals, and how to parachute into enemy territory. The plan was, once these agents were injected into China, they would set up secure bases, use guerilla tactics to recruit locals, gather military intelligence and transmit reports, and engage in sabotage of the Communist regime. As a requirement of the work, both my father and my mother had had to learn to parachute and to shoot. At some point in the operation, according to the scheme, the young Americans would join the Chinese on the Mainland.

My mother piped up, "Yes, we all had to drop onto the beach."

For a moment, the cliff toward which this river was rushing was forgotten. Andy and I were amazed: to think of our mother parachuting! It was like a movie of *America Saves the Biggest Country in the World*, complete with drum rolls and John Wayne.

"The thing is," my father said, "the operation was foolish and wrong. We sent man after man into China and never heard from them again. Most probably, they were immediately picked up and done away with. One of these, Lee, was a close friend." Then my father choked up and his eyes flashed the smoky-black I had witnessed since I was small.

Lee was the first of who knows how many my father had worked with and cared about, and then had to abandon, or worse—and regret forever—in the name of America.

~~

After the visit from the emissary, my father was grimmer. He propped himself on the tenets: *I won't let him take me down. I refuse to lower myself to his level. I will not honor him with my attention.* And: *living well is the best revenge.*

My mother was angrier—rampaging sometimes. Someone had to express the suppressed fury. Her mottoes were: *That son of a gun. Charles, I wish you'd take him on. Call a spade a spade.*

My father was still and always a gentleman. He cleaved to his belief in man's essential goodness and treated people accordingly. "To understand is to forgive," he said; he refused to let anything tamper with that.

I absorbed this maxim of my father's and it would become a core tenet of my own creed. It dovetailed excellently with the social worker's perspective I would take on in graduate school: that, if you learn enough about a person's history, however troubling his behavior, you can forgive him much, or at least soften toward him. It also allowed me to forgive my parents the rice of loss on which they had raised me. Placed in the context of their histories and good intentions, weighing the benefits along with the sacrifices, it allowed me to bring into focus both sides of the Escher print of my childhood.

But my father's laugh now struggled. The mirth had been choked and a deep weariness took up residence. Maybe the true self cannot be suppressed. Looking back, I see these eighteen years, for both my father and me, as a long war fought by our true identities—for emergence. Emergence from the aliases imposed by my father's work, the diplomatic corps, and our culture. Perhaps there is within us all a bright-eyed, real self that doggedly elbows for a world in which it can breathe with complete freedom.

After the news, though you might not have been able to detect it easily—he was a pro at looking fine—my father constricted even more. Although my ordeal had been more dramatic, my father was the one who was emotionally squeezed to the breaking point. He was the one truly straitjacketed. Confined to living multiple lies imposed by the organization that had betrayed him and for which he had done things he regretted, he first became cynical—and then, finally, he collapsed.

One day, almost ten years from that day in Japan, just before he retired, I was with him when, recovering from a minor traffic accident, he broke down. The Japanese believe that the deepest, truest self is hidden and sacred, and cannot be spoken; the soul is so true it cannot be put into words. My father sobbed as though he would never stop. He couldn't keep his private and public selves separate anymore.

What is success? To have towed the company line, brown-nosed the right superiors, cheered or spearheaded arrogant, expensive actions of questionable merit and morality, and thereby risen to the top—would that have been success? Unfair treatment is a bitter elixir that can turn a man into a rampager, and victimhood can be tempting. My father wanted neither. My father loved his country—he insisted that bad always traveled with good, that compromises were inherent to democracy, and that America, even with all its tangled complexity, was the best governmental bet. So, in the end, even though I wanted to reject it for what it had done to him and the world, I couldn't cleanly and freely hate my country. To the end, my father insisted his had been a satisfying career. As always, he claimed grey.

This was how my father went on.

~~

From Japan, during my first year in college, my parents spent a year in Washington and then my father received the inevitable assignment to Vietnam. His job in Saigon was to help manage a radio station, House Seven, which beamed deep-cover "black" propaganda to the North Vietnamese Communists, as well as those in Laos and Cambodia. The work was stimulating—and beaming slanted stories to the enemy didn't kill anyone—but it was in Vietnam that my father's cynicism flowered. Everyone at the embassy knew, despite Ambassador Graham Martin's announcements, that it was just a matter of time before the Viet Cong took the south. Here was an out-in-the-open instance of successful and accurate intelligence gathering that, if heeded, might possibly have changed the course of history, but where the executive branch preferred and promoted an ideologically based false story. Vietnam was such a hoax—the fiction was so blatant, the truth so obvious—that, by this point, my father and his colleagues, drinking beer around the embassy pool, felt they were as much pawns as were the Vietnamese.

But then, at the end of the American odyssey in Vietnam, in April 1975, my father managed to take an action that was the opposite of cynical.

That spring, when it was clear that the Communist takeover was nearing, my father and two colleagues moved the entire House Seven operation—not only the Vietnamese employees but their extended families, which amounted to thirteen hundred people—to Phu Quoc Island off the south coast. From there they were situated to launch an evacuation when the embassy gave up the ghost. As it turned out, Headquarters abandoned my father and his entire group when it fled from the embassy rooftop. My father and his workmates might, in turn, have left the Vietnamese employees to fend for themselves, but they were determined not to abandon the people who had served the CIA for years to a highly uncertain and probably disastrous fate. How many victors look kindly on collaborators? For my father it was a matter of principle. At last he could take an overt, water-surface action for the good. After several attempts, he managed to convince the captain of a passing freighter to take all thirteen hundred people on board, and every last one made it to American shores. Finally my father had been able to take a clean, decisive action for the good.

For the Phu Quoc operation, my father received a medal, a "Certificate of Distinction for Outstanding Performance of Duty," signed by William Colby, director of Central Intelligence. The medal, about which he was not permitted to speak, read, "Mr. Taber's flexibility, imagination, determination, and demonstrated cour-age were in the finest traditions of the service, reflecting credit on him and the Cen-tral Intelligence Agency." This award, however, did not brighten my father's views of many of the Agency's endeavors and the Vietnam debacle.

After Saigon, my father was assigned to The Farm, the CIA training center near Williamsburg, Virginia, and was then rewarded with a plum post: Bonn. Though he loved being in Europe again, it was in Bonn that he received a task from Head-quarters that drove the final nail in the Agency coffin for him. Of late in Germany, there had been massive protests against U.S. nuclear policy. In response, President Reagan had delivered a showy proclamation that Eastern bloc Communists were behind the demonstrations. The assignment my father received promptly thereafter was to find evidence for Reagan's contention. Scoffing as he set off, knowing full well that the German protests were homegrown and sincere, he was unable to find a shred of such evidence. It was yet another instance of a president making up his facts. My father was disgusted. He put in for retirement.

Even retirement from the Agency was not to be smooth sailing, however. Presi-dent Reagan was enamored of secrecy, and under his watch, Agency operatives were expected to retain their cover until death. Once covert, always covert. My father could not abide this. He wanted to cast off his double life at last. He believed in his loyalty oath and would never have dreamed of divulging company secrets; he just wished to no longer have to lie about the nature of his career. The Agency would not have it. But my father wouldn't have *that*. His name had been exposed on a Rus-sian list of American operatives and he felt being honest about this one fact would harm no one with whom he'd worked. So he fought—and the Agency again fought back. He was required to see an Agency psychiatrist and attend a kind of tribunal in which the Agency sought to blame my father's plea on emotional problems. In the end, he won his case, but my mother said, "It was awful." He had been stripped.

When my father got out, he was relieved, but his God-given right to self-assertion had been whittled away. He now poured himself into doing for others, into work for the untainted good. The only man in a committee of women, he lobbied Congress to gain retirement and health benefits for divorced spouses of Agency and State Department employees. He volunteered for the Democratic National Com-mittee, at the National Archives, and in Hillary Clinton's correspondence office. He studied Spanish. He helped my mother carry her physical therapy equipment to and from the car. While he discarded himself, he continued, as always, to nurture others, giving each person the benefit of the doubt, anointing them with goodness.

The one thing my father did for himself, because he needed to, was to write an account of his Phu Quoc odyssey. I had urged him to write a spy story based on one of his espionage missions, such as that in Chigasaki, but he had utterly no interest in that. Phu Quoc was something about which he felt good. As John Dryden wrote in 1666, "To rescue one such friend he took more pride, Than to destroy whole thousands of such foes."

~~

Through all the years, my father refused—no matter how many times they tried, and the Agency tried many—to let them steal the goodness or the truth. He never stopped believing what he knew to be true, never stopped loving what he loved. And he refused to simplify. He insisted on living within an Escher print, with multiple viewpoints flicking, as really the only way to ken what was real—no matter how challenging it made things.

Late in life, my father sank away. He withdrew into a deep passivity. He sat in his old green chair all day, reading the paper, until someone needed his help. He brightened when I visited and told me I was his joy, but it was dismaying. I felt he had handed me his self, a husk to blow into—something that should never have to belong to someone else. In a way, though, I'd always stood for him—from protesting the Vietnam War to falling in love with Japan. Perhaps as long as I was there, he was whole.

It would have been far better if my father had exploded. Instead of breaking out of his walls, he shrank himself down, like Ken at Tachikawa, so as not to feel so keenly their encroachment. He'd received the message: individuals don't matter in the grinding of the geopolitical machine. A man used to being invisible, he just went one better. After a while, even his body seemed to assert: I am nothing. I am disposable. My soul, my talents, and my loves have no importance. I have been, and will be, just a tool for others with more forceful agendas.

Pathology—self-silencing—can be a sanctuary, the only way, sometimes, to express the truth when it is forbidden. The truth is slippery, but once we give up what we do know, what do we have? This is what my father, the spy, gave to his daughter.

So sick at the end, he became a whisper—until, one day, he could no longer be heard. My father, man of mist.

24

my america

On May 20, during my last month of high school, Nixon attended a summit meeting with Brezhnev. After three years of negotiation, President Nixon and Premier Brezhnev now signed the SALT agreement. They had agreed to limit production of the defensive anti-ballistic missiles and to a freeze on missile launchers. It appeared that the superpowers were learning to cooperate. Preparation for global annihilation would continue—an agreement on offensive weapons had not been reached. But Nixon was now viewed all over the world as a champion—China had been opened and détente forged with the USSR.

As tricky Nixon gloried, via his duplicity, my father struggled in the quicksand of his.

~~

Again, events seem paired, white with black.

In June, near graduation, a stark and horrifying photo was beamed around the globe. It was the picture of a naked girl fleeing a Vietnamese village that had been bombed with Napalm. This picture illuminated, with harsh noon light, the shedding of values that rides sidesaddle with bombs.

~~

As I shuttled to and from the American School in Japan on the crowded, hot train, pressed between perspiring bodies, glimpsing the stacked blocks of the Tokyo outskirts, I thought of the girl from the burned village—who blurred into the raggedy girl—and what it meant about being American and a patriot.

To stand with your shoulders back as an American was a tall order. The United States of America had wrought destruction all over the world during the past century. If with great power comes great responsibility, we had ignored ours too often. Up to the age of thirteen, I'd treasured the notion that my country had a nobility unsurpassed by others. The Vietnam war had put this faith to a stringent test.

After living thirty more years, after Chile, Afghanistan, and Iraq, it would be even clearer to me that we were no better than any other country, especially under conditions of war. War is the great leveler—the lowest common denominator.

But, to give my country the benefit of the doubt, neither, perhaps, was America worse than other countries in positions of supremacy. A look at any dominant culture's history—that of the Romans, the English, the Belgians—suggests that power releases a ruthless imperialistic urge, a lust for hegemony.

Ruth, the wise girl who had introduced me to Mishima's novel of early love at the tea shop the previous year, had also brought to my attention the master writer's harsh side. Mishima was a potent and haunting figure to American students, as a man preoccupied with face and honor and who vaunted the ancient Japanese practice of *hara-kiri*. Not a day passed when some boy at my schools in Kobe or Tokyo didn't commit the last act. He'd stab his imaginary dagger into his breast, then— eyes rolling, beginning to stagger—he'd drag the knife in the excruciating, holy, death-dealing square: left, down the left side, right across the gut, up the right side and back to the heart. Then the torso-clutching and the agonized, melodramatic collapse. And, of course, the loyal retainer always stood by ready to lop off his head if by some chance, this maneuver failed to kill the actor.

Ruth lit a cigarette and said at the time, as if it was self-explanatory, "Oh, Mishima is in touch with the underside of Japan. Japan is a country that is known for its serenity and beauty, but smoldering, concealed underneath is a terrible sense of honor and pride—and ferocious violence. Mishima is an ode to violence. He is a terrifying man himself, and in tune with the Japanese potential for explosive, blind aggression. I think he's brilliant."

In a tapping of her cigarette, my young-old friend had revealed the smoky side of Japan, cloaked under the bright brocade cloth. She made me see my new-old country from a new visage: Not only America was warlike. There was potential for violence everywhere.

But still, here at the end of my senior year, it seemed to me, Americans were an especially warlike people. We had, after all, assumed the role of the world's armory. The American penchant for arrogant, unilateral aggression upset me. It seemed to me that we were extravagant: yes, perhaps extravagantly open to newcomers—but also extravagantly violent.

~~~

Over the past two years, I had learned something important from Japan, something that made me take a hard look at America's propensity for hubris and riding roughshod over continents.

One day in Tokyo, when yet another pair of bobby-socked Japanese girls approached me to speak English, with the eagerness that had once annoyed Annie and me, the picture flicked in the frame and the Japanese girls seemed delightfully eager to learn about another culture—and humble in their thirst. An American might ask, Where is the pride of these people? But the Japanese were hungry—maybe a devastating defeat has this consequence—and they were willing to do what it took to obtain the knowledge they desired. A measure of humility—an admission of not yet knowing—is required for learning, and the Japanese girls weren't afraid of this. Put them beside the American man who won't ask for directions, or a president who won't look at the complex truth about the country he's labeled his enemy.

Another experience of Japanese humility: at a Christian-Zen commune Andy and I visited one long weekend, the residents undertook a pilgrimage at the turn of each new year. For a week, to assure their own humility, they donned monks' robes, packed their begging bowls in knotted *furoshiki*-carrying scarves, and walked into the cities and farmlands, offering to clean residents' toilets in exchange for a bowl of rice.

At this same commune, the resident sage gave me a healing massage and then, as he chanted, delivered me his verdict, "Your country need to improve. America need to find humility."

Frequently my family and I stopped at the gleaming chrome bakeries that dotted Tokyo. The pastries were always superb. The humble, eager Japanese bakers had mastered not only French patisserie, but also German kuchen and American donuts. When I would interview master bakers in France as an adult, they would admit that the Japanese could bake a baguette as fine as the French, and sometimes finer.

On this same theme, my major professor in graduate school at Harvard would describe to me Japanese anthropologists' behavior at international conferences. "They're always very quiet during the talks, and never ask questions during a lecture, but invariably, afterward, two or three Japanese will come up to me and they'll have the most trenchant and insightful responses of anyone there. The Japanese learn what we have to offer and then do us one better." It seemed to me that the

Japanese propensity for humble absorption was a great strength, and a source of power. And it could be ours.

~~

To be excellent, as I drew from these experiences, America did not have to be pompous and bellicose. As I'd learned at Tachi, it takes greater courage and strength to be receptive and humble, to admit shortcomings and try something new— which this is ultimately more successful—than to bluster, act cocky, and obfuscate. If open and receptive, we could learn from the Japanese's sense of humility and reverence for beauty and craft; the Netherlander's social ethic; the bracing aphorisms and radical, if flawed, attempts at equality of the Chinese. We could soak up lessons from other cultures, and be the stronger for it. It didn't have to be either-or: My country right or wrong. My country do or die. American *or* Japanese. American *or* Dutch. American *or* Chinese. In my vision, America could *include*.

This is my America: A country that is self-respecting, strong, humble, curious, receptive, empathic, generous, truthful, and wise. A tolerant, plural, cosmopolitan place bound by diplomatic civility. Rather than the tribal, enemy-requiring, "fear and spear" patriotism Senator John Kerry and others have described, our love of country could be large enough and hope-filled enough to embrace all human beings. We could stand for the principles of universal human rights; excellent education for all; generous care for the downtrodden, jobless, sick, and old; and diplomacy and peace. Ours could be a mature love of country. Not the callow infatuation that requires thrill and fireworks to sustain itself, but the deeper love and faith of long-term loves, characterized by self-criticism, adjustment and compromise, and the constant effort to move closer to embracing the whole, complicated messy truth.

If, as William James contends, in his aforementioned 1906 essay, "The Moral Equivalent of War," "the popular imagination fairly fattens on the thought of wars," an "equivalent of war," an outlet for the martial urge, must be provided if there is to be any hope of peace. James's answer to the human need to work with others toward something glorious is the universal conscription of youth:

> *To coal and iron mines, to freight trains, to fishing fleets in December, to dishwashing, clotheswashing . . . to foundries and stoke-holes, and to the frames of skyscrapers, would our gilded youths be drafted off, according to their choice, to get the childishness knocked out of them, and to come back into society with healthier sympathies and soberer ideas. They would have*

paid their blood-tax, done their own part in the immemorial human warfare
against nature; they would tread the earth more proudly.

James's answer still holds. If the martial urge needs to be fed, through conscription we might marshal a youth corps to battle the ongoing worldwide challenges of poverty, ignorance, illness, and environmental degradation. As James said at the beginning of the twentieth century, "It would be simply preposterous if the only force that could work ideals of honor and standards of efficiency into English or American natures should be the fear of being killed by the Germans or the Japanese."

In my vision, America sees itself as part of a community of nations, an integral and wise member of the mutually caring group of nations rather than the fearful, pugnacious, renegade wolf prowling outside the circle of wagons. *E pluribus unum.* Not *E pluribus plures.*

~~

In my ruminations about cultures, it appeared to me that America and Americans, like all countries and all nationalities, of course had some unique and glorious attributes. America *was* the land of free speech and thought. America, founded on a rejection of power and authority and the casting-out of kings, was the place in the world where a person could say what he believed and where having divided sentiments didn't make him unpatriotic or a traitor. A fervent American fourteen-year-old could letter a sign of protest and march for her ideals. To question the status quo was essentially American, to love America was to want it to be the best it could be—and America was a safe place to ask for the best.

America, too, was the place that promised—and delivered on the promise of—a better life. It was the place a poor young couple could land and know that, through the solid, free American schooling, their children could improve their lot. America was the land of possibility. A pair from humble Midwestern roots could, with the GI bill and hard work, get college degrees, move into the upper middle class, and serve their country, as could all those immigrants swearing their allegiance to America in courtrooms across the continent.

America also offered, infinitely, the opportunity for creativity, innovation, and spontaneity. All through my life as a child, and this continued as an adult, when I returned from abroad, a sense of exhilaration flooded through me: a sense of certainty that in America you could conjure and then materialize dreams. In other, more tradition-bound countries, playing it safe, avoiding imposition at all costs, never taking chances were the watch words. Class and propriety were determinative and paramount. Americans were less bound by these strictures, and this allowed them an unusual adventurousness.

In addition, Americans were a wonderfully welcoming people. Upon my childhood arrivals at American airport immigration desks, the officer would always issue a hearty "Welcome home!" and my heart would sing—and upon my adult returns from Latin America or Europe I would always heave a huge sigh of relief to be back in the land where you could wear an old T-shirt and jeans and still receive respect, and where people's predisposition was friendliness. Of his 1950 departure from America, the Czech poet Czeslaw Milosz wrote, "That was probably the most painful decision of my life. . . . During my four-and-a-half-year stay, I had grown attached to this country and wished it the best. . . . I had never come across so many good people ready to help their neighbor, a trait that would be all the more valued by this newcomer from the outer shadows, where to jump at one's neighbor's throat was the rule."

I had reaped from my country-hopping childhood a deep fascination and respect for other cultures, and a staunch belief that all cultures have their own vital integrity. While America was exceptionally open and rich in opportunities, I'd concluded by now, it was no better than any other country. Japan, China, and Holland maximized certain human potentials, and we others—all equally important and valid contributions to the human stew.

~~

What was the personal legacy of all this? The truth is, all my travels would leave me, rather than sated, insatiable: craving other cultures and the stories of other people's lives. At times during my life this tendency would seem a healthy passion, at other times an addiction. In college, I would spin lives in the air like plates. In graduate school, I would study cross-cultural human development, a blend of psychology and anthropology—as close to traversing and tromping the world as I could figure out.

After my globe-sprawling childhood, it would be hard for me to pledge allegiance to a single country. A mobile, international childhood breeds little loyalty to particular nationalities or institutions. What is national loyalty and pride? What are they good for? While they afforded some protection, they mostly got countries into trouble, it seemed to me. Of course it is important to identify with something larger than yourself, to take responsibility and to seek to help your fellow human beings, but why should this stop at a border?

~~

At seventeen in 1972, as I fantasized about staying in Japan forever, I was in danger of idealizing Japan as I had the United States at ten, but the fact was, Japan wasn't all sweet cakes and being a gaijin could be tough.

Some of the very things I loved were the ones that grated most. The Japanese absorption I admired, for instance, was another two-sided matter. On the one hand, the Japanese girls on the street were like supplicants. They stood very close as they talked to me, seeming almost childlike. But, though their eyes looked innocent, there was also something imperative and powerful about their interest. They wanted to drink us in. It was flattering, but it also felt dangerous. Like they were undercover competitors, thieves, or spies.

I hated, also, their pushy indirectness. They seemed to always say "yes" when they meant "no." And while I appreciated them, I also disliked the stiffness of all the rituals and formality. The Japanese always seemed proper and calibrated, never spontaneous. You had to read between the lines too much and I couldn't decipher the lemon juice. What did they really think? I felt like I'd never know. I disliked this Japanese extreme indirectness as intensely as I did extreme U.S. brashness.

Then there were the red-faced, drunken businessmen on the train. They stood close to me, breathing into my face, trying to feel me, as though they had a right to me. Being a gaijin girl was sometimes quite unpleasant.

My ballet class also unsettled me. Three days a week I took dance lessons at a studio two subway stops from home. In the tiny changing room, beside the petite, slim-hipped Japanese girls, I changed into my regulation leotard and pink ballet slippers. The girls hung up their middy-style uniforms, and I hung up my jeans and loose, flowery batik shirts.

In class, in the empty room with the barre looking out over the city ten stories below, we lined up to do our jetés and our twirls. But unlike my ballet classes in America, we performed in order of our mastery. The single boy in the class, and I, the lone American, were the class klutzes. We were always last, and following after the well-practiced pairs of girls in front of us, we were gangling, gawky giraffes.

Removing our leotards after class, a girl asked me, "Don't you take singing too? Do you practice everyday?" For me, ballet was a way to get exercise, and maybe acquire some grace along the way. For the Japanese girls, this was serious business. In Japan, I realized, you did nothing except all the way, aiming for precise mastery, toward some external goal. It seemed there was no such thing as casual, or "just for fun." This was the freedom of America: dabbling.

And then there was this, perhaps most perplexing of all: the homogeneity of the culture. An American could never melt in. You could never *not* be a gaijin in Japan. Everywhere I went, I heard that word whispered as people looked at me. Whether I wanted to be or not, I was stuck with being American. It is logical and exhilarating to declare oneself a citizen of the world. But until that day when the boundaries vanish, we are all stuck with our passports. This is the bitter and the sweet.

~~

And there was growing up as a spy's daughter. As with charm, beware of secrets. As for those raised by mythic, famous parents, growing up in a mythic organization of a mythic country bestowed me blindness and burdens. The romance of the Agency: I see it in the faces of proud CIA kids who'd be horrified at their father's involvements if they looked closely. CIA operations officers are basically missionaries with money and explosives. The romance of secrecy walks hand in hand with the headlongness of aggression.

After my CIA childhood, I'd spend a lot of my life underground in one way or another. And truth would seem wavery, to dwell in the hidden. At parties, I'd slip away.

~~

My mobile Foreign Service life would bequest to me a taste for adventure, an eternal restlessness. Hand me a plane ticket to another culture and I'm on the plane the same day. As Somerset Maugham wrote in his autobiography, *The Summing Up,* "I never felt entirely myself until I had put at least the Channel between my native country and me."

For a long time after my childhood, I'd be best at beginnings. I would never stay anywhere long enough for things to evolve. I would unconsciously subscribe to the CIA tactic: vary routes and times. I would glorify travel and, at the same time, I would be on an eternal search for home. I craved something enduring—a place, a person, a trajectory. It would take me a long time to know nothing stays the same—unless you refuse to grow or let in the world.

I would spend years missing the diplomatic corps—the formal rhythms and rigid civility unique to that culture—my culture. Too, I'd miss the era, the time in history that formed the backdrop to my childhood.

Place is important. Countries are different: of that, my childhood has made me sure. Some places suit better than others. Some supply stimulation, some frustration, some peace. I would spend inordinate amounts of time in my young adulthood trying to find the ultimate place. I was ever restless. No place had all of the landmarks I needed to feel like I was at home. Only the wide world would ever be able to provide that.

On the other hand, being a stranger means you can be at home in many places: I would feel at home at a desolate Patagonian ranch inhabited by two wizened Basques when I was thirty-one; in a bedraggled, nondescript village in France set in a heart-stopping, sere landscape shot with sun when I was in my mid-forties.

Maybe a sense of belonging isn't all it's cracked up to be. It requires choosing this over that, leaving others out—unless your reference group is the human race, which doesn't feel very chummy. Nevertheless, perhaps the most radical and deepest sense of belonging is that of belonging to the world.

~~

For years following my flitting childhood, sometimes it would seem like I was still hauling around those thirteen pieces of luggage (including airline bags), only now they were full of stones of loss and everyone else was traveling luggage-free.

Marooned early, as the child of an ever-moving spy, I was bequeathed young a finely developed sense of vanishing—left with a keen sense that people disappear, and that we are all ultimately alone. I received, too, a piercing sense of time passing, of all the lives one could—and wouldn't get to—live. Moving around makes a kid an existentialist and a Buddhist. *Carpe diem* is the CIA kid's password.

The gypsy traipsing of my childhood left me tentative about love. Touch it, and like spun cotton candy, it might dissolve. And, too, it left me with a spy's outlook: if they find me out they'll vanish.

~~

What of all those different girls? The girl in Taiwan, riding in her crystal coach, trapped between awe and pity of the poor, trying to choose between smocked dresses and the enticements of dragons? The gum-chewing girl who worshipped marines? The girl who adored Holland and yet felt most potently and fiercely American on the Dutch streets? The fourteen-year-old who gorged on war news and grieved both for GIs and Vietnamese children? The sixteen-year-old plopped in Borneo and thunder-struck by its wild and intricate fecundity? And what now of the seventeen-year-old, tempered by lightning and troubled by her father's troubles, who both loves and hates her country and wants the world?

What did it all mean: all these girls, America, the bewildering, mixed-up, contradictory nature of it all? Perhaps a Zen koan with its sense of the world as a many-shaded, intriguing puzzle, says it best:

Two monks were watching a flag flapping in the wind. One said to the other, "The flag is moving."

The other replied, "The wind is moving."

Huineng overheard this: He said, "Not the flag, not the wind; mind is moving."

~~

Close to the end of the year, when I would return to America and college, I met with Dr. Cohen, and all I did was cry.

After all the partings of my childhood, I was laden. I was a sloshing bucket of loss, always missing somewhere. And a treasurer: cupping memories in my hands like alms.

But Dr. Cohen taught me that there was room at the dance for the one who carries the bucket of tears. And he made me realize that I carried, on the other end of my Taiwanese yoke, a pail of brimming, sparkling delight.

~~

Dr. Cohen sent me off with these parting words: "Just water your ability to feel what you feel and you'll be okay." And he handed me a big going-away present, a foot-by-foot-and-a-half book, *The Whole Earth Catalogue*.

~~

I wandered in a moss garden. Trickling lanes of grey stones wended among islands of shapely, gnarled pines and romping pillows of moss. I touched the rough stones with my fingertips, then placed my palm on a mushroom-top of soft green. There was a beauty-drenched stillness. The high, wistful notes of a *shakuhachi* flute reached through in the air. Beauty: the dependable pleasure and solace.

~~

My father shouldered his rucksack and I shouldered mine. The red tulips of the Netherlands, the white lotuses of Taiwan, the blue iris of Japan—all the sweet-sad things: I was lifting them with me to America.

~~

Waters overlap in me. The waters of converging rivers, the tides of different oceans. I am a delta, an Antarctica, a place where oceans meet.

~~

When I landed in California, and stood in a field of rattlesnake grass laced with poppies overlooking the sea, I bowed before the blasting beauty of America.

The majesty of the world.

OF TRUTH

Truth never dies. The ages come and go.
The mountains wear away, the stars retire.
Destruction lays earth's mighty cities low;
    And empires, states and dynasties expire;
But caught and handed onward by the wise,
    Truth never dies.

Though unreceived and scoffed at through the years,
    Though made the butt of ridicule and jest,
Though held aloft for mockery and jeers,
    Denied by those of transient power possessed,
Insulted by the insolence of lies,
    Truth never dies.

It answers not. It does not take offense,
    But with a mighty silence bides its time,
As some great cliff that braves the elements
    And lifts through all the storms its head sublime,
It ever stands, uplifted by the wise,
    And never dies.

As rests the Sphinx amid Egyptian sands;
    As looms on high the snowy peak and crest:
As firm and patient as Gibraltar stands,
    So truth, unwearied, waits the era blest
When men shall turn to it with great surprise.
    Truth never dies.

—FRANCIS BACON, 1625

ABOUT THE AUTHOR

Sara Mansfield Taber was born in Japan and spent her childhood traveling from country to country with her family, as her father, a covert intelligence officer for the CIA, was transferred from post to post. After earning her BA from Carleton College and MSW from the University of Washington, she worked as a psychiatric social worker with troubled families in Massachusetts and California. At Harvard University, where she earned her doctorate, she specialized in cross-cultural human development. Thereafter, as a faculty member of the University of Minnesota, she conducted ethnographic research in Argentina, Spain, and among immigrants to the United States. In 1991 she began a new career as a writer of literary nonfiction. She has published literary journalism, personal essays, memoir, opinion, and travel pieces in literary magazines and newspapers, and had her work produced for public radio. She is the author of *Dusk on the Campo: A Journey in Patagonia*, *Bread of Three Rivers: The Story of a French Loaf*, and *Of Many Lands: Journal of a Traveling Childhood*, a writing guide. She teaches writing and mentors writers in the United States and abroad, and lives just outside Washington, D.C., in Maryland.